MW00818268

THOMAS GOODWIN ON UNION WITH CHRIST

T&T CLARK STUDIES IN ENGLISH THEOLOGY

Series editors

Karen Kilby
Michael Higton
Stephen R. Holmes

THOMAS GOODWIN ON UNION WITH CHRIST

The Indwelling of the Spirit, Participation in Christ and the Defence of Reformed Soteriology

Jonathan M. Carter

t&tclark

LONDON • NEW YORK • OXFORD • NEW DELHI • SYDNEY

T&T CLARK
Bloomsbury Publishing Plc
50 Bedford Square, London, WC1B 3DP, UK
1385 Broadway, New York, NY 10018, USA
29 Earlsfort Terrace, Dublin 2, Ireland

BLOOMSBURY, T&T CLARK and the T&T Clark logo are trademarks of
Bloomsbury Publishing Plc

First published in Great Britain 2022
This paperback edition published 2023

Copyright © Jonathan M. Carter, 2022

Jonathan M. Carter has asserted his right under the Copyright, Designs and Patents Act,
1988, to be identified as Author of this work.

Cover image: clairevis/iStock

All rights reserved. No part of this publication may be reproduced or transmitted
in any form or by any means, electronic or mechanical, including photocopying,
recording, or any information storage or retrieval system, without prior
permission in writing from the publishers.

Bloomsbury Publishing Plc does not have any control over, or responsibility for,
any third-party websites referred to or in this book. All internet addresses given in this
book were correct at the time of going to press. The author and publisher regret any
inconvenience caused if addresses have changed or sites have ceased to exist,
but can accept no responsibility for any such changes.

A catalogue record for this book is available from the British Library.

Library of Congress Cataloging-in-Publication Data
Names: Carter, Jonathan M., author.
Title: Thomas Goodwin on union with Christ : the indwelling of the Spirit,
participation in Christ, and the defence of Reformed soteriology / Jonathan M. Carter.
Description: London ; New York : T&T Clark, 2022. |
Series: T&T Clark studies in English theology |
Includes bibliographical references and index. |
Identifiers: LCCN 2021048818 (print) | LCCN 2021048819 (ebook) |
ISBN 9780567704894 (hardback) | ISBN 9780567704900 (paperback) |
ISBN 9780567704924 (epub) | ISBN 9780567704917 (pdf)
Subjects: LCSH: Goodwin, Thomas, 1600–1680. | Salvation–Puritans–History
of doctrines–17th century. | Mystical union–History of doctrines–17th century.
Classification: LCC BX9339.G64 C37 2022 (print) | LCC BX9339.G64 (ebook) |
DDC 285/.9–dc23/eng/20220114
LC record available at https://lccn.loc.gov/2021048818
LC ebook record available at https://lccn.loc.gov/2021048819

ISBN: HB: 978-0-5677-0489-4
PB: 978-0-5677-0490-0
ePDF: 978-0-5677-0491-7
eBook: 978-0-5677-0492-4

Series: T&T Clark Studies in English Theology

Typeset by Newgen KnowledgeWorks Pvt. Ltd., Chennai, India

To find out more about our authors and books visit www.bloomsbury.com
and sign up for our newsletters.

CONTENTS

PREFACE

I first encountered the ideas of Thomas Goodwin (1600–1680) almost twenty years ago when stumbling across Paul Blackham's doctoral thesis. His stimulating and highly enjoyable study examines Goodwin's pneumatology, and at once I was gripped by Goodwin's account of the work of the Holy Spirit on Christ. I wondered whether many more theological treasures were waiting to be found buried in the volumes of Goodwin. Almost two decades later and now having had the privilege to undertake my own research on Goodwin, I have discovered that this was indeed the case. Goodwin's richly pneumatological Christology is, in fact, part of a grand project to advance a comprehensive vision of Reformed soteriology. What Goodwin said about the work of the Spirit on Christ was what he wanted to say about the work of the Spirit on Christian believers. For Goodwin, soteriology is the application of Christology. To say more is to tell the story contained in this book.

The reader should note that this book is a revision of my 2016 doctoral thesis at the University of Edinburgh entitled ' "Partakers of his Divine Nature": The Reality of Union with Christ in Thomas Goodwin's Defence of Reformed Soteriology'. This revised and updated version includes more footnote material to aid the non-specialist, interaction with studies that have appeared since, a discussion of the distinction of 'real' and 'relative' union with Christ and a reworking of the argument of Chapter 5. The net result is a sharper account of Goodwin's doctrine of union with Christ and the overall vision of his grand project.

A project like this cannot be completed without the support and encouragement of mentors, friends and family. I am especially grateful to my doctoral supervisor, Susan Hardman Moore. Her expertise, feedback and encouragement have been invaluable. I could not have asked for a more supportive supervisor. I also wish to thank David Fergusson, my second supervisor, for his feedback on the final draft of the original thesis. Steve Holmes and James Eglinton, who acted as examiners for my viva, offered incisive comments and the encouragement that has led to this revised version coming to publication. Thanks too go to the Bloomsbury editors involved in getting this work to publication. Among friends, I am especially grateful to Ronald Collinson for proofreading the original thesis and for the stimulating theological conversations that have ensued. Since completing my doctoral studies, I have got married to Laura and I am especially grateful for her support in getting the book ready for publication and the professional editorial skills she has brought to bear on it. As we serve the church family of Christ Church Lowestoft (not far down the coast from the village of Rollesby, Goodwin's birthplace), we have enjoyed numerous conversations teasing out how the kind of ideas that captivated Goodwin transform and impact everyday local church ministry. May union with Christ daily renew and strengthen us.

Lowestoft, September 2021

Chapter 1

THE IMPORTANCE OF GOODWIN'S DOCTRINE OF UNION WITH CHRIST

1.1 Introduction

By the late 1650s and at the height of his influence, Thomas Goodwin (1600–1680), then president of Magdalen College, Oxford, longed to retire from office in order to complete what he considered to be his life's work. This grand project, once completed and edited, would comprise a multivolume defence of Reformed soteriology of a scale unmatched within English puritanism.[1] To date ten doctoral theses have been completed on Goodwin, but no study has offered an account of the soteriological scheme unfolded in these treatises as a coherent project.[2] The

---

1. Within modern scholarship the term 'puritan' has proved notoriously difficult to define. Nevertheless, it has remained useful as a shorthand descriptor of an influential strain of piety within the Church of England. What is important to this study is that by the mid-seventeenth century a clear theological consensus had developed within mainstream English puritanism. The content and bounds of this consensus were hammered out by 'the godly' at the Westminster Assembly (1643–52) but in essence amounted to an English formulation of federal Reformed orthodox theology. For a recent discussion of the issues surrounding the term, see Randall J. Pederson, *Unity in Diversity: English Puritans and the Puritan Reformation, 1603–1689*, Brill's Series in Church History (Leiden: Brill, 2014), chapter 1.

2. Paul Edward Brown, 'The Principle of the Covenant in the Theology of Thomas Goodwin' (PhD thesis, Drew University, 1950); Rembert Byrd Carter, 'The Presbyterian-Independent Controversy with Special Reference to Dr. Thomas Goodwin and the Years 1640–1660' (PhD thesis, University of Edinburgh, 1961); Stanley Fienberg, 'Thomas Goodwin, Puritan Pastor and Independent Divine' (PhD thesis, University of Chicago, 1974); Paul Blackham, 'The Pneumatology of Thomas Goodwin' (PhD thesis, University of London, 1995); Michael S. Horton, 'Thomas Goodwin and the Puritan Doctrine of Assurance: Continuity and Discontinuity in the Reformed Tradition, 1600–1680' (PhD thesis, University of Coventry, 1995); Paul Ling-Ji Chang, 'Thomas Goodwin (1600–1680) on the Christian Life' (PhD thesis, Westminster Theological Seminary, 2001); Thomas Michael Lawrence, 'Transmission and Transformation: Thomas Goodwin and the Puritan Project 1600–1704' (PhD thesis, University of Cambridge, 2002); Mark Jones, *Why Heaven Kissed Earth: The Christology of the Puritan Reformed Orthodox Theologian, Thomas Goodwin (1600–1680)*, Reformed Historical

present study constitutes the first such theological account by demonstrating that Goodwin's scheme holds union with Christ as occupying a fundamental role in the application of salvation.

The importance of this study rises above merely tracing a soteriological theme within the works of a puritan divine (of which there have been many of varied quality) in three respects: (1) by assessing the overall vision, structure and coherency of Goodwin's soteriology; (2) by locating the distinctiveness of Goodwin's theology within the spectrum of puritan and radical theologies of mid-seventeenth-century England; and (3) by contributing to and realigning recent debate over union with Christ in the post-Reformation period.

To establish the case for this study, in this chapter I will show that Goodwin's grand project represents the life's work of an important theologian (§1.2), assess the current state of Goodwin scholarship (§§1.3–1.5) and identify unresolved questions in the ongoing controversy over union with Christ (§1.6). With the literature review complete, I will then outline the trajectory of the argument (§1.7).

1.2 Goodwin's grand project as his life's work

The influences, struggles and experiences of Goodwin's early life shaped him into a convinced Reformed orthodox puritan intent on preaching Christ. Born in 1600 in Rollesby, Norfolk, Goodwin soon moved with his parents to King's Lynn and at twelve years of age arrived at Cambridge to commence his studies. Matriculating at Christ's College, he found himself in a stronghold of puritanism where the influence of the recently deceased William Perkins (1558–1602) and the recently exiled William Ames (1576–1633) was still felt.[3] Goodwin would spend his formative years in this context, but it would not prove to be a straightforward spiritual journey. Using autobiographical material, an account of Goodwin's

---

Theology (Göttingen: Vandenhoeck & Ruprecht, 2010); Jon M. Vickery, 'A Most Lawful Pleasure: The Marriage of Faith and Reason in the Thought of Thomas Goodwin' (PhD thesis, University of Toronto, 2011); Hyo Nam Kim, 'Salvation by Faith: Faith, Covenant, and the Order of Salvation in Thomas Goodwin (1600–1680)' (PhD thesis, Calvin Theological Seminary, 2016). Kim's thesis (which only appeared after the completion of the original thesis of the present study) comes closest to offering such an account but fails to rightly identify the treatises that compose the project and is plagued by other problems. See pp. 16–18.

3. Goodwin [junior], *Works*, V, *The Life of Thomas Goodwin*, ix. Hereafter cited as *Life*. Note: references in this study are given to the original printed edition of Goodwin's *Works*. Thomas Goodwin, *The Works of Thomas Goodwin, D.D.: Sometime President of Magdalene Colledge in Oxford*, 5 vols (1681–1704). See Appendix A. The original formatting and erratic spellings will be preserved in quotations. Italicization will be retained given Mark Jones's remark that manuscripts from Goodwin's hands indicated words to be italicized: *Why Heaven Kissed Earth*, 21. It should also be noted that page numbering in the original edition is sometimes erratic.

life compiled by his son describes Goodwin's conversion as well as the spiritual experiences and struggles of those early years.[4] The account turns on the afternoon of Monday 2 October 1620. Since Whitsuntide 1615, when his tutor had prevented him from taking the Lord's Supper on account of his age, Goodwin had become disillusioned with the puritan way. He desisted from personal prayer, from reading the 'sound Divinity' of Calvin's *Institutes* and Ursinus's *Catechism*, and from sitting under the ministry of Richard Sibbes (1577?–1635).[5] Instead, Goodwin sought to imitate the esteemed preaching of Richard Senhouse (d. 1626) and became attracted to the much discussed tenets of Arminianism. But while listening to a funeral sermon, on the afternoon of 2 October, Goodwin was convicted of his spiritual state. That night, wrestling with the depravity of his nature, Goodwin not only had what he believed was a powerful experience of regeneration but also became convinced of the Calvinist position over the Arminian position.[6] However, over the next seven years Goodwin was diverted from simple living 'by Faith on Christ, and God's free Love'.[7] Struggling to find personal assurance of salvation through self-examination for evidence of sanctification (i.e. the method of the practical syllogism), his sermons were in the main 'for Conviction and Terror'.[8] It was the advice of Mr Price of King's Lynn and the influence of local puritan preachers Sibbes and John Preston (1587–1628) that set Goodwin on a new course.[9] Sibbes instructed him: '*Young Man, if you ever would do good, you must preach the Gospel, and the free Grace of God in Christ Jesus.*'[10]

Despite quickly rising to prominence in Cambridge, Goodwin increasingly devoted himself to the publishing of practical divinity. Having transferred to St Catharine's College in 1619, he became instrumental in securing Sibbes as master of the college. In 1625, Goodwin was licensed as a university preacher, and by 1628 he was curate at St Andrew's church.[11] Not long afterwards, he inherited Sibbes's and Preston's prestigious pulpit at Holy Trinity. However, he resigned this post in 1634, Laud's accession as archbishop having made ministry more difficult for convinced puritans.[12] Remaining for several years in Cambridge, Goodwin focused on writing and publishing works of practical divinity. As will become clear, it was

4. *Life*, v–xix.

5. *Life*, vi.

6. *Life*, xi.

7. *Life*, xv.

8. *Life*, xvi–xvii.

9. *Life*, vi, x, xiii, xiv, xvii.

10. *Life*, xvii.

11. Robert Halley, 'Memoir of Thomas Goodwin, D.D.', in *The Works of Thomas Goodwin, D.D.*, vol. 2, ed. W. Lindsay Alexander, Thomas J. Crawford, William Cunningham, D. T. K. Drummond, William H. Goold and Andrew Thomson, Nichol's Series of Standard Divines: Puritan Period (Edinburgh: James Nichol, 1861), xxiii.

12. *Life*, xvii.

around this time that he first envisaged a much greater project of practical divinity, comprising a comprehensive exposition of salvation in Christ.

Events, however, would put the writing of this grand project on hold. By 1638, Goodwin had emigrated to the Netherlands and there pastored a Congregational church.[13] Having returned to England in the early 1640s, he was engaged in preaching through Ephesians 1:1–2:11 to a gathered church in London,[14] only to find himself swept into national life. He preached several times before parliament, became a prominent figure in the debates at the Westminster Assembly and emerged as the leader of the Congregationalist party. While this party was few in number, Hunter Powell remarks, 'No group in the history of the Puritan Revolution had a more disproportionate impact on the course of events than this vocal minority.'[15] Despite championing the minority ecclesiological view, Goodwin contended for the majority opinion in other matters, especially in the extensive debates over justification, and shared concerns with Presbyterians over the rise of antinomianism. In the 1650s, Goodwin and his Congregational colleague John Owen (1616–1683) arose as the leading clergymen of the protectorate. Goodwin held office in Oxford throughout the 1650s, served as a chaplain to Oliver Cromwell and, along with Owen, was the architect and leader of the Cromwellian national church settlement.[16]

It was in Oxford, as he mentored young men, that Goodwin found opportunity to preach sermon series that could be collected together into his grand project.[17] The context had changed dramatically from the 1630s and, while Arminianism and Catholicism remained opponents, there were new pressing threats of Socinianism[18]

---

13. *Life*, xviii.

14. *Works*, I, *An Exposition of the First and Second Chapters of the Epistle to the Ephesians*. Hereafter cited as *Ephesians*.

15. Hunter Powell, *The Crisis of British Protestantism: Church Power in the Puritan Revolution, 1638–44*, Politics, Culture and Society in Early Modern Britain (Manchester, UK: Manchester University Press, 2015), 3.

16. Lawrence, 'Transmission', 2, 142–87.

17. The major exception is large sections of *An Unregenerate* which were mainly preached in the 1620s–1630s.

18. Socinianism was a theological system that emerged in Poland in the sixteenth and seventeenth centuries. Taking its name from Faustus Socinus (1539–1604), it was widely denounced for its denial of the doctrines of the Trinity and the pre-existence of Christ, as well as questioning a string of orthodox tenets. Yet, as Sarah Mortimer demonstrates, its central idea was 'a claim about religion, freedom and human nature'. Since in Socinus's view authentic religion must be freely chosen, human reason was necessarily the supreme judge of revelation and so fell doctrines that did not conform to human rationality. In the mid-seventeenth century and to the alarm of orthodox divines, Socinian ideas started to gain traction among English scholars and clergy. See Sarah Mortimer, *Reason and Religion in the English Revolution: The Challenge of Socinianism*, Cambridge Studies in Early Modern British History (Cambridge: Cambridge University Press, 2010), 1–3.

and moralism on the one hand and antinomians,[19] enthusiasts,[20] 'ranters'[21] and Quakers[22] on the other. Throughout the 1650s, Goodwin and Owen found themselves at the forefront of refuting these teachings. With the previous decade witnessing fierce debate between Presbyterians and Congregationalists, Goodwin now sought to build consensus around traditional Reformed soteriology against these common foes. Yet, Goodwin's basic concern remained to promote godliness, as in the 1620s–1630s. In particular, despite the institutional reformation to the Church of England accomplished in the 1640s–1650s, Goodwin grieved the lack of personal spiritual reformation among the population. These concerns shaped the sermons that would comprise Goodwin's grand project. Also evident are the influences of his conversion experience and theological formation in Cambridge, his exposition of Ephesians and the disputes of the previous decades.

By the late 1650s, Goodwin longed to retire from office to perfect and edit these sermons together into completed treatises for his grand project. In fact, events would shortly force retirement upon him. Immediately following the Restoration, Goodwin resigned from his post[23] and returned to London where he spent his time in 'prayer, reading and meditation.'[24] While he likely undertook the final

---

19. Reformed orthodox divines of the mid-seventeenth century used the term 'antinomian' to discredit a range of different teachings that purportedly rejected divine moral law. Two distinct strains of antinomianism can be identified; see p. 22.

20. The orthodox used the term 'enthusiasts' to lump together a range of radical spiritual leaders sharing a common impulse. McGregor offers the following helpful definition: 'Enthusiasm may be defined as the immediate guidance of the Holy Spirit superseding any worldly or scriptural authority.' J. F. McGregor and Barry Reay, *Radical Religion in the English Revolution* (Oxford: Oxford University Press, 1984), 121.

21. Orthodox divines made frequent reference to a radical licentious 'ranter' sect which threatened social order and whose chief tenet was a pantheistic conception of God. However, the term will be placed in inverted commas given James Davis's contention that a definable 'ranter' sect was largely a projected myth of the orthodox. Nevertheless, radical pantheistic teachers existed and are relevant to this study. See J. C. Davis, *Fear, Myth and History: The Ranters and the Historians* (Cambridge: Cambridge University Press, 1986); cf. McGregor and Reay, *Radical Religion*, 121–39.

22. The Quaker movement can be traced back to 1652 when George Fox (1624–1691) and other radical preachers moved through rural areas in northern England linking together groups of separatists. In the 1650s, the Quakers were not so much concerned with establishing a doctrinal system as with announcing and experiencing the direct revelation of Christ within each individual apart from external means. Nevertheless, this central conviction led to the rejection of the conventional account of the doctrine of the Trinity as well as other mainstream tenets. Because of these denials and because the movement had quickly gained popularity, it raised considerable concern among mainstream orthodox divines. See McGregor and Reay, *Radical Religion*, 141–7; cf. Barry Reay, *The Quakers and the English Revolution* (London: Temple Smith, 1985).

23. Lawrence, 'Transmission', 9.

24. *Life*, xviii.

editing process during these years, his grand project was not published, perhaps owing to poor health, until the years following his death in 1680. This task fell mainly to his son, who published it along with several other important treatises in five volumes as the *Works*.

What is surprising is that the existence of Goodwin's grand project has only come to light with Michael Lawrence's historical reassessment of Goodwin.[25] This is partly because, despite Goodwin's prominence and theological output, he has only received limited scholarly attention. Mark Jones comments that the description 'the forgotten man of English theology' once ascribed to Owen now rightly belongs to Goodwin.[26] But, as Lawrence uncovers, failure to recognize Goodwin's grand project primarily stems from issues surrounding the original publication of the *Works*.

1.3 Lawrence's historical reassessment

Lawrence's 2002 'Transmission and Transformation' thesis represents a watershed in Goodwin studies and amounts to a broad historical reassessment of Goodwin which subsequent research ought not ignore.[27] Lawrence notes that, prior to his work, studies either focused on the content of Goodwin's theology or studied his significance as a pioneer of Congregationalism.[28] Lawrence's findings expose flaws in both types of studies, showing that both have proceeded on the basis of invalid assumptions.

Studies focusing on the content of Goodwin's theology, Lawrence contends, largely treat the *Works* as an ahistorical systematic theology. To nuance Lawrence, these studies typically read Goodwin in light of the wider Reformed tradition but pay little attention to his immediate historical context. This approach is coupled with two unquestioned assumptions. The first is that the *Works*, which comprise the bulk of Goodwin's output, were written during the final two decades of his life. It is alleged that, forced to live a quiet life, Goodwin turned to writing and theological reflection and that the *Works* are the product of a man in his twilight years who had retired to his private study and was now disconnected from national life. Secondly, it is assumed that Goodwin had no architectonic scheme for his various treatises. Lawrence carefully sifts the evidence to reveal that Goodwin had in mind a definite scheme, long in formation, yet the volumes of the *Works* failed to follow this scheme and instead were published in a rather haphazard

---

25. Lawrence, 'Transmission'.

26. Jones, *Why Heaven Kissed Earth*, 15.

27. The positive reception of Lawrence's historical work is evidenced by the decision of the *Oxford Dictionary of National Biography* for Lawrence to write a new entry for Goodwin. See *Oxford Dictionary of National Biography*, s.v. 'Goodwin, Thomas (1600–1680)' [version: 3 January 2008].

28. Lawrence, 'Transmission', vi.

manner. Moreover, Goodwin's son appropriated his father's treatises to meet the fresh issues of a new day. The prevalence of these assumptions, combined with the treatment of Goodwin's writings as an ahistorical systematic theology, leads Lawrence to conclude, 'Thus while recent expositions of Goodwin's theology have revealed much about the content of his *Works*, they have also served to obscure the theological and polemical agendas and crises that prompted Goodwin to write in the first place.'[29]

Equally problematic are studies on Goodwin as an early pioneer of Congregational ecclesiology. Lawrence observes that little of Goodwin's material is devoted to ecclesiology and so reading Goodwin as principally driven by a Congregational agenda is wrong-headed. Again, Lawrence points to the editorial hand of Goodwin's son who appropriated not only his father's writings but also his biography to further the Congregational cause in the face of new challenges in the decades following his father's death. Goodwin's spiritual journey and his labours were pressed to endorse Congregationalism, with the conforming aspects of his life overlooked. Lawrence contends that the problem with previous studies is that they accept 'without question the basic framework and assumptions provided by the memoir of Goodwin's life.'[30]

By adopting a critical stance towards the editorial hand of Goodwin's son, Lawrence broke new ground to construct a more accurate portrait of Goodwin. Lawrence proceeds by paying careful attention to internal evidence (including marginal notes in the original editions), shedding light upon Goodwin's overall scheme and the immediate historical motivations behind individual treatises. Alongside this, he uncovers references to Goodwin's projects and motivations in the records of Goodwin's colleagues. This methodology leads Lawrence to overturn current historiography and conclude:

> Far from being either narrowly Congregationalist or rigidly Calvinist, Goodwin's platform for the Church of England was both orthodox and inclusive, and sought, above all else, to safeguard a recognisably puritan understanding of salvation against its critics both new and old. Ultimately, the survey of Goodwin's career suggests that he was as much one of the last puritans as the first of the Congregationalists.[31]

Regarding the *Works*, Lawrence argues that the bulk of the treatises were largely written, but not edited, before 1660.[32] In particular, Goodwin, he contends, conceived four treatises to form a coherent theological project in response to theological developments in the 1640s and 1650s. These can be identified as: (1) *Of the Creatures, and the Condition of their State by Creation*; (2) *Of an Unregenerate*

29. Lawrence, 'Transmission', 4.
30. Lawrence, 'Transmission', 3.
31. Lawrence, 'Transmission', 7.
32. Lawrence, 'Transmission', 16.

Mans Guiltiness before God, in respect of Sin and Punishment; (3) *Man's Restauration by Grace;* (4) *Of the Blessed State of Glory which the Saints possess after Death.*[33] The third of these treatises was expanded by three further discourses corresponding to *Of Election, Of Christ the Mediator* and *Of the Work of the Holy Ghost in Our Salvation,* such that Goodwin's grand project is composed of a total of seven treatises.[34] Rather than forming a systematic theology, this project is an extended theological defence of Reformed soteriology. Four pieces of evidence are provided by Lawrence to substantiate this claim. Because these are scattered across his dissertation, each will be summarized here.

First, a letter dated 29 September 1657 by John Thurloe (bap. 1616, d. 1668) refers to Goodwin's desire to retire from his office in Oxford in order to 'separate hymself to his studyes, to perfect severall bookes, which he hath now under his hands, conteyneinge a body of divinity, and without doeing of which he professeth he cannot dye in peace'.[35] Thus, Goodwin already had a major writing project underway by 1657 which included a 'body of divinity' and represented what he considered to be his life's work.

Secondly, *The Creatures* Book II contains a description of Goodwin's intention to write a four-part work which plausibly corresponds to the 'body of divinity':[36]

> This discourse being to handle the State of *Adam* in his purest naturals, with a Comparison between him and Christ, and his State, and our State of Grace under the Gospel. In other Discourses which are to follow, I shall, 1. Treat of Mans sinful and Corrupt Estate and the misery thereof, which serves further by way of Contraries, to magnifie the Glory of God's Grace, and his Christ, as revealed in the Gospel: Then, 2ly, the State of Salvation by Christ, which the Elect are brought and raised up into, by the Grace and work of all three Persons, which is rendred to us the more illustrious, both by the immediately preceeding misery which we are delivered from, and then by its surpassingly excelling, that first and best Estate. Then 3ly, I shall discourse of the last, and best Condition of the Elect, which is the State of Glory.[37]

Briefer comments confirming parts of this architectonic plan appear in other treatises.[38] Lawrence further argues that Book II was written against Socinian teachings and proof-texts. He concludes that, given the prominence of the Socinian

---

33. Lawrence, 'Transmission', 19–22. Hereafter cited as *The Creatures, An Unregenerate, Man's Restauration* and *Blessed State.*

34. Lawrence, 'Transmission', 21; cf. 202–5. Hereafter cited as *Election, Christ the Mediator* and *The Holy Ghost.* See also p. 153.

35. Lawrence, 'Transmission', 16–17.

36. Lawrence, 'Transmission', 18–19.

37. *Works,* II, *The Creatures,* 31–2.

38. *Works,* III, *An Unregenerate,* 1; *Works,* III, *Man's Restauration,* 1; *Works,* V, *The Holy Ghost,* 40; *Works,* V, *Blessed State,* 8. See Lawrence, 'Transmission', 20–1, 205.

threat in the late 1640s and early 1650s as well as Goodwin's strong opposition to Socinianism, it is plausible that Book II should be dated to that period and so this four-part work may be identified with the 'body of divinity' in Thurloe's 1657 letter.[39] Lawrence also argues that Book I should be dated to the immediate wake of the 'ranter' sensation of 1649–50; the bulk of *An Unregenerate* equates to sermons delivered in the 1620s–1630s and the bulk of *Blessed State* composed by 1657.[40] In addition to Lawrence's evidence, Goodwin's *The Holy Ghost* can be dated to the 1650s.[41]

Third, although the original edition of the *Works* did not order the treatises according to this fourfold plan, in the preface to volume III Goodwin's son appeared to acknowledge his father's scheme:[42]

> As the Authors design was to take a careful, and exact survey of Man in the various changes of his State, from Integrity, Innocence, and an answerable blissful Condition, to Sin, and Misery, and from this at last restor'd, and rais'd by Grace to more Glory than he had lost: He accordingly hath shew'd you this Creature fair, and beautiful in Holiness, as he first came out of Gods Hands, and flourishing in all the Joys, and Glories of his Innocence. And He now opens to your sight the ruins of this once noble structure, which would be too sad and melancholy a prospect for any of us to look upon, if we did not at the same time see our Glorious Redeemer raising out of these miserable ruins a Building stronger, and when he once shall have finish'd the Great Work, fairer than the first.[43]

Lawrence suggests that there was some attempt in volume III to follow his father's scheme by publishing *An Unregenerate* followed by *Man's Restauration*, but because of more pressing concerns, this undertaking was not continued into subsequent volumes.

Finally, Lawrence traces the origins of the project back to 1634. In that year, Samuel Hartlib (*c.* 1600–1662) recorded that Goodwin envisioned a grand project called *The History of Truth* which he believed to be a more profitable approach than the work in which he was then engaged.[44] Through the 1620s–1630s, Goodwin had participated in a programme of writing practical divinity under John Dury (1596–1680) and Archbishop Ussher (1581–1656) which was intended for the promotion of godliness not only in England but eventually also in Europe. Lawrence identifies nine treatises published by Goodwin during that period as belonging

---

39. Lawrence, 'Transmission', 50.
40. Lawrence, 'Transmission', 24–41.
41. See Appendix B.
42. Lawrence, 'Transmission', 202.
43. *Works*, III, preface, n.p.
44. Lawrence, 'Transmission', 135.

to this project.[45] It seems, then, as Goodwin penned these tracts, he envisioned a superior multivolume work. Goodwin provided an outline of this project, and in the absence of a matching multivolume publication, Lawrence suggests that the contents are, in fact, to be identified with several treatises published in the *Works*.[46] Moreover, because Goodwin's outline overlaps considerably with his four-part 'body of divinity', it is probable that his grand project was originally conceived in the 1630s but was revised into the four-part scheme. Goodwin's incorporation of sermons from this early period into his final project offers supporting evidence for this contention.

This set of evidence, along with other sources, further allows Lawrence to identify probable motivations behind Goodwin's grand project. The evidence from Hartlib suggests that the project was conceived as an extension of Goodwin's efforts to publish practical divinity. Lawrence summarizes Goodwin's motivations behind these efforts:

> In Goodwin's thinking, practical divinity had merit in itself and in fact was the prime need of the church, both at home and abroad. He did not think 'the State of Grace' had been sufficiently 'set forth' and 'therfore Men commonly slight this kind of Study so much and Socinians and other Heretikes cavil so much at it.'[47]

Like Goodwin's preaching, the purpose of practical divinity was to promote godliness. Thus, while Goodwin opposed Catholicism and Arminianism, his chief intention behind *The History of Truth* was the promotion of godliness through expounding a comprehensive scheme of soteriology. Concerning the Interregnum period when Goodwin returned to his project, Lawrence demonstrates that Goodwin laboured to reinforce a consensus around Calvinistic Trinitarian soteriology despite ecclesiological disagreement. This effort gained new impetus in

---

45. *A childe of light vvalking in darknesse: Or A treatise shewing the causes, by which God leaves his children to distresse of conscience* (1636); *The Returne of Prayers. A Treatise wherein this Case [How to discerne Gods answers to our prayers] is briefly resolved* (1636; repr., 1638); *The Vanity of Thoughts Discovered: with Their Danger and Cure* (1637; repr., 1638); *Aggravation of sinne and sinning against knowledge* (1637); *The Happinesse of the Saints in Glory, Or, A Treatise of Heaven, On Rom. 8. 18* (1638); *The tryall of a Christians growth in mortification, or purging out corruption, vivification, or bringing forth more fruit: a treatise affording some helps rightly to judge of growth in grace by resolving some tentations, clearing some mistakes, answering some questions about growth* (1641); *Encouragements to Faith. Drawn from severall Engagements Both of {Gods Christs} Heart To {Receive Pardon} Sinners* (1642; repr., 1645); *Christ Set Forth In his {Death, Resurrection, Ascension, Sitting at Gods right hand, Intercession,} As the {Cause of Justification [&] Object of Justifying Faith. Upon Rom. 8. ver. 34. Together with A Treatise Discovering The Affectionate tendernesse of Christs Heart now in Heaven, unto Sinners on Earth* (1642; repr., 1651).

46. Lawrence, 'Transmission', 136–7.

47. Lawrence, 'Transmission', 137–8.

the 1650s because of the rise of heterodox teachings opposed by both Presbyterians and Congregationalists. Lawrence describes Goodwin's initiatives to counter these threats:

> The most significant of those means were undoubtedly the attempts in 1652 and 1654 by Goodwin, Owen and their ministerial colleagues to recommend to parliament a confession of faith that would exclude, not only papists, but Socinians, Quakers, ranters and other heretics as well. ... Goodwin was a leading member of the committees that drafted these confessional documents.[48]

This desire to defend Reformed soteriology, Lawrence concludes, also stood behind Goodwin's grand project and his other major treatises:

> Goodwin's posthumous *Works* might best be understood in their authorial context as an attempt to articulate and defend the core of Jacobean puritan soteriology against both its traditional opponents, and the new ones thrown up in the tumultuous decades of the civil wars and interregnum.[49]

However, in the main, Goodwin declined from naming individual opponents in his writings and instead 'constructively and winsomely presented his theological framework in a way that implicitly answered objections and exhorted his audience to embrace by faith the electing love of God in Christ'.[50] Thus, although his work lacks a strongly polemical tone, it is paramount to understand Goodwin's soteriology in its immediate historical context: it was formed in the crucible of pre–Civil War puritan Cambridge, then repeatedly defended over the following decades in the face of the challenges of a new generation.

The overall contentions of Lawrence's work are persuasive and find confirmation in the present study. However, the prominence he grants to the Socinian threat is problematic. He writes,

> The desire to refute Socinianism can explain more than just *Of the Creatures*, Book II. It could also have been the motivation behind the entire theological project, for each part of Goodwin's program could be understood as a response to Socinian error. ... Such a motivation for Goodwin's project can only be speculation, and yet, there are known facts about Goodwin that indicate such speculation is not entirely unreasonable.[51]

The 'known facts' include Goodwin's documented opposition to English Socinian John Biddle (1615/16–1662) but moreover his pastoral mentoring in Oxford of

---

48. Lawrence, 'Transmission', 47.
49. Lawrence, 'Transmission', 16.
50. Lawrence, 'Transmission', 49–50.
51. Lawrence, 'Transmission', 44.

Zachary Mayne (1631–1694), who struggled with Socinian doubts.[52] However, it is questionable whether combatting Socinians was Goodwin's chief motive for his grand project. While he undoubtedly abhorred Socinianism, according to Mortimer it was particularly in 1654–5 that fears over Socinianism came to the fore; at the start of the 1650s, Socinianism was far from the dominant threat and by 1656 this concern had been eclipsed by Quakerism and other issues.[53] Indeed, in the preceding decade, the antinomian threat had been far more prominent at the Westminster Assembly. Chad Van Dixhoorn explains the depth of concern at the Assembly:

> According to the divines, the antinomians were in 'very many places of the kingd[ome][,] but cheifly in and about the citty'. For some divines it appears that the antinomians in London loomed larger than papists in Madrid. It is not unimportant that the minutes of the Assembly record more than twice as many references to antinomians as to papists.[54]

Moreover, some conservative Presbyterians alleged that little separated Congregationalists from the antinomians. The true intent of Thomas Edwards's (c. 1599–1648) *Gangraena* was to discredit Congregationalists by aligning them with radical sectaries and their immoral conduct.[55] In the early 1650s, at least, refuting the libertine threat was the more pressing need for Congregationalists.

As I will demonstrate in this study, while Goodwin refrained from identifying individual opponents, he freely referred to radical teachings and gave greater attention to them than to Socinianism. Lawrence particularly establishes his case on the basis of identifying Socinians as Goodwin's chief target in *The Creatures* Book II. While this identification has some plausibility, Socinians only receive one explicit mention and this is matched by a similar passing reference to radicals.[56] Moreover, in a section of *The Holy Ghost* concerning the nature of regeneration, Goodwin considered the 'Opinions of the Popish Doctors, of the Arminians, and of some Enthusiasticks'.[57] The description Goodwin provided of the 'Enthusiasticks' (who are attacked in various passages in the same treatise) readily agrees with 'ranter' beliefs.[58] Socinians, however, are not explicitly mentioned, which is

---

52. Lawrence, 'Transmission', 48–9.

53. Mortimer, *Reason and Religion*, 205, 220, 230.

54. Chad B. Van Dixhoorn, 'Reforming the Reformation: Theological Debate at the Westminster Assembly, 1643–1652' (PhD thesis, University of Cambridge, 2005), 281; cf. 276, 342.

55. E.g. Thomas Edwards, *The third Part of Gangræna. Or, A new and higher Discovery of the Errors, Heresies, Blasphemies, and insolent Proceedings of the Sectaries of these times* (1646), 191; cf. Ann Hughes, *Gangraena and the Struggle for the English Revolution* (Oxford: Oxford University Press, 2004), 107–8, 434.

56. *Works*, II, *The Creatures*, 27, 105.

57. *Works*, V, *The Holy Ghost*, 173.

58. *Works*, V, *The Holy Ghost*, 175–6.

particularly conspicuous given Goodwin's examination of opposing doctrines of regeneration.[59] Furthermore, combatting 'ranters' was Goodwin's explicit motivation for *Of the Knowledg of God the Father and his Son Jesus Christ*,[60] but no treatise was (explicitly) devoted to refuting Socinian tenets.

While Lawrence also appeals to a correspondence between the topics addressed by Goodwin and Socinian 'errors',[61] he overlooks that Goodwin highlighted and addressed a considerable range of tenets rejected by the radicals, including: infused *habitus*, the God/creation distinction, the Trinitarian union, Christ's hypostatic union, the intermediate state and the relation of Adam's state to the final state.[62] Neither list entirely accounts for the topics covered in Goodwin's project. It is, therefore, preferable to understand Goodwin as defending against a range of threats, while, true to his original intentions, being chiefly motivated by the promotion of godliness.

1.4 Post-Lawrence studies and methodological issues

Lawrence's work has set a new context for Goodwin studies, yet since its appearance only three theses on Goodwin have been forthcoming. Neither of the first two examine his soteriology per se. Nevertheless, both deserve assessment, not least for the methodological issues raised by them. The first to appear was Jones's thesis examining Goodwin's Christology. This is a welcome contribution, not only for elucidating an important aspect of his theology but also for attempting to embrace the implications of Lawrence's historical reassessment. The main impact of Lawrence's findings is evident in Jones aiming to read Goodwin's Christology in light of his opposition to three main opponents: 'much of Goodwin's theology must be understood in the context of his strong reaction to popery, Arminianism, and Socinianism'.[63] Of the three, Jones pays most attention to Socinianism and suggests that this helps to account for the Trinitarian character of Goodwin's theology.

Jones's overarching argument is that Goodwin's Christology was driven by his doctrine of the *pactum salutis*[64] since Christ's incarnation, work and glorification

59. A parallel argument can be made regarding justification: Goodwin frequently disputed the Catholic conception of justification in *Works*, IV, *Of the Object and Acts of Justifying Faith* (hereafter cited as *Object and Acts*) but did not mention the Socinian denial.

60. Hereafter cited as *The Knowledg*.

61. Lawrence, 'Transmission', 44.

62. *Works*, V, *The Holy Ghost*, 148, 150, 175; *Works*, II, *The Creatures*, 1–3, 105–6; *Works*, II, *The Knowledg*, 3, 13.

63. Jones, *Why Heaven Kissed Earth*, 229.

64. The *pactum salutis*, also known as the covenant of redemption, was a doctrine of federal theologians asserting a pre-temporal covenant in which the persons of the Trinity agreed to undertake the salvation of the elect. For a recent introduction, see J. V. Fesko, *The Covenant of Redemption: Origins, Development, and Reception*, Reformed Historical Theology (Göttingen: Vandenhoeck & Ruprecht, 2016).

occurred in fulfilment of its terms. This argument is well-founded, echoing Goodwin's logic in *Christ the Mediator*. Jones believes that the *pactum salutis*, as an intra-Trinitarian agreement, undergirds the Trinitarian shape of Goodwin's Christology.[65] Moreover, as the *pactum salutis* is a covenant concerned with redemption, Goodwin's Christology and soteriology are, therefore, intrinsically intertwined.[66] Accordingly, Jones offers some examination of redemption accomplished but refrains from exploring redemption applied in Goodwin's thought.

However, Jones's work is not without its problems. My primary focus will be on methodological issues, since my intent is not to undermine the value of Jones's contribution but to highlight areas in which this study seeks to adopt an improved methodology.

Jones's study is invaluable for providing points of contact between the Christologies of Goodwin and numerous other Reformed orthodox divines, thus fulfilling Jones's secondary aim of providing an account of Reformed orthodox Christology and establishing Goodwin's orthodox credentials.[67] A weakness, however, is that the distinctiveness of Goodwin's Christology is less evident. Owen serves as the most frequent comparison partner – an appropriate choice given scholarly interest in Owen as well as the overlapping concerns and historical contexts of the two theologians. Nevertheless, the danger is that Goodwin's distinctive theology has been lost in the shadows of the later works of Owen. This may well be the reason why Jones fails to discern Goodwin's fundamental answer to the chief research question – 'Why did God become man?' – that Jones seeks to answer in his study of Goodwin. In Chapter 5, I will note how Jones's account of Goodwin's Christology is lacking and could be improved.

A related failure is the insufficient attention given to the work that Goodwin's Christology does within his overall theological scheme. Jones's exposition would be strengthened by articulating Goodwin's Christology not only in terms of the *pactum salutis* but also in terms of the covenants of works and of grace, which were also important structural categories for Goodwin. Moreover, Jones does not allow the architectonic plan of Goodwin's grand project to shape his analysis. Demonstrating how Christology is located and operates within Goodwin's grand project would have grounded his Christology more fully in his major concerns and within Lawrence's portrait of the puritan.

Also disappointing is a near absence of comparisons with Sibbes and Preston, despite Jones underlining their formative influence upon Goodwin during his early career in Cambridge. Jones is, therefore, unable to answer the question: To what extent does Goodwin move beyond these two puritans and why? Related to this weakness is an overly brief handling of Goodwin's Christology in his earlier published works, which included significant Christological statements.

---

65. Jones, *Why Heaven Kissed Earth*, 144.
66. Jones, *Why Heaven Kissed Earth*, 225–6.
67. Jones, *Why Heaven Kissed Earth*, 222.

Goodwin's writings must not be read exclusively with reference to the issues of the 1640s–1650s but also in light of his formative period in Cambridge.

The greatest shortcoming of Jones's work, however, is the failure to read Goodwin's Christology in the context of the array of heterodox Christologies advocated in the 1650s. Apart from an isolated reference to the pantheistic views of the 'ranters',[68] Jones only considers the Christology of Socinians.[69] This problem is made particularly acute by his desire to hold the moral high ground of appropriate historical contextualization. Three possible factors may underlie this weakness. First, Jones assumes, following Lawrence's suggestion, that Socinianism was Goodwin's chief target. Jones makes this claim for *The Knowledg*,[70] despite Goodwin stating that 'ranters' were his main opponent.[71] Jones advances the same claim for *The Creatures*.[72] While Lawrence does make a case for Socinian ideas as the target of Book II of this treatise, this has been questioned above. Moreover, for Book I, Lawrence on much stronger grounds actually identified 'ranting opinions' as Goodwin's main target.[73] Secondly, Jones focuses on *Christ the Mediator* where the radical threat is less apparent than in Goodwin's other treatises from the 1650s. However, important Christological material elsewhere has radicals primarily in view. Thirdly, Jones tends to read Goodwin through the lens of Owen. Yet, while Owen devoted considerable attention to addressing Socinianism, Goodwin's priorities must not be assumed to be identical to Owen's.

The second thesis to appear since Lawrence's work is Jon Vickery's study of the relation of faith and reason in Goodwin's thought. Again, this is an excellent contribution to the field. By offering a dedicated study to the subject, Vickery seeks to correct previous accounts of Goodwin's view of reason and also challenge recent historiographical claims that puritanism adopted a hostile stance towards reason and natural human learning.

As with Jones's work, I will focus attention on the methodological issues that Vickery's study raises. What is perhaps most significant for future Goodwin research is Vickery's attention to the relationship between Goodwin and medieval scholasticism. Vickery states: 'In the course of this study I will uncover Goodwin's indebtedness to medieval scholasticism, and especially to Thomas Aquinas, deconstructing the false dichotomy ... between the Puritans and the scholastic tradition.'[74] Reading Goodwin in light of medieval scholasticism constitutes the main comparison within Vickery's study, and his conclusion of Goodwin's basic (but not uncritical) acceptance of scholasticism is undoubtedly correct. Vickery's

---

68. Jones, *Why Heaven Kissed Earth*, 102.

69. In fact, Jones only considers three opponents: Catholics, Arminians and Socinians. Jones, *Why Heaven Kissed Earth*, 64–74.

70. Jones, *Why Heaven Kissed Earth*, 147.

71. *Works*, II, *The Knowledg*, 13; cf. 3.

72. Jones, *Why Heaven Kissed Earth*, 69.

73. *Works*, II, *The Creatures*, 1–2; Lawrence, 'Transmission', 24.

74. Vickery, 'A Most Lawful Pleasure', 16–17.

work, together with Jones's own comments concerning Goodwin's usage of scholastic theologians, secures a further methodological principle that future research ought to respect.[75]

The second methodological issue concerns the relation of Vickery's work to Lawrence's. Vickery's consideration of previous Goodwin scholarship, including Lawrence, is typically brief and negative. He offers some important critiques of Lawrence's work regarding Goodwin's formation, arguing that Goodwin contemplated Arminianism for some time before adopting Calvinism and reassesses Goodwin's motivations for resigning from Holy Trinity. Methodologically, Vickery pays attention to details in the biography by Goodwin's son overlooked by Lawrence and so adopts a less dismissive stance towards the memoir.[76] Yet, while these are welcome corrections, they do not overthrow Lawrence's main contentions concerning Goodwin's grand project. It is, therefore, disappointing that Vickery does not seek to build positively upon Lawrence's work. He ignores the architectonic plan of Goodwin's grand project. Moreover, whereas Jones makes frequent comparisons with Goodwin's supposed primary target, Socinianism, the immediate polemical context is virtually absent in Vickery's work. This is disappointing not just from the perspective of Lawrence's suggestion that combatting the new threats of the 1640s–1650s was part of Goodwin's motivations for his grand project but also because these opponents raised questions concerning the place of reason. On the one hand, Socinianism had a rationalistic character; on the other, enthusiastic teachers dismissed formal education and natural learning. Indeed, I will show that the theology of the latter often resembled Goodwin's, albeit more extreme, and thus represent potentially important comparisons. Examples include John Webster (1611–1682), Roger Williams (c. 1606–1683) and Walter Cradock (c. 1606–1659) who promoted the Spirit's direct revelation.[77] For this reason, Vickery's study falls short of offering a full-orbed examination of Goodwin's view of rationality. Vickery, however, advances upon Jones by making repeated comparisons with Preston. Combined with his fresh assessment of Goodwin's early years, he bolsters the case for understanding Goodwin's output also in terms of his formation in Cambridge.[78]

The third thesis, authored by Hyo Nam Kim, appeared in 2016 shortly after the completion of the present study as a doctoral thesis. Unlike the previous two

75. Jones, *Why Heaven Kissed Earth*, 60–2.

76. Vickery, 'A Most Lawful Pleasure', 25.

77. John Webster, *The Saints Guide, Or, Christ the Rule, and Ruler of Saints* (1653), 1; Roger Williams, *The Hirelings Ministry None of Christs, Or, A Discourse touching the Propagating the Gospel of Christ Jesus* (1652), 17; Walter Cradock, *Divine Drops Distilled from the Fountain of Holy Scriptures: Delivered in several Exercises before Sermons, upon Twenty and three Texts of Scripture* (1650), 211; Walter Cradock, *Gospel-Holinesse: Or, The saving Sight of God. Laid open from Isa. 6.5. Together with The glorious Priviledge of the Saints. From Rom. 8.4,5* (1651), 306–7.

78. Vickery, 'A Most Lawful Pleasure', 50.

studies, Kim's work directly concerns soteriology and does so by tracing the theme of faith in Goodwin's thought. He analyses faith in relation to two soteriological frameworks: covenant theology and the *ordo salutis*.[79] Using Goodwin as his case study, he aims to demonstrate that 'faith could serve as a unifying concept in the soteriology of the confessionally Reformed strand of the English Puritans'.[80] Kim contends that the category of faith proved useful to Goodwin for harmonizing divine sovereignty and human responsibility in salvation, thus refuting the denial of human agency by antinomians on one side and an overemphasis upon human obedience by Arminians, neonomians and Socinians on the other.[81] This socio-theological locating of Goodwin and Reformed puritans is neither novel nor controversial.

Unfortunately, however, despite some useful analysis Kim's study fails to escape the poorer quality of scholarship prior to Lawrence and even repeats a number of their errors.[82] Kim's reading of Goodwin is often too cursory to allow for a rigorous analysis of Goodwin's thought. Goodwin's works are demanding and require a closer and more comprehensive reading than Kim offers. His conclusions are most confused concerning Goodwin's views on regeneration and its relation to other doctrinal *loci*. Kim's handling of secondary literature is also wanting. He uncritically accepts many of Paul Ling-Ji Chang's dubious conclusions,[83] misconstrues Lawrence's careful work and entirely ignores Vickery's study despite its relevance to topics addressed.

In terms of methodology, Kim seeks to build upon the findings of Lawrence's work. However, his attempt is significantly flawed and is illustrative of the wider problems in his study. He claims that 'Goodwin's project is broader than Lawrence thought it to be, and that it includes most of his works.'[84] Here Kim criticizes Lawrence for failing to notice that Goodwin's grand project extended beyond four basic treatises when, as already noted, Lawrence had identified three additional treatises.[85] Kim then indulges in a speculative exercise arguing that the majority of Goodwin's works were included in his grand project because elements within each reflect a Trinitarian scheme. In contrast, the argument that Lawrence had put forward for the three additional treatises is far more persuasive and anchored in textual evidence for the interrelation of the different treatises. Furthermore, Kim's motivation for this exercise is to justify the inclusion and primacy of *Object and Acts* in Goodwin's grand project.[86] Such a conclusion would be convenient for

---

79. Kim, 'Salvation by Faith', 15.

80. Kim, 'Salvation by Faith', 1.

81. Kim, 'Salvation by Faith', 83–96. Arguably, Goodwin's attempt to hold together human and divine agency is more clearly addressed in his handling of the relation of created and uncreated grace in the believer. See §3.4.

82. See §1.5.

83. See p. 21.

84. Kim, 'Salvation by Faith', 47.

85. See §1.3.

86. Kim, 'Salvation by Faith', 72–3, 75.

Kim's basic thesis, since it would justify the primacy and importance of faith as a theme in Goodwin's soteriology and grand project. In support, Kim appeals to Chang's unsupported and likely incorrect claim that this treatise should be dated early.[87] However, there is no evidence to suggest that this treatise was intended to be included in, let alone act as an introduction to, Goodwin's grand project. On the contrary, several pieces of evidence identify *Object and Acts* as Goodwin's long-planned sequel to his tract *Christ Set Forth*.[88]

Moreover, Kim's attempt to use faith as the key to expound Goodwin's soteriology must also be brought into question.[89] As I will discuss, for Goodwin and his Reformed colleagues union with Christ is composed of two parts – the indwelling of the Spirit and the faith of the believer – yet Goodwin was emphatic that the Spirit's indwelling takes precedence over faith. This order agrees with the shape of Goodwin's soteriology that prioritizes the action of the triune God over human agency. Union with Christ, therefore, plays a more basic role than faith in Goodwin's thought. And, as I will demonstrate in this study, union with Christ is more successful at unlocking the underlying substructure of Goodwin's soteriology. That said, faith was clearly an important theme for Goodwin and represents his chief category for articulating the human response in salvation.

Where his analysis is accurate, Kim's work serves to complement the present study. In particular, his comments regarding Goodwin's views on the role of faith, the superiority of salvation above creation and the conditionality of the covenant of grace are broadly correct and useful. However, Kim has not succeeded in providing a rigorous analysis of the structure of the soteriology of Goodwin's grand project.

1.5 Approaching Goodwin's soteriology

The need remains for a modern critical study of Goodwin's grand project which builds upon Lawrence's work and engages with Goodwin's immediate historical context. This is not to claim that existing studies have failed to offer any exploration of Goodwin's soteriology. Quite the reverse: most theses have engaged with it at some level. Both Jones and Vickery address themes related to soteriology. Jones gives attention to redemption accomplished within Goodwin's Christology; Vickery traces Goodwin's conception of reason through a creation, fall and redemption schema. Kim directly addresses soteriology but is hampered by the aforementioned issues and choice of approach. The remaining theses predate Lawrence's reassessment and, it can be argued, adopt unsatisfactory methodologies. Since Jones has already provided a competent survey of these studies,[90] attention here will be focused on their contribution to scholarship on Goodwin's soteriology.

87. Kim, 'Salvation by Faith', 73.
88. See p. 256.
89. Kim, 'Salvation by Faith', 71.
90. Jones, *Why Heaven Kissed Earth*, 21–32.

Paul Brown's dissertation is devoted to: 'The Principle of the Covenant in the Theology of Thomas Goodwin'. The covenants of redemption, of works and of grace in Goodwin's writings are examined and this groundwork prepares the way for an exploration of his ecclesiology in which Brown argues that Goodwin's idea of a church covenant dominates his ecclesiology. Brown, in the course of his study, handles several important topics related to soteriology: election, original sin, justification and assurance. While helpfully highlighting the federal character of Goodwin's theology, these *loci* are explored only in so far as they relate to the theme of covenant. Moreover, Brown understands Goodwin's views in terms of major theological positions in the wider Christian tradition, yet these positions are frequently the caricatures of older scholarship or represent twentieth-century issues and debates alien to the seventeenth century. Unfortunately, then, there is little effort to understand Goodwin in his immediate historical context.

Next to appear was Rembert Bryd Carter's 1961 work focusing on Goodwin's ecclesiology in the context of the Westminster Assembly debates. Carter particularly aims to demonstrate doctrinal connections between Goodwin's ecclesiology, scriptural hermeneutics and eschatology. However, apart from some insightful passing remarks concerning the ecclesiological implications of Goodwin's conception of the indwelling Spirit, soteriological categories are left unexplored.[91]

According to Jones, Stanley Fienberg's 1974 thesis 'represents the first meaningful contribution to Goodwin scholarship'.[92] Fienberg provides three portraits of Goodwin, the first of which is Goodwin as a puritan pastor and consists in an examination of his soteriology. Priority is granted to Goodwin's soteriology since Fienberg judged the advancement of soteriology to have been Goodwin's greatest concern.[93] This section on soteriology offers an analysis of the natural state of humanity, justification, sanctification and social ethics. Fienberg's exposition of these doctrines, however, is slanted towards demonstrating connections with his later portraits of Goodwin as a pioneer of Congregationalism and Goodwin as a puritan in power. A notable example is his chapter on justification which in actual fact is devoted to conversion with particular emphasis on the inner revelation of Christ because Fienberg was convinced that such illumination was the defining doctrine of the Congregationalists. Since Goodwin's soteriology is expounded for the purpose of Fienberg's later portraits, the analysis is also plagued by a lack of historical contextualization. Indeed, this is the main weakness that Jones finds in Fienberg's work:

> in his discussion of Goodwin's soteriology, there is almost no interaction with some of Goodwin's seventeenth-century contemporaries, whether orthodox or heretical. So while the question of what Goodwin said has been adequately

---

91. Carter, 'The Presbyterian-Independent Controversy', 35.
92. Jones, *Why Heaven Kissed Earth*, 23.
93. Fienberg, 'Puritan Pastor and Independent Divine', ii.

addressed by Fienberg, with regards to his particular emphases, the equally important question of why he wrote what he did and in what context is altogether missing from his study.[94]

Nevertheless, as well as providing useful exposition, Fienberg's study has value in highlighting how aspects of Goodwin's distinctive soteriology shaped his ecclesiology and eschatology.

Paul Blackham's 1995 work on 'The Pneumatology of Thomas Goodwin' argues that Goodwin's pneumatology was driven by his Christology. It contains an important chapter on 'Pneumatology and Soteriology in Goodwin' where Blackham argues that the work of the Spirit is pivotal to Goodwin's soteriology because Goodwin 'grounds his soteriology firmly in the ontological'.[95] (By 'ontological' Blackham refers to what will be denoted in this study as 'real' and is contrasted with extrinsic or legal categories.[96]) Such an emphasis, Blackham believes, is evident in Goodwin's attention to regeneration by the Spirit and the related notion of 'ontological union' with Christ underpinning a strongly 'ontological' understanding of justification. Blackham argues that such a soteriology was an implication of Goodwin's strongly ontological understanding of original sin and corresponding union with Adam. This emphasis, he concludes, aligned Goodwin with Eastern theology. However, while the insight that Goodwin's soteriology possessed a strong 'ontological' character is important, as I will demonstrate in this study, Blackham misunderstands Goodwin's doctrine of justification and oversimplifies Goodwin's view of the nature of union with Christ. There remains a need for a study of Goodwin's soteriology which exposes its 'ontological' character, yet reads his theology with due care.

Moreover, while Blackham's work is a helpful introduction to some important features of Goodwin's soteriology and locates these in the theologies within the wider Christian tradition, there is minimal interaction with Goodwin's immediate historical context and influences. In fairness, this is a corollary of Blackham's stated aim of bringing Goodwin 'into conversation with the contemporary Pneumatological debates'.[97] This leaves his study lacking as a piece of historical theology, and it is often unclear whether the theology presented is Blackham's or Goodwin's. Furthermore, Vickery has especially and persuasively criticized Blackham's chapter on Goodwin's epistemology, particularly with regard to Goodwin's relation to medieval scholastic theologians. This raises the question of whether similar issues hamper Blackham's exposition of Goodwin's soteriology.

Appearing almost simultaneously to Blackham's work was Michael Horton's 1995 study on Goodwin and the puritan doctrine of assurance. Dedicated to refuting the 'Calvin versus the Calvinists' thesis on the issue of assurance, Horton

---

94. Jones, *Why Heaven Kissed Earth*, 24.
95. Blackham, 'Pneumatology', 192.
96. See §1.5.1.
97. Blackham, 'Pneumatology', 2.

adopts Goodwin as a test case. Jones overstates the matter when he writes that Horton's work is 'as much about Calvin as it is about Goodwin';[98] nonetheless, the driving concern of Horton's argument is not Goodwin's immediate historical context but his theological continuity with earlier Reformed thought. Horton argues that shifts in emphasis can be accounted for on the basis of changed pastoral contexts, rather than fundamental doctrinal change.[99] In mounting this argument, Horton provides a generally competent wide-ranging analysis of Goodwin's theology, including many soteriological *loci*. However, each is only addressed inasmuch as it intersects with the issue of assurance and is not framed within Goodwin's overall theological project.

The final study is Paul Ling-Ji Chang's examination of Goodwin on the Christian life, completed in 2001. Chang's main contention is that Goodwin was a theologian of latter-day glory and that his soteriology was shaped by the development of his millenarianism.[100] To demonstrate this contention, Chang moves through the *ordo salutis* examining each *locus* in turn. Despite some useful exposition, this is a problematic work at multiple levels. Jones remarks that '[r]igorous formal analysis of the aforementioned doctrines is almost non-existent'.[101] Indeed, there is little consideration of how doctrines cohere with the wider structures of Goodwin's thought or careful analysis in his immediate historical context. Perhaps more problematic is that the evidence presented to support Chang's overall contention is at best suggestive. Merely finding some points of contact between Goodwin's eschatology and soteriology does not constitute proof that Goodwin's eschatology is determinative of his soteriology. Proper demonstration will be provided in Chapter 5 where the fundamental movement of Goodwin's soteriology will be shown not to consist in redemption from the Fall but in exaltation from an original earthly state to an eschatological heavenly state. There is little evidence, however, that Goodwin's specific millenarianism as expounded in his writings on Revelation shaped his soteriology.

In conclusion, this survey of Goodwin studies in relation to his soteriology has underlined the need for a modern critical and dedicated study of this principal area of his thought. In this work I aim to fill this major lacuna in Goodwin scholarship. My basic methodology is a close and careful reading of soteriological themes found in Goodwin's entire corpus, but with special consideration of the treatises that comprise his grand project. I will analyse these themes in light of his immediate historical context as identified by Lawrence (with the aforementioned corrections duly noted). This will principally entail an examination of key theological distinctions in light of the concerns of English Reformed orthodox

98. Jones, *Why Heaven Kissed Earth*, 29.

99. Horton, 'Assurance', 39.

100. Chang, 'Christian Life', 338. In effect, Chang's thesis is an attempt to develop Anthony Dallison's article: Anthony R. Dallison, 'The Latter-Day Glory in the Thought of Thomas Goodwin', *Evangelical Quarterly* 58, no. 1 (1986): 53–68.

101. Jones, *Why Heaven Kissed Earth*, 32.

divines in the 1640s-1650s. Compared with Jones, however, I will pay greater attention to the architectonic plan of Goodwin's project, to his early formation (especially noting Sibbes's influence) and to antinomian and radical teachings of the 1640s-1650s. David Como's identification of two discernible strains of antinomian theology – 'imputative' and 'perfectionist' – will prove useful.[102] The former prized the imputed righteousness of Christ; the latter moved in a Familist[103] direction and contended that believers are inherently perfect because of Christ's presence in them. It was out of the perfectionist strain that more extreme mystical and radical pantheistic teachings emerged.[104]

For several reasons in this work I will approach Goodwin's soteriology through the lens of union with Christ. First, while many previous studies have made claims regarding Goodwin's doctrine of union with Christ, none have given proper attention to it. Secondly, by focusing on redemption applied, this work will complement the examination of redemption accomplished included in Jones's study. Thirdly, union with Christ was a matter of heated controversy in the 1640s-1650s because of radical teachings and, therefore, the implications of Lawrence's work will be especially important. Finally, Jones has suggested that union with Christ was a key organizing idea for Goodwin: 'The concept of union with Christ, then, seems to occupy a central position in Goodwin's soteriology.'[105] In this study I will seek to establish the veracity of Jones's suggestion. Noting that Richard Muller has warned that the idea of a 'central dogma' was alien to Reformed orthodox writers,[106] I will take union with Christ to be central in the sense that the whole application of salvation is founded upon it. Thus, the lens of union with Christ opens the possibility of discerning the fundamental structures of Goodwin's soteriology and so the unity of thought underlying his grand project.

102. David R. Como, *Blown by the Spirit: Puritanism and the Emergence of an Antinomian Underground in Pre-Civil-War England* (Stanford, CA: Stanford University Press, 2004), 38-40.

103. Familism (also known as the Family of Love) was a Christian sect that followed the teaching of Dutch mystic Hendrick Niclaes (*c.* 1502-*c.* 1580). Niclaes taught that by the inward presence of Christ disciples could reach a state of perfection. The orthodox were especially outraged by Niclaes's claim that true believers are 'Christed with Christ' and 'Goded with God' and so elevated to the same status as Christ/God. In England, the sect was denounced as heretical in the late sixteenth century and would not survive the restoration in 1660. See Julia G. Ebel, 'The Family of Love: Sources of Its History in England', *Huntington Library Quarterly* 30, no. 4 (1967): 337; Christopher W. Marsh, *The Family of Love in English Society, 1550-1630*, Cambridge Studies in Early Modern British History (Cambridge: Cambridge University Press, 1994), 1, 22.

104. Como, *Blown by the Spirit*, 391.

105. Jones, *Why Heaven Kissed Earth*, 236.

106. Richard A. Muller, *Post-Reformation Reformed Dogmatics: The Rise and Development of Reformed Orthodoxy, ca. 1520 to ca. 1725*, 2nd edn, 4 vols (Grand Rapids, MI: Baker Academic, 2003), volume 1, 187-8.

As evident from his stated intention in *The Creatures* for his grand project, Goodwin sought to defend a high soteriology in which Christ not only reverses the devastating effects of the Fall but also advances believers far above the original Adamic state.[107] The latter aspect constitutes the fundamental movement in Goodwin's soteriology and amounts to what could be described as a Reformed doctrine of Christocentric deification. This study will provide an account of Goodwin's high soteriology and examine his conviction that its application to the believer must be founded in his conception of real union with Christ. The term 'real union' denotes a mystical union with Christ forged by his indwelling within the believer in contradistinction to mere relative union, that is, a legal union external to the believer. Goodwin's particular notion of real union with Christ involves the indwelling of the uncreated grace of the person of the Holy Spirit. I will demonstrate that this conception of real union is essential to the theological logic, pastoral concerns and intentions of Goodwin's grand project.

1.5.1 Excursus: Real and relative unions with Christ

Given the prominence of the notion of real union with Christ throughout this study, it is necessary to offer a brief discussion of this terminology. Some modern writers have employed terms such as 'ontological union'[108] and 'mystical union'[109] seemingly to refer to the same concept. However, both are rather inexact terms and while the latter has the advantage of being used by seventeenth-century writers, it fails to capture an important distinction fundamental to Reformed soteriology. Puritan divines often used the real/relative distinction to distinguish two kinds of union with Christ.[110] The latter referred to union external to the two parties

---

107. *Works*, II, *The Creatures*, 31–2. See p. 8.

108. Blackham, 'Pneumatology', 246.

109. George Hunsinger, 'Justification and Mystical Union with Christ: Where Does Owen Stand?' in *The Ashgate Research Companion to John Owen's Theology*, ed. Kelly M. Kapic and Mark Jones (Farnham, UK: Ashgate, 2012), 200.

110. E.g. Bartholomew Ashwood, *The best treasure, or, The way to be truly rich being a discourse on Ephes. 3.8, wherein is opened and commended to saints and sinners the personal and purchased riches of Christ* (1681), 51; Francis Freeman, *Light vanquishing darknesse. Or a vindication of some truths formerly declared, from those aspersions which have been (by reason of some misapprehensions) cast upon them; now published for the satisfaction and benefit of others* (1650), 48; Edward Leigh, *A Systeme or Body of Divinity: Consisting of Ten Books* (1654), 487; Thomas Manton, *A second volume of sermons preached by the late reverend and learned Thomas Manton* (1684), 'Sermons on the Seventeenth Chapter of St. John', 302; William More, *A short and plaine tractate of the Lords Supper grounded upon I Cor. II, 23, &c* (1645), 18–19; John Shower, *Sacramental discourses, on several texts, before, and after the Lord's Supper* (1693), 5, 10; John Whitefoote, *A discourse upon I Peter IV. VIII. wherein the power and efficacy of charity as it is a means to procure the pardon of sin is explained and vindicated* (Cambridge, 1695), 121. Further examples appear in the discussion that follows.

and was normally forensic in nature. The former was more problematic to define. For these divines, the qualifier 'real' did not merely denote factuality since what is relative was also considered to be factual. Discussing the nature of union with Christ, Richard Baxter (1615–1691) wrote: 'I take not the word Real, as opposite to feigned, but to Relative.'[111] The qualifier 'real', therefore, denoted that which was not relative.[112] However, divines struggled to provide a positive definition and instead turned to scriptural analogies, of which the most frequently appealed to were the head–body and the vine–branches analogies. In these examples, real union amounted to a physical union involving the internal nature of both parts united together. Consequently, an important hallmark of real union was the requirement of the physical spatial proximity of both parts united. In contrast, puritan divines assumed that both parts in relative unions remained physically separate objects and the union did not require spatial proximity. The chief analogies cited to illustrate relative unions were the husband–wife analogy and the analogy of a king and his subjects.[113] The former analogy was appealed to in the sense that marital union is valid even when the husband and wife are geographically separated. Preston remarked: 'What is the union betweene Christ and us? Partly relative, as the union betweene the husband and the wife, and you know if the husband and wife be a thousand miles asunder there might be such an union.'[114]

Both categories of union were applied by puritan divines to the union of Christ and the church. When the category of real union was applied, divines insisted that union with Christ is spiritual[115] rather than physical.[116] While the category 'spiritual' arose from scriptural texts and was rather ill-defined, real union with Christ could be identified by the aforementioned requirement of spatial proximity. For puritan divines, then, the distinguishing hallmark of real

---

111. Richard Baxter, *The saints everlasting rest, or, A treatise of the blessed state of the saints in their enjoyment of God in glory* (1650), 28.

112. Other contrasts were sometimes drawn including the real set in opposition to the imaginary.

113. John Preston, *An elegant and lively description of spirituall life and death* (1632), 87.

114. John Preston, *The saints qualification: Or A treatise I. Of humiliation, in tenne sermons. II. Of sanctification, in nine sermons whereunto is added a treatise of communion with Christ in the sacrament* (1633), 5.

115. Hence, the term 'spiritual union' was also often used by divines, often with 1 Corinthians 6:16-17 in view. E.g. Thomas Case, *Movnt Pisgah, or, A prospect of heaven being an exposition on the fourth chapter of the first epistle of St. Paul to the Thessalonians* (1670), 23–5. Goodwin occasionally employed the term 'spiritual union'. *Works*, V, *The Holy Ghost*, 43; *Works*, I, *Ephesians*, part II, 186; *Works*, II, *The Knowledg*, 29.

116. An exception was Baxter, who, in discussing the idea of real union with Christ, equated it with believers becoming 'Physically one with Christ, and not only Relatively'. Richard Baxter, *Of the imputation of Christ's righteousness to believers in what sence sound Protestants hold it and of the false divised sence by which Libertines subvert the Gospel* (1675), 112.

union with Christ is the requirement of Christ's presence indwelling the believer. Thus, despite lacking rigorous philosophical definition, the term 'real' appeared to operate as a broad category denoting that which has actual inherent physical or spiritual existence.

Here it should be noted that the real/relative distinction was also used by divines to distinguish transformative salvific benefits (e.g. regeneration) from legal salvific benefits (e.g. justification).[117] The qualifier 'real' again denoted what was internal in nature. Henry Burton (bap. 1578, d. 1647/8) wrote, 'the iustification of a sinner ... is relatiue, and not physically inherent in vs'.[118] Some authors linked the real/relative distinction in union with Christ to the same distinction in salvific benefits.[119] This distinction was, therefore, fundamental to Reformed soteriology as expounded by puritan divines. In this study I will employ the real/relative distinction to refer to two kinds of union with Christ as well as to two kinds of salvific benefits.

As I will argue, when Goodwin normally spoke of union with Christ he did not have mere relative union in view but a real union forged by the indwelling of Christ within the believer. Admittedly, Goodwin only employed the term 'real union' on occasion;[120] however, it is clear that he was contending for union with Christ to be understood as real and not merely relative union. That this was the case is evident from a pair of early sermons. In these sermons, Goodwin insisted that both a 'Relative Union' and a 'substantial Union' exist between Christ and believers.[121] Like other puritan divines, Goodwin explained the relative union in terms of the husband–wife analogy, stressing that 'the Husband may be in one place, and the Wife in another ... yet be Man, and Wife'.[122] In contrast, the substantial union, he stressed, involves a 'real In-being' of Christ's person in the believer and so maps on to the category of real union.[123] Why, then, did Goodwin here prefer the term 'substantial union' over 'real union' (the conventional counterpart to relative union)? This question is pointed because the term 'substantial union' was capable of being interpreted as implying the union of God and the believer into one substance, something that Goodwin strenuously argued against elsewhere. Goodwin felt justified in using the term since he was following earlier Reformed

---

117. That real salvific benefits result from union with Christ was sometimes taken as proof that a real union must exist between Christ and believers.

118. Henry Burton, *The Christians bulvvarke, against Satans battery. Or, The doctrine of iustification so plainely and pithily layd out in the severall maine branches of it as the fruits thereof may be to the faithfull, as so many preservatives against the poysonous heresies and prevailing iniquities of these last times* (1632), 58.

119. E.g. Henry Scudder, *The Christians daily walke in holy securitie and peace* (1631), 697–8.

120. E.g. *Works*, IV, *Object and Acts*, part II, 15, 84.

121. *Works*, I, *Thirteen Sermons*, 45–6 cf. 33, 40.

122. *Works*, I, *Thirteen Sermons*, 40.

123. *Works*, I, *Thirteen Sermons*, 40.

writers who had employed it, not to imply substantial union proper but in Goodwin's words to denote 'a union of the substance of [Christ's] person and of ours'.[124] That is, he clarified, Christ's person 'dwelling in us substantially'.[125] Herein lay the reason for Goodwin's choice of this term over 'real union'. For Goodwin, 'substantial union' not only signified real union but real union specifically involving the indwelling of Christ's person rather than a weaker (i.e. mediated) notion of Christ's presence. In later works, Goodwin abandoned the term, perhaps owing to the rise of heterodox radicals who advocated the union of God and the believer into one substance. Nevertheless, he continued to contend that union with Christ must be forged by an indwelling of Christ's person in the believer.[126] In this study I will demonstrate that this contention was Goodwin's conception of union with Christ and will seek to show how Goodwin's high view of real union with Christ is central to his soteriology.

1.6 Controversy over union with Christ

I also aim in this work, by attending to Goodwin's conception of union with Christ, to make an important contribution to significant debate and controversy within academic scholarship in the last decade or so over the doctrine of union with Christ as articulated by sixteenth- and seventeenth-century writers. Broadly speaking two camps have emerged, with the issues of historical theology being brought to the fore most starkly by William Evans and John Fesko. The sharpness of disagreement is particularly evident in a brief exchange between the two scholars precipitated by Evans's review article on the controversy.[127] It is evident

---

124. *Works*, I, *Thirteen Sermons*, 33–4 cf. 40. Likely in view are Calvin, who famously employed the term in his discussion of the sacraments, and Girolamo Zanchi (1516–1590), who had used the term in a work that Goodwin cited later in the same sermon. J. Calvin, *Institutes of the Christian Religion*, trans. F. L. Battles, 2 vols, Library of Christian Classics (Philadelphia, PA: Westminster Press, 1960; repr., Louisville, KY: Westminster John Knox Press, 2006), volume 2, 1382; Girolamo Zanchi, *An excellent and learned treatise, of the spirituall mariage betvveene Christ and the church, and every faithfull man.*, trans. [anon.] ([Cambridge?], 1592), 99.

125. *Works*, I, *Thirteen Sermons*, 34.

126. Although his views underwent some refinement, see §2.4.

127. William B. Evans, 'Déjà Vu All over Again? The Contemporary Reformed Soteriological Controversy in Historical Perspective', *Westminster Theological Journal* 72, no. 1 (2010): 135–51; J. V. Fesko, 'Methodology, Myth, and Misperception: A Response to William B. Evans', *Westminster Theological Journal* 72, no. 2 (2010): 391–402; William B. Evans, 'Of Trajectories, Repristinations, and the Meaningful Engagement of Texts: A Reply to J. V. Fesko', *Westminster Theological Journal* 72, no. 2 (2010): 403–14. For a review article of wider discussions over union with Christ in Reformed theology, see: Michael S. Horton, 'Calvin's Theology of Union with Christ and the Double Grace: Modern Reception and Contemporary Possibilities', in *Calvin's Theology and Its Reception: Disputes, Developments,*

that theological biases are bound up with the historical questions. At stake are two competing visions of applied soteriology according to the Reformed tradition: one scheme grants priority to union with Christ, the other to justification. As Evans remarks, some have referred to a 'Reformed civil war' over union with Christ and related *loci*.[128]

Evans's monograph *Imputation and Impartation* tracks the development of the doctrine of union with Christ from Calvin through to the American Reformed tradition.[129] Most of the contention has been provoked by Evans's chapter on Reformed orthodoxy in which he argues that the generations following Calvin departed from the Reformer's emphasis on union with Christ. Evans claims that Calvin advocated real union with Christ as fundamental in his soteriology, such that the twin salvific benefits of justification and sanctification are bestowed as the immediate result of real union with Christ's human nature. Thus, Calvin held justification as a result of union with Christ, in contrast to the 'Lutheran' scheme in which justification is a divine declaration prior to union with Christ. Evans contends that Reformed orthodox divines, however, departed from Calvin's simple scheme to frame applied soteriology in terms of the *ordo salutis*. Thus, simultaneous bestowal of the twin benefits yielded to a causal sequence in which justification and sanctification are applied in successive and discrete acts. Employing an *ordo salutis* allowed these divines to resolve ambiguities inherent in Calvin's scheme. Theologically, it allowed justification and sanctification to be directly related and allowed the reintroduction of the notion of created grace.[130] Pastorally, it provided grounds for assurance of salvation through the application of the practical syllogism, since according to *ordo salutis* schemes sanctification was viewed as the consequence and therefore evidence of election. In conjunction with this development, the notion of union with Christ was retained but bifurcated into two distinct notions: legal union (i.e. relative union) and real union securing justification and sanctification respectively. Consequently, sanctification and justification were no longer tied together as in Calvin's scheme. The introduction of a legal union resulted from the rise of federal theology and was assumed necessary to ground imputation. Calvin's notion of real union was modified and in effect became equated with sanctification. Finally, accompanying these developments was a depreciation of the significance of Christ's human nature: out of pietistic concerns, interest shifted from union with his human nature to communion with the same, accompanied by a corresponding shift in the significance of the

---

and New Possibilities, ed. J. Todd Billings and I. John Hesselink (Louisville, KY: Westminster John Knox Press, 2012).

128. Evans, 'Déjà Vu', 150.

129. William B. Evans, *Imputation and Impartation: Union with Christ in American Reformed Theology*, Studies in Christian Thought and History (Milton Keynes, UK: Paternoster, 2008).

130. Whereas uncreated grace is the gift of God himself, created grace refers to the gift of transformation of the nature or the disposition of the believer.

Lord's Supper. Evans's study, therefore, helpfully highlights how a wide range of theological *loci* bear relation to union with Christ.

However, Evans's narrative of historical development has been fiercely contested by Fesko.[131] Not only complaining that Evans's work lacks engagement with primary texts, Fesko also perceives methodological problems inherent in Evans's study by accusing him of resurrecting the discredited 'Calvin against the Calvinists' thesis. Fesko's substantial publication *Beyond Calvin* collects together and expands upon a string of articles in which the relation of union with Christ, justification and the *ordo salutis* is explored in the thought of numerous Reformation and post-Reformation theologians. On that basis, he seeks to establish a more accurate picture. Arguing for far greater uniformity and continuity in the early modern Reformed tradition, Fesko states that his work demonstrates four main contentions.[132] First, Calvin's formulations of union were not formative for the Reformed tradition (nor did he diverge in this matter from the Lutheran tradition). Secondly, there was, in fact, no definitive Reformed doctrine of union with Christ or the *ordo salutis*; instead there was variety in articulations of these doctrines. Thirdly, all early modern Reformed theologians embraced some form of the *ordo salutis* alongside union with Christ, with all ordering salvific benefits in some sense. That is, the *ordo salutis* and union with Christ were not deemed incompatible. Fourthly, the hallmark of an early modern Reformed doctrine of union with Christ was logical/theological prioritization of justification over sanctification. In Fesko's mind, this last contention defined the Reformed approach to applied soteriology.

Fesko's work poses a significant challenge to Evans. However, the range of theologians examined is not only the strength but also the weakness of his work. It is often hard to judge whether the evidence cited represents major elements of a theologian's thought or minor inconsistencies. This is especially true in regard to the fourth contention where Fesko's evidence is often slight and lacking in clarity and consistency regarding the nature of the prioritization of justification over sanctification. Fesko enumerates seven senses of prioritization, yet many of these do not address the issues of contention.[133] More problematic is his tendency to assume that the priority of justification over sanctification extends to include priority over real union and regeneration. This leads him to minimize the role of real union as the basis of justification in his handling of primary texts. Indeed, his desire to discover the priority of the forensic over the real leads to dubious interpretations of several texts, especially those of Girolamo Zanchi (1516–1590), Perkins and Owen. These readings evidence confusion of theological categories: real union (indwelling?) is confused with real transformation; the exclusive necessity of justification for divine

---

131. J. V. Fesko, *Beyond Calvin: Union with Christ and Justification in Early Modern Reformed Theology (1517–1700)*, Reformed Historical Theology (Göttingen: Vandenhoeck & Ruprecht, 2012).

132. Fesko, *Beyond Calvin*, 380–4.

133. Fesko, *Beyond Calvin*, 382.

acceptance with theological prioritization; redemption applied with redemption accomplished; and the imputation of Christ's righteousness to believers with the imputation of believers' sin to Christ.

These criticisms underline the need for further exploration of union with Christ and related doctrines in Reformed orthodox theologians. While Fesko offers important correctives to Evans's work and encourages scholars to fresh examination of the texts, his account is overcoloured by theological biases. Since Fesko's publication, two further studies have appeared advancing similar critiques of Evans. Muller has waded into the debate and while his contribution is not plagued by the same problems as Fesko's, union with Christ and the *ordo salutis* receive relatively brief attention.[134] Limited remarks regarding union with Christ and an assessment of Evans's main claims also appear in a recent volume on puritan theology by Jones and Joel Beeke.[135] Significantly, both studies suggest that Goodwin was an important theologian concerning the doctrine of union with Christ but do not offer extended analysis. There remains, then, the pressing need for an examination of Goodwin's conception of union with Christ, which stands outside the theological biases and heat of the ongoing debate, and grants proper attention to both the immediate historical context and theological distinctions.

The inherent weakness of these broad survey approaches highlights the need for detailed studies of individual Reformed thinkers on union with Christ. By restricting the present study to a single divine, my intention is to give proper consideration of both historical and doctrinal issues. Goodwin is a worthy candidate for several reasons. First, as yet Goodwin has not received dedicated attention by Fesko or by any scholar on the topic of union with Christ.[136] Secondly, the three theologians whom Fesko particularly misinterprets – Zanchi, Perkins and Owen – are the three who stand closest to Goodwin theologically.

---

134. Richard A. Muller, *Calvin and the Reformed Tradition: On the Work of Christ and the Order of Salvation* (Grand Rapids, MI: Baker Academic, 2012), chapters 6–7.

135. Joel R. Beeke and Mark Jones, *A Puritan Theology: Doctrine for Life* (Grand Rapids, MI: Reformation Heritage Books, 2012), 481–9.

136. To date the nearest to an extended study of Goodwin's doctrine of union with Christ is a chapter in Jonathan Jong-Chun Won's thesis. However, this study is problematic and of limited value because he claims that 'Goodwin did not give detailed attention to the topic of union with Christ'. Jonathan Jong-Chun Won, 'Communion with Christ: An Exposition and Comparison of the Doctrine of Union and Communion with Christ in Calvin and the English Puritans' (PhD thesis, Westminster Theological Seminary, 1989), 214. As a consequence his chapter is actually devoted to communion and the role of Christ's humanity. Won's study is flawed because he artificially restricts himself to consider only *Christ the Mediator* and *The Heart of Christ*. Unfortunately, Evans appears to reach his conclusion that communion displaced union for seventeenth-century divines on the basis of Won's work. More recently, Kim offers brief remarks on union with Christ, but his analysis is too superficial and tends to rehearse the approach of Fesko. Kim, 'Salvation by Faith', 193–204.

Thirdly, Goodwin's writings are characterized by careful thought, thus opening the possibility that Goodwin gave particularly detailed treatment of union with Christ and related themes. As already noted, Goodwin's grand project amounts to the longest exposition of soteriology to emerge from late puritanism and was penned at a time when the presence of radical teachings forced the nature of union with Christ to come under close scrutiny. For these reasons, a dedicated study of Goodwin's thought on union with Christ where conclusions are reached with sensitivity to the immediate historical context and within Goodwin's wider soteriology and corpus has the potential to make a significant contribution to the ongoing controversy.

Only article length studies have appeared on individual English divines in light of the current debate. In a collected volume, T. Robert Baylor's chapter includes limited comments concerning Owen's doctrine of union with Christ and thereby attempts to resolve some of the divergent conclusions of Fesko and Evans.[137] More relevant is William Edwards's persuasive article arguing that John Flavel's (1627–1691) applied soteriology was structured around the priority of union with Christ rather than justification.[138] Edwards, therefore, finds support for Evans's overarching contention concerning the Reformed shape of applied soteriology but corrects Evans's narrative that union with Christ was displaced in the thought of seventeenth-century divines. However, this brief study pays insufficient attention to the nature of union with Christ and its implications. While in this present study I will paint a similar picture to Edwards, I will make the nature of the union my main focus.

Indeed, the chief matter insufficiently addressed in the Evans–Fesko interchange is the nature of real union with Christ and its significance. Evans contends that in the thought of seventeenth-century divines real union became equated with sanctification and ceased to function as the basis for the application of justification. Fesko assumes that real union involves transformation and so downplays the role of real union with Christ by arguing that legal categories were more primitive. Moreover, in attempting to secure his view of continuity in the tradition and to maintain the compatibility of *ordo salutis* considerations and union with Christ, Fesko tends to overlook the specific nature of union with Christ and instead to identify it with the *ordo salutis* as a whole.[139] Previous Goodwin studies also give

---

137. T. Robert Baylor, '"One with Him in Spirit": Mystical Union and the Humanity of Christ in the Theology of John Owen', in *'In Christ' in Paul: Explorations in Paul's Theology of Union and Participation*, ed. Michael J. Thate, Kevin J. Vanhoozer and Constantine R. Campbell, *Wissenschaftliche Untersuchungen Zum Neuen Testament. 2. Reihe* (Tübingen, Germany: Mohr Siebeck, 2014); cf. Hans Burger, *Being in Christ: A Biblical and Systematic Investigation in a Reformed Perspective* (Eugene, OR: Wipf & Stock, 2009), 30–86; Hunsinger, 'Justification and Mystical Union'.

138. William R. Edwards, 'John Flavel on the Priority of Union with Christ: Further Historical Perspective on the Structure of Reformed Soteriology', *Westminster Theological Journal* 74, no. 1 (2012): 33–58.

139. Fesko, *Beyond Calvin*, 29; cf. Horton, 'Calvin's Theology', 90–1.

conflicting assessments of the nature of union with Christ. Blackham stresses 'ontological union' with Christ,[140] whereas Horton, trying to maintain continuity in the tradition and coherency with covenantal ideas, blurs external and real unions or simply assumes that union with Christ is representative in nature.[141] Furthermore, while several studies have noted the priority of union with Christ in applied soteriology, little attention has been given to disclosing how union with Christ functions as the cause of salvific benefits. In this study, therefore, I will determine the nature of union with Christ in Goodwin's thought and demonstrate how his specific conception of union founds the application of salvation.

1.7 Outline of the argument

My main argument in this book is that Goodwin founded the application of every aspect of salvation upon a real union with Christ forged by the indwelling of the person of the Holy Spirit. To this end, I will expound the different aspects of Goodwin's high soteriology; I will then examine how he founded the application of each aspect in his conception of real union with Christ. Since the theme of union with Christ pervaded much of Goodwin's doctrinal writings, the breadth of his corpus will be considered, but the central texts studied will be the seven treatises comprising his grand project. The argument will unfold in four main doctrinal chapters.

In Chapter 2 I will demonstrate that Goodwin defended a strong notion of real union with Christ and will determine its nature. Goodwin's mature view was that real union with Christ is forged by the indwelling of the Holy Spirit's person in believers and involves the subsequent mystical indwelling of Christ and the believer's response of faith. I will conclude the argument by showing that Goodwin's conception of real union finds fulfilment in communion with God. As a postscript, I will assess Goodwin's understanding of the Lord's Supper in relation to his conception of real union with Christ.

In Chapter 3 I will examine the relation of real union with Christ to the transformation of believers. Goodwin contended for a high notion of transformation in his account of regeneration, bodily resurrection and the renewal of the *imago Dei*. Final salvation, he insisted, requires not only the restoration of a believer's nature from the devastation of the Fall but also transformation to a spiritual state surpassing Adam's original condition. Noting that transformation is distinct from, yet dependent upon, the indwelling of the Spirit, I will conclude by examining how Goodwin believed transformation to be founded in his conception of real union with Christ.

---

140. Blackham, 'Pneumatology', 246.

141. Horton, 'Assurance', 47, 407. In fact, Horton, contra Blackham, states that 'this union is not … ontological'. Horton, 'Assurance', 266.

Chapter 4 provides a parallel analysis for justification. I will demonstrate that Goodwin advocated a high notion of forensic understanding of justification and how he founded the application of justification also in real union. Here I will examine the role of extrinsic/legal union(s) with Christ and the relation of such union(s) to real union. Furthermore, since both transformation and justification result from real union, the question of the priority of justification over transformation will be addressed. This will precipitate an examination of Goodwin's *ordo salutis*[142] and its relation to union with Christ.

In Chapter 5 I will advance the argument by uncovering the reasons why real union occupies a central place in Goodwin's soteriology as the foundation of salvation applied. This question will be addressed by a consideration of Goodwin's conception of participation in Christ. Goodwin's soteriology is governed by a notion of participation as replication and for this reason union with Christ occupies a fundamental role. Finally, I will show that, for Goodwin, the nature of that union is determined by the nature of Christ's person and that participation in Christ's divine nature is central to Goodwin's soteriology.

Throughout these chapters, Goodwin's applied soteriology will be located in the range of major views within his immediate historical context. I will demonstrate that Goodwin maintained a stronger doctrine of union with Christ and salvation than the majority of Reformed puritan divines and that such high views located him near radicals and antinomians. Yet, by repeated and careful employment of key distinctions Goodwin robustly remained within the bounds of Reformed orthodoxy. The consistency of Goodwin's thought, however, is sometimes strained and important tensions will be highlighted.

In Chapter 6 I will conclude the argument by summarizing Goodwin's conception of union with Christ and then assessing its significance within his grand project, his immediate historical context and the ongoing debate over union with Christ. While the findings of this study support the priority of union with Christ as the structure of Reformed applied soteriology, I will contend that neither side of the debate correctly construes the views of Reformed orthodox puritan writers in the mid-seventeenth century. Instead, disagreement among divines over the nature of real union with Christ must be more fully recognized.

1.8 Conclusion

The case for a fresh examination of Goodwin's soteriology with particular reference to union with Christ results from a double-pronged motivation. The first motive arises from the current state of Goodwin scholarship. The legacy of Lawrence's historical reassessment of Goodwin has been to set a new platform for future research. The majority of Goodwin's treatises, Lawrence demonstrates, were

---

142. This term will be used throughout despite only appearing later in the Reformed tradition. See Muller, *Calvin and the Reformed Tradition*, chapter 6.

intended to form a grand project defending Reformed soteriology against new threats of Socinian and radical teachings. Since Lawrence's work, three further studies have appeared, but none offers an examination of Goodwin's soteriology that adequately builds upon Lawrence's findings. Research prior to Lawrence interacted with Goodwin's soteriology through the lens of various theological concerns, but little attention was given to the immediate historical context and did not have Lawrence's findings in view. Therefore, the case was made for a dedicated study of Goodwin's soteriology built upon Lawrence's reassessment. I will offer a close examination of Goodwin's writings with particular reference to his grand project, attempt to locate his theology in the range of views of his day and establish key theological distinctions Goodwin employed to defend his soteriology. As will be demonstrated, union with Christ occupies a central role in Goodwin's soteriology. This study, therefore, will uncover the fundamental structures of his soteriology by focusing on the nature and role of union with Christ.

The second motive stems from current controversy concerning the doctrine of union with Christ in Reformation and post-Reformation thought. Within this debate two groupings of scholars have emerged. The first represented by Evans and advocating a discontinuity thesis argues that the *ordo salutis* and federal theology displaced Calvin's conception of real union with Christ as occupying a fundamental place in applied soteriology. Fesko, representative of the other grouping of scholars, argues for greater uniformity across the tradition and seeks to uphold the priority of the forensic and justification over real categories. Too much of the debate has been characterized by cursory use of primary texts and general narrative claims. The case was made for dedicated studies of union with Christ in the soteriology of key theologians. Goodwin is an obvious candidate not simply because he has been largely ignored in these debates but because his grand project represents the longest account of soteriology to emerge from a seventeenth-century puritan and was written in the midst of controversies surrounding union with Christ. I aim in this book to make a significant contribution to this debate.

This study will demonstrate that Goodwin defended a strong conception of real union with Christ forged by the indwelling of the Holy Spirit's person and upon which Goodwin founded the application of every aspect of salvation. In so doing, I will uncover the nature and architectonic structures of Goodwin's high Reformed soteriology. Goodwin maintained a Trinitarian, federal soteriology in which redemption from the problem of sin is set within a Reformed scheme of Christocentric deification requiring believers to partake of Christ's divine nature.

Chapter 2

THE REALITY OF UNION WITH CHRIST IN HIS MYSTICAL INDWELLING

2.1 Introduction

In Goodwin's mind, the strongest union between a believer and Christ is a real union involving the indwelling of Christ. Focusing on the three works where Goodwin particularly addressed union with Christ, in this chapter I will demonstrate that he defended such a notion of union with Christ and attempt to delimit its nature. Beginning with *The Knowledg*, I will show that in the 1650s Goodwin defended the bounds of real union with Christ against radical teachings (§2.2). Then, by examining an important sermon from the 1620s, I will explore how Goodwin's early understanding of the nature of real union with Christ involved the immediate and primary indwelling of Christ's divine nature (§2.3). By the time he wrote the bulk of his grand project in the 1650s, Goodwin's ideas had undergone significant pneumatological revision and so by analysing *The Holy Ghost*, I will demonstrate Goodwin's mature conception of real union with Christ to be union forged by the person of the Holy Spirit indwelling believers (§2.4). Goodwin's revised conception warrants an investigation of the mode of Christ's mystical indwelling by the Spirit (§2.5). I will complete the argument by demonstrating that Goodwin held real union with Christ to found the application of salvation and, in particular, communion with God (§2.6). As a postscript, Goodwin's doctrine of union with Christ will be shown to be integrated with his understanding of the Lord's Supper (§2.7).

2.2 Defending the bounds of union with Christ

While outside of his grand project, Goodwin's treatise *The Knowledg* also penned in the 1650s provides a suitable point of departure. As his most polemical work, Goodwin stated his target: 'the Ranters of our late Age, as appears by their Writings … which put me upon writing this Discourse'.[1] Thus, while Goodwin made passing critiques of Socinian ideas,[2] the more pressing threat was radical teachings.

---

1. *Works*, II, *The Knowledg*, 13; cf. 3.
2. *Works*, II, *The Knowledg*, 52, 156, 157, 159, 180.

This identification is important because combatting enthusiasts and radicals forced Goodwin to defend the limits of the union of believers with Christ. To this end, Goodwin presented the Trinitarian union, incarnational union and believers' union with Christ as a kind of chain of unions[3] descending in degree.[4] Believers enjoy union with God because of their union with Christ, and in turn the union of Christ's humanity with his divinity, and in turn again the union of Christ's divinity with the Father. Goodwin believed this chain allowed his hearers to 'determine, and state the true Bounds and Condition of our Union with God through Christ.'[5] An examination of these three unions, therefore, allows the bounds of Goodwin's conception of union with Christ to be determined.

2.2.1 The Trinitarian union

In Book I, Goodwin's central concern was to defend the doctrine of the Trinity.[6] While Socinians are most commonly associated with denial of the Trinity in seventeenth-century England, the Reformed orthodox were alarmed that radical protagonists also undermined the doctrine. For this reason, despite divergence on many points, Socinian and radical teachings were often associated in the minds of the Reformed orthodox. However, as Paul Chang-Ha Lim argues, whereas Socinians were anti-Trinitarian, the radicals are better characterized as non-Trinitarian.[7] Unlike Socinians who were anti-Trinitarian because of their literalistic reading of Scripture, radicals were non-Trinitarian as an implication of their chief tenets. Here Lim particularly has in mind pantheistic radicals for whom the uniqueness of the three distinct persons was displaced, since all creatures were understood to be manifestations of God. Citing this rationale, Goodwin accused 'Ranters' of rendering the persons of the Trinity mere 'Manifestations, or else Operations of God'.[8] While Davis has questioned whether an identifiable 'ranter' group promoting licentious pantheism existed, the suspected 'ranter' Joseph Bauthumley (1613–1692), at least, was pantheistic and overtly repudiated the doctrine of

---

3. *Works*, II, *The Knowledg*, 17, 20. Goodwin even employed the term 'Golden Chain': *Works*, II, *The Knowledg*, 139. While this term had been widely associated with Romans 8:28-30 and the *ordo salutis*, here Goodwin took his lead from passages such as 1 Corinthians 3:21-23 and John 17.

4. *Works*, II, *The Knowledg*, 21, 50, 82.

5. *Works*, II, *The Knowledg*, 21.

6. This concern to defend the nature of the Trinitarian union contrasted with his response in *The Creatures* where Goodwin rebutted the same opponents, yet focused on defending the God/creature distinction.

7. Paul Chang-Ha Lim, *Mystery Unveiled: The Crisis of the Trinity in Early Modern England*, Oxford Studies in Historical Theology (Oxford: Oxford University Press, 2012), 73.

8. *Works*, II, *The Knowledg*, 3.

the Trinity.[9] Also likely in Goodwin's purview was an array of radical teachers espousing similar views that undermined the Trinity or were explicitly anti-Trinitarian. Mystical writers such as William Erbery (1604/5–1654) and Thomas Higgenson (fl. 1653–6) abandoned Trinitarian orthodoxy and simply referred to the 'divine nature' united identically to Christ and to believers.[10] Entertaining sympathies with such theology, the Member of Parliament John Fry (c. 1609–1656/7) explicitly abhorred the language of three distinct persons.[11] Regarding Quakers, Hugh Barbour remarks: 'Most Quakers were vague about the Trinity, and called the term itself unbiblical.'[12] Muggletonian leaders John Reeve (1608–1658) and Lodowick Muggleton (1609–1698) were explicitly anti-Trinitarian, favouring a form of modalism.[13] The net result was that the doctrine of the Trinity was under attack from a range of radical voices. Philip Dixon observes that already during the 1640s, the threat posed by these sects was increasingly perceived as far graver than that by the traditional enemy, the Catholics. He recounts how Ephraim Pagitt (1575–1647) 'was indignant with his fellow Protestants because even "the Papists worship God in Trinity, and Trinity in Unity; whereas some of these sectaries blaspheme the holy Trinity"'.[14]

9. Jacob Bauthumley, *The Light and Dark sides of God: Or a plain and brief Discourse of The light side {God, Heaven and Angels.} The dark side} Devill, sin, and Hell. As also of the Resurrection and Scripture* (1650), 10–12; cf. Davis, *Fear, Myth and History*, 44–8.

10. E.g. William Erbery, *The North Star: Or, Some Night-Light Shining in North-Wales. With some Dark Discoveries Of the day of God approaching, that is, the second coming or appearing of Christ in us the hope of Glory* (1653), 8, 25; Thomas Higgenson, *Glory sometimes afar off, Now stepping in; Or, The great Gospel-Mysterie of The Spirit, or Divine Nature in Saints* (1653), 40–1.

11. John Fry, *The Accuser sham'd: Or, A pair of Bellows To Blow off that Dust cast upon John Fry, A Member of Parliament, by Col: John Downs, likewise a Member of Parliament, Who by the Confederacy and Instigation of some, charged the said John Fry of Blasphemy & Error To the Honorable House of Commons* (1648), 20–3.

12. Hugh Barbour, *The Quakers in Puritan England*, Yale Publications in Religion (New Haven, CT: Yale University Press, 1964), 145.

13. John Reeve and Lodowick Muggleton, *A Divine Looking-Glass: Or, The third and last Testament of our Lord Jesus Christ, Whose personal Residence is seated on his Throne of Eternal Glory in another world* (1661), 2. Reeve and Muggleton were tailors by occupation and cousins by relation. In 1651 and the following year both men had profound spiritual experiences which led them to announce that they were the last two witnesses of Revelation chapter 11. Over the years until Reeve's death in 1658, their teachings developed, but were essentially a weaving together of other radical ideas of the time. See *Oxford Dictionary of National Biography*, s.v. 'Reeve, John (1608–1658)' [version: 23 September 2004] and s.v. 'Muggleton, Lodowicke (1609–1698)' [version: 24 May 2008].

14. Philip Dixon, *'Nice and Hot Disputes': The Doctrine of the Trinity in the Seventeenth Century* (London: T&T Clark, 2003), 39.

Goodwin believed that, as well as having a modalistic tendency, the radicals undermined the uniqueness of the Trinitarian union. He responded:

> The Assertion which I undertake to prove, is this, That God, and Christ, and by consequence the Holy Ghost, have an Union and Communion of a higher kind, than what we are ordained ever to receive; and therefore I call it the supream Sovereign Union.[15]

Many radicals, appealing to John 17:21-23, believed that they had scriptural support for asserting the equality of the Trinitarian union and believers' union with God.[16] That this text formed a storm centre of debate in the mid-1650s is evident from the preface penned by Goodwin and Philip Nye (bap. 1595, d. 1672) to their 1656 publication of the late Thomas Hooker's (1586?–1647) exposition of John 17:

> The more eminent Matter of these Sermons, is *our mystical Union* with *God* and Christ; a Subject but rarely handled by *Divines* ... The true stating the Bounds, for kind, or degree of that *Union* with God, which the Saints are admitted to by God, is of great use and necessity *to this Age*; the Fate whereof, is erring ... in the greatest Points of Religion, and in this Point more grossly and wretchedly than in any other ... particularly of some passages and Clauses in this Prayer of our Lord ... as [*that they may be one as we are one, &c.*][17]

Goodwin and Nye claimed that Hooker's work must have resulted from divine guidance. Erbery had notoriously used this text in his 1646 public debate with Francis Cheynell (bap. 1608, d. 1665).[18] Cheynell responded by insisting that 'the union between Christ and the Saints is a true union, a reall though a mysticall and spirituall union'; however, '(As) notes no *equality* in that place of *John*, though it may note a *similitude*, so the proportion and distance be observed between creatures and their Creator ... there is not an union of nature between God and the Saints'.[19] In *The Knowledg*, Goodwin, like Cheynell, insisted that 'as' denotes

---

15. *Works*, II, *The Knowledg*, 13.

16. Especially relevant is John 17:21 which reads, 'that they all may be one; as thou, Father, art in me, and I in thee, that they also may be one in us.'

17. Thomas Hooker, *A Comment upon Christ's last Prayer In the Seventeenth of John. Wherein is opened, The Union Beleevers have with God and Christ, and the glorious Priviledges thereof* (1656), 'To the Reader', n.p.

18. William Erbery, *Nor Truth, nor Errour, Nor day, nor Night; But in the Evening There shall be Light. Zach. 14. 6, 7. Being the Relation of a Publike Discourse in Maries Church at Oxford, Between Master Cheynel and Master Erbury, January 11. 1646* (1647), 12–13.

19. Francis Cheynell, *An Account Given to the Parliament by the Ministers sent by them to Oxford. In which you have the most remarkable passages which have fallen out in the six Moneths service there, divers Questions concerning the Covenant of Grace, Justification, &c. are briefly stated* (1647), 43.

mere similitude rather than exact equality.[20] He asserted that the Trinitarian union is 'superior', 'immediate' and 'incommunicable' whereas the union enjoyed by believers with the divine persons is 'a secondary Union'.[21] Consequently, within the threefold chain of unions, the Trinitarian union is 'the Sovereign, Supream Union' and the 'Original Union'.[22]

Two points, therefore, dominated Goodwin's response to the radicals: the existence of three distinct divine persons and the unique union between them. To ascertain the nature of the Trinitarian union according to Goodwin, it is, therefore, first necessary to examine the notion of divine personhood in his Trinitarianism. Unfortunately, while Jones provides a helpful chapter on Goodwin's doctrine of the Trinity, he pays insufficient attention to this aspect. This is a significant oversight not only because the concept of person coloured much of Goodwin's theology[23] but also because it was at the centre of seventeenth-century Trinitarian controversies. In his study of these debates, Dixon contends that, for various reasons, the category of person in regard to the Trinity was increasingly used in a univocal rather than analogical sense.[24] Fry confessed his bewilderment:

> as for the word Person, I do not understand that it can properly be attributed but to man; it is out of doubt with me, that if you ask the most part of men what they mean by a Person, they wil either tell you 'tis a man, or else they are not able to give you any answer at all[25]

Biddle's Socinian rejection of the Trinity was largely driven by the assumption that in reference to God 'person' must carry the same sense as for humans.[26] That is, for Biddle 'person' imported an absolute, concrete meaning which necessarily implied that three divine persons are three separate gods. Accordingly, Lim writes that Socinians assumed that personhood involves a separate centre of consciousness.[27] Similar critiques were also to be found in the polemics of radical teachers. Bauthumley rejected the Trinity because of the meaning of 'person':

> Surely it is a mystery to mee; But I rather thinke it is a mystery of Iniquity, for I suppose a person cannot be without an essence, so that it plainly appeares there must be three essences in God, and yet these three must be but one[28]

---

20. *Works*, II, *The Knowledg*, 15; *Works*, II, *Election*, 121–44.
21. *Works*, II, *The Knowledg*, 15, 18.
22. *Works*, II, *The Knowledg*, 13, 18.
23. Blackham concurs: 'Goodwin's Trinity is essentially personal. He is quite convinced that it is the concept of person that makes the Trinity what God is.' Blackham, 'Pneumatology', 22; cf. 32–3.
24. Dixon, 'Nice and Hot Disputes', 3.
25. Fry, *The Accuser sham'd*, 22.
26. Dixon, 'Nice and Hot Disputes', 51–3.
27. Lim, *Mystery Unveiled*, 82.
28. Bauthumley, *The Light and Dark sides*, 10–11.

From a different perspective, Reeve and Muggleton closely associated the notion of person with bodily form/existence and so, asserting the corporeality of God, they rejected multiple persons in God.[29]

While Goodwin opposed these writers, he nevertheless operated with a conception of divine personhood which assumed much commonality with human personhood. In part, this resulted from the seriousness with which he took the biblical text, but it also served to refute the modalistic theology of the radicals. Accordingly, Goodwin insisted that the Father, Son and Spirit be denoted as 'distinct persons' or 'persons distinct'.[30] Moreover, he treated the divine persons as distinct personalities involving apparent distinct centres of consciousness. Blackham remarks that, for Goodwin, 'there is no suggestion of God being ultimately but a single person, or a single mind or will'.[31] Thus, while Geoffrey Nuttall contends that puritans such as Goodwin were rediscovering the notion of 'God as a Person' after its medieval neglect,[32] in fact, for Goodwin at least, God is emphatically three persons.

Despite not offering a definition of 'person', Goodwin's strong concept of divine personhood is evident in two main respects. First, he assumed that the divine persons are capable of interpersonal communion. In a chapter devoted to proving that they are distinct from each other, Goodwin's argument turned on scriptural texts containing either conversations between the divine persons, or the speech of one divine person about himself or another: 'they are found speaking, not only *Us*, as Persons but also ordinarily, one to another, in the language of [*I*] and [*Thou*] … One speaks of another, as another Person distinct from himself'.[33] Between the divine persons, he wrote, 'there passeth a Communication of, and imparting of Secrets, a discovery of each others mind'.[34] Elsewhere, Goodwin wrote, 'Speech is the ground of Fellowship'.[35] A strong conception of divine personhood, therefore, was necessary for Goodwin to maintain that the three persons constitute a 'Society among themselves; enjoying Fellowship, and Delights accordingly in themselves'.[36] Goodwin justified this view, arguing 'if the Divine Nature had not afforded, in having in it three Persons really distinct, knowing, rejoycing in, glorying of, and speaking unto each other, there had not been a perfection of Blessedness'.[37] Despite giving insufficient attention to the notion of person, Jones nevertheless rightly remarks that this idea of a divine society 'lies at the very heart' of Goodwin's doctrine

29. Reeve and Muggleton, *A Divine Looking-Glass*, 2–3.

30. E.g. *Works*, II, *The Knowledg*, 11.

31. Blackham, 'Pneumatology', 29.

32. Geoffrey F. Nuttall, *The Holy Spirit in Puritan Faith and Experience* (Oxford: Basil Blackwell, 1946; repr., Chicago, IL: University of Chicago Press, 1992), 171–2.

33. *Works*, II, *The Knowledg*, 11.

34. *Works*, II, *The Knowledg*, 18.

35. *Works*, II, *The Creatures*, 51.

36. *Works*, II, *Election*, 141.

37. *Works*, II, *Election*, 141.

of the Trinity.[38] Indeed, it is striking that Goodwin embraced a social analogy to explain the Trinity but elsewhere rejected the scholastic usage of psychological analogies, warning that 'these all are so obscure and uncertain in their evidence or character of these three Persons and their distinction'.[39] It should be further noted that for Goodwin this conception of divine personhood and communion is not merely an economic phenomenon but pertains to the immanent Trinity. Elsewhere, refuting modalistic teachings, the decisive scriptural proof he offered was that each 'speaks as a person'.[40] Returning to *The Knowledg*, Goodwin asserted that divine interpersonal communion exists before creation: 'an Eternity of Time did pass, when there were no Creatures at all; but the Three Persons wholly enjoyed themselves all that Time without interruption'.[41] Here Goodwin's language stretched the accepted understanding of divine eternity in order to maintain his strong conception of divine personhood.[42]

Secondly, Goodwin's concept of divine personhood is evident in his discussion of the *pactum salutis*. It is vital, in Goodwin's mind, that this agreement be grounded in the Trinity.[43] Ironically, Jones motivates his chapter on Goodwin's doctrine of the Trinity by noting that it underpinned the *pactum salutis*,[44] yet what that most requires is a strong conception of divine personhood – the chief aspect Jones overlooks.[45] In fact, a newly published study by B. Hoon Woo on the *pactum salutis* in the thought of seventeenth-century Reformed divines highlights that Goodwin's account of the doctrine '*seems* to assume three *separate* persons'.[46] In this covenant, Goodwin conceived of the divine persons as distinct personalities entering into a contractual agreement whereby each party binds himself to fulfil his obligations.[47] Goodwin even discussed the motivations of each person for agreeing to the terms of the covenant.[48] Elsewhere, he referred to the mutual trust

38. Jones, *Why Heaven Kissed Earth*, 107.

39. *Works*, III, *Man's Restauration*, 10; cf. 6.

40. *Works*, IV, *Object and Acts*, part II, 105.

41. *Works*, II, *The Knowledg*, 14.

42. Elsewhere, Goodwin articulated a more conventional understanding of God's eternity. *Works*, II, *The Creatures*, 10.

43. *Works*, II, *Election*, 140.

44. Jones, *Why Heaven Kissed Earth*, 100.

45. Jones later includes a brief comment that makes this connection. Jones, *Why Heaven Kissed Earth*, 135. Brown also identifies the importance for the federalists of divine persons characterized by self-consciousness and their ability to enter into agreements. He concludes: 'There must be real distinctions within the Godhead in spite of the cry of tritheism.' Brown, 'The Principle of the Covenant', 114; cf. 88.

46. B. Hoon Woo, *The Promise of the Trinity: The Covenant of Redemption in the Theologies of Witsius, Owen, Dickson, Goodwin, and Cocceius*, Reformed Historical Theology (Göttingen: Vandenhoeck & Ruprecht, 2018), 218.

47. *Works*, III, *Christ the Mediator*, 26; cf. *Works*, III, *Man's Restauration*, 19.

48. E.g. *Works*, III, *Christ the Mediator*, 23–8.

of the Father and the Son in the outworking of the covenant.[49] Similarly, Goodwin appealed to the mutual honouring of the three persons – 'see how the Persons honour one another' – as the consequence of the distinct work each undertakes in salvation.[50]

Given this strong concept of divine personhood, the question of Goodwin's account of the Trinitarian union is more pointed. Adhering to standard Reformed orthodox theology, in *The Knowledg* Goodwin appealed to the oneness of essence, that is, the divine persons possess an essential unity.[51] Hence, his theology did not collapse into the kind of Trinitarianism advocated later in the seventeenth century by William Sherlock (1639/40–1707) or indeed that advocated by modern social Trinitarians, which arguably fails to avoid tritheism.[52] That said, there remains the question of the place of *perichoresis* or mutual interpenetration within Goodwin's account. Goodwin referred to the 'mutual In-being' of the Father and the Son as the ground of being 'one in the Godhead'.[53] Thus, he equated their mutual indwelling with the union of the divine persons: 'as their Union is, and was afore the World was; *I in my Father, and my Father in me* ... as dwelling in one another'.[54] The notion of indwelling, therefore, was intrinsic to his understanding of the Trinitarian union. However, Goodwin appeared unable or unwilling to explain the nature of the Trinitarian union any further. This was tacit recognition of the status of the Trinitarian union, and indeed the whole chain of unions, as a 'great Mystery'.[55]

2.2.2 The incarnational union

If Book I defends the Trinitarian union, then Book II addresses the incarnational union.[56] While Goodwin's target had apparently shifted to opposing claims that the saints enjoy the same status and union as Christ, he believed that the same error of asserting oneness with God was responsible: 'out of the same Principle, they in like manner serve our Lord Jesus Christ's Person ... They must be Christ too'.[57] This claim was borne out in the pantheistic theology of Bauthumley who asserted that God dwells as much in Christ as in any creature.[58] More likely Goodwin

---

49. *Christ Set Forth*, 4; cf. *Works*, IV, *Object and Acts*, part II, 139.

50. *Works*, I, *Ephesians*, part I, 414; cf. *Works*, V, *Of Several Ages*, 196.

51. *Works*, II, *The Knowledg*, 1; cf. 21; *Works*, II, *Election*, 130, 135. Note: Jones remarks that Goodwin treated the terms 'essence', 'being' and 'substance' as practically synonymous. Jones, *Why Heaven Kissed Earth*, 105–6.

52. Woo concurs. Woo, *The Promise of the Trinity*, 222.

53. *Works*, II, *The Knowledg*, 17–18.

54. *Works*, II, *The Knowledg*, 19–20; cf. 14.

55. *Works*, II, *The Knowledg*, 21; cf. *Works*, V, *Glory of the Gospel*, 4.

56. *Works*, II, *The Knowledg*, 50.

57. *Works*, II, *The Knowledg*, 50.

58. Bauthumley, *The Light and Dark sides*, 11–12.

had in mind mystical preachers such as Erbery, Higgenson and William Dell (d. 1669) who, while not pantheists, followed a Familist[59] trajectory and specifically elevated believers to the same status as Christ bar chronological (and perhaps causal) priority.[60] This teaching appeared to be the target of Goodwin's warning against those who add 'the Persons of all the Saints to the individual *one Lord, one Husband, Christ,* … that they all should be Christ as well as he, equal with him, their Union with God the same that he is, this is to un-Christ him'.[61]

As in Book I, Goodwin demarcated the bounds of the respective unions, alleging that the basic error of his opponents was 'Mistakes of Union'.[62] His response is largely absorbed with a scriptural defence of the eternal existence of God the Son as a distinct divine person to whom a human nature was united. Thus, Goodwin contended for a Christology that agreed with the Chalcedonian settlement: 'the Person of Christ is God and Man, joined into one Person'.[63] To secure the reasonableness of the two natures of Christ remaining distinct yet united as one person, Goodwin appealed to the oft-used soul–body analogy.[64] However, contrary to Blackham's judgement, Goodwin's strong concept of personhood was not applied to the person of Christ in the sense of the two natures forming a single centre of consciousness.[65] Indeed, Goodwin held that the human nature of Christ enjoyed fellowship with the Son as he does with the other two divine persons.[66]

Goodwin was emphatic that the incarnational union is the highest possible union that any creature enjoys with God.[67] Reasoning that Scripture presents Christ as the foundation of the salvation of believers, he concluded that Christ's person and union must be of a higher order than, and foundational to, the union enjoyed by them.[68] In the final analysis, however, Goodwin insisted that the qualitative differentiation resides in the unique hypostatic nature of the incarnational union.[69]

---

59. Familist founder Niclaes claimed that true believers are 'Christed with Christ' and 'Goded with God' and so elevated to the same status as Christ/God. See p. 22 fn. 103.

60. William Dell, *The Stumbling-Stone, Or, A Discourse touching that offence which the World and Worldly Church do take against {1. Christ Himself. 2. His true Word. 3. His true Worship. 4. His true Church. 5. His true Government. 6. His true ministry.}* (1653), 34–5; Erbery, *Nor Truth, nor Errour*, 4, 9–10, 15, 21; Erbery, *The North Star*, 9–10; Higgenson, *Glory sometimes afar off*, 40–1.

61. *Works*, II, *The Knowledg*, 93.

62. *Works*, II, *The Knowledg*, 50.

63. *Works*, II, *The Knowledg*, 83.

64. *Works*, II, *The Knowledg*, 86; cf. *Works*, II, *The Creatures*, 86–90.

65. Blackham, 'Pneumatology', 60.

66. *The Heart of Christ*, 196–7.

67. *Works*, II, *The Knowledg*, 50.

68. *Works*, II, *The Knowledg*, 50–2.

69. *Works*, II, *The Knowledg*, 120, 146–7, 148; cf. *Works*, III, *Christ the Mediator*, 51.

2.2.3 Conclusion: Believers' union with Christ

What, then, may be stated concerning the nature of believers' union with Christ? Goodwin maintained that it is a union of a lower order than the Trinitarian and incarnational unions, yet patterned upon them.[70] Like the Trinitarian union, it is a union of persons (here is evident the commonality of divine and human personhood), but it is not a union of essence. Like the incarnation, it is a union of God and creature, but it is not a hypostatic union.

Yet, while Goodwin set upper bounds upon union with Christ, he did not reduce it to the lowest conceivable union. Lawrence alleges that Goodwin and his colleagues who produced the *Principles* distanced themselves from radical teachings by rejecting 'any corporeal or realistic understandings of the doctrine of union with Christ'.[71] The relevant article from the *Principles*, however, merely stated, 'this same Jesus Christ, being the onely God and Man in one Person, remains for ever a distinct Person from all Saints and Angels, notwithstanding their union and communion with him'.[72] Lawrence further appeals to *The Knowledg*. Yet, regarding union with Christ, Goodwin there insisted that

> there have been too many mistakes in these Times; some soaring too high, to Identities and Sameness with God, at least, with Christ … some falling too low, to Unions only by Grace and Assistance, and presence to assist; or in outward Relations to Christ.[73]

This is a crucial passage: While Goodwin insisted that the union of believers with Christ belongs to a lower order than the Trinitarian and incarnational unions, he refused to lower it to a mere legal or external union. Here Goodwin may have had Baxter in view, who was taken to task by Owen over his denial of a mystical union in favour of an external union.[74] Edward Leigh (1603–1671), in his systematic theology also written in the 1650s, stated the same two extremes of how union with Christ was understood at the time: 'Some make our Union with Christ to be

---

70. *Works*, II, *The Knowledg*, 21.

71. Lawrence, 'Transmission', 159.

72. Thomas Goodwin, Philip Nye and Sidrach Simpson, *The Principles of Faith, presented by Mr. Tho. Goodwin, Mr. Nye, Mr. Sydrach Simson, and other Ministers, to the Committee of Parliament for Religion, by way of explanation to the Proposals for propagating of the Gospel* (1654), 6.

73. *Works*, II, *The Knowledg*, 21.

74. Hans Boersma argues that while an external union was the thrust of his view, Baxter did not entirely reject a real union: *A Hot Pepper Corn: Richard Baxter's Doctrine of Justification in Its Seventeenth Century Context of Controversy* (Netherlands: Boekencentrum, 1993; repr., Vancouver: Regent College, 2004), 234–5. Nevertheless, mainstream divines believed that Baxter made such a denial and Baxter, at very least, expressed considerable scepticism regarding the existence of real union with Christ. Baxter, *The saints everlasting rest*, 28; Baxter, *Of the imputation*, 112.

only a relative Union, others an essentiall personall Union, as if we were Godded with God, and Christed with Christ.[75] Like Goodwin, Leigh contended for an intermediate kind of union – a 'real Union' of persons but of a lower kind than the Trinitarian union and the incarnational union.

However, unlike Leigh, Goodwin was also insisting that union with Christ must not be reduced to mere union by created grace, which, as will be discussed, was the majority approach. The radical Higgenson shared Goodwin's assessment that such union is too low. He complained that union by created grace alone amounts to no more than a moral union in which Christ and the saints share the same affections like 'two lovers or friends … of one heart, mind, heart or thought, in a moral conjunction'.[76]

Goodwin, therefore, sought to tread the middle path between low views of union (external union and union by created grace alone) on the one side and high views of union (union which was in danger of assigning believers the same status as Christ or collapsing the God/creation distinction) on the other.

Treading the middle path, Goodwin was capable of making conflicting assessments of the degree of union available to believers. On occasion he ascribed to believers the highest union below the incarnational union enjoyed by Christ: 'all Unions left below him, are left free for us to attain, and shall be obtained by us'.[77] However, he also frequently employed the language of infinity to describe the difference between Christ and believers, such that Christ is at an 'infinite distance' above them.[78] Thus, while Goodwin sought to ascribe to believers the closest of possible unions with Christ/God, this desire conflicted with his commitment to guard the incomparable uniqueness of the Trinitarian and incarnational unions. Here Goodwin may be compared to the more radical Congregationalist preacher Dell. In answering Goodwin's colleague Sydrach Simpson (*c.* 1600–1655), Dell reasoned that since real union involves partaking of the divine nature, affirming real union with Christ is incompatible with affirming an 'infinite distance' between believers and Christ.[79] Dell's theology was generally more restrained than Erbery's, although even he was far less worried than Goodwin about staying within the bounds of orthodoxy.

Nevertheless, Goodwin's views on the nature of union with Christ resembled the position of the enthusiasts.[80] Cradock, who had served under Erbery yet narrowly

---

75. Leigh, *A Body of Divinity*, 487.

76. Higgenson, *Glory sometimes afar off*, 14.

77. *Works*, II, *The Knowledg*, 50.

78. E.g. *Works*, II, *The Knowledg*, 16, 71.

79. William Dell, *A Plain and Necessary Confutation Of divers gross and Antichristian Errors Delivered … by Mr. Sydrach Simpson* (1654), 41.

80. While real union was not a central conviction of 'imputative antinomians', nevertheless John Eaton (1574/5–1630/1), for example, also stressed the nearness and reality of union with Christ: 'though mystically and spiritually, yet, truly, really and substantially so ingraffed and united into Christ, that wee are made one with him, and he one with us'. John Eaton, *The Honey-Combe of Free Justification by Christ alone. Collected out of the meere*

stayed within the bounds of orthodoxy,[81] similarly stressed the real nature of union with Christ.[82] As well as insisting that believers and Christ enjoy 'the most *reall* union', he stipulated that it is 'a very *neere union*', a '*totall* union' and 'an *inseparable* union'.[83] The commonality between Goodwin and Cradock may be explained by the shared influence of Preston. By far Cradock's most frequently referenced authority, Preston was cited in support of Cradock's conception of union with Christ: 'as that reverend Doctor *Preston*, I remember, observes, it signifies a *greater union* than any other in the world'.[84] In a sermon from the 1640s, Goodwin used similar language: 'It is the strongest tie in the World.'[85]

Having identified upper and lower bounds of union with Christ, the question remains as to the nature of the union. Baxter was sceptical that a real union could be conceived which is neither a union of essence nor a union of hypostasis:

> A Real Conjunction (improperly called Union) we may expect. And a true Union of Affections, A Moral Union, (improperly still called Union,) And a true Relative Union, such as is between the members of the same political body and the Head, yea such as is between the husband and the wife, who are called one flesh. And a real communion, and Communication of Real Favors, flowing from that Relative Union. If there be any more, it is acknowledged unconceiveable, and consequently unexpressable, and so not to be Spoken of. If any can conceive of a proper Real Union and Identity, which shall neither be a unity of Essence, nor of person with Christ (as I yet cannot) I shall not oppose it[86]

In a later work, he put the matter even more sharply, demanding that those who insist on a real union with Christ answer the question: 'ONE What?'[87] Baxter, however, found himself isolated in holding this view. Like other puritan divines, Goodwin, while unable to provide a direct answer to this question, insisted that union with Christ must be a real union. In the face of this ineffability of real union, divines employed scriptural analogies to describe the union. As will become clear,

---

Authorities of Scripture, and common and unanimous consent of the faithfull interpreters and Dispensers of Gods mysteries (1642), 429.

81. E.g. Cradock differentiated the incarnational union from the union believers enjoy: 'betweene him and the person of the Father, there is an *Essentiall* union, and ours is virtuall by the power of the Spirit of God, he by his union hath all good things without measure, and wee by ours in measure'. Walter Cradock, *The Saints Fulnesse of Joy in their fellowship with God: Presented In a Sermon preached July 21. 1646. Before the Honorable House of Commons* (1646), 24–5.

82. Cradock, *Saints Fulnesse*, 21–2.

83. Cradock, *Saints Fulnesse*, 20–3.

84. Cradock, *Divine Drops*, 71.

85. *Works*, I, *Ephesians*, part I, 490.

86. Baxter, *The saints everlasting rest*, 27–8.

87. Baxter, *Of the imputation*, 112.

two analogies dominated Goodwin's understanding of real union with Christ: the marriage analogy such that believers share interpersonal communion with Christ, and the head–body analogy such that believers are united in sharing Christ's spiritual life. As will be explored in Chapter 5,[88] the latter analogy was the more fundamental of the two, suggesting that Goodwin's notion of Christ and believers united by the same spiritual principle of life was the closest he came to answering Baxter's question: 'ONE What?' While this answer lacks the theological precision of the unions involved in the received doctrines of the Trinity and the incarnation, Goodwin was able to provide significant theological reflection on the nature of Christ's indwelling involved. Examining the mode of indwelling in Goodwin's thought, however, reveals a key development in his theology.

2.3 *The early Goodwin: The immediate and primary indwelling of Christ*

Among the earliest extant works of Goodwin are a set of sermons '*preached in his younger Time at* Cambridge *in his Lecture at Trinity Church*.'[89] The notions of union and mystical indwelling were major themes in several of these sermons and so provide an invaluable window onto Goodwin's early thought concerning real union with Christ. The first of two sermons on Ephesians 3:17 is worthy of especial attention. It is unsurprising that in this early sermon Goodwin was apparently attempting to think himself clear on the nature of mystical indwelling. This is evident from expressions of hesitancy on certain points.[90] Moreover, as will be noted, the scheme that he expounded was neither entirely satisfactory nor consistent with his later views. Nevertheless, this sermon comprises Goodwin's most extended treatment of the notion of indwelling and what is clear is a close identification of union with indwelling.

Whereas Goodwin's later treatise *The Knowledg* outlined the boundaries within which the three unions of his chain must be understood in the face of heterodox teachings, this early sermon reveals Goodwin's assumptions concerning the commonality of the three unions. Goodwin assumed throughout the sermon that indwelling forges or entails union. For example, he wrote that the Spirit indwelt the prelapsarian Adam by infused grace and was 'the only Bond of that Union' such that once lost the 'Union was instantly dissolved'.[91] This indwelling Goodwin presented as inferior to that experienced by believers. Superior union, he remarked, involves superior indwelling. In the second sermon on the same text, Goodwin asserted that union with Christ involves 'both a substantial Union, and a communicative Union, which is expressed here by *In-dwelling*'.[92] Granting

88. See especially §§5.4.2–5.4.3.
89. *Works*, I, *Thirteen Sermons*, 'To the Reader', n.p.
90. *Works*, I, *Thirteen Sermons*, 31.
91. *Works*, I, *Thirteen Sermons*, 34.
92. *Works*, I, *Thirteen Sermons*, 46.

the existence also of an external 'relative' union between Christ and believers, he insisted that 'the relative Union serves for' union involving indwelling.[93] Goodwin, therefore, assumed that the strongest unions involve indwelling.

Moreover, for the three unions belonging to the chain of salvation, Goodwin insisted that union specifically involves indwelling by a divine person. Concerning the Trinitarian union, Goodwin understood the unity of the three divine persons in one essence as entailing their mutual indwelling:

> All three Persons are *essentially* one God; although Persons distinct enjoying that God-head. … the Father, and Spirit do dwell naturally, or essentially in him; as he is the second Person, simply considered: And thus do each of the Persons dwell one in another, and hold an intimate in-dwelling … this mutual Union of the Persons one in another, is the highest, and nearest that can be; and is indeed founded on the Identity of the God-head.[94]

Thus, the key distinctive is that the Trinitarian persons indwell each other 'essentially'.[95] Goodwin declined to give further content, stating that it involves 'a Circum-incession' belonging uniquely to the three divine persons 'which I cannot stand to explain'.[96]

Likewise, Goodwin cast the incarnational union in terms of indwelling by a divine person. Here the parallel with the other two unions of the chain was strained, since the incarnational union was not forged by one person indwelling another person but by a person indwelling a human nature. This raises the question of an incipient Nestorian tendency in Goodwin's Christology.[97] Here it should be recalled that Nestorius's primary model of the divine–human relationship in Christ was that of indwelling: the Word indwelt the man Jesus. His nemesis, Cyril of Alexandria, well aware of this metaphor's scriptural basis, did not reject such language altogether but neither believed that it adequately described nor allowed it to drive his conception of the union of Christ's two natures. While Goodwin primarily referred to the incarnational union in terms of indwelling, unlike Nestorius he was careful to insert deliberate qualifiers to insist upon Christ's singular personhood. For example, he described the incarnation as: 'the Son of God dwelling in the Man, as personally one Person with him'.[98] Goodwin regularly used

---

93. *Works*, I, *Thirteen Sermons*, 46.

94. *Works*, I, *Thirteen Sermons*, 35–6.

95. *Works*, I, *Thirteen Sermons*, 36.

96. *Works*, I, *Thirteen Sermons*, 35.

97. The same propensity was inherent in the Reformed tradition in light of stress upon the integrity of Christ's two natures in contradistinction to the perceived Lutheran confusion of the natures. By the 1650s, the rise of pantheistic radical teachers reinforced Goodwin's instinct to protect the God/creation distinction and therefore the distinction of Christ's two natures.

98. *Works*, I, *Thirteen Sermons*, 34.

the qualifier 'personally' to specify hypostatic union/indwelling. In comparison, he also cast the union of Christ's human nature with the Father and the Spirit in terms of indwelling by divine persons, but unlike the incarnational union added the disclaimer that these unions are not hypostatic: 'the Persons both of the Father, and the Spirit, should dwell therein, according to its utmost capacity of having Union with them; which is not Personal'.[99] In the final analysis, Goodwin assumed that the relation established, whether hypostatic or interpersonal, is the critical factor. Nevertheless, while he had no intention to depart from Chalcedonian Christology, Goodwin's stress upon union as the indwelling of one person by another was so dominant that his Christology moved in a Nestorian direction and was only kept in check by assertions of the hypostatic nature of the incarnational union. Moreover, his frequent referral of Christ's human nature as 'the Man' or 'that Man Jesus' was also suggestive of an incipient Nestorian tendency in his thought.[100]

In view of this evidence, it is unsurprising that Goodwin equated the union of believers with Christ with the indwelling of believers by Christ's person. The sermon as a whole constituted an extended argument for the immediate and primary indwelling of Christ in the believer. It is immediate in the sense that Christ indwells neither merely by created grace nor by the Spirit as a proxy but rather by 'an actual In-being of his Person ... as the Soul dwells in the Body'.[101] Moreover, by the indwelling of Christ's person, Goodwin specifically had in mind Christ in his divine nature indwelling believers. Thus, as the Trinitarian union involves the mutual indwelling of divine persons and as the incarnational union involves the indwelling of the second person in the human nature, so Christ's union with believers involves the indwelling of his divine person in their persons.

Here Goodwin believed that he was merely affirming the same conception of union with Christ as 'Other Divines' who denoted it 'a *substantial Union*, or dwelling in us substantially, whereby I understand ... that the Person of the Son doth dwell in our Persons'.[102] However, Goodwin's position was far from universally accepted by English Reformed divines. Ronald Frost contends that English Reformed theology had divided over the mode of indwelling. Complaining that scholarship has overlooked this division, he remarks, 'while Perkins and Sibbes, might appear to have much in common in the language of union, they maintained fundamentally different positions'.[103] Following Aquinas

---

99. *Works*, I, *Thirteen Sermons*, 36.

100. E.g. *Works*, I, *Thirteen Sermons*, 34, 39.

101. *Works*, I, *Thirteen Sermons*, 40. Goodwin further distinguished Christ's immediate indwelling from his indwelling by faith. This notion consists in the revelation of Christ within the believer as a consequence of his actual indwelling (see §2.5). *Works*, I, *Thirteen Sermons*, 29–31, 41–50.

102. *Works*, I, *Thirteen Sermons*, 34; cf. 33. See discussion on pp. 25–6.

103. Ronald Norman Frost, 'Richard Sibbes' Theology of Grace and the Division of English Reformed Theology' (PhD thesis, University of London, 1996), 103; cf. 8.

and concerned about the incommensurability of the created and uncreated, Perkins had understood the Spirit's indwelling in terms of his effects and so buffered God from the creature. Perkins stated that the Spirit 'is said to dwell in men, not in respect of substance (for the whole nature of the H. Ghost cannot be comprised in the body or soule of man) but in respect of a particular operation'.[104] He then proceeded to define this 'particular operation' in terms of the bestowal of created grace. Elsewhere, Perkins even equated the reception of the Spirit with the reception of created grace:

> the Spirit doth manifest his presence by diuine effects in vs. In this respect he is saide to be sent, or giuen of the Father and, the Sonne. ... Men are saide to receiue the spirit, when they receiue some new gift of the spirit, or the increase of some old gift.[105]

Real union with Christ, therefore, was defined by Perkins in terms of the Spirit's infusion of created grace.[106] Consistent with his comment in *The Knowledg*, Goodwin complained that such an interpretation brought union with Christ 'unto so great a lowness'.[107]

Frost contends that Sibbes following Augustine (and also Luther and Calvin) had departed from Perkins and affirmed that the Spirit's person is 'locally present' in believers.[108] Unfortunately, Frost's description oversimplifies the subtle, but profound, difference in Sibbes's conception of indwelling. In one passage, Sibbes employed similar language to Perkins:

> the holy Ghost is not in us personally as the second Person is in Christ man ... nor is the holy Ghost in us essentially only: for so he is in all creatures: nor yet is in us onely by stirring up holy motions, but he is in us mystically, and as Temples dedicated to himselfe ... The holy Spirit dwels in those that are Christs after another manner then in others in whom he is in, in some sort by common gifts; but in his owne, he is in them as holy ... as the soule is in the whole body in regard of divers operations ... so the holy Ghost is in his, in regard of more noble operations, and his person is together with his working[109]

---

104. William Perkins, *An Exposition of the Symbole or Creede of the Apostles, according to the Tenour of the Scriptures, and the consent of Orthodoxe Fathers of the Church: reuewed and corrected* (Cambridge, 1596), 331; cf. William Perkins, *A Commentarie or Exposition, vpon the fiue first Chapters of the Epistle to the Galatians* (Cambridge, 1604), 265–6.

105. Perkins, *Exposition, vpon the fiue first Chapters of the Epistle to the Galatians*, 204–5.

106. Perkins, *An Exposition of the Symbole*, 391.

107. *Works*, I, *Thirteen Sermons*, 31.

108. Frost, 'Sibbes' Theology of Grace', 29; cf. 8, 71, 105–7, 137, 143.

109. Richard Sibbes, *A Fountain Sealed: Or, The duty of the sealed to the Spirit, and the worke of the Spirit in Sealing* (1637), 8–11.

Sibbes, therefore, also affirmed the Spirit's omnipresence and contended for his special operation in believers. For Sibbes, however, the key point was that the person of the Spirit related directly to the believer. The Spirit's person assumes a relation to the believer of mystical union, here likened to the soul's relationship to the body. Thus, in the Spirit's operations, his person is always 'together with his working'. Goodwin, in stressing the primary and immediate indwelling of the person, sided with Sibbes rather than Perkins. Thus, Nuttall's characterization of puritanism as a movement concerned with 'immediacy in relation to God' was really valid for those who followed Sibbes's approach.[110]

Where Goodwin's pursuit of immediacy departed from Sibbes was in his rejection of indwelling by the proxy of the Holy Spirit.[111] Indeed, the early Goodwin granted no significant place to the Spirit in his account of mystical indwelling.[112] This was entailed in his assertion that the indwelling of Christ is primary: that is, he did not deny the indwelling of the Spirit (or of the Father) but argued that the indwelling of Christ is primary and allows the other two divine persons to indwell: 'Christ joins himself to us first and immediatly, and then we are made one with the Father, and then he sends his Spirit into our Hearts.'[113] Reasoning that Christ is the means of union with God and so is the 'prime Object and *Terminus* of our Union', Goodwin concluded that Christ himself, therefore, must indwell in the nearest conjunction with the believer.[114] In this scheme there is a Trinitarian concern – Goodwin argued that the believer experiences the fullness of God dwelling within (i.e. all three divine persons indwell) – but the Christocentric priority won out. Consequently, in this sermon Goodwin was forced to address the objection: '*What need the Spirit of God to dwell in us, if that the Person of Christ, the Son of God, in his own Person, immediately dwell in us, and doth all for us, and in us?*'[115] His main reply was to argue that the Holy Spirit in addition to the Son indwelt the human nature of Christ, therefore the Spirit's indwelling the believer cannot be redundant.

An important corollary of Goodwin's scheme was his claim that believers are united directly to Christ's divine nature, rather than mediated through his human nature.[116] For Goodwin, Christ's human nature is a precondition of believers' union with the divine nature, but it is not the medium of that union.[117] In other

110. Nuttall, *The Holy Spirit in Puritan Faith*, 134.

111. Richard Sibbes, *The Saints Cordials* (1629), 105.

112. Nuttall, *The Holy Spirit in Puritan Faith*, 91–2.

113. *Works*, I, *Thirteen Sermons*, 33.

114. *Works*, I, *Thirteen Sermons*, 33.

115. *Works*, I, *Thirteen Sermons*, 34.

116. *Works*, I, *Thirteen Sermons*, 38; cf. *Works*, V, *Glory of the Gospel*, 76. See §§5.4.2–5.4.3 for a discussion of the significance of this point for Goodwin's soteriology.

117. While in one passage in *The Knowledg* Goodwin wrote that Christ's human nature is the means of union, he must have intended the same sense as in this early sermon since in both contexts he employed the analogy of a lodestone set in steel to illustrate the role of Christ's two natures. *Works*, II, *The Knowledg*, 145; cf. *Works*, I, *Thirteen Sermons*, 40.

words, the human nature is the 'moral cause' but not the 'physical cause' of union. Goodwin held to this position emphatically: 'I utterly deny, that the Divine Nature in Christ should work an Act of Mediation in us, and for us, but by the physical Virtue or Instrumentality of the Human Nature, and particularly this of Union with us.'[118] As he recognized, there was diversity of opinion on this matter among Reformed divines.[119] From Goodwin's perspective, his view went hand in hand with his conviction that the divine nature of Christ indwells believers. In contrast, since Sibbes held that Christ indwells believers by the Spirit, there was no necessity for believers to be united immediately to Christ's divine nature.[120] Moreover, those who restricted indwelling to created grace were arguably more likely to advocate union with Christ's human nature, since to receive the same created grace as Christ corresponds to receiving his human nature. Perkins wrote, 'A faithfull man first of all and immediatly is vnited to the flesh, or humane nature of Christ, & afterward by reason of the humanitie, to the *Word* it selfe, or diuine nature.'[121] Perkins made the same distinction elsewhere and argued that the reception of Christ's humanity equates to the imputation of his righteousness and the infusion of his created grace.[122]

Goodwin's early notion of union with Christ, therefore, was conceptually close to the incarnational union. Indeed, Goodwin employed the indwelling experienced by Christ's human nature as a model to understand Christ's indwelling of believers. As the second person primarily and immediately indwells Christ's human nature and then as a consequence the Father and the Spirit indwell, so it is with believers: Christ in his divine nature primarily and immediately indwells the believer and then as a consequence the Father and the Spirit indwell.[123] Employing such logic can be viewed as providing the conditions in which the kind of radical teachings propounded by figures such as Erbery could develop – namely, that the saints experience the same kind of indwelling that Christ experienced bar a chronological priority. Thus, some of the strands of radical teaching later combatted in *The Knowledg* find their roots in the kind of theology espoused by Goodwin here. Indeed, Erbery himself would later explicitly mention Goodwin as an earlier stage in the development of increasingly enlightened theology.[124]

118. *Works*, I, *Thirteen Sermons*, 39.

119. Hooker also noted the division of opinion. Thomas Hooker, *The Soules Exaltation. A Treatise containing The Soules Union with Christ, on I Cor. 6. 17. The Soules Benefit from Union with Christ, on I Cor. 1. 30. The Soules Justification, on 2 Cor. 5. 21* (1638), 39–53.

120. Sibbes, *The Saints Cordials*, 105.

121. William Perkins, *A golden Chaine: Or, The Description of Theologie, containing the order of the causes of Saluation and Damnation, according to Gods word* (Cambridge, 1600), 116.

122. Perkins, *An Exposition of the Symbole*, 388–9.

123. *Works*, I, *Thirteen Sermons*, 37.

124. William Erbery, *The Testimony of William Erbery, Left Upon Record for The Saints of succeeding Ages being A Collection of the Writings of the aforesaid Authour, for the benefit*

This link can be interpreted in light of Nuttall's meta-argument: there is a natural movement from the insistence upon the indwelling of uncreated grace by puritans such as Goodwin to that of the radical preachers of the 1650s. Como, therefore, is mistaken in stating that radicals alone advocated the indwelling of believers by a divine person: 'Here, then, was a mode of divinity that smashed the molds of puritan religion … It suggested not only a new law … but a different God, a God that dwelled, essentially and personally, within every believer.'[125]

While there was commonality between Goodwin's doctrine of the indwelling experienced by believers and that of later radical teachings, even in this early sermon Goodwin provided distinctions to remain within orthodox bounds. The Trinitarian union involves the essential indwelling of persons and, therefore, is incommunicable to the elect.[126] The incarnational union is a hypostatic union and remains an 'infinite distance' above the union enjoyed by believers – yet, even here Goodwin added: 'we have the next Union unto that.'[127] Moreover, the union of believers with the divine is dependent upon Christ's hypostatic union.[128] Similar considerations featured in Goodwin's use of the Father and the Spirit indwelling Christ as a model of the corresponding indwelling of believers. He urged that, while it is the same mode of indwelling, there remains a difference in measure and basis.[129]

For Goodwin, then, the immediate and primary indwelling of Christ's person enabled him to maintain that the believer enjoys the strongest of possible unions with Christ. Negatively, Goodwin argued that to permit any mediation between Christ and the believer would not allow the strongest union.[130] Positively, he argued that Christ himself must indwell in order to function as a higher principle of life in believers.[131] Christ, he alleged, is '*intimior intimo nostro*; more within us, than we our selves are within our selves'.[132] Christ's divine nature indwelling the soul of believers allows for a close union, since as Goodwin reasoned, 'Spirits do, and can easily mingle'.[133] Goodwin's logic is clear: Christ's immediate and primary indwelling of the believer, therefore, allows a close and strong union with Christ to be established.

---

of Posterity (1658), 68, although Erbery's claim was not specifically relating to the matter of union with Christ.

125. Como, *Blown by the Spirit*, 361; cf. 37, 166.
126. *Works*, I, *Thirteen Sermons*, 35–6.
127. *Works*, I, *Thirteen Sermons*, 34.
128. *Works*, I, *Thirteen Sermons*, 38.
129. *Works*, I, *Thirteen Sermons*, 35.
130. *Works*, I, *Thirteen Sermons*, 33.
131. *Works*, I, *Thirteen Sermons*, 31–2. See §5.4.2.
132. *Works*, I, *Thirteen Sermons*, 32.
133. *Works*, I, *Thirteen Sermons*, 37.

2.4 The mature Goodwin: Honouring the Spirit

Goodwin's categorical assertions of the immediate and primary indwelling of Christ had been quietly forgotten by the time he penned *The Holy Ghost*. Part of his grand project, this treatise is composed of sermons delivered in the 1650s. The tone of the treatise is pastoral, rather than polemical, yet several features suggest that Goodwin expounded his understanding of the work of the Holy Spirit with an eye to the rising influence of radical and heterodox ideas. While refraining from naming individuals, Goodwin freely identified opposing viewpoints: Familist ideas,[134] Quakers,[135] 'Enthusiasticks' (a probable allusion to 'ranters')[136] as well as Catholic and Arminian teaching.[137] Absent is any explicit mention of Socinianism.

The basic contention of the treatise is that there must be a distinct honouring of the Spirit alongside the Father and the Son. Reasoning that equal honouring of the divine persons demands that each must have a distinct work, Goodwin identified the distinct work assigned to the Spirit not simply as the application of salvation but specifically as the Spirit's indwelling of believers. If the Son's love was manifested in his incarnation and atoning death, then Goodwin reasoned, the Spirit's love is manifested in his indwelling of unholy people.[138] This point echoed Sibbes, who had declared, 'Next to the love of Christ in taking our nature, and dwelling in it; we may wonder at the love of the holy Ghost, that will take up his residence in such defiled soules.'[139] For Goodwin there is a greatness which belongs to both demonstrations of love which in turn demands an honouring of both persons. This logic rooted in the distinct work of each person reflected his frequently stated commitment to the principle that the external works of the Trinity are undivided.[140] In other words, it was a manifestation of his commitment to expound a Trinitarian soteriology. Indeed, *The Holy Ghost* was the third treatise in a Trinitarian account of redemption.

What then were Goodwin's motives in contending for the honouring of the Spirit? It is possible that Goodwin may have been responding to Biddle's version of Socinianism. Biddle had explicitly argued against ascribing honour to the Son and the Spirit in the same degree as to the Father.[141] The Spirit should not even be held in as high dignity as Christ, he reasoned, because Christ sends the Spirit.[142] Thus,

---

134. *Works*, V, *The Holy Ghost*, 149.

135. *Works*, V, *The Holy Ghost*, 309.

136. *Works*, V, *The Holy Ghost*, 173, 175–6.

137. *Works*, V, *The Holy Ghost*, 173.

138. *Works*, V, *The Holy Ghost*, 34.

139. Sibbes, *A Fountain Sealed*, 12.

140. *Works*, V, *The Holy Ghost*, 8; *Works*, I, *Ephesians*, part I, 401.

141. John Biddle, *A confession of faith touching the Holy Trinity, according to the Scripture* (1648), preface, n.p.

142. Biddle, *A confession of faith*, 23.

arguably, the opening section of *The Holy Ghost* emphasizing the Spirit's distinct honour was a later insertion before the main treatise and could be explained as a veiled attack on such teaching.[143] However, Goodwin had opened by stating his driving concern:

> There is a general Omission in the Saints of God, in their not giving the Holy Ghost that Glory that is due to his Person, and for his Great Work of Salvation in us; insomuch that we have in our Hearts almost lost this *Third Person*.[144]

Moreover, Goodwin's pneumatological revision of indwelling and real union was already evident elsewhere.[145] His concerns were pastoral not polemical. He desired to impress upon his readers the reality of the Spirit's indwelling.

Significantly, Goodwin's basic contention implied that the Spirit must uniquely and primarily indwell believers; otherwise the grounds for the Spirit's distinct honouring would be rendered void. Therefore, in a reversal of his early opinion, Goodwin asserted that Christ indwells as a consequence of the Spirit's indwelling. Indeed, this applies to both the Father and the Son: 'their dwelling in us is attributed to his'.[146] In adopting this position, Goodwin conformed to the Reformed consensus: 'our Divines have generally affirmed it, that Christ is said to dwell in us, because first his Spirit dwells in us, from *Rom.* 8.9,10. compared'.[147] Goodwin now presented Christ's indwelling by proxy as a sign of Christ's exalted position: 'Great Persons woo not by themselves, but employ Embassadors, and Ministers of State, and so doth Christ'.[148] Thus, Goodwin believed his revised scheme appropriately honours both the Son and the Spirit. How the Spirit's indwelling causes Christ's indwelling remains to be addressed. What may be noted here is Goodwin's restriction of Christ's indwelling to an indwelling by faith in contradistinction to the actual indwelling of the Spirit's person.[149] This difference in mode of indwelling was the necessary implication of Goodwin's desire to uphold a distinct honouring of the Spirit.[150]

143. See pp. 81–2.

144. *Works*, V, *The Holy Ghost*, 1.

145. *Works*, V, *Glory of the Gospel*, 62, 71.

146. *Works*, V, *The Holy Ghost*, 56.

147. *Works*, V, *The Holy Ghost*, 56.

148. *Works*, V, *The Holy Ghost*, 44.

149. *Works*, V, *The Holy Ghost*, 35.

150. Unfortunately, Chang misconstrues the nature of Goodwin's argument. He writes, 'The essence of Book I of his *The Work of the Holy Spirit in our Salvation* is devoted to demonstrating the implications of *filioque* in the Christian life.' See Chang, 'Christian Life', 121.

In Goodwin's mature thought, therefore, real union with Christ is forged by the indwelling of the Holy Spirit in believers.[151] In his early view, it is self-evident that Christ's primary indwelling in his divine nature allows believers to be united to his divinity. The question raised for his mature view is, what qualifies the Spirit to act as a proxy for Christ? Goodwin's appeal to the Trinitarian and incarnational unions should be noted:

> That same Person that made that happy match, the Personal Union between Christ's Humane Nature and the Divine, the same Person makes the Union between Christ and our Souls; and so we become one Spirit with the Lord, 1 *Cor.* 6.17. The same Person that made the Man Christ Partaker of the Divine Nature, maketh us also. There is an higher correspondency yet: The Holy Ghost is *Vinculum Trinitatis*, the Union of the Father and the Son, as proceeding from both by way of Love, and who so meet to be the Union of God and Man in Christ, of Christ and Men in us, as he that was the Bond of Union among themselves?[152]

151. It should be noted that one passage in his grand project appears to contradict this claim. Goodwin wrote,

> That Union with Christ is the first fundamental thing of Justification and Sanctification, and all. Christ first takes us, and then sends his Spirit. He apprehends us first. It is not my being regenerate that puts me into a right of all those priviledges, but it is Christ takes me, and then gives me his Spirit, Faith, Holiness, &c It is through our Union with Christ, and the perfect Holiness of his Nature, to whom we are united, that we partake of the priviledges of the Covenant of Grace.

Works, III, *Christ the Mediator*, 347. Some scholars have made valiant but unsuccessful attempts to offer reconciliations. Beeke and Jones argue that the union Christ establishes first only refers to his side of union, not the believer's side; however, as the argument of this section makes clear Goodwin repeatedly wrote that Christ establishes his side of union by sending the Spirit. Beeke and Jones, *A Puritan Theology*, 484. Kim, rightly rejecting this resolution, argues that the union Christ first establishes with the believer is an external representative union; however, Goodwin's language here must be read as referring to real union since it causes actual justification (see §§4.3.2–4.3.3). Kim, 'Salvation by Faith', 202–4. One possible resolution is that the 'Spirit' may be referring to the Holy Spirit in his work of transformation (which was Goodwin's concern in context) rather than the Spirit's basic work of indwelling. However, the simplest explanation is that this passage may be an artefact of Goodwin's early views on union with Christ in which Christ's indwelling takes precedence over the Spirit's indwelling. This resolution requires a relatively early composition for this chapter which is plausible given the content may well have been written during or in the wake of the justification debate at the Westminster Assembly in September 1643. Of course, the passage may simply represent a moment of inconsistency on Goodwin's part, especially since it also appears to contradict statements concerning the relation of regeneration and justification (see §4.4.2 and pp. 157–8).

152. *Works*, V, *The Holy Ghost*, 43.

Here Goodwin's main comparison was the Spirit's role in the incarnational union, presenting the Spirit as the bond of the two natures of Christ.[153] Yet, pages earlier Goodwin had apparently denied this to be the case:

> I have not found a ground why to attribute the Personal Union more particularly to the Holy Ghost; but rather … that Action is more peculiarly to be Attributed to the Son Himself; as Second Person[154]

Blackham offers a possible reconciliation by arguing that the Spirit functions as the bond but not the active agent of the incarnational union.[155] To state the matter more accurately: Goodwin was not denying the Spirit's agency (indeed, he was convinced that each divine person shares in every divine act), rather his concern was to establish to which divine person this divine act may be especially attributed.[156] There was consistency of thought in terms of agency: just as the Son by his Spirit establishes the incarnational union, so by his Spirit he establishes real union with believers. As I will discuss in Chapter 5, consistency of thought, however, was less exact in terms of the Spirit as bond of the two unions.[157]

Nevertheless, as Goodwin indicated, the more fundamental relation is the Spirit as the bond of the Trinitarian union.[158] Here the doctrine of the double procession of the Spirit is crucial.[159] Regarding this doctrinal point, Blackham argues that other statements in Goodwin suggest a degree of ambiguity and that his view was, in fact, closer to the Eastern Orthodox position.[160] Jones, however, has persuasively demonstrated that Goodwin's language can be adequately understood within the Western *filioque* tradition.[161] Importantly, here the *filioque* appears to have been Goodwin's grounds for asserting that the Spirit is 'meet to be the Union of God and Man in Christ, of Christ and Men in us'.[162] Thus, only because the Spirit proceeds from the Son is he able to unite Christ's human nature to his divine nature and unite believers to Christ's divine nature. While this rationale was implicit, Goodwin's colleague Owen explicitly expounded the

---

153. Elsewhere, Goodwin wrote, 'It was the Spirit who … knit that indissoluble knot between our nature and the second Person.' *The Heart of Christ*, 174.

154. *Works*, V, *The Holy Ghost*, 8.

155. Blackham, 'Pneumatology', 43–5.

156. *Works*, V, *The Holy Ghost*, 8; *Works*, I, *Ephesians*, part I, 439. Jones is inconsistent in this matter: Jones, *Why Heaven Kissed Earth*, 108–9, 165.

157. See pp. 217–20.

158. *Works*, V, *The Holy Ghost*, 43.

159. *Works*, V, *The Holy Ghost*, 2, 33, 46; cf. *Works*, III, *Christ the Mediator*, 43; *Works*, II, *Election*, 137; *The Heart of Christ*, 153.

160. Blackham, 'Pneumatology', 14–21.

161. Jones, *Why Heaven Kissed Earth*, 116–21.

162. *Works*, V, *The Holy Ghost*, 43.

filioque as the grounds for the Spirit's actions upon Christ's human nature.[163] Ultimately, then, the Spirit's procession from the Son qualifies the Spirit to act as a proxy for Christ.

Goodwin's stress upon the Spirit as the bond between the Father and the Son raises the question of how this notion integrates with the aforementioned unity of the Trinity in the divine essence and corresponding mutual indwelling.[164] Unfortunately, Goodwin did not address this question. Arguably, this ambiguity reflected a double-mindedness that had developed in the Western tradition of whether Trinitarian unity resides in the Holy Spirit or in the oneness of essence. However, Owen, also arguing for the Spirit as the bond in the Trinitarian, incarnational and mystical unions, held that the Father and Son indwell each other by the Spirit, and distinguished this union from the unity of the Trinity in the divine essence. Alluding to the standard person/essence distinction, Owen remarked that the union of the Father and Son in the Spirit is the union 'that they have with themselves, in their distinct Personality; and not their *Unity* of Essence'.[165] In this light, it is the Trinitarian union in the Spirit (rather than the essential union) that constitutes the appropriate analogue to the union of believers with Christ, since both are person-to-person unions. Thus, Goodwin's pneumatological concept of union with Christ advanced beyond his earlier view by allowing for greater consistency of thought in this respect.

Goodwin's insistence upon real union with Christ by the Spirit was the consensus view among Reformed divines.[166] Where Goodwin dissented from the majority opinion was in his insistence that the Spirit in his person indwells believers rather than by his graces alone.[167] Goodwin's stance here was a further implication of his intent to ascribe distinct honour to the Spirit. If the Spirit receives honour by indwelling sinful humans, then he is only honoured if he actually indwells in person. Goodwin contended that just as the person of the Son was given in his

163. John Owen, *Pneumatologia: Or, A Discourse Concerning the Holy Spirit. Wherein An Account is given of his Name, Nature, Personality, Dispensation, Operations, and Effects* (1674), 130.

164. See p. 42.

165. John Owen, *The Doctrine of the Saints Perseverance, Explained and Confirmed. Or, The certain Permanency of their {1. Acceptation with God, & 2. Sanctification from God. Manifested & Proved from the {1. Eternal Principles 2. Effectuall Causes 3. Externall Meanes} Thereof* (1654), 195. The essential union of the Trinity, Owen insisted, is the '*substratum* and Ground' of the union of persons. What may have worried Owen was that without a distinct essential unity radical teachings would be conceded which advocate that saints enjoy union with God of the same order as the Trinity.

166. E.g. Leigh, *A Body of Divinity*, 487; Owen, *Saints Perseverance*, 195; John Owen, *Exercitations on the Epistle to the Hebrews, Concerning the Priesthood of Christ. Wherein, The Original, Causes, Nature, Prefigurations, and Discharge of that Holy Office, are Explained and Vindicated* (1674), 143.

167. *Works*, V, *The Holy Ghost*, 56.

sacrificial death, 'answerably … the Gift of the Holy Ghost is the Gift of his Person to dwell in us'.[168] Goodwin was adamant that 'the Gift of his Person is … greater infinitely than that of his Benefits'.[169]

Here Goodwin recognized that he was dissenting from the majority position: 'It hath been generally almost asserted that he dwells no otherwise in us, then by having wrought such and such Graces'.[170] The staunch Presbyterian Richard Hollingworth (bap. 1607, d. 1656) represented the conservative majority when he wrote,

> when I speak of the *Spirits being*, or *dwelling in a Saint*: I mean not an essential or personal in-being or in-dwelling of the Spirit, as he is God, or the third Person of the Holy Trinity … this Scripture phrase of *in-being* and *in-dwelling*, doth import only inwardness, meer relation and close union. … we partake of his Gifts and Graces, though these be not the Spirit it self[171]

Fellow Presbyterian Christopher Love (1618–1651) defended this interpretation of scriptural language by appealing to an oft-used analogy: 'The Sunne that is in the firmament, we use to say that it is in such a house, or such a window; but when we say so, we do not mean that the body of the sunne is there, but only that the light, heat, or influence of the Sunne is there'.[172]

However, Goodwin was not alone among the orthodox. In a 1654 treatise refuting John Goodwin (c. 1594–1665), Owen felt compelled to digress and devote a chapter to the indwelling of the Spirit and bullishly argued for the indwelling of his person:

168. *Works*, V, *The Holy Ghost*, 52.

169. *Works*, V, *The Holy Ghost*, 51.

170. *Works*, V, *The Holy Ghost*, 55.

171. E.g. Richard Hollingworth, *The Holy Ghost on the Bench, other Spirits at the Bar: Or the Judgment of the Holy Spirit of God upon the Spirits of the Times* (1656), 8–11; cf. Samuel Rutherford, *Christ Dying and Drawing Sinners to Himself. Or, A survey of our Saviour in his soule-suffering, his lovelynesse in his death, and the efficacie thereof* (1647), 464–5; Samuel Rutherford, *Influences of the Life of Grace. Or, A Practical Treatise concerning The way, manner, and means of having and improving of Spiritual Dispositions, and quickning Influences from Christ the Resurrection and the Life* (1659), 241; Rowland Stedman, *The Mystical Union of Believers with Christ. Or, A Treatise wherein, That great Mystery and Priviledge, of The Saints Union with the Son of God is opened* (1668), 124–5; John Flavel, *The Method of Grace, In bringing home the Eternal Redemption, Contrived by the Father, and accomplished by the Son through the effectual application of the Spirit unto God's Elect; being the Second Part of Gospel Redemption* (1681), 404. Further examples appear in the discussion that follows.

172. Christopher Love, *The Combate between the Flesh and Spirit. As also The wofull with-drawing of the Spirit of God, with the Causes thereof: And walking in, and after the Spirit, together with the blessednesse thereof* (1654), 100.

Whereas some may say, it cannot be denied, but that the *Spirit dwels* in Believers, but yet this is not *personally*, but only by his Grace, though I might reply, that this indeed, and upon the matter, is not to distinguish, but to deny, what is positively affirmed. ... If such distinctions ought to be of force, to evade so many positive and plaine Texts of Scripture, as have been produced; it may well be questioned, whether any Truth be capable of proofe from Scripture or no.[173]

By the 1650s, the subtle difference between Perkins and Sibbes on the mode of indwelling had therefore become the source of sharp disagreement, with proponents of the two sides roughly corresponding to the two sides of the Presbyterianism–Congregationalism dispute.[174] Indeed, several older studies suggest that differences over the mode of indwelling explain, at least in part, ecclesiological differences.[175] The correlation, however, was not perfect. The New England Congregationalist Hooker, conservative in outlook, denied the indwelling of the Spirit apart from his operations in believers.[176] Anthony Burgess (d. 1664), a moderate Presbyterian, was trapped in the middle: he felt the force of the theological arguments for the majority position but was reluctant to deny the clarity of scriptural texts suggesting the indwelling of the Spirit's person.[177] Obadiah Sedgwick (1599/1600–1658), also a moderate Presbyterian, was adamant that the Spirit's person indwells.[178]

The typical argument provided by the conservative majority was to appeal to the Spirit's omnipresence and conclude that the Spirit cannot be specially located in believers.[179] In fact, Hollingworth reasoned that if the Spirit resided specifically in the saints, then the Spirit's deity would be denied, for he would be divided and limited.[180] Recognizing divine omnipresence as the main objection advanced against his view, Goodwin responded with a *reductio ad absurdum* argument: the same logic, if valid, must be applied to Christ, yet the divine nature of the second

---

173. Owen, *Saints Perseverance*, 191; cf. John Cotton, *The Covenant of Grace: Discovering The Great Work of a Sinners Reconciliation to God* (1655), 145–6.

174. Nuttall also sketches the variety of opinions on the mode of indwelling. Nuttall, *The Holy Spirit in Puritan Faith*, 49–50.

175. Nuttall, *The Holy Spirit in Puritan Faith*, 119–20; Carter, 'The Presbyterian-Independent Controversy', 35; Fienberg, 'Puritan Pastor and Independent Divine', 350.

176. Thomas Hooker, *The Application of Redemption, By the effectual Work of the Word, and Spirit of Christ, for the bringing home of lost Sinners to God* (1656), book 9, 3–4.

177. Anthony Burgess, *Spiritual Refining: Or A Treatise of Grace and Assurance* (1652), 91–2.

178. Obadiah Sedgwick, *The Bowels of Tender Mercy Sealed in the Everlasting Covenant wherein is set forth the Nature, Conditions and Excellencies of it, and how a Sinner should do to enter into it, and the danger of refusing this Covenant-Relation* (1661), 585–6.

179. E.g. Henry Wilkinson, *The hope of Glory, Or, Christs Indwelling in true Believers Is an Evident Demonstration of their hope of Glory* (Oxford, 1657), 11.

180. Hollingworth, *The Holy Ghost on the Bench*, 9.

person did not indwell the human nature merely by graces but enjoyed hypostatic indwelling.[181] Goodwin concluded, therefore, that the key factor is the relation that Christ's (omnipresent) divine nature assumes to Christ's human nature. While for Christ the relation was hypostatic, for believers the divine Spirit assumes a union of persons akin to marriage.[182] In Goodwin's mind, the issue turns on a direct person-to-person relationship between the Spirit and the believer. Elsewhere, Goodwin often conceived of this direct relation in terms of the person of the Spirit operating as the principle of spiritual life in the believer's person.[183] Goodwin's answer, therefore, effectively rehearsed Sibbes's approach, albeit stated with greater clarity.[184]

What really fuelled emotions among the conservatives, however, was the association of the indwelling of uncreated grace with enthusiasts and radicals. Samuel Petto (*c.* 1624–1711) insisted that the Spirit must indwell in person otherwise believers could not experience direct inner revelation.[185] Joshua Sprigg (bap. 1618, d. 1684) championed the immediacy of the Spirit's indwelling and complained about the controversy over the mode of indwelling.[186] Sprigg's theology moved in a direction similar to Erbery's. Despite defending himself against claims that he denied Christ's divinity, Sprigg offered little in the way of a clear adherence to Chalcedonian two-nature Christology.[187] The longest critique against the denial of the indwelling of the Spirit's person however was published by Higgenson who explicitly denied Christ's hypostatic union.[188]

The conservative majority typically voiced their position in opposition to such radicals. Love believed that affirming the indwelling of the Spirit's person would 'make humanity the Deity' as the Familists taught.[189] In a work dedicated to refuting Erbery, Henry Nicholls (1612/13–1670) similarly warned that it would 'render us Goded, and Christed, (as the Familists expound …) is high blasphemy'.[190] Nicholls instead restricted indwelling to created grace alone and union with Christ to an external legal union.

---

181. *Works*, V, *The Holy Ghost*, 57.

182. *Works*, V, *The Holy Ghost*, 58.

183. See §5.4.2.

184. Sibbes, *A Fountain Sealed*, 8–11. See pp. 50–1.

185. Samuel Petto, *The Voice of the Spirit. Or An Essay towards a Discoverie of the witnessings of the Spirit* (1654), 27.

186. Joshua Sprigg, *A Testimony to An Approaching Glory Being An Account of certaine Discourses lately delivered* (1649), preface, n.p.; 141.

187. Joshua Sprigg, *Christus Redivivus, The Lord is risen being Some Account of Christ, what, and where he is; of the glory and mystery of his Person and Office, so miserably mangled now adaies* (1649), preface, n.p.

188. Higgenson, *Glory sometimes afar off*.

189. Love, *The Combate*, 100.

190. Henry Nicholls, *The Shield Single against The Sword Doubled. To defend the Righteous against the Wicked* (1653), 47–8.

Moreover, this association led some conservatives to believe that little substantial difference existed between the views of divines such as Goodwin and these radicals. The Presbyterian Henry Wilkinson (1616/17–1690) asked: 'But how neare do they come to the campe of their Adversaries?'[191] Despite recognizing that orthodox writers such as Goodwin and Owen distinguished between personal (hypostatic) union and a union of persons, Wilkinson worried their position veered perilously close to that of the enthusiastic radicals.[192]

In reacting so strongly to radical ideas, the conservative majority found themselves adopting the same position as Biddle, although ironically with opposite rationale.[193] Biddle departed from Socinus by affirming the personhood of the Holy Spirit: 'it will be impossible … to embrace either the opinion of *Athanasius*, who held the holy Spirit to be a Person of supream Deity, or that of *Socinus*, who believed him to be the divine power or efficacy, but no Person'.[194] In Biddle's mind, holding the Spirit to be 'the divine power or efficacy' permitted the omnipresence of the Spirit, but as a created person possessing omnipresence was impossible and so he concluded that the Spirit must indwell by graces. He accused the conservative majority of forgetting their own doctrine of the Spirit's divine omnipresence in their denial of the Spirit's person indwelling believers. For conservative divines, however, radical teachers who collapsed the God/creation distinction presented the graver threat.

In Goodwin's mind, too much had been sacrificed. While he equally opposed the radicals, he demarcated his position by insisting upon the unique hypostatic nature of the incarnational union along with the unique indwelling of the second person in Christ's human nature. And, while the person of the Spirit indwells believers in the same mode as in Christ, Goodwin maintained that he indwells believers in an inferior measure and on a different basis.[195]

For Goodwin the indwelling of the Spirit's person, rather than by his graces, is necessary for believers to enjoy the strongest of unions with Christ. He employed the same categories as he had used in his early sermon. Thus, he likened the Spirit's indwelling the believer to the soul indwelling the body, such that the Spirit indwells as the soul of the soul.[196] Thus, 'the Spirit is *intimior intimo*, is so nearly

191. Wilkinson, *The hope of Glory*, 11.

192. Indeed, Wilkinson here may have had Goodwin in view. Not only did Wilkinson also sit at the Westminster Assembly, but he and his uncle were closely associated with Magdalen College, Oxford.

193. John Biddle, *The Apostolical And True Opinion concerning the Holy Trinity, revived and asserted; partly by Twelve Arguments Levyed against the Traditional and False Opinion about the Godhead of the Holy Spirit: partly by A Confession of Faith Touching the three Persons*, Enlarged edn (1653), 35; cf. 30.

194. Biddle, *A confession of faith*, 51.

195. *Works*, V, *The Holy Ghost*, 58.

196. *Works*, V, *The Holy Ghost*, 377; cf. *Works*, I, *Ephesians*, part II, 186, 191. Admittedly, on occasion Goodwin conceded that the Spirit also indwells the body: 'Our Persons (Bodies and Souls) are the Temples of his Person immediately'. *Works*, V, *The Holy Ghost*, 55. Behind

and intimately united to us, dwells in us as our own Souls do in us'.[197] A strong and close union can be achieved because 'The substance of the Soul (which he comes to) is his own'.[198] What results is 'an immediate union of our persons to and with [the Spirit's] person, so as to have an eternal right personal to each other, and everlastingly to dwell each in other'.[199] The Spirit and the believer enjoy an immediate union of persons akin to marriage.[200] Yet, because the Spirit mediates Christ's presence, Goodwin argued that union with Christ also results. Taking his lead from 1 Corinthians 6:17, Goodwin wrote that the Spirit's indwelling constitutes the union of Christ with the believer's soul, such that the believer becomes 'one Spirit with the Lord'.[201]

2.5 Union with Christ in his mystical indwelling by faith

The question which Goodwin's revised scheme raises is the manner in which the Spirit mediates Christ's presence and so allows Christ to indwell the believer. Already in his early sermon, Goodwin had distinguished on the basis of Ephesians 3:17 Christ's indwelling by faith (an 'Objective' indwelling) from his indwelling in person.[202] The former notion appears frequently in Goodwin's works but found fullest treatment in his *Glory of the Gospel*.[203] Here Goodwin likewise granted a more significant place to the Holy Spirit and assumed that the Spirit was responsible for union with Christ.[204] Contending that the glory of the gospel is 'Christ in you', he explained that the Spirit mediates Christ's presence by revealing an image of

---

Goodwin's comment was scriptural language of the body as the temple of the Holy Spirit. Cradock, on the basis that Christ possesses the whole believer, similarly concluded that union with Christ is a '*totall* union … that is, *whole* Christ is united to the *whole believer*, soule and body'. Cradock, *Saints Fulnesse*, 22–3. Goodwin's claim, at least, was qualified by asserting that the Spirit indwells the soul by a nearer conjunction than the body. *Works*, V, *The Holy Ghost*, 377. While it might seem that Goodwin was merely contending that the Spirit indwells the body by virtue of indwelling the soul and in turn the soul indwelling the body, he also claimed that the Spirit remains united to the body following death. *Works*, V, *The Holy Ghost*, 35; cf. *Works*, I, *Ephesians*, part I, 221. Nevertheless, the dominant focus in Goodwin's thought is on the Spirit indwelling the soul.

197. *Works*, V, *The Holy Ghost*, 33; cf. *Works*, II, *The Creatures*, 95.

198. *Works*, V, *The Holy Ghost*, 54 cf. 62.

199. *Works*, V, *The Holy Ghost*, 35.

200. *Works*, V, *The Holy Ghost*, 58.

201. *Works*, V, *The Holy Ghost*, 43; cf. *Works*, I, *Ephesians*, part II, 186; *Works*, II, *The Knowledg*, 29.

202. *Works*, I, *Thirteen Sermons*, 40.

203. Briefer discussions appear elsewhere. E.g. *Works*, I, *Thirteen Sermons*, 31; *Works*, V, *The Holy Ghost*, 16, 54; cf. 178–9.

204. *Works*, V, *Glory of the Gospel*, 62.

Christ, not just to, but within, the mind of the believer.[205] To this end, Goodwin was intent on securing the reality of the revealed image. His favourite analogy was of the image of a person perceived in a looking glass, since the image beheld in a glass, while not direct sight, is nevertheless a 'lively Image' of the person.[206] It surpasses a painting because the image in the glass is the person (albeit indirectly). Likewise, the inwardly revealed image of Christ can properly be called 'Christ'.[207] The reality of the image, therefore, allowed Goodwin to equate the revealed image with Christ's indwelling by faith.[208]

The indwelling of the Spirit's person, Goodwin maintained, is vital for the production of such a real image in the believer. The Spirit 'to whom all things are continually present, tho' absent from us, and therefore he dwelling in the man, can set those things before him'.[209] The Spirit's divinity, therefore, was crucial to portray an absent Christ as though present. Moreover, the Spirit must be in close union with the believer: 'the Spirit of Christ is present, and joineth with his Spirit, for always sight hath as a certainty so a reality joined with it'.[210] The resulting knowledge of Christ 'hath a Certainty in it' and 'hath a Reality in it'.[211] As well as the Spirit's illumination, Goodwin contended that the Spirit 'put a principle into us, to behold those things'.[212] This new spiritual sense is required for the mind of the believer to behold the reality of the revealed image of Christ. While the faculty of the fancy enables the natural mind to imagine ordinary objects, such appearances lack reality and subsistence in the mind.[213] In contrast, a spiritual mind having spiritual sight is continually able to apprehend the reality of Christ himself.[214]

Goodwin's conception of Christ's indwelling by faith contrasted with the tendency of the conservative majority. Restricting indwelling to created grace, Rowland Stedman (d. 1673), for example, equated Christ's indwelling with transformation into Christ's image and argued that created grace can be deemed 'Christ in you' since it originates from Christ.[215] Goodwin's view was closer to

205. See especially *Works*, V, *Glory of the Gospel*, 68–74. While Goodwin here admitted other supplementary senses of 'Christ in you', these were secondary effects of the inner revealed image of Christ. Elsewhere, Goodwin argued that the inner revelation of Christ is so profound that it exceeds 'Visions and Revelations extraordinary'. *Works*, IV, *Object and Acts*, part II, 10.

206. *Works*, V, *Glory of the Gospel*, 55.

207. *Works*, V, *Glory of the Gospel*, 70–1.

208. *Works*, V, *Glory of the Gospel*, 71; cf. *Works*, III, *An Unregenerate*, 151.

209. *Works*, III, *An Unregenerate*, 151; cf. *Works*, I, *Ephesians*, part I, 327.

210. *Works*, IV, *Object and Acts*, part II, 10.

211. *Works*, IV, *Object and Acts*, part II, 2. Goodwin stressed this in the strongest terms: 'it is a real, solid, substantial Sight'. *Works*, IV, *Object and Acts*, part I, 127.

212. *Works*, III, *An Unregenerate*, 151. This idea is examined further in Chapter 3.

213. *Works*, V, *Glory of the Gospel*, 70–1.

214. This idea can also be found in his second sermon on Ephesians 3:17. *Works*, I, *Thirteen Sermons*, 47.

215. Stedman, *Mystical Union*, 132.

enthusiastic preachers. Cradock also equated spiritual sight with indwelling[216] and insisted that such revelation grants 'such *reall* impressions upon the heart, as that they can bare up the Soule in any outward reall miserie'.[217] Goodwin, by insisting upon revelation within rather than to the believer, claimed that he had advanced beyond Calvin and many other interpreters.[218]

Yet, Goodwin sought to avoid collapsing into the mysticism of the enthusiasts. The last chapter of his *Glory of the Gospel* was appended later and addresses Galatians 1:15-16 with the Quakers in view: 'This Phrase [Revealing Christ within me] hath made a great deal of do among Interpreters, as well as amongst us of late Days ... the very Notion of the *Quakers*'.[219] Consequently, he stressed, 'It is the same Christ without us, and the same Christ within us; only what He is, or did for us without us, the same is applied to us'.[220] Moreover, in the earlier part of the treatise, Goodwin had insisted that the revealed image of Christ is produced by the Spirit in conjunction with 'the Gospel'; here Goodwin was referring to the New Testament, which in his view was a written account of the historical Christ or truths about him.[221] Accordingly, in his favourite analogy Goodwin repeatedly identified the looking glass with the text of the New Testament.[222] While Quakers were famed for advocating the inner revelation apart from external means,[223] many earlier enthusiasts also prized revelation as the result of divine indwelling. Even in the early 1640s Goodwin felt compelled to distance himself from '*Enthusiasms*', warning of 'Revelations that are without the Word', and instead he insisted upon 'the Spirit applying the Word'.[224] This is striking since elsewhere Goodwin advocated the more mystical idea of the Spirit overhearing Christ interceding before the Father and, consequently, making the saints aware of Christ's petitions.[225] In Goodwin's mind, though, the indwelling of Christ by faith produced in conjunction with the New Testament comprised inner revelation of Christ of a superior kind.

Nevertheless Goodwin also insisted that the inner revealed image of Christ surpasses the words of the New Testament.[226] This he supported by another analogy: just as it is impossible to picture the sun fully in all its life, glory and heat, so Christ can never be fully represented by words.[227] Without the Spirit

---

216. Cradock, *Gospel-Holinesse*, 41; cf. 57.

217. Cradock, *Gospel-Holinesse*, 43.

218. *Works*, V, *Glory of the Gospel*, 78-9.

219. *Works*, V, *Glory of the Gospel*, 78.

220. *Works*, V, *Glory of the Gospel*, 77.

221. *Works*, V, *Glory of the Gospel*, 5.

222. *Works*, V, *Glory of the Gospel*, 7, 56-7, 65.

223. E.g. George Fox, *A Message from the Lord, to the Parliament of England* (1654), 6-7.

224. *Works*, I, *Ephesians*, part I, 214.

225. *The Heart of Christ*, 157; cf. *Works*, V, *The Holy Ghost*, 44, 386; *Works*, II, *The Knowledg*, 8, 19.

226. *Works*, V, *Glory of the Gospel*, 35, 57; *Works*, I, *Ephesians*, part I, 327.

227. *Works*, V, *Glory of the Gospel*, 35.

accompanying the words of the New Testament into the heart, the believer would receive 'meer Words of Christ'.[228] It would amount to knowledge of Christ 'in the Doctrine of the Gospel', but stop short of his indwelling.[229] Thus, the unbeliever while hearing the same words does not have Christ revealed to them.[230] Strictly speaking, then, the glass represents the New Testament text accompanied by the Spirit.[231] This theology Goodwin had developed in two early sermons preached in 1625 also entitled *Glory of the Gospel* upon which the longer treatise was based.[232] Here he was responding to the provocative publications of the Laudian Richard Montagu (1575?–1641) and, as Lawrence explains, Goodwin's motivation was to uphold the preaching of Scripture rather than 'the more "lively" images of ceremony' of Laudian religion.[233]

The consequence of Goodwin's scheme is that Christ's indwelling by faith must be subsequent (causally, if not chronologically) to the indwelling of the Spirit. In other words, Christ's indwelling by faith is not simply a consequence of the indwelling presence of the Spirit who proceeds from the Son. His procession may be a necessary foundation, but the mediation of Christ's presence requires an additional work of the Spirit. This reflects Goodwin's desire to assign a distinct work to the Spirit. Moreover, it also manifests an important aspect of his pneumatology: while the person of the Spirit permanently indwells believers, the Spirit may perform fresh works within the believer.[234] In particular, causing Christ to indwell by faith must be distinguished from the Spirit's work of preparation and assurance.

Regarding preparation, Goodwin believed that the Spirit's indwelling requires no preparation, whereas Christ's indwelling by faith requires a work of preparation.[235] The Spirit indwells prior to faith, producing conviction of sin, regeneration and faith in the believer; only then may Christ indwell by faith. Kim's claim that Goodwin held preparation to result from regeneration is incorrect.[236] Goodwin envisaged a period of preparation resulting from the indwelling of the Holy Spirit, but with regeneration as the end: '[The Spirit] must be a *Regenerator*, ere a *Comforter*. Receive him they may, to convert them; but not thus to assure them, until he hath wrought Regeneration in them.'[237]

---

228. *Works*, V, *Glory of the Gospel*, 56.

229. *Works*, V, *Glory of the Gospel*, 57.

230. *Works*, III, *An Unregenerate*, 152.

231. *Works*, V, *Glory of the Gospel*, 7, 57.

232. *Works*, I, *Thirteen Sermons*, 67–8.

233. Lawrence, 'Transmission', 83.

234. *Works*, V, *The Holy Ghost*, 4, 41–2, 55.

235. *Works*, V, *The Holy Ghost*, 54. For the significance of Goodwin insisting upon the Spirit's indwelling prior to preparation, see Horton, 'Assurance', 317.

236. Kim, 'Salvation by Faith', 210–11, 226.

237. *Works*, V, *The Holy Ghost*, 55.

Regarding assurance, Goodwin is famed for his doctrine of the sealing of the Spirit as an inner state of assurance subsequent to regeneration.[238] In contrast, the conservative majority, advocating the indwelling by created grace alone, typically appealed to the practical syllogism for obtaining assurance. It was the indwelling of the Spirit's person that allowed Goodwin to promote assurance by the immediate internal witness of the Spirit.[239] While in his early sermon Goodwin equated the indwelling of Christ by faith with the sealing of assurance,[240] in his later works he argued that the former can occur without the latter: 'When Christ is represented to the Soul by the Father, the Soul is not deceived, tho it hath not the Assurance personal of its own Interest: his Presence is real, and it is called the real Presence of the Lord Jesus.'[241] Both experiences involve inner revelation; the former concerned revelation of Christ, whereas the latter concerned revelation of personal assurance of salvation. Admittedly, however, tensions remained within Goodwin's thought at this point, since elsewhere he assumed that assurance arose out of communion with the three divine persons.[242]

Despite this tension, Goodwin was unequivocal that the indwelling of Christ by faith rests upon a distinct work of the Spirit subsequent to the Spirit's indwelling. The question is raised, therefore, as to whether Goodwin included Christ's indwelling by faith as intrinsic to real union with Christ. In *Glory of the Gospel*, he equated Christ's indwelling by faith and real union with him.[243] The strongest confirmation, however, arises from his conviction that real union finds completion in the believer's act of faith in the faculty of the will. In *Object and Acts*, Goodwin repeatedly contended that faith in the will is an intrinsic part of real union with Christ. For example,

> Yea, by this act of the Will is the Union on our parts compleated between Christ and us, and we are thereby made ultimately one with him. ... for the making a real Union with him (so far as on our part it is made) it lyes not primarily in believing Christ is mine, or that Christ is, but in joining my self to his Person, in the shooting in of my Will into him, in taking him, and consenting to be his ... to rest in him, to cleave to him as the Fountain of Life ... 'tis that makes the real Union[244]

What must be noted, however, is that Goodwin believed this act of faith in the will is a consequence of faith in the intellect and that he equated the latter with spiritual

238. *Works*, I, *Ephesians*, part I, 212.

239. See Horton, 'Assurance', 308.

240. *Works*, I, *Thirteen Sermons*, 29.

241. *Works*, IV, *Object and Acts*, part I, 128; cf. part II, 8, 77–8; *Works*, I, *Ephesians*, part I, 207, 210.

242. *Works*, IV, *Object and Acts*, part II, 106.

243. *Works*, V, *Glory of the Gospel*, 74.

244. *Works*, IV, *Object and Acts*, part II, 15; cf. 14; part III, 6.

sight of Christ: "Faith in the Understanding is a spiritual Sight and Knowledge of Christ."[245] In the will, faith is expressed by the will embracing Christ revealed by the Spirit. Here should be noted Vickery's assessment that the overall movement of Goodwin's theology was intellectualist and, in particular, that Goodwin was convinced that faith's 'chief seat is in the intellect'[246] despite making ostensible voluntaristic affirmations.[247] In such comments, Goodwin's intent was not to deny the causal priority of faith in the intellect but to insist that faith must be completed in the voluntary response of the believer.[248] That spiritual sight of Christ has causal priority strongly suggests that Goodwin understood it to be integral to real union with Christ.

Thus, real union with Christ has two parts: Christ's part involves the Spirit's indwelling, the believer's part in the will joining to Christ. While the former represents the fundamental act of union,[249] it is incomplete without the latter.[250] The priority of the Holy Spirit's work is evident since even faith results from his operations. Such a scheme protected not only the Calvinist priority of divine initiative but also the distinct honour of the Holy Spirit as responsible for the entire application of redemption.[251] The second part incorporates the believer's agency and allows the union to be strengthened through increased meditation upon Christ in Scripture.[252]

245. *Works*, IV, *Object and Acts*, part II, 1; cf. 10. To this Goodwin added assent as a secondary act of faith in the intellect. *Works*, IV, *Object and Acts*, part II, 14.

246. Vickery, 'A Most Lawful Pleasure', 219; cf. 69–72, 190–9, 219–26. Vickery misreads Horton in alleging that Horton believed Goodwin was ultimately a voluntarist. Vickery, 'A Most Lawful Pleasure', 71. Horton states his conclusion: 'If one faculty does appear to find supreme place in Goodwin's theology, in spite of his explicit location of faith's seat in the heart, it is the intellect.' Horton, 'Assurance', 147; cf. 143, 145.

247. E.g. 'It principally is seated in the Will.' *Works*, IV, *Object and Acts*, part II, 77; cf. 14–15, 44, 78; part III, 41. On the basis of one of these texts, Kim argues that Goodwin was inclined to locate faith in the will, yet in the end preferred to locate faith not in an individual faculty but in the whole heart. Kim, 'Salvation by Faith', 380–7. However, Kim overlooks Vickery's important study devoted to demonstrating the priority of the intellect in Goodwin's thought.

248. See §4.3.3 for further discussion. Goodwin was emphatic that both faculties exercise faith. *Works*, I, *Ephesians*, part I, 248; *Works*, IV, *Object and Acts*, part I, 175; part II, 14. Here he reflected mainstream Puritan opinion; see John Von Rohr, *The Covenant of Grace in Puritan Thought*, American Academy of Religion Studies in Religion (Atlanta, GA: Scholars Press, 1986), 70.

249. *Works*, V, *The Holy Ghost*, 389.

250. *Works*, IV, *Object and Acts*, part II, 77.

251. Leigh made the same point: 'There is no one branch of our partaking of Christ, but what is totally ascribed to the holy Ghost.' Leigh, *A Body of Divinity*, 486.

252. *Works*, V, *Glory of the Gospel*, 75.

This two-part scheme was widely held among Reformed divines.[253] Like Goodwin, Cheynell also stressed the role of the Spirit in both sides of the union: 'The bond ... on Gods part is *the Spirit*, and on our part *Faith*, which is wrought in us by the same Co-essentiall Spirit.'[254] Where Goodwin advanced beyond more conservative divines was in insisting upon the inner revelation of the Spirit in addition to the infusion of faith. A two-part scheme was, however, questioned by 'imputative antinomians' such as Tobias Crisp (1600–1643). Contending for justification prior to faith, Crisp concluded that faith cannot be intrinsic to union: 'faith is not the instrument radically to unite Christ and the soul together, but rather is the fruit that follows and flows from Christ the root, being united beforehand to the persons that do believe.'[255] The significance of Crisp's denial of faith as part of real union with Christ will be explored in Chapter 4.

In conclusion, then, Goodwin explained real union with Christ in terms of the indwelling of the person of the Spirit, the subsequent inner revelation of Christ by the Spirit and the believer's response of faith in the will. Even Goodwin, however, conceded that in the final analysis union with Christ and, in particular, the corresponding indwelling of Christ by faith remained beyond full comprehension: 'great is the Mystery of our Union with Christ, and Christ with us.'[256] Citing the same passage, Jonathan Won concludes that since Goodwin deemed union a mystery he 'did not give detailed attention to the topic of union with Christ'.[257] However, the quotation in question appears at the end of Goodwin's explanation of Christ's indwelling by faith entailed in real union. What, then, did Goodwin mean by 'Mystery'? Earlier he had defined 'mystery' not simply as hidden knowledge but that which involves 'a Profoundness and Depth of Knowledge'.[258] The term did not prohibit any level of explanation. Goodwin encouraged believers to search and pry into the depths of the gospel,[259] yet he recognized a limit at which even the apostle Paul had to admit: 'I have gone as far as I can.'[260]

---

253. E.g. Leigh, *A Body of Divinity*, 486; Anthony Burgess, *CXLV Expository Sermons upon The whole 17th Chapter of the Gospel According to St. John: Or, Christs Prayer Before his Passion Explicated* (1656), 587.

254. Francis Cheynell, *The Divine Trinunity of the Father, Son, and Holy Spirit: Or, The blessed Doctrine of the three Coessentiall Subsistents in the eternall Godhead without any confusion or division of the distinct Subsistences, or multiplication of the most single and entire Godhead* (1650), 429.

255. Tobias Crisp, *Christ Alone Exalted In the Perfection and Encouragements of the Saints, notwithstanding Sins and Trialls* (1646), 226.

256. *Works*, V, *Glory of the Gospel*, 74.

257. Won, 'Communion with Christ', 214.

258. *Works*, V, *Glory of the Gospel*, 12.

259. *Works*, V, *Glory of the Gospel*, 19.

260. *Works*, V, *Glory of the Gospel*, 13.

The mysterious nature of real union was commonplace for the Reformed orthodox and entailed in the widely used term 'mystical union'.[261] In fact, Goodwin designated the Trinitarian union, the incarnational union and believers' union with Christ each a mystery.[262] Viewing the embrace of mysteries as a hallmark of orthodoxy, the gospel, he remarked, contains many 'seeming Contradictions' which Arians, Catholics, Socinians, antinomians and Arminians failed to understand.[263] The heterodox teachers of the 1640s–1650s were divergent on the category of mystery. As manifest in the title of Paul Best's (1590–1657) work *Mysteries Discovered*, Socinians deplored appeals by orthodox divines to the notion of mystery to secure doctrines.[264] Biddle wrote, 'I found that the Adversaries, who so much cry down Reason, saying that we must renounce it when we speak of Divine Mysteries'.[265] Radical preachers, in contrast, readily embraced the notion of mystery.[266] Like Goodwin, Colossians 1:27 was important for Erbery's theology: 'The Gospel is a mystery, the mystery of the Gospel is *Christ in us the hope of Glory*, Col. 1.27'.[267] Yet, Erbery claimed that he only comprehended the import of this mystery by direct revelation. The two strands of heterodox teaching on this matter, therefore, were diametrically opposed, to the extent that Erbery lambasted Socinians for eradicating the notion of mystery from their theology.[268] Goodwin was positioned between the two – attempting to offer some understanding of the nature of real union with Christ and his indwelling by faith, yet acknowledging that it ultimately resides beyond full comprehension.

2.6 Union with Christ as the foundation of salvation and communion with God

Goodwin held that his conception of real union with Christ by the indwelling of the Spirit's person is the basis for the application of salvation to the believer. Real

---

261. E.g. Wilkinson, *The hope of Glory*, 16–17; Stedman, *Mystical Union*, 23; Leigh, *A Body of Divinity*, 488.

262. *Works*, V, *Glory of the Gospel*, 4, 14, 74.

263. *Works*, V, *Glory of the Gospel*, 16–17.

264. Paul Best, *Mysteries Discovered. Or, A Mercuriall Picture pointing out the way from Babylon to the holy City, for the good of all such as during that night of generall Errour and Apostasie* (1647), 2–3.

265. Biddle, *The Apostolical And True Opinion*, 30.

266. Reeve and Muggleton, *A Divine Looking-Glass*, the epistle, 25; William Dell, *The Way of True Peace and Unity among The Faithful and Churches of Christ, In all humility and bowels of love presented to them* (1649), 16–17; William Dell, *The Tryal of Spirits Both in Teachers & Hearers. Wherein is held forth The clear Discovery, and certain Downfal of the Carnal and Antichristian Clergie of These Nations* (1653), 15; Dell, *A Plain and Necessary Confutation*, 37; Erbery, *Nor Truth, nor Errour*, 3–4; Erbery, *The North Star*, 21–2.

267. Erbery, *The Testimony*, 93.

268. Erbery, *The Testimony*, 71–2.

union with Christ, he asserted, is 'the Foundation of all good they must receive from him'.[269] Elsewhere he wrote, 'Union with Christ is the first fundamental thing of Justification and Sanctification, and all. ... It is through our Union with Christ ... that we partake of the priviledges of the Covenant of Grace'.[270] Real union with Christ was widely accepted among mainstream puritans and enthusiasts as the foundation for the application of salvific benefits.[271] The wide acceptance is evidenced by the *Westminster Larger Catechism* which, having insisted upon a real union with Christ, stated,

> The Communion in grace, which the members of the invisible Church have with Christ, is their partaking of the vertue of his Mediation, in their justification, Adoption, Sanctification, and whatever else in this life manifests their Union with him.[272]

However, for Goodwin, the mode of indwelling involved in real union is also essential for the application of salvation. He presented the indwelling of the Spirit as the foundation from which the Spirit performs all other operations within an individual: 'the shedding forth, or entring in of the Holy Spirit, is the first foundation to all wrought in us ... therefore this his coming upon us and entring into us, is immediately without any preparation, when men are unregenerate'.[273] Moreover, Goodwin believed that the entire application of salvation is founded in his conception of Christ's mystical indwelling by faith. 'All then, that God works upon you savingly, from First to Last'[274] is founded, he insisted, upon spiritual sight of Christ. For this reason, Goodwin declared that 'The main Sum and Substance of Christianity then is, That Christ be revealed *in us*, and not only *to us*'.[275] I will determine how applied soteriology is founded in this conception of real union with Christ in the remainder of this study.

---

269. *Works*, V, *The Holy Ghost*, 356.

270. *Works*, III, *Christ the Mediator*, 347.

271. Owen, *Exercitations on the Epistle to the Hebrews*, 144; John Owen, *Meditations and Discourses on the Glory of Christ, in His Person, Office, and Grace with The differences between Faith and Sight* (1684), 143. Flavel, *The Method of Grace*, 25, 33, 68; Burgess, *CXLV Expository Sermons*, 589; Cotton, *Covenant of Grace*, 31; John Saltmarsh, *The Fountaine of Free Grace Opened by Questions and Answers: Proving the Foundation of Faith to consist only in Gods Free Love in giving Christ to dye for the sins of all, and Objections to the contrary Answered* (1645), 22.

272. Westminster Assembly, *The Confession of Faith, And the Larger and Shorter Catechisme, First agreed upon by the Assembly of Divines at Westminster* (Edinburgh, 1649), 93–4.

273. *Works*, V, *The Holy Ghost*, 54.

274. *Works*, V, *Glory of the Gospel*, 79.

275. *Works*, V, *Glory of the Gospel*, 79.

In Goodwin's mind, however, the ultimate purpose of union with Christ is the enjoyment of communion with God. Other salvific benefits, most notably transformation and justification, are secondary in importance to communion. In fact, as will be discussed, both are required in order to make communion with God possible.[276] Goodwin's conception of communion with God and its relation to union with Christ must, therefore, be examined. For him, the two ideas are bound together: communion is the end of union and, accordingly, communion is necessarily grounded in union.[277] While this conviction was shared by enthusiasts and conservatives alike,[278] Goodwin entertained a specific notion of communion which required his conception of real union with Christ as the foundation.

Goodwin understood communion with God chiefly in interpersonal terms.[279] Foundational was his Trinitarianism in which, as already discussed, the three persons comprise a 'Society among themselves; enjoying Fellowship, and Delights accordingly in themselves.'[280] He reasoned that the enjoyment of this communion moved them 'to take up Creature-fellowship and Communion into a participation of that sweet Society.'[281] While the communion enjoyed by the three divine persons ultimately remains incommunicable, nevertheless in a limited sense believers may participate in that communion.[282] This underscores the significance of the aforementioned commonality of divine and human personhood in Goodwin's thought.

Believers, therefore, enjoy a distinct communion with each of the divine persons.[283] Distinct communion, Goodwin reasoned, is also necessitated by the narrowness of the human mind which can only commune with one divine person at a time.[284] True to classical Trinitarian theology, Goodwin balanced this stress upon distinct communion with an affirmation that each person is the same God and, therefore, communion with one person entails implicit communion or a 'secret under-Communion' with the other two.[285] In this theology of distinct communion, Goodwin was close to Owen who also developed the idea at length,

---

276. E.g. *Works*, V, *Blessed State*, 39.

277. *Works*, II, *Election*, 100–1, 122.

278. Cradock, *Saints Fulnesse*, 13; Burgess, *CXLV Expository Sermons*, 587; Hooker, *The Application of Redemption*, 490; Wilkinson, *The hope of Glory*, 41.

279. On occasion, Goodwin employed the term 'communion' to denote participation in Christ's actions and salvific benefits, but he normally reserved the term for experiential fellowship with God.

280. *Works*, II, *Election*, 141; cf. *Works*, IV, *The Government of the Churches*, 241.

281. *Works*, II, *Election*, 130.

282. *Works*, II, *The Knowledg*, 13–21.

283. *Works*, IV, *Object and Acts*, part I, 132; part II, 104–6.

284. *Works*, IV, *Object and Acts*, part I, 132.

285. *Works*, V, *Of Several Ages*, 198; cf. *Works*, IV, *Object and Acts*, part II, 104. This was also an idea advanced by Owen. See Ryan M. McGraw, *A Heavenly Directory: Trinitarian Piety, Public Worship and a Reassessment of John Owen's Theology*, Reformed Historical Theology (Göttingen: Vandenhoeck & Ruprecht, 2014), 55.

especially in his work *Of Communion with God.*[286] Drawing upon Brian Kay's work, Ryan McGraw remarks, 'it was rare for seventeenth century theologians to root their devotional works in the Trinity ... it held little practical or devotional value beyond adoring God for his incomprehensibility.'[287] McGraw notes that along with Owen, the chief exception was Goodwin.

Admittedly, on occasion Goodwin also made reference to communion with the divine perfections and the divine nature.[288] However, even this must be understood in interpersonal terms. Since each divine person has an enjoyment of the one Godhead, they were also moved, Goodwin reasoned, to allow believers to enjoy all their perfections.[289] Moreover, the common divine nature allows all that each person is and has to be shared with the other two persons.[290] Similarly, believers commune with the divine perfections because the divine persons share their fullness with believers.

For Goodwin, then, such interpersonal communion with God is the height of salvation and the end to which the elect are ordained.[291] While in the present believers enjoy communion by faith, fullness of communion with God awaits eschatological glory where saints will enjoy communion by sight.[292] Thus, Goodwin proclaimed: 'let ... all the World know, that the Top and Summity of our Religion is to obtain, and then to retain and hold Fellowship with the Person of God the Father, and of Christ.'[293]

Why, then, did Goodwin promote communion with God so vigorously? In the first instance was Goodwin's own experiential religion. On his deathbed, he reassured his two sons: '*I am going ... to the three Persons, with whom I have had Communion.*'[294] In his writings, Goodwin urged his readers to seek assurance of salvation not by 'Argument or Deduction' but in communion with the Trinitarian persons.[295] Consequently, since Goodwin believed it is possible to possess saving faith without assurance, so he believed it is possible to have union without communion.[296] Given his struggle for assurance of salvation for seven years

---

286. John Owen, *Of Communion with God The Father, Sonne, and Holy Ghost, Each Person Distinctly; in Love, Grace, and Consolation: Or, The Saints Fellowship With the Father, Sonne, and Holy Ghost, Unfolded* (Oxford, 1657). For an analysis, see Kelly M. Kapic, 'Communion with God: Relations between the Divine and the Human in the Theology of John Owen' (PhD thesis, University of London, 2001), 152–212.

287. McGraw, *A Heavenly Directory*, 31.

288. *Works*, IV, *Object and Acts*, part I, 60; *Works*, II, *Election*, 143.

289. *Works*, II, *Election*, 130.

290. *Works*, II, *The Knowledg*, 17–18.

291. *Works*, II, *Election*, 96.

292. *Works*, V, *Blessed State*, 73; cf. *Works*, IV, *Object and Acts*, part II, 107; *Works*, I, *Thirteen Sermons*, 38.

293. *Works*, V, *Of Several Ages*, 183.

294. *Life*, xix.

295. *Works*, IV, *Object and Acts*, part II, 106.

296. *Works*, IV, *Object and Acts*, part II, 84.

following his conversion in 1620, it is tempting to conclude that Goodwin believed that he had only truly discovered communion with the divine persons from 1627 onwards.[297] According to his son's biographical account, Goodwin wrote the *Glory of the Gospel*, which stresses the mystical indwelling of Christ, as a result of his new confidence.[298]

What also drove Goodwin to stress communion with the divine persons as the height of salvation was his abhorrence of Catholic and moralistic religion. He complained, 'The Height of Popish Religion, and of many others also, is to converse with Maxims and Articles of Faith.'[299] Catholic religion, he alleged, displaced interpersonal communion by general faith, created grace and communion with the saints.[300] Since Goodwin also denounced a '*practical Catechism*' in context, the 'many others' almost certainly included Henry Hammond (1605–1660) who, while not openly denying the Trinity, believed it had little bearing upon the Christian life. Tracing the Socinian influence upon Hammond, Mortimer notes the popularity of his *A Practical Catechisme*; by 1650, it was on its seventh printing.[301] Goodwin complained that Hammond treated salvation as mere moral restoration 'unto the State of Holiness which Adam was created in.'[302] In contrast, contending that salvation advances the believer beyond the Adamic state, Goodwin asserted that 'Knowledg of and Communion with these Persons, is both that which is the ultimate End and Tendency of all the other part of our *practic Religion*.'[303]

On the other side of Goodwin were radicals who advocated participation of essence in the divine nature. Goodwin believed his notion of interpersonal communion readily demarcated his position from such opponents. A believer, he contended, 'cannot otherwise be Partaker of the God-head than by such Communion with him as our Person with another Person, who never become one in Nature and Essence, but continue two several Beings'.[304] Thus, his notion of 'distinct persons' was crucial for advancing a high view of communion with God, while protecting the ontological boundary between God and creation. Indeed, provided ontological distinctions were maintained, Goodwin urged his audience to aspire to the highest degree of communion possible beyond which any attempts of his radical opponents were in vain.[305] Thus, Goodwin was not excluding all notions of deification but here championed deification in terms of interpersonal

297. *Life*, xv.

298. *Life*, xvii.

299. *Works*, V, *Of Several Ages*, 182.

300. *Works*, V, *Of Several Ages*, 182–3. This passage suggests Goodwin's strong concept of divine personhood was originally forged in opposition to Catholicism rather than the heterodox teachings of the 1640s–1650s.

301. Mortimer, *Reason and Religion*, 119–46.

302. *Works*, V, *Of Several Ages*, 184.

303. *Works*, V, *Of Several Ages*, 184.

304. *Works*, V, *The Holy Ghost*, 176.

305. *Works*, V, *The Holy Ghost*, 149.

communion with the divine persons. In fact, I will identify two further senses of deification in later chapters.[306]

The proper conception of communion with God, therefore, arises from grasping the true nature of union with Christ. As Goodwin stated, 'Where there is an Union of Persons, there is, or shall follow in the end, a making each other known one to the other.'[307] For Goodwin, then, interpersonal communion with God is the inevitable consequence of his inherently interpersonal concept of real union with Christ.

Moreover, Goodwin's conception of real union with Christ founds a distinct communion with each divine person. This is immediately apparent regarding communion with Christ. Stipulating that communion requires a person to be 'real and present', Goodwin directly connected communion with Christ and Christ's mystical indwelling of the believer.[308] Elsewhere, Goodwin stated that Christ's indwelling by faith allows 'real Communion with him'.[309] Communion with Christ, therefore, is inherent in Goodwin's conception of real union with Christ. It is both the chief work of the indwelling Spirit and the primary benefit of real union. In contrast, lower conceptions of union with Christ lack the Spirit's inner revelation of Christ and, therefore, cannot allow interpersonal communion with him.

Believers enjoy communion with the Father derivatively, Goodwin reasoned, because the Father is revealed in Christ: 'in beholding him, we behold the Glory of God the Father also'.[310] For Goodwin, the mediation of communion with the Father through Christ was vital for refuting radicals who advocated immediate communion with the Father.[311]

Goodwin's conception of real union also provides the foundation for communion with the Spirit, albeit in a different mode to communion with the Father and the Son. In the case of the latter two, Goodwin wrote, 'our Fellowship is objectively with the Father, and with his Son'.[312] By objective, he meant that communion results from revelation of their persons. However, because the Spirit reveals the Father and the Son, rather than himself,[313] communion with the Spirit is not objective.[314] In Goodwin's mind, this explains why, despite the Spirit's status

306. See p. 92 and §5.4.3.

307. *Works*, II, *The Knowledg*, 18.

308. *Works*, IV, *Object and Acts*, part III, 14.

309. *Works*, V, *Glory of the Gospel*, 7; cf. *Works*, IV, *Object and Acts*, part III, 6; *Works*, III, *An Unregenerate*, 151.

310. *Works*, V, *Of Several Ages*, 198.

311. *Works*, IV, *Object and Acts*, part II, 106–7.

312. *Works*, IV, *Object and Acts*, part I, 110; cf. *Works*, V, *Of Several Ages*, 198.

313. *Works*, V, *The Holy Ghost*, 21, 44; *Works*, IV, *Object and Acts*, part III, 15.

314. *Works*, V, *The Holy Ghost*, 54. Admittedly, Goodwin was occasionally inconsistent by advocating that the Spirit produces a lively image of all three persons. E.g. *Works*, I, *Ephesians*, part I, 327.

as a divine person, many believers neglected communion with him.[315] Yet, such believers still experience communion with the Spirit: given the aforementioned idea of implicit communion, communion with the Father and the Son also involves communion with the Spirit.[316] Nevertheless Goodwin urged believers to seek communion with the Spirit and called them to reflect on the reality of the person of the Spirit indwelling within, reasoning that the indwelling of his person demonstrates his closeness and love for them.[317]

Goodwin's conception of real union with Christ, therefore, imposed a Trinitarian structure upon communion with God. Goodwin wrote,

> [The Spirit] leads us by Christ to the Father, for we come to God by and through Christ, being led in the Hand of the Spirit. Thus the Soul comes to have Communion with all the three Persons, Fellowship with the Father, and with the Son, and with the Holy Ghost, till this Fellowship is perfected in Heaven.[318]

Furthermore, communion with God also necessarily requires the believer's part of real union with Christ. Goodwin wrote, 'the Union, on which this our Communion is founded, is of all other the closest, which by the help of Faith in the Understanding, and of Love in the Will, joins God and the Soul into one Spirit.'[319] Given the relational nature of interpersonal communion with God, it is unsurprising that Goodwin believed that both of the soul's chief faculties must be engaged in faith.

For Goodwin, then, participation in God as interpersonal communion is entirely founded in his conception of real union with Christ. This deified state, Goodwin contended, surpasses the Adamic state. Adam experienced 'Communion with God in a Natural way,'[320] since his knowledge of God was mediated by creation and through natural means.[321] Believers, in contrast, experience spiritual communion on the basis of faith and the inner revelation of Christ by the Spirit. Thus, Goodwin's conception of real union with Christ allowed him to advance a deification soteriology in which believers are raised above the Adamic state to interpersonal participation in God.

2.7 Postscript: The Lord's Supper and union with Christ

The question of the relation of the sacraments to union with Christ may now be examined. Much of Calvin's theology of union with Christ was developed in

---

315. *Works*, V, *The Holy Ghost*, 32–3.
316. *Works*, V, *Of Several Ages*, 198.
317. *Works*, V, *The Holy Ghost*, 33–4.
318. *Works*, IV, *Object and Acts*, part I, 115.
319. *Works*, IV, *Object and Acts*, part II, 123.
320. *Works*, II, *The Creatures*, 48.
321. *Works*, II, *The Creatures*, 35–6, 38, 41–4; *Works*, V, *The Holy Ghost*, 149.

relation to the Lord's Supper. While this was not the case for Goodwin, his limited remarks concerning the sacraments nevertheless manifest a tight connection with his conception of real union with Christ. Goodwin insisted that the sacraments 'signifie' and 'seal up' not only Christ's death but also 'our being one with him therein'.[322] Thus, he understood the sacraments both to symbolize and to convey real union with Christ. Whereas baptism symbolizes the initial 'ingrafting' of individuals into this union, the Lord's Supper symbolizes the ongoing 'common participation' of the church's union with Christ.[323] The latter signifies participation in this union, since union is implied in eating and drinking: 'what we Eat, or Drink, becomes one with our Bodies'.[324] Moreover, Goodwin contended that the bread and the wine primarily signify the person of Christ, rather than his benefits.[325] In his early sermon on Ephesians 3:17, Goodwin argued that the Reformed view of the Lord's Supper supported his conception of union with Christ as the immediate and primary indwelling of Christ's person:

> I find that Divines say, That our Union with Christ is a *substantial Union*; that is, it is an Union of the Substance of his Person, and of ours, which the Lord's Supper is the Symbol of, and is ordained to signify; and therefore not only by his Spirit or Graces.[326]

What could be questioned, however, is whether Goodwin's dismissal of the proxy of the Spirit in this early sermon found support from the received Reformed doctrine of the Lord's Supper in which Christ's presence is mediated by the Spirit.[327] In keeping with Goodwin's pneumatological revision of union with Christ, his later comments on the sacraments granted a clearer role to the Holy Spirit. Referring to the wine, he wrote, 'We are yet said *to drink into one Spirit*; For that Blood is *Vehiculum Spiritus*, the Spirit runs in and with this Blood.'[328] Thus, while the sacraments symbolize Christ, the mature Goodwin associated their efficacy with the Holy Spirit.

This examination must therefore turn to the manner in which the Spirit seals union with Christ through the sacrament. In an important passage, quoted here at length, Goodwin compared the representation of Christ in the Supper with that in the Scriptures:

322. *Works*, IV, *Object and Acts*, part II, 37.

323. *Works*, IV, *The Government of the Churches*, 378. For baptism, see *Works*, V, *The Holy Ghost*, 317; *Works*, IV, *Object and Acts*, part II, 130; *Works*, IV, *The Government of the Churches*, 30.

324. *Works*, II, *The Knowledg*, 16.

325. *Christ Set Forth*, 12.

326. *Works*, I, *Thirteen Sermons*, 33.

327. His son mentioned that Goodwin was well acquainted with Calvin's *Institutes* from his formative years in Cambridge. *Life*, vi.

328. *Works*, V, *The Holy Ghost*, 46.

In the Word read or heard, we have directly and first to do with some Truth, and so with Christ considered but either as the Author and Deliverer of the Truth, or at most but as that particular Truth concerneth him and treats of him, or of some particular Benefit of his, or some Excellency of his, or some action of his for us. And these are singled out to be treated on by piecemeal, unto which our Thoughts are required immediately to be intent … But in this Ordinance of the Lord's Supper, we have to do with Christ himself, his Person, &c. We are put upon him, let into him immediately and directly, and are to converse with him, as a Spouse with her Husband in the nearest Intimacies. … Yea, and we have to deal with all this in the most expressive real manner; it is whole Christ represented as to the Eye: whereas a Sermon, if it did represent whole Christ, yet it would be but to the Ear; and you know things by the Ear strike more dully and slowly, but by Sight more really, and make a lasting Impression.[329]

Kelly Kapic notes that this section from Goodwin parallels Owen's beliefs concerning the sacrament and that both do so against the devaluation of the sacrament by non-conformists.[330] The key question is, in what sense did Goodwin here hold the sacrament to be superior to the Word? Won suggests, 'What Goodwin is distinguishing from this is the act of actual communion with the person of Christ which goes beyond (albeit it is based on) objective knowledge about Christ'.[331] However, as discussed above, Goodwin elsewhere insisted that Christ indwells by faith through the means of the written Word and such indwelling involves inner revelation of Christ surpassing the mere letter.[332] Thus, Won's judgement, if correct, is at odds with Goodwin's comments elsewhere concerning the written Word. Indeed, Fienberg detects inconsistency between this passage and Goodwin's otherwise high evaluation of Scripture's representation of Christ.[333] However, both scholars may have misunderstood the force of Goodwin's comments here. What differed between Scripture and the sacrament was not the possibility of communion but the mode of representation of Christ. The mode of representation in the Lord's Supper, devoid of the mental processes required to receive the written Word, allows the believer to behold Christ in his totality and therefore more readily permits unhindered communion with him. Accordingly, Goodwin claimed elsewhere that, in comparison to the preached Word, 'partaking of the Holy Ghost, is especially in Baptism and the Sacraments; and he usually is powred forth more abundantly at the Sacrament'.[334]

Like Scripture, the Lord's Supper, therefore, allows Christ to indwell by faith. In this way, Goodwin was able to integrate his theology of real union with Christ

---

329. *Works*, V, *Gospel Holiness*, 153; cf. *Works*, IV, *The Government of the Churches*, 344.
330. Kapic, 'Communion with God', 228.
331. Won, 'Communion with Christ', 255.
332. See §2.5.
333. Fienberg, 'Puritan Pastor and Independent Divine', 30.
334. *Works*, IV, *The Government of the Churches*, 262.

with the efficacy of the sacrament. While Goodwin rejected transubstantiation and consubstantiation, he affirmed the real presence of Christ with the elements and understood Christ's presence in terms of the inner revelation of Christ by the Spirit.[335] The efficacy of the sacrament, then, results from the Spirit's operation and requires faith for Christ's presence to be made real in the believer.[336] Thus, while his doctrine of union with Christ was far less strongly associated with the Lord's Supper than was the case with Calvin, nevertheless, Goodwin readily integrated the sacrament within his theology of real union with Christ.

2.8 Conclusion

Goodwin expounded his conception of union with Christ, bounded by two competing concerns: on the one hand, he desired to attribute to believers the strongest of unions with Christ and therefore the closest of communions with the divine (here he distanced himself not only from conservative figures but also from Socinians). On the other hand, he wanted to define clearly the boundaries of union with Christ to respect the orthodox understanding of the Trinity and Christ (here he distanced himself from radicals). Treading the middle path, Goodwin contended for a real union of believers with Christ but not amounting to the essential union of the Trinity or the hypostatic union of the incarnation. His mature position affirmed that, while ultimately a mystery, real union involves the indwelling of the Holy Spirit's person who mediates Christ's presence through inner revelation of Christ's person. The Spirit can function as the bond of this union because he proceeds from Christ's divine nature and so is able to truly reveal Christ. Against mystical and enthusiastic teachings, Goodwin insisted that this revelation must be coupled with the external Scripture and sacraments. This revelation of Christ is necessary to complete real union with him because only through spiritual sight of Christ can the will of the believer be moved to cleave to him in faith. Goodwin maintained this conception of real union against the conservative majority who restricted indwelling to created grace alone. In Goodwin's mind, their view of union was too low and unable to sustain the application of salvation and communion with God.

What has become clear from this examination is that Goodwin's concept of person was vital to his conception of real union with Christ. He was emphatic that the strongest unions involve the indwelling of one person in another. Thus, the notion of *perichoresis* was important within his doctrine of the Trinity. His conception of the incarnational union veered towards the indwelling of a divine person in a human person, but here he was careful to insist that Christ was one person. The same conviction also governed his understanding of the union of believers with Christ: this union did not simply involve the indwelling of graces

---

335. *Works*, V, *Gospel Holiness*, 155; cf. 150.
336. *Works*, V, *Gospel Holiness*, 156.

but the indwelling of Christ's person. In an early sermon, Goodwin insisted that Christ's indwelling entailed the immediate and primary indwelling of Christ in his divine nature. This view later underwent pneumatological revision: Goodwin's concept of divine personhood necessitated that each person receive equal honour and therefore his mature position was that Christ indwells by the Spirit's indwelling. This scheme honours both the Son (for great persons have ambassadors) and the Spirit (whose act of love is to indwell sinful believers). Goodwin's emphasis upon the indwelling of persons climaxed in his advocacy of interpersonal communion with God as the goal of salvation. Since salvation ultimately consists in interpersonal communion with the persons of the Trinity, real union requires the indwelling of the divine persons. Interpersonal communion with God, therefore, was for Goodwin one aspect of participating in the divine nature. Crucially, it was the category of 'distinct persons' which allowed communion without confusion of the God/creation distinction. What will become evident in the following two chapters is Goodwin's belief that both transformation and justification are required, in different respects, for the believer to commune with the divine persons.

Chapter 3

REAL UNION WITH CHRIST AND THE REALITY OF TRANSFORMATION

3.1 Introduction

In his grand project, Goodwin gave considerable attention to the transformation of believers which, he believed, must involve a radical change in nature. In this chapter I will examine Goodwin's high notion of transformation and demonstrate how he understood transformation to result from his conception of real union with Christ. In Goodwin's mind, transformation consists in two principal stages – regeneration and bodily resurrection. I will begin by examining the necessity and nature of regeneration (§3.2). Goodwin argued that regeneration consists in the infusion of created grace which functions as new spiritual life. The corresponding reality of bodily resurrection will then be shown to consist in the same infused grace (§3.3). Both sections raise the question of the relation of the created grace of transformation to the indwelling Holy Spirit which will be addressed in the next section (§3.4). The argument will then culminate in establishing that the renewal of the *imago Dei* in Christ encompasses the different aspects of transformation and in examining how Goodwin believed its renewal is founded in his conception of real union with Christ (§3.5).

I will pay greatest attention to four treatises belonging to Goodwin's grand project: *The Creatures, An Unregenerate, The Holy Ghost* and *Blessed State*. Apart from large sections of *An Unregenerate* composed in the late 1620s, these works were largely, if not entirely, composed in the 1650s.

3.2 The reality of regeneration

The importance of regeneration in Goodwin's thought is evident from the opening of chapter 7 of *The Holy Ghost* Book I. Having outlined the Trinitarian structure of the three central treatises of his grand project, Goodwin announced his intention for the third: 'That which I have to do, is more particularly to demonstrate … both *That*, and *Why*, this last part of Salvation, *viz.* Application, and so principally this of Regeneration, is attributed to the Holy Ghost.'[1] Within Goodwin's grand

---

1. *Works*, V, *The Holy Ghost*, 40.

project, regeneration, therefore, occupied a foundational role upon which the application of salvation rests. Given this importance of regeneration, the question of its relation to indwelling is raised. In short, while placing indwelling logically and chronologically prior to regeneration,[2] Goodwin held regeneration to be the Spirit's 'prime work in us'.[3] Accordingly, though he opened the treatise arguing that the Spirit's indwelling of believers is the Spirit's foundational work, the bulk of the treatise was devoted to the nature and necessity of new birth. Indeed, the opening of chapter 7 of Book I operates as a second introduction to the treatise announcing the subject proper.

That regeneration was important in Goodwin's theology is also highlighted by noting the history of development of the doctrine. In his survey of the puritan doctrine of regeneration, James Shields remarks, 'It was the English Puritans who gave doctrinal structure to the idea of regeneration after it was rediscovered in the Reformation.'[4] While both Perkins and Sibbes had often appealed to the doctrine, arguably Goodwin's treatment in *The Holy Ghost* was the first robust exposition.[5] At the very least, Goodwin was a leading architect in establishing the doctrine within the concerns of a Calvinistic soteriology. No doubt the Arminianism debate that came to a head at the Synod of Dort in 1618–19 focused the minds of later puritans such as Goodwin to secure a more robust notion of regeneration.

Yet, what primarily drove Goodwin to examine regeneration at length was a growing pastoral concern very much alive in the 1650s. This is clear from the conclusion of a sermon originally preached in Oxford during this period, included within the treatise and quoted here at length:

> Let us see, and make this necessity of the New Birth. We are faln into times in which the thing and Doctrine of it is forgotten and laid aside: In which there are multitudes of Professors, but Few Converts … There is a Zeal amongst us to advance this or that Reformation in Religion … But my Brethren, where is Regeneration call'd for or regarded? We have seen the greatest outward Alterations that ever were in any Age, Kingdoms turned and Converted into Commonwealths, the Power of Heaven and Earth shaken: But men, although they turn this way and that, from this or that way, from this opinion to that, yet their Hearts generally turn upon the same Hinges they were hung on, when they came into the World. In this University of *Oxford* we have had puttings out and puttings in, but where is putting off the Old Nature and putting on the New? Where do we hear (as we had wont) of Souls carrying home the Holy Ghost from Sermons, of their being changed and altered, and made new, and

---

2. *Works*, V, *The Holy Ghost*, 52–3, 380.

3. *Works*, V, *The Holy Ghost*, 13.

4. James L. Shields, 'The Doctrine of Regeneration in English Puritan Theology, 1604–1689' (PhD thesis, Southwestern Baptist Theological Seminary, 1965), 232; cf. 1–2; Beeke and Jones, *A Puritan Theology*, 463.

5. Shields, 'The Doctrine of Regeneration', 34–5.

of Students running home weeping to their Studies, crying out *What shall I do to be saved?* This was heretofore a wonted Cry. Conversion is the only standing Miracle in the Church, but I may truly say these Miracles are well nigh ceased; we hear of few of them.[6]

The importance of this concern is also evident from Goodwin's stated intention in the opening of his treatise *An Unregenerate*:

That which I intend therein, is a Conviction of all those Sorts of Persons, (that are the Generality of the Church) that they are still in the State of Nature, and without true Regeneration will eternally perish.[7]

Other puritans similarly convinced of the necessity of personal regeneration were likewise distressed by the extent of nominal Christianity in the 1650s.[8] Calls for true reformation were also issued by enthusiastic preachers who were far more sceptical of the reformation of institutional structures.[9] It should be noted that for Goodwin this pastoral concern cannot be isolated from his own conversion experience in 1620. In autobiographical material, Goodwin recounted the moment of his conversion:

God was pleased on the sudden, and as it were in an instant, to alter the whole Course of his former Dispensation towards me … as he created the World and the Matter of all things by a Word, so he created and put a new Life and Spirit into my Soul, and so great an Alteration was strange to me.[10]

He proceeded to interpret his conversion in terms of the apostle Paul's Damascus road experience and also a certain Mr Price 'who was in all Mens Eyes the greatest and most famous Convert, known to the whole University of *Cambridge*'.[11] Goodwin's son's editorial remarks suggest that his father's profound sense of regeneration also led him to discount the Arminian low view of corruption of nature. In a sermon from the early 1640s, Goodwin dismissed reducing corruption and divine transforming power to mere metaphors and, instead, asserted that 'they have the greatest reality in them in the world'.[12]

New in the 1650s was the need to defend a strong doctrine of regeneration against the rising tide of heterodox teachings. Mainstream puritans warned that

6. *Works*, V, *The Holy Ghost*, 145.

7. *Works*, III, *An Unregenerate*, 1.

8. E.g. Burgess, *Spiritual Refining*, 209.

9. E.g. William Dell, *Right Reformation: Or, The Reformation of the Church of the New Testament, Represented in Gospel-Light* (1646), 4–5.

10. *Life*, xi.

11. *Life*, xii.

12. *Works*, I, *Ephesians*, part I, 312.

Socinians reduced regeneration to mere moral reformation.[13] In the 1670s, Owen attacked this view: 'We say and believe that Regeneration consists ... in a Spiritual Renovation of our Nature: Our Modern *Socinians*, that it doth so ... in a Moral Reformation of Life.'[14] However, if Goodwin intended to undermine Socinian teaching in *The Holy Ghost*, then this motive remained veiled.[15] In one section he identified three opposing opponents to his doctrine of regeneration – Catholics, Arminians and enthusiasts – but Socinians were omitted.[16] For Goodwin, then, the dominant new threat of the 1650s was not Socinianism but radical ideas. Without naming individual proponents, he repeatedly warned against radicals who confused the God/creation distinction in their account of transformation.

3.2.1 *The necessity of a change in nature*

Goodwin defined regeneration in the following terms: 'Regeneration ... consists in the Mortification of Lusts, and quickning us with Christ, and Faith that marries us to him.'[17] Later he enumerated 'Three parts of our Regeneration: 1. Humiliation for Sin, and the Necessity thereof in order to Faith. 2. Faith in Christ for Justification. 3. Turning from Sin unto God, or Holiness of Heart and Life.'[18] As a broad category, regeneration defined 'the Passage' between the states of nature and grace.[19] Normally, however, Goodwin understood regeneration to consist narrowly in a change of nature.[20] Noting that the main change in conversion consists in the '*Moral, Legal, Forinsecal* change', Goodwin remarked that 'over and above such as these, there is a *Physical* change, which is more properly the impress *of Regeneration*, which is a work in us'.[21]

Regeneration must involve a change of nature, Goodwin contended, in order for God to respect the integrity of creation. Since a nature is received through birth, scriptural language of new birth implies that regeneration entails a change

---

13. Christopher Harold Cleveland, 'Thomism in John Owen' (PhD thesis, Aberdeen University, 2011), 83. See *The Racovian Catechism, with Notes and Illustrations, Translated from the Latin: To Which Is Prefixed a Sketch of the History of Unitarianism in Poland and the Adjacent Countries.*, trans. Thomas Rees (1818), 326, 330–1.

14. Owen, *Pneumatologia*, 182.

15. Given the introduction in chapter 7 of Book I, it is possible that chapters 1–6 were inserted later as a new opening designed to meet the Socinian threat, but the rest of the treatise concerning regeneration did not especially have Socinian teachings in view.

16. *Works*, V, *The Holy Ghost*, 173–6. Elsewhere, Goodwin attacked 'imputative antinomians' who undermined the necessity of regeneration by championing free justification.

17. *Works*, V, *The Holy Ghost*, 71.

18. *Works*, V, *The Holy Ghost*, 335.

19. *Works*, V, *The Holy Ghost*, 65.

20. Goodwin employed the language of a 'new Nature'. E.g. *Works*, V, *The Holy Ghost*, 184.

21. *Works*, V, *The Holy Ghost*, 377.

in nature.[22] Moreover, stating that it is a law of nature for a creature's behaviour to flow from its created nature, he further reasoned that only a change in nature accounts for behavioural change from regeneration.[23] God proceeds by the same law in his new creation as in his first, such that the actions of believers are natural to them.

However, what really dictated the necessity of regeneration in Goodwin's mind were two soteriological concerns. First was the depravity of human nature; the second was the heavenly nature of the eschatological state. Regarding the former, Goodwin asserted that corruption of nature involves 'an universal, total, sinful Defilement, spread over all Faculties of Soul and Body, containing in it a Privation or Want of all Good, and an inclination to all Evil ... which is traduced unto us by Birth and fleshly Generation.'[24] Thus, the understanding, the will and the affections were all corrupted.[25] Here Goodwin was consistent with the Reformed tenet of total depravity. Calvin wrote, 'Original sin, therefore, seems to be a hereditary depravity and corruption of our nature, diffused into all parts of the soul.'[26] Total depravity, Goodwin contrasted with the stance of Catholics and others who 'exclude some of the Faculties of the Soul from being infected with it.'[27] Likely in view here were medieval scholastics such as Duns Scotus (c. 1266–1308) and other Franciscans who excluded the mind from corruption.[28] As I will discuss later, Goodwin countered that the understanding was even to blame for corruption in the other faculties.[29]

For puritans like Goodwin, regeneration involves a radical change of nature to undo corruption.[30] Burgess likewise asserted: '*The great Corruption of mans Nature is the ground of the necessity of Regeneration.*'[31] Both divines concluded that since every faculty has been corrupted, in regeneration there must be a commensurate change in all the faculties.[32] For Goodwin, at least, the necessity of regeneration to undo corruption was a conviction that had grown out of personal experience. In his conversion narrative he recounted,

22. *Works*, V, *The Holy Ghost*, 141.

23. *Works*, V, *The Holy Ghost*, 188–9; cf. 181.

24. *Works*, III, *An Unregenerate*, 36; cf. 102, 117; *Aggravation of Sinne*, 4.

25. *Works*, III, *An Unregenerate*, 83–5.

26. Calvin, *Institutes of the Christian Religion*, volume 1, 251. See also Peter Harrison, *The Fall of Man and the Foundations of Science* (Cambridge: Cambridge University Press, 2007), 59.

27. *Works*, III, *An Unregenerate*, 37; cf. 161; *Works*, I, *Ephesians*, part II, 96–7.

28. Harrison, *The Fall of Man*, 61. The English writer Jeremiah Taylor (bap. 1613, d. 1667) also explicitly denied the corruption of every faculty. Jeremy Taylor, *Deus justificatus. Two Discourses of Original Sin* (1656), 39.

29. See pp. 122–3.

30. *Works*, III, *An Unregenerate*, 38.

31. Burgess, *Spiritual Refining*, 218.

32. *Works*, V, *The Holy Ghost*, 364. Burgess, *Spiritual Refining*, 204.

I found my Spirit clothed with a new Nature, naturally inclining me to good; whereas before it was inclined only to evil. ... I found a new Indweller or habitual Principle of opposition to, and hatred of Sin indwelling[33]

Because of the corruption of nature, Goodwin was convinced that the change of nature in regeneration must involve mortification. True mortification is not a mere 'deading the Soul to a present act of sinning, then it were no more but restraining Grace.'[34] Instead, mortification is the destruction of inherent corruption applied to every aspect of human nature.[35] As well as mortification, Goodwin was adamant that regeneration involves vivification.[36] Indeed, vivification is as decisive a change as mortification: 'Vivification, or quickening, is of as large an extent as mortification can be supposed, for they are commensurable ... God's work in quickening is no less then what is seen in mortifying.'[37] Without vivification, regeneration would return an individual to a neutral state, rendering the believer vulnerable to future corruption.[38]

Ultimately, human depravity must be reversed in order to bring the believer into eschatological glory. Shields remarks,

The somewhat surprising thing ... is that in the whole of the writings of these men the deliverance from the state of sin and corruption was emphasized more than the deliverance from the eternal consequences of sin. ... It was sin, that inherent corruption of nature, which caused the most concern to the Puritans.[39]

However, while Shields rightly identifies an emphasis upon deliverance from corruption, puritans like Goodwin believed that transformation of human nature was required to achieve deliverance from the eternal consequences of sin. Often appealing to John 3:3-7 and Hebrews 12:14, Goodwin repeatedly stressed that transformation from corruption to holiness is essential preparation for eschatological glory.[40] He explained, 'Glory in Heaven is an Inheritance undefiled, and no unclean thing can enter in ... Without Holiness no man can see God; that is, so see him as to be happy in him.'[41] The final words encapsulate the key theology: transformation does not merit acceptance, but instead fits the believer to enjoy heavenly life and, especially, knowledge of God.[42] Entailed were two key

33. *Life*, xii; cf. xvii.

34. *Works*, V, *The Holy Ghost*, 186.

35. *Works*, II, *Election*, 272.

36. *Works*, V, *The Holy Ghost*, 420.

37. *Works*, V, *The Holy Ghost*, 186.

38. *Works*, V, *The Holy Ghost*, 186.

39. Shields, 'The Doctrine of Regeneration', 167–8.

40. *Works*, V, *The Holy Ghost*, 41, 75; *The Tryall of a Christians Growth*, 62; *Works*, IV, *Object and Acts*, part III, 25.

41. *Works*, V, *The Holy Ghost*, 145; cf. *Works*, V, *Gospel Holiness*, 19–20, 92.

42. *Works*, V, *Blessed State*, 39; *Works*, I, *Ephesians*, part I, 72; part II, 200.

convictions: first, glory primarily consists in communion with God;[43] secondly, the believer must be conformed to God in holiness in order to commune with him.[44] Here Goodwin occupied the mainstream position among his colleagues on the necessity of regeneration and sanctification. Many puritan divines, appealing to the same scriptural texts, also contended for the necessity of transformation for final salvation. Sedgwick, for example, warned against thinking that forgiveness alone is necessary for salvation.[45] Like Goodwin, Sedgwick reasoned that transformation is necessary for communion with God.[46]

However, the mainstream view was opposed on both sides. On the one side of the mainstream position was Hammond who, seeking to promote moral conduct, argued from Hebrews 12:14 that justification must be rooted in sanctification.[47] In the Westminster Assembly debate on justification, Richard Vines (1599/1600–1656) rejected the imputation of Christ's active obedience and instead apparently advocated that personal obedience merits eternal life, with Christ's passive obedience addressing any lapses. Van Dixhoorn comments, 'Vines suggested that believers are adopted and given a right to heaven because they are sanctified and thus in a sense righteous themselves, and not because of the merits of Christ that are first imputed to them and then seen as their own merits.'[48] Contrary to Goodwin, both Hammond and Vines in their differing ways treated sanctification as necessary for meriting heaven.

On the other side, the 'imputative antinomian' Crisp argued from the incompleteness of sanctification and accordingly interpreted 'No uncleane thing can enter into the Kingdom of heaven' as referring to justification, not sanctification.[49] This cohered with Crisp's controversial teaching that justification removed sin from God's sight.[50] In *Gospel Holiness*, Goodwin warned of antinomians who advocated that justification renders a change in nature unnecessary.[51] Crisp differed from 'perfectionist antinomians'. Cradock, for example, insisted that Hebrews 12:14 refers to '*Personall* holinesse ... not of the imputed holinesse of Christ.'[52] Dealing with the objection from the incompleteness of sanctification, Cradock replied that sanctification is continually increasing and that the believer's innermost part has been decisively made pure.

---

43. *Works*, V, *Blessed State*, 71; cf. 94.

44. *Works*, I, *Ephesians*, part I, 72, 74; *Works*, V, *The Holy Ghost*, 112, 121.

45. Sedgwick, *The Bowels*, 490.

46. Sedgwick, *The Bowels*, 491.

47. Henry Hammond, *A Practical Catechisme* (1645), 49.

48. Van Dixhoorn, 'Reforming the Reformation', 304.

49. Tobias Crisp, *Christ Alone Exalted; In seventeene Sermons: Preached In or neare London* (1643), 308.

50. Crisp, *Christ Alone Exalted; in seventeene Sermons*, 374–7.

51. *Works*, V, *Gospel Holiness*, 104; cf. 20, 92.

52. Cradock, *Gospel-Holinesse*, 51; cf. 63–4.

Upholding the mainstream position, Goodwin contended that sanctification must be completed for the enjoyment of eschatological glory. Its incompleteness will be resolved at death: 'Either at the instant of Death, or in that Passage to Heaven, thy Soul shall be fully purified from Sin, and made perfectly Holy.'[53] This claim was an implication of Goodwin's belief in the intermediate state of the soul in glory, a belief he defended at length in the final part of his grand project, *Blessed State*.[54] Sanctification must be completed at death, he there insisted, so that the soul may enjoy the heavenly glory of communion with God. Like regeneration, then, sanctification prepares the soul for glorification, so it is also necessary for glorification.[55] Goodwin asserted, 'God *afore* our Deaths *hath wrought* all of Grace he intends to work, in Preparation to Glory.'[56] Yet, Goodwin also appealed to the 'Furnance of Gods immediate Presence arrived unto at Death' to complete transformation in an instant.[57] Goodwin, therefore, insisted upon the necessity of sanctification, while avoiding the Catholic doctrine of purgatory which assumed a protracted period of purification removed from God's presence.[58]

Beyond the problem of the depravity of human nature, Goodwin believed that regeneration is necessary because salvation also involves the advancement of believers above the original Adamic earthly state to a heavenly existence,[59] that is, advancement from a natural to a spiritual state. This eschatological state was the ultimate divine intention for humanity at creation. Thus, rather than destroying creation, grace transforms it: 'as Nature is a Ground-work to Grace, so was the Animal Substance to that which was Spiritual, even to be cloathed with it, and swallowed up by it.'[60] For Goodwin, then, regeneration involving a radical transformation is necessary to fit the believer for a spiritual existence. On different grounds, this second soteriological concern returns to the matter of communion with God as the centre of eschatological glory: since God is a spirit (as well as holy),

---

53. *Works*, V, *Blessed State*, 101; cf. 102; *Works*, V, *Gospel Holiness*, 20.

54. *Works*, V, *Blessed State*, 6. Goodwin may have had in view the leveller Richard Overton (fl. 1640–63) and radical teachers Reeve and Muggleton. Richard Overton, *Mans Mortalitie: Or, A treatise Wherein 'tis proved, both Theologically and Philosophically, that whole Man (as a rationall Creature) is a Compound wholly mortall, contrary to that common distinction of Soule and Body: And that the present going of the Soule into Heaven or Hell is a meer Fiction: And that at the Resurrection is the beginning of our immortality, and then Actual Xondemnation, and Salvation, and not before* (Amsterdam, 1644); Reeve and Muggleton, *A Divine Looking-Glass*, 100; John Reeve and Lodowick Muggleton, *A Transcendent Spiritual Treatise Upon several heavenly Doctrines, from the holy spirit of the man Jesus, the only true God* (1652), 42–6.

55. *Works*, V, *Blessed State*, 20, 39, 68, 72.

56. *Works*, V, *Blessed State*, 70.

57. *Works*, V, *Blessed State*, 64.

58. *Works*, V, *Blessed State*, 51, 72.

59. *Works*, V, *The Holy Ghost*, 149; *Works*, I, *Ephesians*, part I, 47–8.

60. *Works*, II, *The Creatures*, 80.

to commune with God believers must be made spiritual (as well as holy).[61] As I will demonstrate, the dual soteriological necessity – the requirement for holiness and for spiritualization – dictated the nature of regeneration and transformation.

3.2.2 Transformation of qualities into the divine nature

Basic to Goodwin's account of the nature of transformation involved in regeneration is the substance/quality distinction from his received Aristotelian tradition. Unfortunately, Vickery, Chang and Blackham all overlook the importance of this distinction, despite their studies addressing aspects of Goodwin's doctrine of transformation.[62] While regeneration consists in a radical change in nature, Goodwin insisted that 'the substance of a Mans Nature … is one and the same afore and after.'[63] Regeneration instead effects a change in quality (an accident).[64] His favourite analogy to secure this distinction was to liken regeneration to the dyeing of the believer with a new colour.[65]

In Goodwin's mind, a key argument for this distinction arises from the nature of sin.[66] Asserting that sin is a corruption of nature, Goodwin reasoned that it is self-evident that sin must be a quality.[67] Since regeneration addresses sin, he concluded that it too must involve a change in quality. He believed that such logic is entailed in the scriptural flesh/spirit contrast.[68] Moreover, stating that within a regenerate man flesh and spirit are two contrary inherent principles, Goodwin argued that both must be understood as qualities: 'For Qualities only, not Substances, are contrary.'[69] Thus, corresponding to mortification and vivification, the change in nature in regeneration must involve both the removal of the quality of corruption and the addition of a new quality.[70]

This distinction applied to transformation predated Goodwin. In particular, it had been employed in a dispute among Lutheran theologians concerning original sin and so had been enshrined in the *Formula of Concord*.[71] Goodwin had long been familiar with this debate; in his earlier work, *An Unregenerate*, he made reference

---

61. *Works*, V, *The Holy Ghost*, 152.

62. Blackham comes closest to discussing this distinction. Blackham, 'Pneumatology', 218.

63. *Works*, V, *The Holy Ghost*, 377. Shields, 'The Doctrine of Regeneration', 163.

64. *Works*, V, *The Holy Ghost*, 377; cf. 184.

65. E.g. *Works*, V, *The Holy Ghost*, 24.

66. *Works*, V, *The Holy Ghost*, 147; cf. 187; *Works*, I, *Ephesians*, part II, 69–72.

67. See also *Works*, III, *An Unregenerate*, 38.

68. *Works*, V, *The Holy Ghost*, 147; cf. *Works*, I, *Ephesians*, part II, 69–72.

69. *Works*, V, *The Holy Ghost*, 147.

70. *Works*, V, *The Holy Ghost*, 186–8.

71. See Robert C. Schultz, 'Original Sin: Accident or Substance: The Paradoxical Significance of FC I, 53–62 in Historical Context', in *Discord, Dialogue, and Concord: Studies in the Lutheran Reformation's Formula of Concord*, ed. Lewis W. Spitz and Wenzel Lohff (Philadelphia, PA: Fortress Press, 1977).

to the views of the Lutheran Flacius Illyricus (1520–1575) who had provoked the controversy.[72] By Goodwin's day, the distinction had obtained orthodox status and was employed by divines including his mentor Sibbes.[73]

While not an innovation on his part, it took on a more prominent role in Goodwin's soteriology because this distinction proved decisive in combatting radical teachings. He referred to teachers of 'high-flown Perswasions'[74] who espoused transformation into the divine substance, that is, a 'real Transubstantiation to be Goded with God'.[75] Goodwin reported that part of their argumentation was that 'flesh' in Scripture refers to the substance of human nature and so regeneration must involve its complete transformation. In *An Unregenerate*, denouncing the views of Flacius, Goodwin had noted that for Flacius corruption involved 'the very substantial Nature of Man, turn'd or transform'd substantially into the Image of the Devil; that as Christ is the substantial Image of his Father, so our Nature is the substantial Image of the Devil'.[76] In *The Holy Ghost*, though, Goodwin's contemporary opponents are readily recognizable as the radicals of the 1650s, such as Bauthumley and Laurence Clarkson (1615–1667), who subverted the God/creation ontological distinction.[77] For these radicals, the issue was not flesh as corrupt but as creaturely and thus required transformation into the divine substance. Goodwin opposed this view vigorously: 'Our Souls, by Christ's Restauration of them, do remain created Substances still, He doth not Transubstantiate them into the Being of the Divine Nature.'[78] Believing it to be a sufficiently live threat, Goodwin warned his hearers: 'take heed of being seduced and drawn into Opinions under the pretence and allurement of still more Spiritualness … The nature of Things must not be destroyed, God must alone be God, and that Eternal Spirit.'[79] Also writing in the 1650s, Burgess appealed to the same distinction against radical ideas.[80] In a sermon published in 1652, he alleged, 'some have confusedly talked of a transubstantiation into the being of God, and tels us of a strange deification, or being God with God. … grace where it is, makes a wonderfull alteration, though not in the essence, yet in the qualities.'[81] In contrast, in the 1670s when 'ranters' were no longer a significant threat, Owen in

---

72. See article on Flacius Illyricus in Hans J. Hillerbrand, *The Oxford Encyclopedia of the Reformation*, 4 vols (Oxford: Oxford University Press, 1996), volume 2, 110–11.

73. Sibbes, *The Saints Cordials*, 369–70.

74. *Works*, V, *The Holy Ghost*, 148.

75. *Works*, V, *The Holy Ghost*, 359; cf. 146.

76. *Works*, III, *An Unregenerate*, 303.

77. See pp. 101–2.

78. *Works*, V, *The Holy Ghost*, 148.

79. *Works*, V, *The Holy Ghost*, 149.

80. Burgess, *Spiritual Refining*, 202–3, 258, 266–7, 290; Anthony Burgess, *The Doctrine of Original Sin Asserted & Vindicated against The old and new Adversaries thereof, both Socinians, Papists, Arminians and Anabaptists* (1659), 5, 14.

81. Burgess, *Spiritual Refining*, 202–3; cf. 290.

his *Pneumatologia* barely employed the substance/quality distinction to explicate regeneration.

As Goodwin explained, many 'Enthusiasticks'[82] objected that transformation 'meerly by Accidents and Qualities' would be too weak.[83] Such attacks did not just come from radicals who transgressed the God/creation distinction. The moderately enthusiastic Congregationalist Cradock complained that mere change in quality rendered regeneration too weak and invoked tedious and recent distinctions.[84] In his mind, scriptural language of a new creature demands that regeneration involves more than a change in quality. Cradock was unlikely, however, to have been one of Goodwin's targets, since he did not espouse transubstantiation into the divine substance, but rather, as will be demonstrated, he advocated the addition of new faculties. Nevertheless, Cradock was less wary than Goodwin of the threat from extreme radicals.

Anticipating this objection, Goodwin stressed that the new quality of regeneration is more valuable than the substance of the soul.[85] Returning to the dyed cloth analogy, he reasoned that when a cloth is dyed scarlet, the dye is worth more than the cloth itself.[86] The new quality has greater worth than the substance because it is a likeness to the divine nature (and so is the highest of all qualities).[87] Noting that some teachers interpreted the infamous phrase 'divine nature' in 2 Peter 1:4 as a 'Participation of the Essence of God', Goodwin insisted that it refers to the quality of divine holiness bestowed in regeneration.[88] Here he was in good company, for Burgess contended for the same interpretation, noting that it was the opinion of Augustine and the schoolmen.[89] Goodwin, however, held that the new quality bestowed in regeneration is the quality equivalent of the divine substance not only in respect of divine holiness but also in respect of divine substance as a spirit: it is the 'Divine Quality of Spirit'.[90] For Goodwin, this stronger notion is entailed in the scriptural designation of the new quality as 'Spirit':

> this very word *Spirit* ... speaks a Sublimated Work, the most Refined and most Raised Work that Mans Heart in this Life is capable of: For the Extract, the Quintessence of things (leavings the gross parts behind them as severed) you still call *Spirits*. ... Also in the Creation, those things which are of highest Rank, Strength and Excellency, and nearest God himself in their Natures, are termed

---

82. *Works*, V, *The Holy Ghost*, 173.

83. *Works*, V, *The Holy Ghost*, 175.

84. Cradock, *Gospel-Holinesse*, 403–4.

85. *Works*, V, *The Holy Ghost*, 377; cf. 179; *Works*, III, *An Unregenerate*, 500.

86. *Works*, III, *An Unregenerate*, 512. Here the analogy was employed to a different end, nevertheless the point stands.

87. *Works*, V, *The Holy Ghost*, 192.

88. *Works*, V, *The Holy Ghost*, 141; cf. 41, 54, 184; *Works*, IV, *Object and Acts*, part I, 60–1.

89. Burgess, *Spiritual Refining*, 266–7.

90. *Works*, V, *The Holy Ghost*, 179; cf. 146, 192.

Spirits ... And the Substance of his own pure Nature, is set out by this, *God is a Spirit*[91]

The substance/quality distinction implied that a believer does not become a spirit but becomes spiritual. Herein was Goodwin's second notion of participation in God: whereas radicals 'boldly Assert that they are Partakers of the Divine Nature by being Transubstantiated into God',[92] Goodwin asserted conformity in quality to the divine nature as far as possible.[93] Elsewhere, restricting this new quality to the equivalent of God's communicable attributes, Goodwin insisted that it truly becomes a 'new and *divine Nature* in us' as far as a quality allows.[94] Far from a mere concession in the face of the radicals, as I will argue, this notion of participation drove his account of regeneration.

3.2.3 *Infused grace as spiritual life*

To understand the function of this new quality in the believer, Goodwin's usage of the scholastic category of infused grace must be examined. Goodwin understood the new quality from regeneration to be infused in a fresh creative work of the Holy Spirit.[95] Thus, Goodwin simultaneously underlined the radical change involved in regeneration and the corresponding monergism.[96] He therefore insisted that believers 'are altogether passive' in regeneration.[97] Yet, as created grace these qualities become truly part of the individual.[98] Such an account of regeneration as an infused quality by the Spirit's work was standard fare among Goodwin's mainstream contemporaries.[99]

The question narrows to whether Goodwin understood infused grace in terms of the scholastic notion of *habitus*. The Thomistic tradition had embraced Aristotle's notion of *habitus* to explain the nature of infused grace. In so doing, the Aristotelian notion was redesignated as acquired *habitus* and thus differentiated from the extended notion of infused *habitus*. Infused *habitus* could readily be equated with an inherent inclination to holy acts.[100] Both Aristotle and Aquinas had, of course, understood habits to be qualities.[101] Thus, it was natural for Goodwin to cast regeneration as infused *habitus*. Blackham, however, portrays

---

91. *Works*, V, *The Holy Ghost*, 151.
92. *Works*, V, *The Holy Ghost*, 175.
93. *Works*, V, *The Holy Ghost*, 40–1, 179, 184, 192.
94. *Works*, IV, *Object and Acts*, part I, 61.
95. *Works*, V, *The Holy Ghost*, 396.
96. *Works*, I, *Ephesians*, part I, 316, 340.
97. *Works*, III, *Christ the Mediator*, 310.
98. *Works*, III, *Christ the Mediator*, 358.
99. E.g. Burgess, *Original Sin*, 20; Burgess, *Spiritual Refining*, 37.
100. E.g. *Works*, V, *The Holy Ghost*, 181, 183.
101. See Cleveland, 'Thomism in John Owen', 75.

Goodwin as rejecting the category altogether: 'Regeneration is not the infusion of Christ's righteousness into the old humanity in the form of *habitus*.'[102] In a footnote, Blackham claims that Goodwin, Sibbes and John Cotton (1585–1652) rejected the notion of *habitus*, believing that 'The old nature must be replaced by a completely new nature, or rather it must be re-created into a new nature, not simply "enabled" with the addition of righteous *habitus*.'[103] While he rightly detects here in Goodwin's soteriology a marked difference from scholastic thought, Blackham's claim that the notion of *habitus* finds no place in Goodwin's theology is an overstatement. Goodwin defined his own position in opposition to Catholics, Arminians and enthusiasts who, in different ways, denied infused grace and only permitted the Spirit's direct movings.[104]

Outlining the Catholic view, Goodwin wrote, 'the Papists very much speak of Habitual Grace as a Principle by which the Soul acts'[105] but then complained that, in their scheme, the infusion of grace is subsequent to conversion. In order to protect free will, Catholics maintained that, while aided and assisted by uncreated grace, conversion does not involve a change in nature.[106] This, according to Goodwin, implied that 'the Understanding and Will are but as of a man in the dark that can see imperfectly'.[107]

Yet, stronger criticism was directed at Arminians. In contrast to Catholics, Goodwin complained that Arminians 'utterly deny any infusion of Habits or Principles abiding in the Soul'.[108] Mark Ellis, in his discussion of Arminius's doctrine of grace, observes that despite the language of infusion Arminius held that 'Grace *is* the Holy Spirit' (i.e. identified solely with the indwelling of the Spirit's person).[109] Thus, Goodwin wrote that the Arminian view of regeneration coincided with 'the Popish Doctrine of free Will and exciting Grace'.[110] Regarding sanctification, however, Arminians departed from Catholic theology by insisting that uncreated grace is sufficient to move the soul to obedience and that the repetition of such acts forms acquired habits in the believer. For Goodwin, the Arminian rejection of infused habits manifested an equally inadequate assessment of sin. In their view, human nature does not require a radical renovation but mere assistance by the indwelling Spirit. Goodwin's critique followed the judgement of the Synod of Dort which had enshrined infused *habitus* as orthodoxy.[111]

102. Blackham, 'Pneumatology', 208.

103. Blackham, 'Pneumatology', 192–3.

104. *Works*, V, *The Holy Ghost*, 177; cf. 191.

105. *Works*, V, *The Holy Ghost*, 174.

106. Blackham muddles this point, see Blackham, 'Pneumatology', 221.

107. *Works*, V, *The Holy Ghost*, 174.

108. *Works*, V, *The Holy Ghost*, 174.

109. Mark A. Ellis, *Simon Episcopius' Doctrine of Original Sin*, American University Studies 7, Theology and Religion (New York: Peter Lang, 2006), 80.

110. *Works*, V, *The Holy Ghost*, 174.

111. Synod of Dort, *The Iudgement of the Synode Holden at Dort, Concerning the fiue Articles: As also their sentence touching Conradus Vorstius* (1619), 37–8.

Goodwin's final target was 'Enthusiasticks' who 'reject and despise all Habits, and Effects of Grace'.[112] This claim was true of some 'perfectionist antinomians' such as John Traske (*c.* 1585–1636), who believed that the immediate indwelling of Christ in the soul is sufficient for sanctification, since Christ possesses holy habits in his human nature.[113] But Goodwin's comments appear to have had more radical 'ranters' in view.[114] As already noted, these radicals advocated union with God, such that believers are transformed into the divine substance. Accordingly, the flesh must be destroyed and then the individual raised up as Spirit. For 'Enthusiasticks' of both kinds, there was a tendency to see the Spirit as overriding the flesh, rather than the Spirit assisting the flesh as with Catholics and Arminians.

In Goodwin's mind, infused habitual grace is essential because the corruption of human nature results in 'habitual Principles and dispositions unto evil'.[115] He concluded, 'Nature is not healed if the Holy Ghost only works Acts in a man, and did not work Habits.' Goodwin, therefore, was emphatic in defining regeneration as 'the infusion of a new Habit'.[116] However, Goodwin radically reworked the notion of infused *habitus*, such that created grace is to be understood as an entirely new permanent principle of spiritual life. In his judgement, many schoolmen erred by understanding infused habits too readily in terms of acquired habits. Goodwin contended that infused habits could not be alternatively formed by repeated action and instead belong 'wholly to another Rank, and Order, and Kind of Life' than acquired habits.[117] The reason schoolmen erred was an overly optimistic assessment of human nature. Goodwin insisted that infused grace does not merely enhance or aid natural abilities as many schoolmen presumed;[118] rather, infused grace contains entirely new dispositions and abilities.[119] As will become clear, what particularly allowed Goodwin to secure this newness was his conviction that regeneration not only restores Adamic grace but actually bestows higher 'spiritual' grace unknown to Adam.[120]

Moreover, whereas acquired habits concern individual faculties and so are 'seated but finger deep',[121] Goodwin pleaded for created grace infused into 'the Spirit of a Man ... Center of the Soul'.[122] Infused grace, therefore, is imparted at

112. *Works*, V, *The Holy Ghost*, 175.

113. John Traske, *The True Gospel Vindicated, From the Reproach of A new Gospel. In which many things are opened that tend to the comfort of sad Soules, and for their understanding of the Scriptures and their assurance of Faith* (1636), 22–3.

114. *Works*, II, *The Knowledg*, 146, 148–9, 175–6.

115. *Works*, I, *Ephesians*, part I, 316; cf. *Works*, V, *The Holy Ghost*, 147–8.

116. *Works*, I, *Ephesians*, part II, 16.

117. *Works*, V, *The Holy Ghost*, 194.

118. *Works*, V, *The Holy Ghost*, 193.

119. *Works*, V, *The Holy Ghost*, 192.

120. *Works*, V, *The Holy Ghost*, 190.

121. *Works*, V, *The Holy Ghost*, 194.

122. *Works*, V, *The Holy Ghost*, 151.

the deepest level and so does not merely amount to new abilities but 'deserves as much to be styled a new Power, and Life in the Soul'.[123] Goodwin likened infused grace to the life a soul supplies to an otherwise dead body; infused grace is a new soul to the soul.[124] As a consequence of the impartation of new life to the soul, the different faculties of the soul receive grace. The mind, for example, receives spiritual understanding whereas the will receives love for God.

To secure the concept of created grace as new life, Goodwin distinguished between faculties, principles and acts of the soul.[125] The latter two are readily distinguished: 'All Men may Understand the difference between an *Inherent Power* in the Soul, or *Principle* wherewith to Act; and the *Act*, or *Operation* it self ... proceeding from it, as the effect thereof'.[126] Principle, therefore, is a power by which the soul is enabled to act. The more significant distinction is between faculties and principles. Individuals possess a range of natural faculties within their souls, yet each faculty requires a principle in order to act. Hence Goodwin could assert that, alongside the natural principle in each faculty, regenerate individuals are endowed with a spiritual principle enabling spiritual actions. This spiritual principle equates to the new spiritual life infused in regeneration and consequently manifested in each faculty. (In part, this explains why Goodwin referred to created grace in both the singular and the plural.) For Goodwin, the new abilities received in regeneration are to be explained by the reception of the infused new quality. He therefore differed from Cradock who advocated the addition of new faculties in regeneration.[127] Cradock's scheme was not an option for Goodwin, since it amounted to a change in substance. Indeed, the faculty/principle distinction is a manifestation of the substance/quality distinction: whereas faculties are essential to the soul (i.e. belong to substance), the new principle is a superadded quality.

The faculty/principle distinction was crucial for demarcating Goodwin's conception of regeneration from the views of many medieval theologians. Schoolmen erred, Goodwin alleged, because they failed to distinguish the category of faculty from principle.[128] In this matter, Vickery remarks that 'Goodwin quarrels most fiercely with those schoolmen'.[129] Goodwin's logic was that if infused grace is not a new principle enabling the faculties of the soul to act in entirely new ways, then infused grace merely enhances natural abilities and such a scheme betrays an inadequate doctrine of sin.[130] In contrast, Goodwin's distinction between faculty and principle allowed him to maintain that natural human abilities contribute nothing to faith and spiritual acts. From a similar rationale, Owen warned: 'to

---

123. *Works*, V, *The Holy Ghost*, 195.
124. *Works*, V, *The Holy Ghost*, 195.
125. *Works*, V, *The Holy Ghost*, 178.
126. *Works*, V, *The Holy Ghost*, 177.
127. Cradock, *Gospel-Holinesse*, 378.
128. *Works*, V, *The Holy Ghost*, 193.
129. Vickery, 'A Most Lawful Pleasure', 215.
130. *Works*, V, *The Holy Ghost*, 193.

deny such a *quickning Principle* of Spiritual Life superadded unto us by the Grace of Christ, distinct and separate from the Natural Faculties of the Soul, is upon the matter to renounce the whole Gospel.'[131]

It is therefore clear that Goodwin was convinced that the quality of divine nature imparted in regeneration equates to new spiritual life infused into the soul. In each faculty, it functions as a new principle enabling the faculty to act in an entirely new way. Owen also fiercely contended for regeneration as 'the infusion of a *new real Spiritual* Principle into the soul and its Faculties'.[132] For Owen, however, the term 'spiritual' also applied to Adamic created grace. And, while Owen allowed regeneration to convey some advancement beyond the Adamic state, this aspect remained undeveloped in his *Pneumatologia*, and the idea that regeneration fits the believer for a higher existence was absent.[133] In contrast, Goodwin defined the term 'spiritual' as superior to Adam's earthly or natural state.[134] Believers receive spiritual created grace, he insisted, in order to suit them for a spiritual existence: '*The Soul is inwardly fitted, capacitated, inclined, and quicken'd unto the Operations of a spiritual Life.*'[135] Positively, Goodwin defined 'spiritual' in relation to God: 'God is the measure, the Standard of all things Spiritual.'[136] Deification as interpersonal communion and deification as transformation are thereby connected. Spiritual created grace as a divine quality fits believers for a spiritual existence centring on communion with God.[137]

This, then, raises the question of the relation within Goodwin's thought of regeneration as fitting the believer for a spiritual state to regeneration as reversing corruption. A further comparison with Cradock is illuminating. Cradock believed that regeneration involved the addition of both new qualities and new substance. He explained,

I doe find in the Scripture that a man is made a *Saint*, made *spirituall*, and holy, *two* wayes. One is by *renewing* a man to that which he was in *Old Adam*. Secondly, by *creating* things in him that were *never* there before.[138]

He aligned the first transformation to quality and the second to substance. Thus, Cradock's scheme readily distinguished the dual transformation accomplished in regeneration, with both 'earthinesse' and 'sinfulnesse' being addressed distinctly.[139] In contrast, Goodwin tried to hold both emphases within his concept

---

131. Owen, *Pneumatologia*, 243.
132. Owen, *Pneumatologia*, 182; cf. 280.
133. Owen, *Pneumatologia*, 241–2.
134. *Works*, V, *The Holy Ghost*, 190.
135. *Works*, V, *The Holy Ghost*, 173; cf. 149.
136. *Works*, V, *The Holy Ghost*, 152.
137. *Works*, V, *The Holy Ghost*, 176.
138. Cradock, *Gospel-Holinesse*, 404.
139. Cradock, *Gospel-Holinesse*, 294.

of an infused quality. Arguably, this resulted in switching between casting created grace as a disposition to holiness and as new abilities. The new principles in the faculties 'dispose them for holy Actions, and give spiritual Abilities for the performance of them'.[140] It is tempting to find resolution by noting that Goodwin particularly associated the disposition to holiness with the renewed will whereas he associated new abilities with the renewed understanding.[141] However, this cannot be absolute because Goodwin stipulated that the new disposition to holiness pervaded all the faculties.[142] Moreover, he contended that the new disposition to holiness is also spiritual in nature, thus enabling a higher communion with God than Adamic natural holiness had permitted.[143] In Goodwin's mind, regeneration infuses a single spiritual principle resulting in both spiritual holiness and spiritual abilities.

For Goodwin, then, the leading idea in regeneration is the conveyance of spiritual life. Here a difference with Burgess may be detected. Burgess issued brief remarks concerning the superiority of the regenerate state over the Adamic state.[144] However, his account of regeneration was otherwise consumed with the problem of corruption: 'For the grace of Regeneration is chiefly and principally intended to subdue sinne, as it did corrupt the nature, and so by consequence, as we were personally corrupted.'[145] While Goodwin clearly advocated regeneration as the antidote to sinful corruption, he assumed that the leading idea in regeneration is the reception of new spiritual grace. In fact, mortification of corruption occurs not as a distinct process but as the consequence of receiving infused spiritual life: 'The meaning is not, that first God kills a Man's Sin, and then puts a principle of Life in him; but by a principle of Life he kills Sin.'[146] Here Goodwin shared common ground with John Saltmarsh (d. 1647) who stated the same theology more forcefully: 'Conversion takes not away corruption from the nature of man, but ingrafts or plants in a *new nature* of *spirit* into the nature of man, which weakens, and impaires and works out the *flesh*.'[147] For both writers, regeneration strictly denotes vivification; mortification occurs as an implication, since the old is supplanted by the new. Thus, while Goodwin was convinced that regeneration is essential to address sinful corruption, regeneration actually consists in the impartation of new spiritual life fitting believers for a spiritual existence. Goodwin's

---

140. *Works*, V, *The Holy Ghost*, 173.

141. *Works*, V, *Of Several Ages*, 208; *Works*, V, *The Holy Ghost*, 176.

142. *Works*, V, *The Holy Ghost*, 364.

143. *Works*, V, *The Holy Ghost*, 149, 151.

144. Burgess, *Spiritual Refining*, 266–7.

145. Burgess, *Original Sin*, 20; cf. Burgess, *Spiritual Refining*, 217–23.

146. *Works*, I, *Ephesians*, part II, 184.

147. John Saltmarsh, *Free-Grace: Or, The Flowings of Christs Blood freely to Sinners. Being an Experiment of Iesus Christ upon one who hath been in the bondage of a troubled Conscience at times for the space of about twelve years, till now upon a clearer discovery of Iesus Christ and the Gospel* (1648), 60.

assumption here may have been that new infused grace in Christ is able to displace sinful corruption because it is of a higher order than Adamic grace.

3.2.4 Sanctification as the increase of spiritual life

For Goodwin, progressive sanctification is the increase of the spiritual life infused in regeneration. Claiming that when Adam sinned 'the Holiness that was in him, was that very Moment Expeld', he argued that there must be an instantaneous reversal at the moment of regeneration.[148] Yet, he also distinguished this '*Specifical* change' of regeneration from 'Other changes, by growings up in Grace; are but Gradual'.[149] In relation to regeneration, these 'other changes are the consequents, or concomitants thereof'[150] and 'the encreasing of those permanent Qualities and Vertues' infused at regeneration.[151] Goodwin, then, understood sanctification to be the extension of regeneration.[152] As regeneration contained 'two parts, *Mortification* and *Vivification*', so sanctification contains the same 'two parts also'.[153] While initial mortification inflicts a deadly wound to corruption, daily mortification is also required.[154] Moreover, like regeneration, the substance/quality distinction underpins his conception of sanctification. Indeed, the question of whether saving grace can be increased or decreased arose in one session of the Westminster Assembly and it was Goodwin who stated the general principle: 'Grace being a quality, it is capable of diminution as well as augmentation.'[155] Returning to the dye analogy, Goodwin argued that the reception of more grace is like a cloth receiving more dye.[156] The increase of grace, therefore, spreads through every faculty.[157]

Consequently, Goodwin referred to two principles in a regenerate person – flesh and spirit – locked in conflict.[158] Recounting his own experience of this conflict, Goodwin wrote, 'I found not by reading, or hearing any one speak of it, but (as *Austin* did) I perceived it of my self, and wonder'd at it; for I may say of this Combat,

---

148. *Works*, V, *The Holy Ghost*, 191.

149. *Works*, V, *The Holy Ghost*, 377; cf. *The Tryall of a Christians Growth*, 66.

150. *Works*, V, *The Holy Ghost*, 377.

151. *Works*, V, *The Holy Ghost*, 185.

152. This relationship was widely accepted among Goodwin's Reformed colleagues. Owen wrote: 'And this Regeneration is the Head, Fountain or Beginning of our Sanctification virtually comprizing the whole in it self.' Owen, *Pneumatologia*, 254.

153. *The Tryall of a Christians Growth*, 55–6. Cradock stated that sanctification is usually taken to be '*mortification*, and *vivification* (as we say) the *killing* of sin, and the *quickning* of grace'. Cradock, *Gospel-Holinesse*, 50.

154. *Works*, V, *The Holy Ghost*, 212–13.

155. Chad B. Van Dixhoorn, *The Minutes and Papers of the Westminster Assembly, 1643–1652*, 5 vols (Oxford: Oxford University Press, 2012), volume 2, 190.

156. *The Tryall of a Christians Growth*, 165.

157. *The Tryall of a Christians Growth*, 163.

158. *Works*, V, *The Holy Ghost*, 147; *Works*, III, *An Unregenerate*, 141–2, 273, 281.

that 'tis proper and peculiar to a Man that is regenerate.'[159] The ongoing presence of corruption may be reconciled with the decisive mortification in regeneration, since grace is first infused into 'the inner Man'[160] and thence transforming the whole believer. This scheme came to the fore in Goodwin's comments on the infamous 'I' of Romans 7:14-24. Embracing Augustine's interpretation of this text as referring to a regenerate person, Goodwin claimed that the inner man is for God, whereas the remainder continues to experience the principle of the flesh.[161] To overcome sin, the inner man must, therefore, be strengthened.[162] However, in keeping with the Reformed tradition, Goodwin resisted collapsing the spirit–flesh conflict to a struggle of the soul against the body as many Catholics contended.[163] He wrote, 'It is not a Fight of one Faculty against another, but of the same Faculties against themselves, and this through the whole Man.'[164] While redemption must involve the right ordering of the faculties, ultimately, true to his substance/quality distinction, the problem of corruption pervades every faculty. Accordingly, mortification does not merely destroy a specific sin but destroys the corruption of nature.[165] A believer may target one particular sin, but as Goodwin argued the effects are much wider. This point was important to enthusiasts such as Petto and Saltmarsh who sought to establish the nature of true mortification.[166]

In Goodwin's mind, the key difference between regeneration and sanctification is entailed in their divergent relationship to faith. Mainstream divines widely agreed that regeneration equated to the initial infusion of sanctification, but some contended that the grace of faith was infused in advance, thereby permitting regeneration to follow the act of faith. Goodwin stated the opposite opinion: 'many Divines hold, (and I think not without ground,) that all the principles of Sanctification are wrought in the heart before an act of Faith, they are all wrought together ... the working of the Image is presupposed before Faith, in order of nature.'[167] That Goodwin found this position persuasive is understandable given his conviction that regeneration consists in a single infused principle of life permeating all faculties. The principle of faith, Goodwin held, is contained within regeneration as its chief part.[168] All principles of sanctification are infused prior to faith and are subsequently increased by faith.

---

159. *Life*, xiii.

160. *Works*, V, *The Holy Ghost*, 364. Elsewhere, Goodwin defined the inner man as 'strictly the Soul with its Graces' and the outer man as 'the Body with its Appurtenances'. *Works*, V, *Blessed State*, 65; cf. 68.

161. *Works*, V, *The Holy Ghost*, 264; cf. 244, 359-60.

162. *Works*, III, *An Unregenerate*, 69.

163. *Works*, III, *An Unregenerate*, 161; cf. Shields, 'The Doctrine of Regeneration', 180-1.

164. *Works*, III, *An Unregenerate*, 119; cf. Burgess, *Original Sin*, 12.

165. *The Tryall of a Christians Growth*, 158-60.

166. Petto, *The Voice of the Spirit*, 127; Saltmarsh, *Free-Grace*, 56, 66.

167. *Works*, I, *Ephesians*, part I, 197.

168. *Works*, III, *Man's Restauration*, 16; *Works*, V, *The Holy Ghost*, 179.

While dependent upon faith, Goodwin believed that sanctification differs from the natural improvement of habits. Christopher Cleveland claims that Owen explicitly taught that progress in sanctification resulted from the strengthening of habits by repeated holy acts: 'For both Thomas and Owen, actions corresponding to an infused habit strengthen the habit, and make it grow ... For Owen, this is how sanctification works.'[169] However, while Owen allowed the increase of habits in this way,[170] he also insisted that the Spirit increases graces 'by working *immediately* an Actual *Encrease* of these graces in us' and that 'this is the principal Cause and Means of the *gradual Encrease of Holiness* in us, or the carrying on of the Work of Sanctification.'[171] Likewise, Goodwin rarely advocated strengthening habits by repeated action. One exception appears in a treatise:

> For therein his Grace is seen to give Grace, that he may be mov'd to give more Grace: and thus it come to pass, that habitual Grace being increas'd by the exercise and using of it it self, where it is once begun by Regeneration; that then the Influences of active and overcoming Grace from God come to abound more, as habitual Grace through long exercise hath abounded.[172]

Yet, unlike Owen, Goodwin understood that such strengthening occurs not through a natural mechanism as in the case of acquired habits but from further divine impartation: 'God increaseth the inward stock of habitual Grace within us, by gracious Diligence in holy actings.'[173] Elsewhere, he warned,

> when we thinke graces ... are so rooted in our selves, that we neglect God and Christ, for the upholding, increase, and exercise of them; then God withdraws the light of these, that we may have recourse to the spring, and well-head.[174]

A naturalistic conception of growth would not sit well with his theology of regeneration as the infusion of a new principle of spiritual life. For Goodwin, sanctification is the increase of the transformation begun in regeneration.

3.3 The reality of resurrection

While regeneration occupied Goodwin's main attention, bodily resurrection was also important in his doctrine of transformation and discussed in several sections of his grand project. Like regeneration, Goodwin sought to uphold a radical

---

169. Cleveland, 'Thomism in John Owen', 101.
170. Owen, *Pneumatologia*, 340, 417.
171. Owen, *Pneumatologia*, 342.
172. *Works*, V, *Of Several Ages*, 207.
173. *Works*, V, *Of Several Ages*, 207.
174. *A Childe of Light*, 130.

transformation in resurrection as necessary for final salvation. 1 Corinthians 15:50 was determinative. In *The Creatures*, Goodwin insisted,

> *Flesh and Blood cannot inherit the Kingdom of Heaven*; that is, take these poor earthly bodies of ours, we are so unsuited to that glory that it would sink us, so that if a Man could be put into Heaven with this body as it is now, that glory would kill him, he were not able to bear it, he were not able to inherit.[175]

The body, therefore, must be transformed to cope with heavenly glory. Glorification of the body and the soul is the end of the divine purposes for the believer.[176] However, glorification primarily concerns the soul, since glorification centres on communion with God and the body is incapable of knowledge of God.[177] The glorification of the body is derivative of the glorification of the soul 'as the Lanthorn shines with the Light that is put into it'.[178] Yet, even this derived glory would destroy the body prior to the resurrection.[179] For this reason, the soul cannot receive glory until separated from the body at death.[180]

What is significant was Goodwin's assumption that the body must be transformed, not because of sinful corruption but because the body's earthly state is inadequate for heavenly existence. As Adam's natural body was suited to the first creation, so the resurrection body must become a spiritual body suited to the heavenly world.[181] The resurrection body, therefore, will be greater than Adam's body which, while possessing conditional immortality, was dependent upon creation and subject to weakness.[182] Thus, despite advocating total depravity, the sinful corruption of the body had little impact upon Goodwin's account of bodily resurrection. For Goodwin, then, final salvation demands that the body must be made spiritual.

It was in the 1650s that Goodwin had to defend this conception of a spiritual bodily resurrection against heterodox ideas regarding the resurrection body. Goodwin warned,

> He doth not say our Bodies shall be turned into Spirits, as some have thought, but they shall be made Spiritual. As for example: Go take a piece of Iron, and put it in the Fire, it is one thing to have this Iron to be turned into Fire, and another

---

175. *Works*, II, *The Creatures*, 107; cf. *Works*, V, *The Holy Ghost*, 180; *Works*, V, *Blessed State*, 71.

176. *Works*, V, *Blessed State*, 92.

177. *Works*, V, *Blessed State*, 71.

178. *Works*, V, *Blessed State*, 63.

179. *Works*, V, *Blessed State*, 71.

180. *Works*, V, *Blessed State*, 76.

181. *Works*, V, *The Holy Ghost*, 153; *Works*, II, *The Creatures*, 46–7, 75, 110; *Works*, I, *Ephesians*, part I, 324.

182. *Works*, II, *The Creatures*, 93, 116.

thing to have it to be filled with Fire, and to be fiery, that if you look upon it, you shall not see Iron, but see Fire; yet Iron it is still … I speak thus much; the rather because it is a great Heresie that is risen up in these latter times, that we shall not have the same Bodies in Heaven for substance, that we have here below.[183]

Lawrence suggests that Goodwin here had in view Socinians, such as Biddle, who advocated that the bodies of believers will be transformed into spirits.[184] But radicals also promoted similar ideas. Clarkson in his 'ranter' phase rejected 'the Resurrection of that body consisting of Flesh, Bloud and Bone' as a 'palpable Tenent of Darkness'.[185] His hope was that 'flesh be made Spirit, and Spirit flesh'.[186] Along similar lines, Bauthumley also denied a bodily resurrection in favour of a spiritual and inward resurrection.[187] He puzzled over the orthodox opinion: 'men imagine that there is a fleshly resurrection, and that the same body flesh and bones shall rise and remain a corporall and visible substance: how this should be I am sure they do not know themselves.'[188] Instead, Bauthumley propounded an alternative view: 'the Scripture speaks of a spirituall body … which … I apprehend to be nothing but the divine Being, or God in spirit.'[189] Consequently, he declared, 'flesh is swallowed up of spirit'.[190]

Seeking to maintain a strong notion of transformation, Goodwin turned again to the substance/quality distinction and maintained that bodily resurrection involves a change in qualities only: 'what is that new Spiritualizing of the Body, but an endowing it with new Qualities and Abilities as shall fit the Body unto a spiritual Condition and Actings.'[191] Against heterodox ideas, Goodwin applied his substance/quality distinction, insisting that the resurrection body 'is the same Body for substance'.[192] Moreover, he wrote, 'it is the same body with all the parts of it: And … That all these Parts have their use.'[193] In his mind, this was an implication of the body being designed primarily for the next world, rather than this world.[194] Sibbes had also applied the substance/quality distinction to the resurrection

183. *Works*, II, *The Creatures*, 105–6.

184. John Biddle, *A Brief Scripture-Catechism for Children. Wherein, notwithstanding the brevity thereof, all things necessary unto Life and Godliness are contained* (1654), 32; Lawrence, 'Transmission', 43–4.

185. Laurence Claxton [pseud.], *A Single Eye: All Light, no Darkness; or Light and Darkness One* (1650), 13.

186. Claxton [pseud.], *A Single Eye*, 14.

187. Bauthumley, *The Light and Dark sides*, 55.

188. Bauthumley, *The Light and Dark sides*, 57.

189. Bauthumley, *The Light and Dark sides*, 58.

190. Bauthumley, *The Light and Dark sides*, 65.

191. *Works*, V, *The Holy Ghost*, 180; cf. 377; *Works*, II, *The Creatures*, 111.

192. *Works*, II, *The Creatures*, 105; cf. 72.

193. *Works*, II, *The Creatures*, 107.

194. *Works*, II, *The Creatures*, 92, 109.

body.[195] While Goodwin was not innovating, the threat of Socinian and radical ideas in the 1650s caused him to appeal to this distinction far more pervasively.

As with regeneration, the substance/quality distinction allowed Goodwin to maintain a strong doctrine of transformation without confusing the God/creation distinction. This commonality with regeneration was no coincidence. In Goodwin's mind, regeneration and bodily resurrection are, in fact, one transformation applied in two stages.[196] Noting that Scripture interchanges language, Goodwin believed it is justifiable to speak of regeneration as the '*Resurrection* to the Soul' and bodily resurrection as 'the Regeneration of the Body'.[197] More frequently, Goodwin appealed to the nature of bodily resurrection to defend the nature of regeneration. Shields remarks,

> The term resurrection seemed to be made for the Puritans' use in describing the nature of regeneration. The idea fit so very well into their concept of man's deadness in sin and their contention that nothing short of a miraculous resurrection could change his condition.[198]

Indeed, Burgess, for example, also used the analogy of bodily resurrection to stress the radical renovation involved in regeneration.[199] For Goodwin, however, resurrection was more than a convenient analogy: regeneration and resurrection are two stages in the same transformation, since both result from the infusion of the same principle of spiritual life.[200] As the faculties of the soul receive new capabilities at regeneration, so the same spiritual life produces new capabilities in the faculties of the body.[201] A spiritual body has spiritual endowments granting the 'agility and nimbleness to move as an Angel'.[202] Elsewhere, Goodwin wrote that as a spiritual body, it will be removed of all earthly uses, suited to spiritual objects and possess the agility of spirits.[203] Since transformation is applied in two stages, Goodwin contended that glorification occurs in two stages: the soul is glorified immediately following death;[204] the body is glorified at the resurrection.[205] In the

---

195. Richard Sibbes, *Evangelicall Sacrifices. In XIX. Sermons* (1640), 'The Hidden Life', 46; Richard Sibbes, *Exposition of the Third Chapter of the Epistle of St. Paul to the Philippians* (1639), 241; Sibbes, *The Saints Cordials*, 309.

196. *Works*, V, *The Holy Ghost*, 420; cf. *Works*, IV, *Object and Acts*, part I, 138; *Works*, I, *Ephesians*, part II, 207, 220–1.

197. *Works*, V, *The Holy Ghost*, 180–1; cf. *Works*, I, *Ephesians*, part I, 381–3.

198. Shields, 'The Doctrine of Regeneration', 156.

199. Burgess, *Spiritual Refining*, 254.

200. *Works*, V, *The Holy Ghost*, 180–1.

201. *Works*, V, *The Holy Ghost*, 179, 156.

202. *Works*, I, *Ephesians*, part I, 324.

203. *Works*, II, *The Creatures*, 107–8.

204. *Works*, V, *Blessed State*, 28, 31, 67.

205. *Works*, V, *Blessed State*, 50.

intermediate state the soul is clothed with the glory that the body will enjoy in the eternal state.[206] This sequence was necessitated because glorification requires the prior reception of grace which the body only receives at the resurrection.[207]

Significantly, Goodwin believed that the case of bodily resurrection allowed him more powerfully to defend his conception of created grace as new spiritual life.[208] He repeatedly argued from the nature of transformation in resurrection to the nature of transformation in regeneration.[209] This is significant. For Goodwin, resurrection involves the transformation of bodies from an earthly to a heavenly state, rather than primarily undoing sinful corruption.[210] By implication, then, the leading idea in his concept of regeneration must also be the impartation of new spiritual life. That is, fundamental in Goodwin's account of transformation is the movement of natural to spiritual, rather than corrupt to restored.

3.4 The relation of infused grace to the indwelling Spirit

Having established Goodwin's doctrine of transformation as the infusion of created grace, what I must now address is the relation of created grace to the indwelling of the Spirit. On one side of Goodwin were conservative Reformed orthodox divines who affirmed infused grace but denied the indwelling of the Spirit's person; on the other side were Arminians and radicals who affirmed the Spirit's indwelling but denied infused grace. Goodwin affirmed both uncreated and created grace as essential to salvation. A crucial question to address, then, is their relation in his soteriology. In particular, how did the priority of uncreated grace shape Goodwin's account of created grace? Or, did the priority of the indwelling of the Spirit's person effectively give way, such that created grace had functional priority in his soteriology?

Goodwin set John 3:6 – 'That which is born of the Spirit is Spirit' – as the central text in *The Holy Ghost*, believing it encapsulated the doctrine of regeneration for which he contended. From this verse, he argued that the indwelling Holy Spirit and the new nature must be distinct, despite both being termed 'Spirit'.[211] Sibbes had also distinguished the created grace of regeneration from the grace of the Spirit's indwelling,[212] yet he had so stressed the divine origin of grace that the distinction

206. *Works*, V, *Blessed State*, 35. Admittedly, Goodwin held that at the resurrection not only will the body be glorified but the soul will receive further glorification. *Works*, V, *Blessed State*, 22, 70, 64–5, 92–3.

207. *Works*, V, *The Holy Ghost*, 145; *Works*, V, *Blessed State*, 70–1.

208. *Works*, V, *The Holy Ghost*, 180.

209. *Works*, I, *Ephesians*, part I, 324.

210. *Works*, V, *The Holy Ghost*, 145.

211. *Works*, V, *The Holy Ghost*, 146, 51–2.

212. Richard Sibbes, *A Learned Commentary or, Exposition, upon The fourth Chapter of the second Epistle of Saint Paul to the Corrinthians* (1656), 250.

was stretched to the limit: 'consider all habituall graces in us, not as they are streams derived to us, and resting in us, but as they are knit to a Spring which is never drawn dry: which besides is a free Spring, therefore they are graces.'[213] For Goodwin, at least, the two concepts were clearly distinct since he contended for a period of preparation in which the Holy Spirit indwells the individual but without the infusion of the created grace of regeneration.[214]

While distinct, Goodwin maintained that created grace is dependent upon the Spirit's person for existence. Appealing again to John 3:6, he argued that created grace is 'born of the Spirit' and, for that reason, also is termed 'Spirit.'[215] The infusion of graces is only possible because the Spirit's person contains 'virtually all other parcels and particular Gifts which he after works.'[216] In particular, the Holy Spirit is able to infuse qualities imitating both his holiness[217] and spirit nature.[218] As well as the initial act of infusion, the ongoing existence of created grace is sustained by the Spirit.[219]

Moreover, Goodwin insisted that the Spirit's person must indwell in order to perform his work of transformation: 'The substance of the Soul (which he comes to) is his own, and comes to make it clean, which he cannot do, unless he gets within it.'[220] Indeed, Goodwin explained that transformation is an inevitable consequence of the Spirit's indwelling: 'Our Persons (Bodies and Souls) are the Temples of his Person immediately; his Graces are hangings, the Furniture, that he may dwell like himself ... that he may dwell handsomely.'[221] Alluding to the preparationism debate, he noted that here he was departing from divines who argued for transformation prior to the Spirit's indwelling.[222] Goodwin also insisted that the ongoing sustaining of created grace depends upon the Spirit's indwelling. Comparing the Spirit to the breath breathed into Adam, he wrote, 'as Life comes with the breath God breathed at first, and goes away with it; so doth Spiritual Life upon the going or coming of the Holy Ghost upon us.'[223] Infused graces, therefore, are evidence of the Spirit's indwelling, as a functioning body manifests

---

213. Richard Sibbes, *A Learned Commentary or Exposition upon The first Chapter of the Second Epistle of S. Paul to the Corinthians* (1655), 290.

214. *Works*, V, *The Holy Ghost*, 55.

215. *Works*, V, *The Holy Ghost*, 40.

216. *Works*, V, *The Holy Ghost*, 51; cf. 46.

217. *Works*, V, *The Holy Ghost*, 41, 54, 184.

218. *Works*, V, *The Holy Ghost*, 146, 153.

219. *Works*, V, *Of Several Ages*, 209.

220. *Works*, V, *The Holy Ghost*, 54.

221. *Works*, V, *The Holy Ghost*, 55.

222. *Works*, V, *The Holy Ghost*, 54; cf. Owen, *Pneumatologia*, 453. For a discussion locating Goodwin's views within the wider preparationism debate, see Horton, 'Assurance', chapter 9.

223. *Works*, V, *The Holy Ghost*, 43.

an indwelling soul.[224] In Goodwin's mind, the dependency of created grace for its existence upon the indwelling Spirit secured the priority of uncreated grace.[225]

Furthermore, Goodwin believed that created grace is dependent upon the indwelling Spirit not just for its existence but more importantly for its actions. Accordingly, the resurrection body depends upon the immediate influence of the indwelling Spirit.[226] More frequently, he applied this principle to the soul:

> Let us go over the *particular* Actings of the Soul, which are as a *drawing out* of those created Principles, whether *at* or *in* our first Conversion or *afterwards*; and we shall find that each, and every particular thereof, are attributed to this *Spirit*.[227]

The 'same Spirit' who created the new creature 'doth cause him to operate, and act, as such a New Creature'.[228] Thus, although created grace grants inherent abilities to the believer, it remains 'in dependance still on his renew'd enlivening us, both to *Will, and to Do*' (Philippians 2:13).[229] This dependency was commonly advanced by divines who insisted on the indwelling of both uncreated and created grace.[230] Identifying this as a crucial difference with the conservative majority, Cotton insisted, 'the Holy Ghost hath not only an external efficacy in begetting and preserving our Sanctification; but also an internal concourse and cooperation in the duties of Sanctification.'[231] Otherwise, he contended, believers would only be restored to a prelapsarian state.

Given this dependency upon uncreated grace, Goodwin was not inconsistent in referring to both created grace as a principle of new spiritual life and, as will become evident in Chapter 5, the indwelling Spirit in the same terms. Created spiritual life is continually dependent upon uncreated spiritual life. Moreover, this dependency was in effect an implication of restricting created grace to a quality, since in order for the believer to operate as a spiritual being, the spirit quality infused into the believer must be paired with the corresponding substance supplied in the person of the Holy Spirit.

Thus, while Goodwin defended a strong notion of created grace, he prioritized the uncreated grace of the Spirit's indwelling. He referred to the 'double spiritual Strength' of created grace and the divine Spirit operating together, yet 'our spiritual Strength lies principally in the *Supplies of the Spirit* … and not in our habitual

---

224. *Works*, V, *The Holy Ghost*, 57.

225. *Works*, V, *The Holy Ghost*, 55.

226. *Works*, II, *The Creatures*, 118; *Works*, I, *Ephesians*, part II, 186–7.

227. *Works*, V, *The Holy Ghost*, 14; cf. 193, 196.

228. *Works*, V, *The Holy Ghost*, 25.

229. *Works*, V, *The Holy Ghost*, 177.

230. Cotton, *Covenant of Grace*, 149; Owen, *Pneumatologia*, 273.

231. David D. Hall, *The Antinomian Controversy, 1636–1638: A Documentary History*, 2nd edn (Durham, NC: Duke University Press, 1990), 103; cf. 67, 102.

Graces'.[232] The pastoral utility was to discourage believers from diverting attention from Christ to inherent grace.[233] Cotton warned against trusting in created graces rather than Christ[234] and complained that many other ministers granted far too much independence to created grace.[235] Here Goodwin and Cotton followed Sibbes who argued that 'habitual graces' remain dependent upon 'the continual work of the Spirit' for their 'acting, enlivening, quickening and strengthening'.[236]

This dependency, therefore, dictated the character of created grace. Since it is inherently reliant upon the inner movings of the Spirit, Goodwin contended that created grace 'makes the Heart to be nothing in its own Abilities to do any Thing, but Jesus Christ to be all'.[237] Cotton argued similarly: 'For the very Habit and gift of Faith is of an Emptying Nature, emptying the soule of all confidence in it self and in the creature, and so leaving and constituting the soule as an empty vessel, empty of its owne worth, and goodnesse, but full of Christ'.[238] Because created grace transforms the believer to receive uncreated grace, Goodwin concluded that the strength of God's assisting grace received from the indwelling Spirit is normally proportionate to infused grace.[239] Cotton drew the negative conclusion: 'the stronger and the more your gifts are, if you sit loose from Christ, the emptier your hearts are of him'.[240] Here Goodwin and Cotton were close to the radical Higgenson who wrote, 'graces without Christ in them, leave a man dead, his soul empty'.[241] Thus, it was insisting upon the indwelling of the Spirit's person which further caused these divines to construe created grace in very different terms to acquired *habitus*. Not only did Goodwin cast created grace as a new principle of life, but he believed that its very nature is in dependency upon Christ mediated by the indwelling Spirit.

However, here was perhaps tension within Goodwin's thought, for he also wanted to avoid rendering the new nature passive: 'the holy Actions, tho' the Spirit excites, and stirs us up to them, are our own, and we are the intrinsecal Agent

---

232. *Works*, V, *Of Several Ages*, 204–5; cf. 210.

233. *Works*, V, *Of Several Ages*, 208, 211.

234. Cotton, *Covenant of Grace*, 153.

235. William K. B. Stoever, *'A Faire and Easie Way to Heaven': Covenant Theology and Antinomianism in Early Massachusetts* (Middletown, CT: Wesleyan University Press, 1978), 45.

236. Sibbes, *Exposition: upon The first Chapter of the Second Epistle to the Corinthians*, 297; cf. Sibbes, *Exposition, upon The fourth Chapter of the second Epistle to the Corrinthians*, 164–5.

237. *Works*, V, *Glory of the Gospel*, 73–4; cf. *Works*, IV, *Object and Acts*, part III, 9.

238. Hall, *The Antinomian Controversy*, 40. Where Cotton went further than Goodwin was by seeking to remove the act of faith from real union and insisting only upon the habit of faith.

239. *Works*, V, *Of Several Ages*, 207–8.

240. Cotton, *Covenant of Grace*, 168.

241. Higgenson, *Glory sometimes afar off*, 32.

of them and constituted to be so by vertue of a divine Seed convey'd to us in our spiritual Birth.'[242] Created grace secures human agency, Goodwin contended, because it is part of the believer.[243] Wishing to protect human responsibility, Samuel Rutherford (c. 1600–1661) used the same logic to restrict the Spirit's indwelling to created grace alone.[244] While arguably the indwelling of uncreated grace alone cannot avoid perfectionism, Goodwin's additional insistence upon created grace allowed him to affirm the indwelling of uncreated grace without conceding perfectionism. Here, though, Goodwin had departed from Sibbes who preferred the term 'graces' over 'habits' fearing the latter implied it could be accredited to the individual.[245] For Goodwin, then, while the initial creation of grace rested exclusively upon the operation of the Spirit, the believer cooperates with the Spirit's continuing operations. This correlates with Goodwin's conviction that regeneration is passive whereas sanctification involves faith[246] and the entailed conviction that initial mortification is passive whereas the believer is a co-worker in ongoing mortification.[247] Yet, in the final analysis, Goodwin conceded that the Spirit 'mingleth his Power (unperceivably to us) with the Activity of our Wills, in the new Creature'.[248]

Moreover, Goodwin balanced his conviction of the dependency of created grace upon the motions of the Spirit with his conviction that created grace enables believers to respond to the Spirit's motions. This applied to the faculty of the mind:

> for the discerning of these things Spiritually, a man must not simply have the Spirit of God to reveal them objectively … but he must subjectively be made by that Spirit a Spiritual man, and have Spiritual Senses given him, else tho' the Spirit should reveal them, he could not receive them.[249]

Thus, the Spirit's work of illumination and regeneration are both required for revelation.[250] Goodwin believed the same is also true for the will:

> As He is a *Spirit of Counsel* to our *Understanding* part, so an Effectual Perswader, and Conductor of our *Wills* … For altho' the Will of a Man Regenerate is endowed with a new vital Principle of Spiritual Life; so as in its willing and

242. *Works*, V, *The Holy Ghost*, 182; cf. 147.

243. *Works*, V, *The Holy Ghost*, 147–8, 194.

244. Rutherford, *Christ Dying*, 468.

245. Sibbes, *Exposition: upon The first Chapter of the Second Epistle to the Corinthians*, 298–9.

246. *Works*, IV, *Object and Acts*, part II, 1–2; part III, 19; *Works*, I, *Ephesians*, part I, 197.

247. *Works*, V, *Blessed State*, 102; *Works*, III, *An Unregenerate*, 161; *The Tryall of a Christians Growth*, 94, 167.

248. *Works*, V, *Of Several Ages*, 209.

249. *Works*, V, *The Holy Ghost*, 155–6; cf. 154.

250. *Works*, V, *The Holy Ghost*, 399; *Works*, III, *An Unregenerate*, 151–2.

acting Spiritually it doth it freely, and as a *Living Principle* of its own Acts, yet it Acts concurring with the Movings and Influences of the Spirit.[251]

In Goodwin's mind, then, regeneration is contained within his conception of real union with Christ. Since the believer's part of real union is faith in the mind and the will, both faculties require the enablement of created grace as well as the direct operation of the Spirit.

By insisting upon both indwelling and regeneration, Goodwin believed he upheld the gracious and high nature of salvation.[252] From Ephesians 1:17-18, he contended for a 'double gift' requirement for salvation.[253] He impressed this upon his hearers by employing the analogy of a man whose hands had been cut off and so could not hold a rope thrown down to save him. Goodwin concluded, 'God must not only find him Christ, but his Grace must give him hands to lay hold of him also ... the apprehension of this, serves both to drive him out of himself, and to magnifie Gods free Grace in working Faith.'[254] Again, here Goodwin was close to Cotton and Cradock who also argued that both are required for salvation.[255]

3.5 Real union with Christ and the renewal of the imago Dei

Having determined the nature of transformation as infused grace and its relation to the Spirit's indwelling, the question of how Goodwin understood transformation to result from his conception of real union with Christ may now be addressed. As will become evident, here Goodwin's doctrine of the renewal of the *imago Dei* is crucial. Representing the totality of the believer's transformation, this category appears frequently in his writings.

3.5.1 The Adamic imago Dei

Goodwin held that the Adamic *imago Dei* was not a functional likeness but resided in Adam's nature: 'it consisted not in bare acts of Holiness, for he is said to be created in it.'[256] Specifically, it consisted in graces corresponding to inherent holiness, distinct from and yet concreated with the soul.[257] As with

---

251. *Works*, V, *The Holy Ghost*, 28.

252. *Works*, V, *The Holy Ghost*, 377.

253. *Works*, I, *Ephesians*, part I, 259–62; cf. 326.

254. *Works*, V, *The Holy Ghost*, 358.

255. Cotton, *Covenant of Grace*, 149; Cradock, *Gospel-Holinesse*, 378.

256. *Works*, V, *The Holy Ghost*, 187. Unlike Aquinas and other scholastic theologians, Goodwin did not make a theological distinction between image and likeness. Instead, he often equated the two. E.g. *Works*, V, *The Holy Ghost*, 140, 184, 221, 361; *Works*, II, *The Creatures*, 87.

257. *Works*, V, *The Holy Ghost*, 187.

regeneration, these graces were dependent upon, but distinct from, the indwelling Spirit.[258]

As Vickery notes, in addition to this holiness image Goodwin referred to an image of substance.[259] This second image resides 'in the substance and natural Faculties of the Soul'.[260] While the substantial image is not restricted to a particular faculty, Goodwin chiefly associated it with the mind.[261] Human souls/spirits, he reasoned, bear greatest similarity to the divine nature since they are created ex nihilo.[262] Nevertheless, the priority of the mind was advocated without excluding the body from image bearing: 'The Image of God appeareth in the Head, more than in all the Body'.[263] Indeed, Adam's body participated in the image by consequence of the indwelling soul.[264] Burgess likewise taught the existence of a substantial image besides the holiness image, but noted that 'many learned Divines' only held to the latter.[265] To compensate, Burgess immediately insisted that the holiness image is 'the principal and chief, the other is but remote and secundary, for the lat[t]er abideth even in the Devils and the damned in hell'. Goodwin and Burgess here reflected the emerging Reformed orthodox consensus,[266] which can be traced back at least as far as Zanchi.[267]

Unfortunately, Vickery overlooks the structural relation of Goodwin's two notions of the *imago Dei*. Since the holiness image was accidental rather than substantial,[268] the two notions manifested the substance/quality distinction fundamental to Goodwin's doctrine of transformation.[269] Moreover, Goodwin argued that the Adamic image cannot be singular, since creatures do not possess divine simplicity. While God's holiness is his essence, this cannot be true of humans.[270] Furthermore, Goodwin believed that the substantial image necessitated

---

258. *Works*, V, *The Holy Ghost*, 47. This differed from Goodwin's early sermon on Ephesians 3:17 where he denied that the Holy Spirit indwelt Adam other than by graces. *Works*, I, *Thirteen Sermons*, 34.

259. Here Vickery corrects Blackham. Vickery, 'A Most Lawful Pleasure', 94–5.

260. *Works*, V, *The Holy Ghost*, 247. The substantial image demarcated humans from animals and enabled humans to rule over other creatures.

261. *Works*, III, *An Unregenerate*, 129; cf. Vickery, 'A Most Lawful Pleasure', 100.

262. *Works*, V, *Blessed State*, 78.

263. *Works*, I, *Ephesians*, part I, 482; cf. *Works*, I, *Thirteen Sermons*, 66.

264. *Works*, II, *The Creatures*, 74, 92.

265. Burgess, *Original Sin*, 113.

266. See Suzanne McDonald, 'The Pneumatology of the "Lost" Image in John Owen', *Westminster Theological Journal* 71, no. 2 (2009): 328.

267. Kalvin S. Budiman, 'A Protestant Doctrine of Nature and Grace as Illustrated by Jerome Zanchi's Appropriation of Thomas Aquinas' (PhD thesis, Baylor University, 2011), 88.

268. *Works*, II, *The Creatures*, 29–30.

269. *Works*, III, *An Unregenerate*, 129.

270. *Works*, II, *The Creatures*, 27–8; *Works*, IV, *Object and Acts*, part I, 61.

the holiness image. Had God not bestowed the holiness image upon Adam to enjoy communion with him, then Adam, Goodwin argued, would have been created unfulfilled: 'the very Nature of such a Creature required it as convenient, meet, and suitable to its Nature, and without which, it had been imperfect, yea, miserable: For otherwise, those vast Faculties of Understanding and Will, had been left empty, and like an hungry Stomach.'[271] In this sense, Goodwin insisted that Adam's holiness was natural to him, while stipulating that his holiness was not 'any part or ingredient into the Essence' of him.[272]

Thus, Goodwin's basic justification for the classification of the holiness image as natural resulted from the holiness image being Adam's creaturely due and thus given according to the covenant of works.[273] Burgess similarly insisted that the Adamic image was natural since it was Adam's due as a creature.[274] Here Goodwin and Burgess were standing in the mainstream Reformed orthodox opinion.[275] This point was vital to distance Reformed theology from the Thomistic scheme which held Adam's holiness to be supernatural.[276] Catholics argued their case on the basis that what is natural cannot be lost,[277] but, as will be discussed, the theological motivation was their desire to maintain their account of original sin.

Yet, while viewing Adam's state as natural was the mainstream Reformed opinion, Mark Herzer remarks that 'Goodwin seems to have gone further than most Reformed divines in depicting Adam almost as pure nature.'[278] What was driving Goodwin was his intent to uphold salvation in Christ as surpassing the Adamic state. Here it should be noted that Catholic position of supernatural Adamic grace was also argued on the basis that Adam needed to be suited for potential translation to heaven.[279] The majority of Reformed divines held that Adamic grace was natural, yet maintained that the reward available to Adam was heavenly. Here Goodwin was more consistent: Adam had natural grace and

---

271. *Works*, II, *The Creatures*, 22; cf. 40.

272. *Works*, II, *The Creatures*, 30; cf. 45; *Works*, IV, *Object and Acts*, part I, 60–1, 81–2.

273. *Works*, II, *The Creatures*, 40–1.

274. Burgess, *Spiritual Refining*, 204; cf. 324; Burgess, *Original Sin*, 19.

275. E.g. Zanchi had already advanced the same scheme. Budiman, 'Nature and Grace', 89, 197.

276. Goodwin allowed Adam's original righteousness to be classified as supernatural in the limited sense that it was created by God. *Works*, II, *The Creatures*, 30.

277. *Works*, II, *The Creatures*, 30; *Works*, V, *The Holy Ghost*, 186.

278. Mark A. Herzer, 'Adam's Reward: Heaven or Earth?' in *Drawn into Controversie: Reformed Theological Diversity and Debates within Seventeenth-Century British Puritanism*, ed. Michael A. G. Haykin and Mark Jones, *Reformed Historical Theology* (Göttingen: Vandenhoeck & Ruprecht, 2011), 171. Following Herzer's lead, Kim highlights Goodwin's construal of the Adamic *imago Dei* as entirely natural and offers a helpful discussion of how it relates to Goodwin's characterization of the covenant of works. Kim, 'Salvation by Faith', 109–14.

279. *Works*, II, *The Creatures*, 53.

was offered a corresponding earthly reward. For Goodwin, then, the Adamic state was natural in order to maintain a superior supernatural state in Christ.[280]

3.5.2 Original sin and the loss of the image

The substance/quality distinction along with the corresponding designation of the holiness image as natural was in Goodwin's mind vital for securing the correct account of sin and the devastation of the *imago Dei*. Appealing to Augustine, Goodwin attempted to explain the nature of the first sin in Adam: '*The Deficient Will of Man need no innate Principle to Sin, its Frailty was Sufficient, or rather Insufficient to it.*'[281] Adam's inherent vulnerability to the possibility of sin, he contended, was entailed in his holiness as a natural quality: creatures are inherently mutable (and consequently defectible) by nature and therefore God was not obliged to constrain Adam from falling.[282]

Adam's sin resulted in the destruction of the image. The holiness image was severely damaged: 'Man had ras'd and defaced that Image or Likeness to God in Holiness and Righteousness, wherein he was at first created.'[283] However, the substance image remained intact.[284] There is 'nothing of the substance of the Body, or of the Soul, destroyed.'[285] This preservation was due to the divine intent for redemption.[286] Moreover, this scheme was an implication of Goodwin's substance/quality distinction: as an accidental quality, the holiness image could be lost; the substantial image, however, must endure.[287] While substantially the natural faculties remain intact, they are misguided because of the loss of the holiness image.[288]

The destruction of the holiness image, in Goodwin's assessment, was total. Taking issue with those who interpreted morally positive elements in fallen humans as 'Relicks of the former Image of God', Goodwin insisted upon 'the totally ruined Condition of man's Nature; out of which by the Curse, all Stems were utterly rooted out and stubbed up ... nothing but Flesh ... devoid of all good.'[289] In contrast, the conservative Hooker, for example, advocated that relics of the *imago*

---

280. See §3.5.3.

281. *Works*, V, *The Holy Ghost*, 191.

282. *Works*, II, *The Creatures*, 41, 28–9; *Works*, V, *The Holy Ghost*, 191; *Works*, III, *An Unregenerate*, 5.

283. *Works*, V, *The Holy Ghost*, 361; cf. 187.

284. Here Goodwin followed Zanchi and Aquinas. See Budiman, 'Nature and Grace', 198; Vickery, 'A Most Lawful Pleasure', 107.

285. *Works*, I, *Ephesians*, part II, 80.

286. *Works*, II, *The Creatures*, 29.

287. *Works*, II, *The Creatures*, 29–30.

288. *Works*, III, *An Unregenerate*, 64, 304.

289. *Works*, V, *The Holy Ghost*, 234; cf. *Works*, II, *The Creatures*, 43; *Works*, III, *An Unregenerate*, 91–2, 432.

Dei remained.[290] For Goodwin, while positive elements are present in unregenerate individuals, he posited that these result from a conscience installed by God after the Fall to curb sin.[291] Goodwin pictured Adam left naked in body and soul, 'stript of this Robe of God's Image'.[292] Adam 'lost every piece of that Image, and so had no Goodness to cover him'.[293] If the holiness image was not entirely eradicated, then, Goodwin reasoned, regeneration would be rendered unnecessary since Adam would merely be in the state of a believer fallen into sin.[294] Moreover, if the loss of grace was not total, then the Spirit must remain indwelling Adam, he argued, since graces must be sustained by the indwelling Spirit.[295]

Goodwin's scheme of the loss of the image was representative of the emerging Reformed orthodox consensus.[296] Those who did not adopt a twofold *imago Dei* scheme had difficulty accounting for a severe loss, yet some remnant, of the image. The scholastic distinction between *similitudo* and *imago* permitted the loss of the latter but retention of the former. This distinction, however, was rejected by the Reformers, resulting in conflicting remarks concerning the enduring state of the post-Fall image. Despite attempts at resolution of Calvin's comments, his interpreters complain that his varied assessments are plain incoherent or at least confusing.[297] Owen, as Suzanne McDonald notes, restricted the *imago Dei* to the holiness image and accordingly contended for the total loss of the image: 'Owen is therefore distinctive even within his own tradition for his evident reluctance to speak of any remnant of the image outside the elect'.[298] In contrast, Goodwin's twofold scheme allowed him simultaneously to hold both a total loss alongside a well-defined continuation of the *imago Dei*.

Furthermore, in addition to the loss of the holiness image, Goodwin contended that Adam had gained a depraved image.[299] The corruption of Adam's nature did not come about as 'an Habit follows upon Acts in a Philosophical way'.[300] Indeed, the

---

290. Hooker, *The Application of Redemption*, books 1–8, 318, 382.

291. *Works*, III, *An Unregenerate*, 94.

292. *Works*, III, *An Unregenerate*, 43.

293. *Works*, III, *An Unregenerate*, 80.

294. *Works*, III, *An Unregenerate*, 79.

295. *Works*, III, *An Unregenerate*, 80.

296. E.g. Anthony Burgess, *Vindiciæ Legis: Or, A Vindication of the Morall Law and the Covenants, From the Errours of Papists, Arminians, Socinians, and more especially, Antinomians* (1646), 65. See McDonald, 'The "Lost" Image', 328.

297. Thomas F. Torrance, *Calvin's Doctrine of Man* (London: Lutterworth Press, 1949), 88ff; Mary Potter Engel, *John Calvin's Perspectival Anthropology*, American Academy of Religion Academy Series (Atlanta, GA: Scholars Press, 1988), 54–61; Jason Van Vliet, *Children of God: The Imago Dei in John Calvin and His Context*, Reformed Historical Theology (Göttingen: Vandenhoeck & Ruprecht, 2009), 22–3.

298. McDonald, 'The "Lost" Image', 329.

299. *Works*, III, *An Unregenerate*, 43; cf. 77.

300. *Works*, III, *An Unregenerate*, 8.

one sin of Adam did not merely weaken his holiness but expelled it.[301] Since Adam was under the covenant of works, the change in his nature arose 'by way of Curse and Forfeiture, even of the Spirit of all inherent Holiness'.[302] Thus, Adam's single transgression caused the departure of the indwelling Spirit and by consequence his graces (i.e. the holiness image) and by further consequence Adam's nature was corrupted. The first consequence resulted from the dependence of created grace upon the indwelling Spirit. Regarding the second consequence, Goodwin explained 'that positive Pravity is a consequence of that Privation' of created grace in the same way bodily corruption follows the soul's departure.[303] Thus, depravity was not directly imparted by divine intervention.[304] The net effect was that Adam's single transgression caused the total loss of the holiness image and its replacement with a sinful image. This depraved image, Goodwin evocatively described as the image of the devil[305] and defined its essence as self-love.[306]

It was against traditional opponents that Goodwin contended for the depravity of nature in addition to loss of original righteousness. The real dispute over the designation of Adam's holiness as either natural or supernatural concerned the question of whether original sin merely involved deprivation or also involved depravity: 'This Point I will not now dispute, but may well take for granted, it being Fundamental to all the Protestant Opinions about Original Sin, &c. wherein we differ from the Papists'.[307] The Thomistic system defined sin in terms of the removal of original righteousness. Original righteousness restrained the lower faculties from leading the mind and will astray, but since nothing natural was lost, it did not cause the depravation of nature. Thus, Catholics, as Goodwin noted, accepted the loss of original righteousness but denied a 'positive Inclination to all Evil'.[308] The influential Jesuit Robert Bellarmine (1542–1621) declared, 'The state of man following the fall of Adam differs from the state of Adam in what was purely natural to him … no more than a man who has been stripped differs from a naked man'.[309] The Thomistic scheme, therefore, permitted a lower doctrine of the Fall in which human nature did not become inherently evil and so a positive assessment of its natural abilities could be maintained.[310]

To the alarm of Reformed divines, this lower doctrine was the position towards which Arminius also moved. He stated, 'Though we think it much more probable, that this absence of original righteousness only is original sin itself'.[311]

301. *Works*, III, *An Unregenerate*, 45.

302. *Works*, III, *An Unregenerate*, 8.

303. *Works*, III, *An Unregenerate*, 48.

304. *Works*, III, *An Unregenerate*, 323.

305. *Works*, V, *The Holy Ghost*, 361.

306. *Works*, V, *The Holy Ghost*, 157; *Works*, I, *Ephesians*, part I, 353, 355.

307. *Works*, II, *The Creatures*, 41.

308. *Works*, III, *An Unregenerate*, 37.

309. Quoted in Harrison, *The Fall of Man*, 67–8.

310. *Works*, III, *An Unregenerate*, 324–5.

311. Quoted in Ellis, *Simon Episcopius' Doctrine of Original Sin*, 76.

Like Goodwin, Arminius also held to a twofold notion of the image of God. Ellis notes that, for Arminius, there was a natural image consisting in the faculties of will and intellect, and there was a supernatural image consisting in the three *habitus* of wisdom, righteousness and holiness.[312] The difference with Goodwin's scheme was entailed in the term 'supernatural'. Arminius held that these graces were supernatural 'because they are actually the presence and ministry of the Holy Spirit operating within the intellect and the will'.[313] While Arminius's conception of supernatural grace differed from the Thomistic scheme, the same implication results: the supernatural image was not intrinsic to human nature and so its removal does not inevitably cause depravity of nature.

While Goodwin seldom made reference to Socinians, he was explicit in accusing them of holding Adam to be created in a neutral state: 'The *Socinians*, who hold Man's Nature in his first Creation not to have been holy, but only indifferent unto good and evil'.[314] In other words, Socinians rejected the notion of a holiness image. The 1652 English translation of the *Racovian Catechism* stated, 'Yes, for it is certain, that the first Man was so created by God, as that he was endued with Free-will'.[315] Mortimer explains that behind this view was Socinus's belief that 'only voluntary actions were praiseworthy'.[316] Accordingly, Socinus denied that Adam was created with inherent graces/original righteousness and also denied the corruption of his nature by sin.

Moreover, Goodwin contended that Adam's depraved nature was transmitted to the human race. This transmission he explained by appealing to the law of nature: '*That Man should beget in his own Image or Likeness*.'[317] On the basis of this law not only was the substance of Adam's nature conveyed but its qualities too.[318] Thus, Goodwin held that had Adam not fallen into sin, the holiness image would have been transmitted to the human race.[319] Instead, according to the same law 'the Image of inherent Corruption' was conveyed.[320] In support, Goodwin often appealed to the first part of John 3:6: '*That which is born of the Flesh, is Flesh*.'[321]

---

312. Ellis, *Simon Episcopius' Doctrine of Original Sin*, 64–5.

313. Ellis, *Simon Episcopius' Doctrine of Original Sin*, 66.

314. *Works*, II, *The Creatures*, 27.

315. *The Racovian Catechisme; vvherein You have the substance of the Confession of those Churches, which in the Kingdom of Poland, and Great Dukedome of Lithuania, and other Provinces appertaining to that Kingdom, do affirm, That no other save the Father of our Lord Jesus Christ, is that one God of Israel, and that the man Jesus of Nazareth, who was born of the Virgin, and no other besides, or before him, is the onely begotten Sonne of God* (Amsterledam, 1652), 142.

316. Mortimer, *Reason and Religion*, 16.

317. *Works*, III, *An Unregenerate*, 15.

318. *Works*, III, *An Unregenerate*, 18, 47.

319. *Works*, III, *An Unregenerate*, 15.

320. *Works*, V, *The Holy Ghost*, 188; cf. *Works*, III, *An Unregenerate*, 18.

321. *Works*, III, *An Unregenerate*, 35–42.

Goodwin, therefore, appealed to a realistic understanding of union with Adam in order to explain the means by which Adamic nature is transmitted.[322] Thus, he wrote,

> in this first Man the whole Nature of Man being reposited as a common Receptacle or Cistern of it, from whence it was to flow to others; therefore what befals this Nature in him by any Action of his, that Nature is so to be propagated from him.[323]

However, Goodwin distanced himself from the Augustinian notion of generation as the cause of corruption, stressing that generation functions as the instrumental cause alone.[324] This distinction allowed Goodwin to assert that while actual sins 'addeth to their natural defilement, makes the tincture of that Dye deeper,'[325] increased corruption is not conveyed to children.[326] Moreover, this distinction allowed him to hold to the soul's corruption while also holding a creationist position on the soul's origin.[327]

Goodwin defended his Reformed account of the transmission of corruption of nature against weaker schemes. In conventional fashion, he dismissed Pelagius as advocating the transmission of corruption merely by imitation of Adam's example.[328] He denounced Albert Pighius (c. 1490–1542) and those schoolmen who accepted the transmission of Adamic guilt but not corruption.[329] Socinians, he warned, denied the transmission of both Adamic guilt and corruption.[330] Indeed, the *Racovian Catechism* stated, 'There is no such thing as Originall sinne.'[331] As Mortimer highlights, the doctrine of original sin was perceived as denying human liberty and personal responsibility, so fundamental to Socinus's soteriology.[332] In the mid-1650s, a Socinian-style rejection of original sin was especially propagated

---

322. *Works*, III, *An Unregenerate*, 20.

323. *Works*, III, *An Unregenerate*, 15.

324. *Works*, I, *Ephesians*, part II, 112. Note: Christ was exempted because of the virgin conception. *Works*, III, *An Unregenerate*, 8.

325. *Works*, I, *Ephesians*, part II, 122; cf. 11, 17.

326. *Works*, III, *An Unregenerate*, 16–17; *Works*, I, *Ephesians*, part II, 112.

327. See p. 142.

328. *Works*, III, *An Unregenerate*, 36.

329. *Works*, III, *An Unregenerate*, 36–7.

330. *Works*, III, *An Unregenerate*, 342.

331. *The Racovian Catechisme*, 142. See also John Biddle, *A Twofold Catechism: The One simply called A Scripture-Catechism; The Other, A brief Scripture-Catechism for Children. Wherein the chiefest points of the Christian Religion, being Question-wise proposed, resolve themselves by pertinent Answers taken word for word out of the Scripture, without either Consequences or Comments* (1654), 24–5.

332. Mortimer, *Reason and Religion*, 16–17.

by the episcopalian Jeremiah Taylor (bap. 1613, d. 1667), who published multiple works debunking the orthodox opinion.[333]

3.5.3 The renewal of the image in Christ

Having outlined Goodwin's doctrine of the *imago Dei* in creation and the Fall, I will now complete the argument by demonstrating that Goodwin founded the renewal of the *imago Dei* in his notion of real union with Christ. Goodwin contended that Christ is uniquely able to function as the archetypal image: 'he being the Image of God, therefore to restore it in Man when 'twas lost, the best way was to set forth the Original Image, and to bring our decayed Image to this to be conformed.'[334] Thus, 'God set up Christ as the Masterpiece; first Patern, and Draught of his Decree.'[335] The renewed image, therefore, is the image of Christ.

The renewed image, Goodwin argued, must include restoration of the forfeited image: 'Christ must convey at least the same, if not higher: Else God doth not so much for us in restoring his Image, as he did at our first Creation.'[336] Thus, renewal restores the holiness image.[337] Yet, Goodwin also contended that the renewed image surpasses the original Adamic image: 'The Image which he renews is a better Image than that of *Adams*.'[338] Owen affirmed the same point: 'God, in the *Humane Nature* of Christ did perfectly renew that blessed Image of his on our Nature, which we lost in *Adam*, with an addition of many glorious endowments which *Adam* was not made partaker of.'[339] However, Goodwin's language was much stronger: the Adamic image 'fell infinitely short' and 'was but a Shadow' of the renewed image.[340] Driving these comments was Goodwin's conviction that renewal does not merely address corruption but also Adam's earthly natural state.[341] Here Goodwin differed from more conservative thinkers who tended to deny that the renewed *imago Dei* surpassed the Adamic image. For example, Hooker insisted, 'The image of God was restored to the whole man by Christ. What Christ restores, *Adam* had. Christ renewes what was before made.'[342] In fact, this was a point of disagreement in the New England antinomian controversy, as evident

333. Mortimer, *Reason and Religion*, 137–46.

334. *Works*, III, *Christ the Mediator*, 42.

335. *Works*, V, *The Holy Ghost*, 202.

336. *Works*, V, *The Holy Ghost*, 187.

337. *Works*, V, *The Holy Ghost*, 187.

338. *Works*, III, *Christ the Mediator*, 101.

339. John Owen, *Christologia, Or, A Declaration of the Glorious Mystery of the Person of Christ, God and Man* (1679), 213.

340. *Works*, I, *Thirteen Sermons*, 51. Goodwin was more restrained in his language in another passage. *Works*, II, *Election*, 131.

341. *Works*, II, *The Creatures*, 20.

342. Thomas Hooker, *The Paterne of Perfection: Exhibited in Gods Image on Adam: And Gods Covenant made with him* (1640), 34–5; cf. 6–7; Thomas Hooker, *An Exposition of the Principles of Religion* (1645), 24.

from an exchange between Cotton, whose ideas were similar to Goodwin's, and the more conservative elders. Responding to Cotton, the elders stated, 'wherein you add other things besides the Image of God in Adam concurring to the making up of Christian sanctification, we cannot assent.'[343] As will become apparent, this divergence of opinion accompanied divergent conceptions of real union with Christ.

It should be noted that although Goodwin advocated the renewal of the *imago Dei* in Christ as the archetypal image, he conceded that the law also functions as a restorative image.[344] By affirming that the law operates in this manner, Goodwin differed from antinomian teaching. Enthusiastic preacher Dell wrote, 'this *Word* by which *Christ* reforms the *Church*, is not the *Word* of the *Law*; *for the Law made nothing perfect*, but the *Word* of the *Gospel*; *This, this*, is the *onely Word*, that *works Reformation*.'[345] Also acknowledging the impotency of the law to change hearts,[346] Goodwin believed that the law could, however, effect transformation if combined with the efficacy of Christ's death and resurrection.[347] In Goodwin's mind, the key difference is that the law is an inferior image to Christ because it is merely a written representation of the inferior Adamic image.[348] For this reason, application of the law cannot produce more than mere restoration of the Adamic image. Therefore, while conformity to the law is true sanctification, Goodwin insisted that it is not the whole of sanctification, since Christ is a superior image.[349] In this way, Goodwin avoided antinomianism, yet promoted a Christocentric view of renewal. Cotton similarly insisted that the renewed image surpasses the Adamic image because it is patterned upon Christ in his death and resurrection.[350] These Christocentric views contrasted with the approach of more conservative divines such as Burgess and Hooker who, both enamoured with defending the law, advocated mere restoration and so equated the renewed image with conformity to the law. Burgess wrote, 'What is Regeneration, but the writing of the Morall Law in thy heart? This is that image of God, which *Adam* was created in.'[351] This view reflected a tendency in conservative theology to reduce salvation to mere moral restoration, rather than casting salvation as advancement to communion with God.

Goodwin, then, was adamant that only transformation into Christ's image represents the sum total of transformation: 'To be Conformed to the Image of Christ ... it contains fully all that can be said of what we were ordained to.'[352]

343. Hall, *The Antinomian Controversy*, 67; cf. 51, 104.

344. *Works*, V, *The Holy Ghost*, 359.

345. Dell, *Right Reformation*, 17.

346. *Works*, V, *The Holy Ghost*, 201.

347. *Works*, V, *The Holy Ghost*, 360; cf. 242.

348. *Works*, V, *The Holy Ghost*, 200; cf. *Works*, V, *Glory of the Gospel*, 54, 59.

349. *Works*, V, *The Holy Ghost*, 359–60.

350. Hall, *The Antinomian Controversy*, 104.

351. Burgess, *Vindiciæ Legis*, 193.

352. *Works*, V, *The Holy Ghost*, 203; cf. 14, 173.

Believers will be conformed to Christ's image as far as possible.[353] Guarding against radicals, Goodwin insisted again that transformation is limited to qualities.[354] Consistent with his questioning of the substance/quality distinction, Cradock pressed for the transformation of 'all our whole man, soule and body, in respect of *substance* as well as *quality*'.[355] As already noted, Goodwin was more wary of heterodox teachings than was Cradock.

The superiority of the renewed image is entailed in Goodwin's characterization of it as supernatural or spiritual as opposed to the natural image of Adam. First, the renewed image is supernatural because it derives from grace, rather than Adam's due as a creature.[356] In other words, whereas the Adamic image was rooted in the covenant of nature/works, the renewed image is rooted in the covenant of grace and so is permanent. While conservatives also accepted this difference in legal basis, the renewed image was otherwise deemed identical to the Adamic image. In contrast, Goodwin and Cotton believed that the legal difference must be matched by the indwelling of the Holy Spirit to sustain its permanency. Cotton wrote, 'the indwelling Power of the Spirit, to act and keep Holinesse in us all, which Adam wanted.'[357] Along similar lines, Goodwin contended that whereas Adam was assisted only by the grace of providence common to all creation and therefore defectible, believers enjoy superior assistance because the Spirit fulfils all that Christ has undertaken to work in them.[358] Moreover, in keeping with its basis in grace, Cotton also argued that the content of the renewed image must be superior, since it contains faith and repentance.[359] Goodwin likewise maintained that faith is part of the image of Christ,[360] yet also advanced further, arguing that the character of the virtues infused in believers surpasses what Adam received by nature.[361] For example, in Adam the virtue of humility was derived from his status as a creature, yet for the believer, humility also derives from the believer's status as a sinner. Thus, as Goodwin concluded, the renewed image founded in Christ is 'suted and fitted to Gospel-Motives and Considerations, unto which Holiness in *Adam* was not suted.'[362]

Secondly, the renewed image is supernatural because it consists in principles capable of spiritual existence: 'Both the Condition of our Souls here, and of our Bodies and Souls hereafter, is Spiritual, and Supernatural. And such is, Christ whole Image; whereas *Adam's* was but Natural.'[363] The renewed image, therefore, equated

353. *Works*, V, *The Holy Ghost*, 58, 183, 202.
354. *Works*, II, *The Creatures*, 105; cf. 91.
355. Cradock, *Gospel-Holinesse*, 293.
356. *Works*, II, *The Creatures*, 40–1, 50; cf. *Works*, I, *Thirteen Sermons*, 51.
357. Hall, *The Antinomian Controversy*, 51; cf. 104.
358. *Works*, V, *The Holy Ghost*, 210; cf. 47–50; *Works*, II, *Election*, 316.
359. Hall, *The Antinomian Controversy*, 51; cf. 67, 104.
360. *Works*, I, *Ephesians*, part I, 197.
361. *Works*, V, *The Holy Ghost*, 207–10.
362. *Works*, V, *Gospel Holiness*, 34.
363. *Works*, II, *The Creatures*, 44.

to the infused grace of new spiritual life bestowed in regeneration and resurrection. Thus, it has a divine character. Goodwin wrote, '[it] is of a more Divine Temper, Genius and Aspirement than the Image of God in *Adam* was.'[364] This principle he especially applied to the knowledge of God. While the knowledge of God already enjoyed by believers far surpasses that enjoyed by Adam in paradise,[365] ultimately the renewed image allows the immediate knowledge of God in the beatific vision. The renewed image 'is ordained in the end to see God in himself, and will be raised up thereto; and at present hath such a way of knowing and enjoying God, and such Objects Spiritual suited to it, as *Adam's* state was not capable of'.[366]

Crucially, the argument turns on Goodwin's conviction that this spiritual *imago Dei* can only be formed in the believer as a result of real union with Christ. Alluding to 2 Corinthians 3:18, Goodwin repeatedly stated that believers are transformed into the *imago Dei* by beholding Christ as presented in the New Testament: 'we in this Glass of the Gospel, *behold the Glory of the Lord*, and are thereby changed into the same Image'.[367] Indeed, renewal into Christ's image solely rests upon beholding Christ, such that the extent of transformation is limited by the extent to which the New Testament reveals him.[368] In part, transformation via spiritual sight of Christ is possible because the image in Christ, as the truest image, possesses inherent potency.[369] Yet, Goodwin also insisted that spiritual sight has transformative power because of the reality of the inner knowledge of Christ.[370] For this reason, Goodwin urged believers not simply to have notions about Christ: 'You may come to a Sermon and hear Notions indeed, but if you get a real sight of Christ you will be changed; and I say so far as we see Him, so far we are changed.'[371] Revelation of Christ to the believer is insufficient; for transformation revelation within the believer is required.[372] Importantly, this inner revelation of Christ equates to Christ's mystical indwelling by faith intrinsic to real union with Christ.

364. *Works*, V, *The Holy Ghost*, 149; cf. 207.

365. *Works*, II, *The Creatures*, 38–9.

366. *Works*, V, *The Holy Ghost*, 149; cf. *Works*, II, *The Creatures*, 48; *Works*, I, *Thirteen Sermons*, 51.

367. *Works*, V, *Glory of the Gospel*, 64.

368. *Works*, V, *The Holy Ghost*, 202–3. In this life, believers are conformed to Christ's image in his graces and example. *Works*, V, *The Holy Ghost*, 205. Regarding the completion of transformation at the resurrection, Goodwin again appealed to revelation of Christ: when Christ is seen in glory, then believers will be transformed into his glorified image. *Works*, V, *The Holy Ghost*, 205; *Works*, V, *Glory of the Gospel*, 65. Their bodies will be conformed to Christ's glorious resurrection body. *Works*, II, *The Creatures*, 104; cf. 99. It would be consistent within Goodwin's thought for Christ to indwell saints in glory by sight and for real union with Christ to be strengthened.

369. *Works*, III, *Christ the Mediator*, 101.

370. *Works*, V, *Glory of the Gospel*, 71; *Works*, I, *Thirteen Sermons*, 68; *Works*, IV, *Object and Acts*, part II, 12; *Works*, V, *The Holy Ghost*, 203.

371. *Works*, V, *Glory of the Gospel*, 65.

372. *Works*, I, *Thirteen Sermons*, 47–8.

Here, then, is the crucial dependence of renewal of the image upon Goodwin's conception of real union with Christ. Within this scheme, both the Spirit's part and the believer's part in real union may be examined in relation to transformation. The indwelling Spirit plays a vital role, not only in revealing Christ but also in accompanying revelation with transforming power. The indwelling presence of the Spirit impresses the inner revelation of Christ upon the heart such that the believer is transformed into Christ's image.[373] Goodwin, therefore, was emphatic that the transforming power of the Spirit accompanies the Gospel 'as the prolifique *Vertue* in the Word'.[374] He was adamant that the Spirit's transforming power must not be identified with the natural strength and force of the written Word.[375] This claim paralleled Goodwin's contention that the Spirit reveals Christ in a greater manner than the words of Scripture, while tied to the instrument of Scripture.[376] Here Goodwin wanted to distance himself from Arminians and others promoting a low doctrine of regeneration who held that the power of the Spirit was but the 'moral persuasion' of the Word. Instead, Goodwin shared ground with moderate enthusiasts. Cradock, for example, wrote,

> The *Gospel* bids me *deny* selfe, and subdue my lusts, if it did give no *power* it were a terrible thing: but if withall the *Gospel* carry the Spirit of Christ into the heart and kill *sin*, and make me able to *deny* my selfe, then it is good newes.[377]

Goodwin, however, guarding against more radical theology insisted that the Spirit constrains himself to work through the Word.

The believer's part of real union is also crucial in transformation since transformation results from the beholding of Christ by faith.[378] A major inconsistency, however, was that Goodwin equated the initial renewal of the image with regeneration preceding faith: 'the working of the Image is presupposed before Faith, in order of nature'.[379] Indeed, Goodwin held regeneration to include the created grace necessary for faith and spiritual sight of Christ. This *ordo salutis* problem ought to exclude regeneration from transformation by spiritual sight of Christ. Nevertheless, regeneration is still rooted in real union with Christ, but restricted to the Spirit's part of the union. Assigning regeneration and sanctification to different aspects of real union with Christ would have followed the lead of the

---

373. *Works*, V, *The Holy Ghost*, 14; *Works*, I, *Ephesians*, part I, 247; *Works*, IV, *Object and Acts*, part III, 19–20.

374. *Works*, V, *The Holy Ghost*, 49; cf. *Works*, III, *Of the Unregenerate*, 66–7.

375. *Works*, V, *The Holy Ghost*, 393.

376. See pp. 65–6.

377. Walter Cradock, *Glad Tydings from Heaven; To The Worst of Sinners on Earth* (1648), 23.

378. *Works*, V, *The Holy Ghost*, 201; cf. *Works*, I, *Thirteen Sermons*, 48. Although the emphasis is decidedly upon faith in the mind rather than in the will.

379. *Works*, I, *Ephesians*, part I, 197.

influential William Pemble (1591/2–1623). Pemble, also advocating two parts of real union, explicitly assigned regeneration to the Spirit's part and sanctification to the believer's part.[380] However, Goodwin did not appear to embrace this approach and instead maintained that the Spirit performs regeneration through the means of the Word, despite the *ordo salutis* problem.[381]

Why, then, did Goodwin so insist upon transformation by beholding Christ? Renewal of the *imago Dei* must occur, he believed, via the faculty of the understanding.[382] This must be the case, he reasoned, since 'we are not wrought on as a piece of dead Clay, but according to the nature of the Soul, which being an understanding Creature, the Heart is wrought upon by means of it'.[383] The other faculties are transformed as a result of the renewal of the mind. Goodwin, therefore, was committed to the priority of the mind over the will and other faculties. In this I am in agreement with Vickery's assessment that the overall movement of Goodwin's theology was intellectualist and that faith and renewal begin in the intellect with the will following its guidance.[384] Elsewhere, Goodwin wrote, 'there is no act of Will, but an Understanding Goes before it, and leads on to it'.[385]

This priority of the mind was vital in addressing the problem of corruption. In his earlier work, *An Unregenerate*, Goodwin was adamant that the infusion of grace must begin with the mind because, in contradistinction to many Catholic divines, the mind of all the faculties 'is primarily and most deeply depraved'.[386] Moreover, the corruption of sin 'beginning at the Understanding, eats into the Will and Affections, soaks through all'.[387] The darkened mind is not only the prime seat of many sins but also fails to guide the lower faculties and is frequently the direct cause of sin in them.[388] Thus, other faculties are transformed as a result of renewal of the understanding.[389] In later works, however, Goodwin stressed that sin is normally aroused in the lower faculties and that 'the Workings of Grace are perfectly contrary'.[390] Here he apparently identified the lower faculties as the chief seat of sin. Nevertheless, Goodwin assumed that since 'the strength that must sway the man lies' in the mind, the underlying problem is the mind abdicating its responsibility.[391] In his sermons on Ephesians, he explained that the order of the

---

380. William Pemble, *Vindiciæ Gratiæ. A Plea For Grace. More especially the Grace of Faith. Or, Certain Lectures as touching the Nature and Properties of Grace and Faith* (1627), 15.

381. E.g. *Works*, V, *The Holy Ghost*, 49, 392–3.

382. *Works*, I, *Ephesians*, part I, 116.

383. *Works*, V, *The Holy Ghost*, 363.

384. See pp. 67–8.

385. *Works*, II, *Election*, 383.

386. *Works*, III, *An Unregenerate*, 126; cf. 129, 161.

387. *Works*, III, *An Unregenerate*, 500; cf. 124.

388. *Works*, III, *An Unregenerate*, 127–8, 199; cf. *Works*, I, *Ephesians*, part II, 68.

389. *Works*, III, *An Unregenerate*, 126.

390. *Works*, V, *The Holy Ghost*, 152.

391. *Works*, V, *The Holy Ghost*, 152.

faculties remains despite the Fall and so while lusts begin in the lower faculties, the higher faculties must still give 'consent'.[392] Similarly, he referred to the will as 'the proper Seat of Sin', but also in the context of the mind ceasing to guide the will properly.[393] Thus, while Goodwin was inconsistent in his identification of the faculty most corrupted by sin, nevertheless he consistently maintained that the mind is the key to addressing corruption.

Transformation must also begin with the mind since infused grace not only addresses corruption but also comprises new spiritual life. Holding 'the Spirit of a Man' as the highest part of the mind, Goodwin believed it constituted 'the very *Spirit*, Quintessence, and Center of the Soul'.[394] Thus, only transformation applied to this part of the mind may operate as a new life principle and, consequently, be diffused to all other faculties.[395] Moreover the highest part of the mind is most capable of spiritual realities and so permits the reception of spiritual life in particular.[396] For these reasons, Goodwin was convinced that transformation must occur through the mind in order to maintain his conception of transformation as new spiritual life infused into the centre of the soul.

Goodwin's scheme of transformation, therefore, went hand in hand with his anthropology and his conception of real union with Christ. In this regard, his scheme may be compared with other views. Goodwin's stress upon transformation by spiritual sight of Christ resembled Sibbes's approach in his exposition of 2 Corinthians 3:17-18 brought to publication by Goodwin.[397] Owen repeatedly made the same connection between spiritual sight of Christ and transformation.[398] Where Goodwin differed from these divines was in putting more stress upon the necessity of revelation of Christ within the believer. In this respect, he was closer to enthusiasts like Dell who stressed that the Word of Christ must be within the believer to transform.[399] In contrast, conservatives who denied the indwelling of the Spirit's person were much more reticent to affirm inner revelation of Christ by the Spirit. Consequently, conservatives tended to downplay the connection between transformation and revelation of Christ. For example, in Stedman's treatise *The Mystical Union*, the renewal of the *imago Dei* does not depend upon inner revelation of Christ. Indeed, for Stedman, the indwelling of Christ equated to created grace.[400] In this light, Vickery's thesis that Goodwin was an intellectualist

392. *Works*, I, *Ephesians*, part II, 84; cf. 34.

393. *Works*, II, *The Creatures*, 29.

394. *Works*, V, *The Holy Ghost*, 151. Vickery rightly contends that Goodwin was not assuming a tripartite anthropology but treating the spirit as the highest part of the soul. See Vickery, 'A Most Lawful Pleasure', 63–4.

395. *Works*, V, *The Holy Ghost*, 151–2.

396. *Works*, V, *The Holy Ghost*, 152.

397. Richard Sibbes, *The Excellencie of The Gospell above the Law* (1639).

398. Owen, *Christologia*, 212, 215–16; Owen, *The Glory of Christ*, 204–5, 210–11.

399. Dell, *Right Reformation*, 18–19.

400. Stedman, *Mystical Union*, 132.

could be further established by noting the connection with the mode of the Spirit's indwelling. For Goodwin, the Spirit indwells in person and, therefore, immediately reveals Christ to the mind, whereas restricting indwelling to created grace tended to promote the enablement of the will apart from revelation. Thus, Hooker, advocating the will as the main faculty, understood sanctification to result from the impartation of created grace to the will enabling obedience to the law.[401] While grace is also imparted to the understanding, for Hooker the mind is merely restored to an Adamic state and is not the source of transformation of the will. In different ways, then, both Goodwin and Hooker assumed a direct connection between the nature of transformation and the nature of real union with Christ. While it is beyond the scope of this study, it could well be that among mainstream puritans there was a correlation between intellectualist/voluntarist positions and the mode of the Spirit's indwelling.

3.6 Conclusion

In his defence of Reformed soteriology, Goodwin was deeply concerned to maintain a high doctrine of transformation. The decisive moment of transformation is regeneration, although regeneration along with progressive sanctification and bodily resurrection were understood to be part of one work of transformation effected by the Holy Spirit. All of which, Goodwin insisted, are necessary for final salvation and eschatological glory. Transformation, he argued, is essential to enjoy heavenly life and communion with God because the believer must be transformed from corrupt to holy and from earthly to spiritual. While Goodwin strove to maintain such a high conception of transformation against Catholics and Arminians, by the 1650s, when he wrote the bulk of his grand project, he was particularly defending against 'Enthusiasticks' and radicals who advocated an extreme deification theology. His key theological move was to exploit the substance/quality distinction to his advantage and thus insist that transformation does not involve transubstantiation into the divine nature but involves a change in qualities equivalent to the divine nature. (Herein was a second notion of deification in Goodwin's theology.) Importantly, he believed that this new quality functions as new spiritual life. To this end, while he employed the scholastic language of *habitus*, Goodwin markedly reworked the notion to avoid perceived errors of scholastic theologians. Concerned that their assessment of human corruption was too low, he insisted that infused grace is implanted at the centre of the soul as new spiritual life. Thus, the leading idea in Goodwin's account of transformation is not so much addressing corruption but the fitting of the believer for a spiritual, that is heavenly, existence. The former occurs as the result of the latter.

This created grace, Goodwin insisted, is entirely dependent upon the presence of the indwelling Spirit. Not only does the Spirit infuse and sustain created grace,

401. Hooker, *The Paterne of Perfection*, 36–7, 65.

but he also constantly activates created grace such that even its actions remain entirely dependent upon his motions. For Goodwin, infused grace enables the believer to be moved by the direct operations of the Spirit and, in particular, the Spirit's inner revelation of Christ. Thus, Goodwin believed that the indwelling of both uncreated and created grace is essential for transformation, but with the former having clear priority. He contended for this scheme against, on one side, conservatives who denied the indwelling of the Spirit's person and, on the other, Arminians and perfectionist antinomians who denied infused grace.

The entire work of transformation, according to Goodwin, is summed up in the renewal of the *imago Dei* and this renewal, he held, depends upon real union with Christ. His dual notion of the image – the holiness and substantial images – corresponds to his quality and substance distinction. The former was entirely lost at the Fall; the latter remained intact. In contrast to conservative divines, Goodwin insisted that renewal is not only the restoration of the original image but also transformation to a higher spiritual image. Crucially, Goodwin contended that Christ is the superior image and only by beholding him could believers be transformed into his image. In other words, transformation results from Christ's mystical indwelling intrinsic to his conception of real union with Christ. Goodwin insisted upon transformation by revelation because of his intellectualist convictions. In contrast, conservatives who denied the indwelling of the Spirit tended to downplay the Spirit's inner revelation and understand transformation principally in terms of enablement of the will. Goodwin, therefore, found himself articulating a similar view of transformation to others who advocated the indwelling of uncreated grace, including Sibbes, Owen and many enthusiasts.

Chapter 4

REAL UNION WITH CHRIST AND THE REALITY OF JUSTIFICATION

4.1 Introduction

Having explored indwelling and transformation, I will now focus on the relation of these 'real' notions to extrinsic categories in Goodwin's thought and, in particular, how he founded the reality of justification in his conception of real union with Christ. First I will show that Goodwin maintained a high account of justification consisting solely in the forensic imputation of Christ's righteousness (§4.2). I will then discuss the relation of justification to union with Christ (§4.3). I will demonstrate that while Goodwin believed the imputation of Christ's righteousness to have its immediate basis in an external union, he also insisted that imputation must be founded in real union with Christ. Given that both justification and transformation result from real union with Christ, I will then examine the relation of justification and transformation (§4.4). I will show that Goodwin prioritized justification over transformation, yet this did not overthrow his conviction that justification must be founded in real union. This final section will draw the various threads of this chapter and the main theological ideas from the previous chapters together into a consideration of Goodwin's understanding of the *ordo salutis* and its relation to real union with Christ. In this chapter, therefore, I will address the central points of contention in current debates over union with Christ.[1]

Of especial relevance will be Goodwin's sermons on Ephesians, his treatise *Object and Acts*, and, from his grand project, *An Unregenerate, Election* and *Christ the Mediator*. *Ephesians* dates to the early 1640s; the other works to the 1650s. I will also give attention to the Westminster Assembly, where Goodwin was the second most frequent speaker in the justification debate of September 1643.[2] Van Dixhoorn, as a result of his research, remarks that 'we currently have more information on this debate than on any other debate in the Assembly and much of this information is new'.[3]

---

1. See §1.6.
2. Van Dixhoorn, 'Reforming the Reformation', 333.
3. Van Dixhoorn, 'Reforming the Reformation', 273.

4.2 The reality of justification

Goodwin declared that the protestant doctrine of justification is 'the Glory of our Religion'.[4] In keeping with his protestant heritage, he sharply delineated justification from real transformation. To this end, Goodwin distinguished two sorts of mercies bestowed upon believers:

> 1st. Such as impress something on us, work some real new Being in us, which we call a physical Change. 2dly. There are Privileges granted us, which work a mighty Change in us in our State and Condition before the Lord.[5]

The change in 'State or Condition' includes adoption, justification and the divine call into the church; the 'Physical change' includes regeneration, sanctification and bodily resurrection.[6] (Regeneration belongs to the latter category, despite Kim's contention that Goodwin placed regeneration in the former category along with justification and adoption.[7]) The former are 'external Workings as to the Person'; the latter 'internal Workings on the Person'.[8] Accordingly, Goodwin differentiated justification and sanctification: 'Justification is a Work of God upon us, but Sanctification is a working Holiness in us'.[9] In *The Holy Ghost* Goodwin stated that while conversion includes the '*Physical* change' of regeneration as a work in believers, the greatest change consists in '*Moral, Legal, Forensecal* change' of justification and adoption.[10] In upholding justification as a purely forensic benefit, Goodwin was of one accord with the Reformed orthodox consensus.[11]

---

4. *Works*, V, *The Holy Ghost*, 167.

5. *Works*, IV, *Object and Acts*, part I, 25.

6. *Works*, IV, *Object and Acts*, part I, 25–7.

7. Kim, 'Salvation by Faith', 205–7 cf. 186, 191. Kim's argument appears to be based on a single text where Goodwin referred to regeneration as a soteric benefit bestowed 'upon us'. *Works*, V, *Gospel Holiness*, 89. However, this is a fallacy of argumentation: Goodwin employed the prepositional phrase not in contrast to transformation worked 'in us' but in contrast to the indwelling of the Spirit 'in us'. Indeed, Goodwin immediately delineated a third category of soteric benefits (distinct from regeneration) in which he placed justification.

8. *Works*, IV, *Object and Acts*, part I, 26; cf. 27.

9. *Works*, IV, *Object and Acts*, part I, 26.

10. *Works*, V, *The Holy Ghost*, 377; cf. *Works*, I, *Ephesians*, part II, 122. Chang misunderstands Goodwin as equating moral and physical changes. Chang, 'Christian Life', 196.

11. E.g. Anthony Burgess, *The True Doctrine of Justification Asserted and Vindicated, From The Errours of Papists, Arminians, Socinians, and more especially Antinomians. In XXX. Lectures* (1651), 167; Samuel Rutherford, *A Survey of the Spirituall Antichrist. Opening the secrets of Familisme and Antinomianisme in the Antichristian Doctrine of John Saltmarsh, and Will. Del, the present Preachers of the Army now in England, and of Robert Town, Tob. Crisp, H. Denne, Eaton, and others* (1648), part II, 229.

Also true to his tradition, Goodwin held that justification results not from the impartation but from the imputation of Christ's righteousness.[12] Thus, Goodwin rejected the Catholic position: 'We detest that Doctrine of Infusion of Habits for Justification, or as a Foundation of works, to make them meritorious.'[13] The matter of the formal cause of justification – whether by infusion or imputation – was widely accepted to be the central point of division against Rome's view.[14] Also representative of the clarity of the Reformed orthodox consensus was Leigh's comment: 'The Papists confound Justification and Sanctification, they say to justifie signifies to make righteous by infusion of grace.'[15] Imputation of Christ's righteousness was also rejected by Socinians such as Biddle in favour of the imputation of faith.[16] However, unlike Burgess and Owen,[17] Goodwin did not explicitly defend the Reformed orthodox doctrine of justification against Socinian teaching.[18]

While strictly forensic in nature, Goodwin stressed that justification is as much a reality as the physical changes of regeneration and sanctification. Thus, he employed the term 'real' and its derivatives in two different ways. When set in opposition to relative (i.e. extrinsic) changes, real denotes changes in the nature of the believer. Accordingly, Goodwin contended that there are two kinds of salvific benefits, exemplified in justification and sanctification:

One is a Relative Change, which consisteth meerly in Title. And The other is a real Change, which consisteth in Works in us. The Relative Change in us consisteth in all those things which depend upon God's accounting, and reputing, and actual reckoning as such.[19]

Yet, Goodwin also used the term 'real' to denote true or actual.[20] For example, justification causes a 'real moral change, as truly and as really as Sanctification is a

---

12. E.g. *Works*, III, *Christ the Mediator*, 350; *Works*, IV, *Object and Acts*, part I, 104.

13. *Works*, V, *The Holy Ghost*, 175; cf. *Works*, I, *Ephesians*, part II, 283.

14. C. FitzSimons Allison, *The Rise of Moralism: The Proclamation of the Gospel from Hooker to Baxter* (Wilton, CT: Morehouse Barlow, 1966), 6.

15. Leigh, *A Body of Divinity*, 512.

16. Biddle, *A Twofold Catechism*, 82.

17. Anthony Burgess, *The True Doctrine of Justification Asserted & Vindicated From the Errours of many, and more especially Papists and Socinians. Or A Treatise of the Natural Righteousness of God, and Imputed Righteousness of Christ* (1654), 292–3; John Owen, *The Doctrine of Justification by Faith Through the Imputation of the Righteousness of Christ, Explained, Confirmed, & Vindicated* (1677), 67–76.

18. An exception is *Works*, II, *Election*, 440.

19. *Works*, I, *Ephesians*, part II, 280. This relative/real distinction applied to soteric benefits was widely accepted among Reformed orthodox puritans. E.g. Leigh, *A Body of Divinity*, 510.

20. *Works*, I, *Ephesians*, part II, 294.

physical Change'.[21] Again, 'the greatest Benefits in Grace do impress nothing upon us, make no physical Change … and yet are things of the greatest Make, and have the greatest Reality in them'.[22] This was not uncommon. Burgess, like Goodwin, held justification to be a relative change and also defended its reality. He stressed that justification is rooted in the 'real' work of Christ and God, received through the 'real' means of faith, producing 'real' effects.[23]

What Goodwin was seeking to protect was the soteriological significance of justification. In the first instance, forensic justification is essential to address the forensic problem of guilt and so redeem believers from God's wrath.[24] Yet, in common with the majority of mainstream Reformed divines, Goodwin contended that justification is also necessary as the entitlement to heaven and final salvation.[25] This was an important point, for debate over the imputation of Christ's active obedience turned upon it.[26] The majority of divines assigned entitlement to heaven specifically to the imputation of Christ's active obedience. Thus, Owen wrote,

> *Pardon of sin* doth not give right and title unto eternal life. It is true, he whose sins are pardoned shall inherit eternal life; but not meerly by vertue of that pardon, but through the imputation of Righteousness which doth inseparably accompany it, and is the ground of it.[27]

For Owen, then, the imputation of Christ's passive and active obedience corresponds to freedom from condemnation and entitlement to eternal life respectively.[28] Burgess likewise argued that remission of sins is insufficient for entitlement to heaven.[29] For him, the granting of heaven is an additional benefit joined by divine appointment to freedom from condemnation.[30] Goodwin, therefore, was embracing the mainstream opinion when he wrote, 'Remission of Sins is rather attributed to Christs Death, Justification of Life to his Active Obedience.'[31]

---

21. *Works*, IV, *Object and Acts*, part I, 107; cf. *Works*, I, *Ephesians*, part II, 300.

22. *Works*, IV, *Object and Acts*, part I, 25; cf. 26–7.

23. Burgess, *Justification (1654)*, 135–6.

24. *Works*, V, *The Holy Ghost*, 114.

25. *Works*, V, *The Holy Ghost*, 208; cf. Richard Sibbes, *Light from Heaven, Discovering The {Fountaine Opened. Angels Acclamations. Churches Riches. Rich Povertie* (1638), 'The Churches Riches', 19; Leigh, *A Body of Divinity*, 512; Burgess, *Justification (1654)*, 122, 176; Burgess, *Justification (1651)*, 176; Owen, *Justification*, 1, 199.

26. A fine analysis of other aspects of Goodwin's argument for the imputation of Christ's active obedience in the Westminster Assembly and in *Christ the Mediator* has been provided in Jones, *Why Heaven Kissed Earth*, 179–88.

27. Owen, *Justification*, 478.

28. Owen, *Justification*, 484–6.

29. Burgess, *Justification (1654)*, 278.

30. Burgess, *Justification (1654)*, 270, 282.

31. *Works*, III, *Christ the Mediator*, 345; cf. 339.

The imputation of Christ's active obedience had been a matter of sharp dispute in the protracted debate in the proceedings of the Westminster Assembly over the revision of Article XI.[32] Van Dixhoorn summarizes the range of views expressed:

> When defining justification, there are three parties: those who equate justification with remission of sins, those who add to remission of sins the imputation of Christ's righteousness, and Gataker, who equates justification with vindication and is a party to himself. However, when discussing the basis of justification – that is, whether the active obedience of Christ is credited to the believer – the Assembly divides into two theological parties: there are those who hold closely to a more traditional Anselmic understanding of Christology and the atonement, and there are those who adopt a more developed post-Reformation covenant of works or something similar to it.[33]

The vocal minority were concerned that the notion of the imputation of Christ's active obedience lacked exegetical support, displaced the atonement and, more worryingly in their eyes, entailed antinomianism.[34] Francis Taylor (1589–1656) stated this third concern: 'this seemes to give a great bent to the Antinomians: if it be granted that Christ hath performed the law for me then it will follow I am not bound to keepe this lawe myselfe.'[35] Goodwin, fighting for the majority opinion, responded by arguing that the imputation of Christ's active obedience only concerns justification and therefore does not cancel the obligation to holiness.[36] Discussion of this matter also raised the question of the entitlement to heaven. Goodwin contended that the phrase 'justification of life' appearing in Romans 5:18, 21 signifies 'the right to eternall life'.[37] This right, he argued, results from the imputation of Christ's active obedience:

> 'Justification of life'. I did not meane of Christs life, but this: wheras eminently our title to eternall life is founded upon the active be[cause] suited to the law which runs upon doing, dot suffering, by his doing properly this law is fulfilled.[38]

32. For analysis of this debate see Van Dixhoorn, 'Reforming the Reformation', chapter 5; Alan D. Strange, 'The Imputation of the Active Obedience of Christ at the Westminster Assembly' in *Drawn into Controversie: Reformed Theological Diversity and Debates within Seventeenth-Century British Puritanism*, ed. Michael A. G. Haykin and Mark Jones, *Reformed Historical Theology* (Göttingen: Vandenhoeck & Ruprecht, 2011).
33. Van Dixhoorn, 'Reforming the Reformation', 337.
34. Van Dixhoorn, 'Reforming the Reformation', 317.
35. Van Dixhoorn, *Minutes*, volume 2, 69. The same concern is evident in Baxter's account of justification. For a helpful discussion, see: Kim, 'Salvation by Faith', 236–43.
36. Van Dixhoorn, *Minutes*, volume 2, 70, 96.
37. Van Dixhoorn, *Minutes*, volume 2, 64.
38. [Note: 'dot' should be read 'and not'.] Van Dixhoorn, *Minutes*, volume 2, 78. Goodwin also nuanced this one-to-one relationship: 'I thinke to say his death served only to free from condemnation or his active obedience to Justification is not soe good: it is all to all. But soe

In opposition, Vines objected: 'I question whether Christ's active obedience is a <proper> distinct foundation of title to heaven.'[39] He had already argued that entitlement to heaven is rooted in adoption rather than justification.[40] Thomas Gataker (1574–1654), who denied the imputation of Christ's active obedience and also assigned entitlement to adoption,[41] argued that justification places believers in a position no higher than the prelapsarian Adam.[42] Goodwin contended against such a view:

> I desire [it] likewise to be considered, [that] if the passive obedience of Christ only ware it that ware imputed, it would but set us in the same state we ware in [when] Adam was in the moment of his creation. Though the passive cut of[f] all omissions past, yet I must have an eternall active righteousnesse, soe Adam was to have. & wher shall we have this, unlesse it be active?[43]

What controlled the majority opinion in this matter was covenant theology. In *Christ the Mediator*, Goodwin explained that there was a double demand upon Adam: negatively, punishment for transgression; positively, obedience to procure the reward of eternal life.[44] The former was demanded upon Adam as a sinner; the latter upon Adam as a creature.[45] The implication is that reception of eternal life requires the imputation of Christ's active obedience, without which believers would only be restored to the Adamic state under the covenant of works at the moment of creation. Leigh explained that the covenant of works demanded such a relation between entitlement to eternal life and the imputation of Christ's active obedience:

> We are justified in part by Christs active obedience, for by it we obtain the imputation of that perfect righteousnesse which giveth us title to the Kingdom of Heaven. Seeing it was not possible for us to enter into life, till we had kept the Commandments of God ... and we were not able to keep them our selves, it was necessary our Surety should keep them for us[46]

as eminently to one more than another.' Van Dixhoorn, *Minutes*, volume 2, 70. This can be explained by an earlier comment whereby Goodwin had acknowledged that Christ's active obedience only has soteriological effectiveness in combination with the imputation of Christ's passive obedience: 'It is true, "without bloud noe remission". The active obedience would not save us without this.' Van Dixhoorn, *Minutes*, volume 2, 64.

39. Van Dixhoorn, *Minutes*, volume 2, 76.

40. Van Dixhoorn, *Minutes*, volume 2, 61.

41. Thomas Gataker, *An Antidote Against Errour Concerning Justification, Or, The True Notion of Justification, and of Justifying Faith* (1670), 3.

42. Van Dixhoorn, *Minutes*, volume 2, 58.

43. Van Dixhoorn, *Minutes*, volume 2, 77.

44. *Works*, III, *Christ the Mediator*, 337–41.

45. *Works*, III, *Christ the Mediator*, 85.

46. Leigh, *A Body of Divinity*, 518.

This logic clarifies Charles Herle's (1598–1659) comment at the Assembly that entitlement to heaven would be rooted in the works of believers if the imputation of Christ's active obedience is denied.[47] Thus, it was this covenantal framework which really determined Goodwin's position, rather than his exegesis which at best was theologically driven.[48]

In Goodwin's mind, then, the reality of justification is crucial not only for securing salvation from the guilt of sin but also for advancing the believer above the Adamic state. Christ's active obedience obtains a permanent state of righteousness for believers and so secures eternal life.[49] Yet, Goodwin advocated a far more significant advancement in salvation. As Herzer notes, Goodwin was particularly vigorous in defending the minority position that, upon obedience, Adam could only have merited earthly eternal life.[50] In the case of Christ, Goodwin adopted Anselmic logic and argued that Christ's divine nature granted his merits greater worth and therefore entitled the believer to heavenly eternal life.[51] In fact, Goodwin may have assumed a tight connection between the worth of Christ's person and the nature of eternal life it secures. As an earthly man, Adam was (in principle) able to merit earthly eternal life, whereas the obedience of Christ as the God-man entitles the believer to partake of the divine nature (i.e. heavenly eternal life).

Moreover, in addition to the imputation of Christ's passive and active obedience, Goodwin contended for a third aspect of justification:

> There be three parts of Justification: First, … His Passive Obedience takes away the guilt of Actual Sin. But Secondly, We ought to have an Actual Righteousness reckoned to us … The Active Obedience of Jesus Christ made many Righteous. … But the Law is not fulfilled yet; for we have corruption of Nature in us? The Apostle … brings in the third part of Justification, *viz.* That Christ came into the World in our Nature, and fulfilled the Righteousness of the Law, in having that Nature perfectly holy. And now the Righteousness of the Law is fulfilled in all parts of it; here is a perfect Justification[52]

Blackham, Chang and Kim each identify this third aspect as regeneration and therefore conclude that Goodwin advocated only a partially forensic conception of justification. Contending that Goodwin included the 'ontological change'

---

47. Van Dixhoorn, *Minutes*, volume 2, 94.

48. Van Dixhoorn, 'Reforming the Reformation', 316.

49. *Works*, III, *Christ the Mediator*, 81–2; *Works*, V, *The Holy Ghost*, 208; *Works*, I, *Ephesians*, part II, 190.

50. Herzer, 'Adam's Reward', 165–8. See *Works*, III, *Christ the Mediator*, 81–2; *Works*, II, *The Creatures*, 45–9.

51. *Works*, III, *Christ the Mediator*, 117–18, 132–3; *Works*, II, *The Knowledg*, 136, 172. Here Goodwin followed Sibbes. Sibbes, *Evangelicall Sacrifices*, 'The Hidden Life', 14.

52. *Works*, III, *Christ the Mediator*, 348; cf. *Works*, V, *The Holy Ghost*, 358.

of regeneration in justification, Blackham aligns Goodwin with an 'Eastern' view.[53] Consequently, he claims that 'Goodwin has significantly changed the way the doctrine works' and so departed from Calvin who kept justification and regeneration distinct.[54] And he further alleges that, despite his leading role at the Westminster Assembly, Goodwin departed from the 'Westminster scheme'.[55] Independently, Chang expresses surprise at discovering the same non-forensic aspect in Goodwin's conception of justification.[56] Kim follows Blackham and Chang, although his account is confused and also tries to maintain that Goodwin's doctrine of justification was 'purely forensic'.[57]

However, these scholars have misinterpreted Goodwin's scheme. In *Christ the Mediator*, Goodwin's aim was to establish the imputation not only of Christ's passive obedience but also of his whole righteousness.[58] Noting 'Controversie' among Reformed divines over '*whether the whole Righteousness of Christ be imputed*', he explained: 'There are some who not only exclude that Sanctity of his Nature, but all the Active Righteousness of his Life, from that Righteousness which is imputed to us ... they deny all this to be together with his Passive Obedience imputed to us in the room of our Righteousness.'[59] The third aspect of justification, therefore, is the imputation of Christ's sanctified nature. That imputation, not impartation, is in view is repeatedly made clear:

> That that absolute, complete, and universal Conformity, and Satisfaction to the Law in suffering the punishment and Death, or Obedience of Life, and Holyness of Nature required of Sinners, being found in Christ, and communicated unto us by imputation is said to be fulfilled in us, as if we had accomplished it. The whole Righteousness therefore of Christ, as it ought to be imputed, so *de facto* it is imputed unto us.[60]

Contra Blackham, Chang and Kim, Goodwin was adamant that justification is an entirely legal category, distinct from the physical change of regeneration. Indeed elsewhere, Goodwin denounced Catholic theologians who 'according to their Doctrine, habitual Sanctification is to come in also ... as that which helps constitute us righteous'.[61]

---

53. Blackham, 'Pneumatology', 208.

54. Blackham, 'Pneumatology', 207.

55. Blackham, 'Pneumatology', 209.

56. Chang, 'Christian Life', 196–8.

57. Kim, 'Salvation by Faith', 260; cf. 248–50, 305–6.

58. *Works*, III, *Christ the Mediator*, 335; cf. *Works*, II, *Election*, 272, 276. Jones asserts that this principle was central to Goodwin's soteriology, yet ignores the third aspect of justification. Jones, *Why Heaven Kissed Earth*, 180; cf. 179–88.

59. *Works*, III, *Christ the Mediator*, 336.

60. *Works*, III, *Christ the Mediator*, 344; cf. 336, 343.

61. *Works*, III, *Man's Restauration*, 16–17. Here 'habitual' designates what belongs to infused *habitus*.

Although not an innovation on his part, Goodwin especially championed this third aspect of justification. Hans Boersma traces the differentiation of active and passive obedience in imputation of Christ's righteousness back to Theodore Beza (1519–1605) and observes that Beza also advocated the imputation of Christ's habitual righteousness.[62] While Goodwin did not cite Beza as his source in *Christ the Mediator*, this is apparent in the minutes of the Westminster Assembly. In one speech, he declared: 'Beza['s] notion: the ep. to Ro[mans] handles the doctrine of justification most exactly in all the parts'[63] and then contended that the imputation of Christ's passive obedience, active obedience and holiness is taught in Romans 4, 5 and 8 respectively. While many sought to defend the imputation of Christ's active obedience at the Assembly, it was Goodwin who almost single-handedly championed this third aspect.[64] He encountered some resistance to this idea. Vines called into question Goodwin's interpretation of Romans 8: 'I am not cleare that here is spoken of a holynesse of Christs nature Imputed',[65] and, later, 'Habituall righteousnesse. I cannot digest the Imputation of it.'[66] Even as a supporter of the majority opinion, Herle remained unconvinced of the third aspect: 'It is yet a question whether this habituall righteousnesse be imputed to us.'[67] Goodwin found himself defending an interpretation of Romans 8 that he would later defend again in *Christ the Mediator*.[68] The imputation of Christ's holiness also found little support in arguably the two most important puritan defences of justification: Owen did not mention the notion; Burgess recognized and then dismissed it.[69]

Like Beza, what drove Goodwin to champion the imputation of Christ's nature was a conviction concerning original sin. The Reformed consensus held that corrupt nature constitutes a sin.[70] Goodwin not only embraced this position but

62. Boersma, *Hot Pepper Corn*, 220–1.

63. Van Dixhoorn, *Minutes*, volume 2, 63; cf. 85.

64. Van Dixhoorn believes that Joshua Hoyle (bap. 1588, d. 1654) alluded to the same notion: 'Reforming the Reformation', 295. Also, Lazarus Seaman (d. 1675) assumed the legitimacy of Goodwin's contention. Van Dixhoorn, *Minutes*, volume 2, 71, 79. Here Jeffrey Jue misunderstands this third aspect of justification in his comment: 'By "habituall," Seaman was referring to the active righteousness of Christ demonstrated in his active obedience.' Jeffrey K. Jue, 'The Active Obedience of Christ and the Theology of the Westminster Standards: A Historical Investigation', in *Justified in Christ: God's Plan for Us in Justification*, ed. K. Scott Oliphint (Ross-shire: Christian Focus, 2007), 122.

65. Van Dixhoorn, *Minutes*, volume 2, 77.

66. Van Dixhoorn, *Minutes*, volume 2, 98.

67. Van Dixhoorn, *Minutes*, volume 2, 93.

68. Van Dixhoorn, *Minutes*, volume 2, 78, 97. Cf. *Works*, III, *Christ the Mediator*, 343–4, 346–8.

69. Owen, *Justification*; Burgess, *Justification (1654)*, 346–7.

70. Note: this tenet was included in Article IX of the *Thirty-Nine Articles* and the Westminster Assembly's revision of the article. Church of England, *The Proceedings of the Assembly of Divines upon the Thirty nine Articles of the Church of England* (1647), 7–8.

agreed with Sibbes that the guilt of corrupt nature outstrips that of actual sins.[71] Both divines were convinced that as well as acts, the orientation of nature is crucially significant before God. Goodwin, at least, warned that this doctrine was under attack:

> there is a rotten Generation of Divines, sprung up in this Age, which do flatly deny original Corruption to be a Sin: acknowledg they do a Guilt of *Adam's* Sin, and a Corruption thence derived, but that Corruption they say, is only to be considered as the Punishment of the first Sin, but in it self not properly a Sin[72]

The 'Generation of Divines' Goodwin later identified as Arminians.[73] By the late 1650s, extra impetus may have been given by the prominent writer Taylor who openly rejected the tenet 'that our naturall corruption in the regenerate still remains, and is still properly a sin.'[74] In Goodwin's mind, the imputation of Christ's nature is the required remedy for the guilt of corruption. He entitled one chapter: '*That the perfect Holiness of Christs Nature is Imputed to a Believer to justifie him against the Condemnation of Original Sin.*'[75]

In conclusion, Goodwin was convinced that justification is essential for salvation. In keeping with his Reformed heritage, he insisted upon a purely forensic conception of justification. The dimensions of justification were determined by the necessity of justification within Goodwin's soteriology. The guilt of Adam's transgression demands the imputation of Christ's passive obedience; the guilt of corruption demands the imputation of Christ's sanctified nature; and the granting of eternal life demands the imputation of Christ's active obedience under the law. Moreover, since in Goodwin's soteriology believers are not merely restored to an (permanent) Adamic state but raised to a heavenly existence, the value of Christ's righteousness must surpass any possible Adamic righteousness. It was Goodwin's high soteriology, therefore, which drove him to contend for a notably high doctrine of justification among his orthodox colleagues.

4.3 Justification and real union with Christ

Goodwin was convinced that the reality of forensic justification could only be secured if founded in union with Christ. Justification occurs, he insisted, 'through Faith as laying hold upon Christ; it is *in* Christ, *in in* Christ, and *in in* only him.'[76]

---

71. *Works*, III, *An Unregenerate*, 381; *Works*, I, *Ephesians*, part II, 119.

72. *Works*, III, *An Unregenerate*, 50; cf. 37.

73. *Works*, III, *An Unregenerate*, 342. For a discussion of Arminius's rejection of corruption as sin, see Ellis, *Simon Episcopius' Doctrine of Original Sin*, 78.

74. Taylor, *Deus justificatus.*, 39; cf. 49–52.

75. *Works*, III, *Christ the Mediator*, 346.

76. *Works*, IV, *Object and Acts*, part II, 37.

Thus, he was emphatic that both justification and transformation result from union with Christ:

> there was a twofold righteousness ... both flowing from union with Christ and a Mans being one with him, or being found in him. 1. One being a righteousness of Sanctification ... wrought in himself ... 2. Another, which is the righteousness of Justification ... imputed to him upon believing[77]

In part, insisting upon union with Christ allowed divines such as Goodwin to defend the imputation of Christ's righteousness from Catholics and Socinians who repudiated the idea.[78] At the Westminster Assembly, George Walker (bap. 1582?, d. 1651) particularly contended that imputation is not a legal fiction, if founded in union:

> Gods judgement is allwayes according to truth & if God doe acount us soe, we are made soe. Therfore, as we are made sin by Adam, soe righteous by Christ. We are made righteous by communion of Christ's righteousnesse. & the ground of this is our union with Christ.[79]

Justification founded in union with Christ, Walker believed, transcended the false choice between the Catholic notion of justification resulting from infused grace and justification as a bare divine declaration: 'It is an Imperfect devision to say that to Justify is either by inherency or *verbum forense*, for ther is a Justification by communion of the righteousnesse of Christ.'[80] Like Walker, Goodwin also rejected justification as divine declaration apart from union. He explained,

> the Promises of Forgivenesse are not as the Pardons of a Prince, which merely containe an expression of his royall word for pardoning ... but Gods Promises of pardon are made in his Son, and are as if a Prince should offer to pardon a Traytor upon marriage with his child[81]

Goodwin assumed that adoption (the other major legal benefit) also is grounded in union with Christ.[82] Again appealing to the marriage analogy, he reasoned, 'For it is to be a Son in Law by marriage unto, and union with, the Natural Son of God.'[83]

---

77. *Works*, III, *Christ the Mediator*, 353.
78. *Works*, II, *Election*, 440–1. Goodwin's mentor Sibbes likewise contended that union with Christ provides the grounding for justification. Sibbes, *An Exposition of the Third Chapter of Philippians*, 103.
79. Van Dixhoorn, *Minutes*, volume 2, 51; cf. 45. See also Leigh, *A Body of Divinity*, 514.
80. Van Dixhoorn, *Minutes*, volume 2, 51.
81. *Christ Set Forth*, 12–13.
82. *Works*, I, *Ephesians*, part I, 71. See p. 180 for the relation of adoption and justification in Goodwin's thought.
83. *Works*, V, *The Holy Ghost*, 166; cf. *Works*, I, *Ephesians*, part I, 81.

4.3.1 External union as the basis of imputation

What, then, must be determined is the nature of union with Christ upon which justification is founded. By considering the grounds of different imputations in Goodwin's thought, it becomes evident that he believed that the immediate basis for the imputation of Christ's righteousness is an external union with Christ.

4.3.1.1 The imputation of Adam's sin to the human race Besides inherited corruption, Goodwin also defended the transmission of Adamic guilt.[84] By the time of the Westminster Assembly there was increased stress on this latter tenet. Article IX of the *Thirty-Nine Articles* had stated an unflinching declaration of inherited corruption and the resulting guilt of corrupt nature, yet the imputation of Adam's guilt was absent. The revised article produced by the Assembly begins as follows:

> Original sin standeth not in the following of *Adam*, as the Pelagians do vainly talk: But, together with his first sin imputed, it is the fault and corruption of the nature of every man, that naturally is propagated from *Adam*[85]

This followed the original closely apart from the insertion: 'together with his first sin imputed'. With the rise of covenant theology, the representative headship of Adam had brought new clarity to this doctrinal point. Maintaining the dual nature of the problem of sin implied sanctification and justification as distinct and necessary realities. Sanctification addresses corruption; justification addresses guilt. Moreover, the Arminian rejection of the imputation of Adam's guilt had particularly made the Reformed orthodox sensitive on this point.[86] It would also become subject to attacks from vocal English clergy, most notably from Taylor in the 1650s.[87]

Accounting for the basis of the imputation of Adamic guilt to his progeny, however, was considered a difficult task. Perkins expressed caution over determining the precise mechanism.[88] Leigh wrote, 'Nothing is more known then that original sin is traduced, and nothing more obscure then how it is traduced.'[89] Despite admitting the difficulty of the task,[90] Goodwin nevertheless offered one of the most detailed accounts of original sin of his time and gave careful attention to the relation between guilt and corruption. Unfortunately, his statements have been subject to diverging interpretations: Brown aligns Goodwin with 'the

---

84. *Works*, III, *An Unregenerate*, 7–19; *Works*, I, *Ephesians*, part II, 108–19.

85. Church of England, *The Proceedings of the Assembly*, 7.

86. E.g. John Owen, *Theomachia A'vtexousiatike: Or, A Display of Arminianisme* (1643), 70, 72. See Ellis, *Simon Episcopius' Doctrine of Original Sin*, 158–64.

87. Jeremy Taylor, *Vnum Necessarium. Or, The Doctrine and Practice of Repentance* (1655), 364–5.

88. Perkins, *An Exposition of the Symbole*, 90.

89. Leigh, *A Body of Divinity*, 313.

90. *Works*, I, *Ephesians*, part II, 109.

Federalist point of view' as opposed to an Augustinian realist view,[91] whereas Blackham claims that Goodwin held to a 'strong Augustinian view'.[92] Part of the problem is that the federalist and realist categories only became well delineated in later Reformed theology and Goodwin's statements defy this division. A second problem is a paucity of scholarly attention to the doctrine of original sin as taught by puritan divines. George Fisher's study remains one of the most helpful in which he argues that a middle position – 'the Augustino-federal or the Semi-federal' position – was common among divines during this period.[93] This more accurately locates Goodwin: the overall movement of his theology was to understand original sin in Augustinian realist terms, but he superimposed a covenantal framework to legitimize imputation.

Goodwin constructed his account of the transmission of Adamic guilt on the premise that 'God exerciseth no Punishment where there is no Fault'.[94] Thus, 'if we be the *Children of Wrath* by virtue of our natural Birth, then first *Children of Sin* thereby; for God is not angry with us but for Sin'.[95] For Goodwin, then, guilt is the necessary legal grounding for punishment. Later, Owen would labour the same point in his defence of justification: 'There can be no *punishment* but with respect unto the *guilt of sin* personally contracted, or imputed. It is guilt alone that gives what is materially evil and afflictive, the *formal* nature of punishment and nothing else.'[96]

Goodwin's second premise was the inclusion of the corruption of nature in the penalty inflicted by God.[97] By sinning, an individual's nature is depraved. As noted in the previous chapter, this 'comes to pass not upon that mistaken Ground that an Habit follows upon Acts in a Philosophical way ... But Depravation followeth by way of Curse and Forfeiture.'[98] The indwelling Spirit was removed as a direct result of Adam's sin, then by natural consequence the *imago Dei* was forfeited and a depraved nature resulted. Thus, while corruption was a natural corollary of the loss of the Spirit, Goodwin also insisted that it was a punishment.[99] In other words, corruption was a punishment but inflicted through natural cause and effect, rather than by direct divine agency.[100] Accordingly, Goodwin stated that Adam's corruption was contracted by guilt[101] and arose from his sinful act as 'the

91. Brown, 'The Principle of the Covenant', 139.

92. Blackham, 'Pneumatology', 192.

93. George P. Fisher, 'The Augustinian and the Federal Theories of Original Sin Compared', *New Englander and Yale Review* 27, no. 3 (1868): 470–1.

94. *Works*, III, *An Unregenerate*, 7; cf. 360.

95. *Works*, III, *An Unregenerate*, 8.

96. Owen, *Justification*, 287; cf. 282.

97. This was denied by Socinians. See *The Racovian Catechisme*, 142.

98. *Works*, III, *An Unregenerate*, 8.

99. *Works*, III, *An Unregenerate*, 45.

100. *Works*, III, *An Unregenerate*, 48.

101. *Works*, III, *An Unregenerate*, 8.

sole efficient or meritorious Cause of it'.[102] In this way, Goodwin distinguished the meritorious cause of corruption from its physical cause.[103]

Having established these two premises, Goodwin concluded that Adamic guilt must function as the cause of inherited corruption in the whole race:

> That *Adam* committing that Act of Disobedience, his Nature was thereby first in himself for ever defiled by it. … If therefore we also be proved guilty of that Act in him, then by the like reason also must that Nature we received from him by natural Propagation, be tainted with Sin, as his was by virtue of that Act[104]

Goodwin therefore claimed that the true cause of inherited corruption is the imputation of Adam's guilt, whereas natural generation is but the conduit.[105] Thus, Goodwin did not merely defend the transmission of both guilt and corruption, but specifically defended inherited guilt as the legal ground of corruption.[106] He had become convinced of this doctrinal point in his conversion experience. As he stared at his inherent depravity and contemplated its origin, he concluded 'that it was the Guilt or Demerit of that one Man's Disobedience, that corrupted my Nature'.[107]

Goodwin's belief in guilt as the cause of corruption represented the emerging Reformed orthodox consensus as is evident from the Placeus dispute.[108] The continental theologian Josué de la Place (1596–1655?) caused controversy by teaching that Adam's guilt is mediated through inherited corruption (arguably, this mediate imputation view finds support in Calvin). In 1645, the Third Synod of Charenton condemned Placeus's position and so rejected the idea that corruption precedes guilt. Reformed orthodoxy had already reached a consensus that Adam's guilt is directly imputed to his offspring on account of Adam's federal relationship to the race. Goodwin's defence of guilt as the meritorious cause of corruption, therefore, reflected the Reformed consensus.[109]

That guilt as the cause of corruption was a decisive tenet for Goodwin was especially evident in his argument for Adam's status as a public person representing the whole race.[110] Dismissing the views that Adam became a public person by the

102. *Works*, III, *An Unregenerate*, 16.

103. *Works*, III, *An Unregenerate*, 45.

104. *Works*, III, *An Unregenerate*, 9.

105. *Works*, I, *Ephesians*, part II, 113–16.

106. *Works*, I, *Ephesians*, part II, 108.

107. *Life*, ix.

108. See Evans, *Imputation and Impartation*, 72–5; Donald Macleod, 'Original Sin in Reformed Theology' in *Adam, the Fall, and Original Sin: Theological, Biblical and Scientific Perspectives*, ed. Hans Madueme and Michael Reeves (Grand Rapids, MI: Baker Academic, 2014), 140–4.

109. E.g. Leigh, *A Body of Divinity*, 314; Burgess, *Original Sin*, 32.

110. *Works*, III, *An Unregenerate*, 12–13.

absolute appointment of God or by a simple covenant, Goodwin argued that the order and principles of creation necessitated that Adam must function as a public person.[111] In particular, Adam was subject to the law of nature which stipulated that he should beget according to his likeness. Adam therefore would convey the holiness image to his descendants upon obedience, but if he fell, his corrupt nature would instead be conveyed. Next followed Goodwin's key move: if Adam's descendants receive his corrupt nature, then they must also receive his guilt as the necessary legal basis for receiving corruption.[112] Thus, Adam was necessarily appointed as a public person in order to provide the legal grounds for the law of nature:

> if he will convey this *Image* acquired *by his Sin as sinful*, there must be a Guilt of that act of his Sin, which was the cause of it; and therefore he must be a publick Person in that first act of Sin; so as without this, as the Case stood, the Law of Nature could not have had its course.[113]

By this logic, Goodwin concluded that Adam was 'naturally and necessarily' appointed a public person.[114]

Significantly, in this scheme Goodwin assumed that the imputation of Adamic guilt occurs on the immediate basis of an external federal relation. This is confirmed by his statement that Adamic guilt and corruption are conveyed on the basis of two different unions between Adam and the human race: a representative union in which Adam functions as a public person and a real union in which Adam is the organic root of humanity, such that the whole race originally resided in him.[115] Crucially, the imputation of Adamic guilt was assigned to the former; transmission of corruption to the latter.

What complicates matters is Goodwin's contention that real union by itself is inadequate to account for the transmission of corruption. Natural generation functions as the instrumental cause,[116] but the primary cause is 'the common Law that lies upon Generation' or 'annexed unto Generation'.[117] In effect, this law of nature which stipulated that Adam should beget according to his image employed natural generation as the means to fulfil itself.[118] Thus, in the final analysis, Goodwin held that the transmission of both corruption and guilt ultimately find their basis in this external law. Yet, the means for conveying guilt and corruption are representative and real unions respectively.

---

111. *Works*, III, *An Unregenerate*, 15.
112. *Works*, III, *An Unregenerate*, 15.
113. *Works*, III, *An Unregenerate*, 16.
114. *Works*, III, *An Unregenerate*, 357.
115. *Works*, III, *An Unregenerate*, 20; cf. 17–18.
116. *Works*, I, *Ephesians*, part II, 115; cf. *Works*, III, *An Unregenerate*, 17, 19.
117. *Works*, I, *Ephesians*, part II, 112.
118. *Works*, I, *Ephesians*, part II, 117–18.

The exception to real union as the means for the transmission of corruption is the case of the soul. This exception was a consequence of Goodwin adopting the standard Reformed creationist position on the origin of the soul.[119] Assuming a creationist stance, Perkins outlined two common explanations for the soul's corruption.[120] The first postulated an immediate divine withdrawal of grace from the soul as a consequence of the imputation of Adamic guilt. The second opted for a more realistic explanation: the soul is corrupted by the natural cause and effect of the soul indwelling the corrupted body. Consistent with his appeal to the law of nature, Goodwin adopted the first position.[121] Nevertheless, the corruption of the soul remained the exception and otherwise Goodwin held that real union is the instrumental cause of inherited corruption.

More importantly, several factors suggest that Goodwin was not entirely consistent in maintaining federal union as the basis for the imputation of Adamic guilt. First, his exposition of original sin opened in Augustinian terms of universal participation in Adam's sin.[122] Secondly, Fisher points out that under the federal scheme personal responsibility may not be attributed for Adam's transgression.[123] Yet, Goodwin devoted Book IX of his *An Unregenerate* to calling his readers to repent of Adam's sin.[124] Such an act of repentance was integral to Goodwin's account of his conversion: 'I ... rose out of bed being alone, and solemnly fell down on my knees before God ... and did on my own accord assume and take on me the Guilt of that Sin, as truly as any of my own actual Sins.'[125] Thirdly, Augustinian explanations are among Goodwin's justifications for the legitimacy of the imputation of Adamic guilt.[126] In particular, he argued, 'all *Adam*'s Posterity be as truly said to have committed Sin in *Adam*, for that yet they were in his Loins.'[127] Can these apparent inconsistencies be resolved? In Goodwin's mind, universal real participation in Adam's transgression occurs in terms of nature but not person. He explained, 'a Man begets not his like in Person, but in the common Nature.'[128] So while there is real participation at the level of common nature, an external covenantal union is required to render the person guilty of Adam's transgression.[129] Owen stated this more explicitly. Regarding Adam's sin,

119. *Works*, V, *Blessed State*, 78; *Works*, V, *The Holy Ghost*, 379; *Works*, IV, *Object and Acts*, part III, 105.

120. Perkins, *An Exposition of the Symbole*, 89–90.

121. *Works*, I, *Ephesians*, part II, 118.

122. *Works*, III, *An Unregenerate*, 7.

123. Fisher, 'The Augustinian and the Federal Theories of Original Sin Compared', 472.

124. *Works*, III, *An Unregenerate*, 341–92; cf. 26.

125. *Life*, ix.

126. *Works*, III, *An Unregenerate*, 17–19.

127. *Works*, III, *An Unregenerate*, 19; cf. *Works*, III, *Christ the Mediator*, 195.

128. *Works*, III, *An Unregenerate*, 18.

129. If the soul is the seat of personhood, then this distinction cohered with Goodwin's creationist account of the origin of the soul.

he wrote, 'though that be extrinsecall unto us, considered as particular persons, yet it is intrinsecall, as we are all parts of one common nature: as in him we sinned, so in him we had a will of sinning'.[130] Goodwin, however, appeared to venture further. He was suggesting that it is appropriate for the person to be deemed guilty since the person's nature participated in Adam's sin. Nevertheless, the person can only be legally accounted guilty by means of Adam's federal relation to his descendants.

What emerges is an essentially Augustinian account of original sin chiefly concerned with corruption conveyed through real union to which external union and imputation of Adamic guilt are superadded to provide the legal basis. Here Goodwin reflected the development of incorporating federal ideas within Augustinian realism. Earlier writers had attempted to explain the imputation of Adamic guilt by appealing to real union. For instance, Robert Rollock (1555–1599), whom Goodwin often cited, wrote, 'the first apostasie was not *Adams* only, but did appertaine to vs al … for we were all as then in his loynes, and as parcelles of the substance and nature of the first man; and so we all fell in him and with him'.[131] Perkins appealed to both federal and real unions to explain inherited guilt.[132] Elsewhere, he noted that opinion was divided over the grounds for the transmission of corruption and was reluctant to decide the matter.[133] Edward Reynolds (1599–1676), in his influential 1640 treatise on anthropology and hamartiology, clearly distinguished two unions to account for imputation and corruption:

> We were *all one in Adam, and with him*; In him *legally* in regard of the stipulation and covenant between God and him, we were in him parties in that covenat, had interest in the mercy, & were liable to the curse which belonged to the breach of that Covenant; and in him *naturally*, and therefore unavoidably subject to all that bondage and burden which the *humane nature* contracted in his fall.[134]

As already noted, Owen adopted the same distinction of a twofold union with Adam.[135] Goodwin's and Owen's contribution in this development is displayed by a comparison of the *Westminster Confession of Faith* and the *Savoy Declaration*. The former only appealed to a realistic connection to validate the imputation of Adam's sin: 'They being the root of all man-kind, the guilt of this sin was imputed, and the same death in sin and corrupted nature, conveyed to all their posterity

130. Owen, *A Display of Arminianisme*, 74.

131. Robert Rollock, *A Treatise of Gods Effectual Calling*, trans. Henry Holland (1603), 135.

132. Perkins, *A golden Chaine*, 16.

133. Perkins, *An Exposition of the Symbole*, 89–90.

134. Edward Reynolds, *Three Treatises of the Vanity of the Creature. The Sinfulness of sinne. The Life of Christ* (1631), 134.

135. Owen, *A Display of Arminianisme*, 73–4.

descending from them by ordinary generation.'[136] The latter added the federal explanation: 'They being the Root, and by Gods appointment standing in the room and stead of all mankind, the guilt of this sin was imputed, and corrupted nature conveyed to all posterity descending from them by ordinary generation.'[137]

Goodwin's account of original sin was unique in his attempt to integrate the two theories. Representative union is superimposed onto an essentially Augustinian account of original sin principally concerned with corruption conveyed by real union. An external union is introduced to provide the immediate basis for the imputation of guilt and so legally ground the transmission of corruption. Yet, Goodwin also appealed to a real connection to secure the legitimacy of the imputation of the external union.

4.3.1.2 The imputation of sin to Christ As to the imputation of sin to Christ, Goodwin insisted that Christ was made both sin and a curse.[138] He was made sin by the imputation of guilt; a curse by the infliction of punishment.[139] To demonstrate the necessity of the imputation of guilt, Goodwin again appealed to his premise that guilt is the necessary legal basis for punishment.[140] Thus, in his mind, penal substitutionary atonement required the imputation of guilt to Christ.

For Goodwin there was a crucial difference, however, between the imputation of Adamic guilt to his descendants and the imputation of the elect's guilt to Christ.[141] The former imputation occurs by derivation, since the covenant with Adam was 'a *natural* and *necessary* Covenant'; the latter imputation by 'voluntary Assumption'. The voluntary nature of Christ's imputation was widely advocated by Reformed orthodox puritans.[142] The corollary, according to Goodwin, is that while the human race inherits Adam's guilt necessarily from 'being *one* in him', this is not the case for Christ receiving the guilt of the elect, since he is the head of the union.[143] If anything, Christ's voluntary assumption of guilt establishes a (representative) union with the elect.

4.3.1.3 Conclusion: The imputation of Christ's righteousness Therefore, of these two different grounds for the imputation of guilt, which explained the imputation of

---

136. Westminster Assembly, *The Humble Advice of the Assembly of Divines, Now by Authority of Parliament sitting at Westminster, Concerning A Confession of Faith: With the Quotations and Texts of Scripture annexed* (1647), 12.

137. Savoy Assembly, *A Declaration of the Faith and Order Owned and practised in the Congregational Churches in England: Agreed upon and consented unto By their Elders and Messengers in Their Meeting at the Savoy, Octob. 12. 1658* (1659), 8.

138. *Works*, III, *Christ the Mediator*, 193.

139. *Works*, III, *Christ the Mediator*, 194, 200.

140. *Works*, III, *Christ the Mediator*, 195–6. The problem Goodwin had to explain was why the imputation of guilt to Christ did not inflict a corrupt nature upon him. *Works*, III, *Christ the Mediator*, 194.

141. *Works*, III, *Christ the Mediator*, 194.

142. E.g. Leigh, *A Body of Divinity*, 513; Owen, *Justification*, 237–8.

143. *Works*, III, *Christ the Mediator*, 195.

Christ's righteousness to the elect? While on occasion Goodwin paralleled the imputation of guilt to Christ with the imputation of Christ's righteousness to the elect, in his mind these two imputations were quite distinct.[144] This is evident from their chronological separation: whereas the imputation of guilt to Christ occurred on the first Good Friday, the imputation of Christ's righteousness to the believer occurs at conversion.[145] Moreover, the two imputations do not share the same basis:

> in this doth the Imputation of his Righteousness to us differ from the Imputation of our Sins to him, that his Righteousness is so imputed to us, as we by reason of that Covenant between God and him, may be said to have fulfilled the Law in him, and the Law is said to be fulfilled in us, because we were in him, but not so are our sins imputed to him. It cannot be said in any sense, he was made Sin *in us*, but *for us* onely: or the sin which was committed first in us, and by us, considered in ourselves, was made his; for though we were in him, yet not he in us: for the Root bears the Branches, and not the Branches the Root.[146]

Goodwin insisted upon an asymmetry: whereas the imputation of guilt to Christ occurs by voluntary assumption (and so establishes the union), the imputation of Christ's righteousness to believers results from the necessary consequence of union with Christ. Owen similarly contended that these two imputations hold different relations to real union with Christ:

> The imputation of sin unto Christ, was *antecedent* unto any real union between him and sinners ... But the *imputation* of his Righteousness unto Believers, is consequential in order of nature unto their union with him, whereby it becomes theirs in a *peculiar manner*; so as that there is not a parity of reason that he should be esteemed a sinner, as that they should be accounted Righteous.[147]

Unfortunately, Fesko fails to notice Owen's distinction between the two imputations in this passage. Judging Owen to have held that 'imputation is both antecedent to union and consequent to it', Fesko believes he has key evidence to refute the contention that 'union was more foundational to justification and sanctification' than legal considerations in Owen's thought.[148] However, Owen was consistent: imputation of Christ's righteousness occurs on the basis of a real union between Christ and believers.[149]

144. *Works*, III, *Christ the Mediator*, 194; cf. 196.
145. *Works*, I, *Ephesians*, part II, 296.
146. *Works*, III, *Christ the Mediator*, 195.
147. Owen, *Justification*, 511–12.
148. Fesko, *Beyond Calvin*, 296–7.
149. Inconsistency in fact appeared in the opposite direction: Owen occasionally grounded the imputation of guilt to Christ in union with him: 'That our sins were *transferred* unto Christ and made his, that thereon he underwent the *punishment* that was due unto us for them, and that the Ground hereof, whereinto its Equity is resolved, is the *Union* between

Where similarity in the basis of imputation actually exists is between the imputation of Adam's guilt to his descendants and Christ's righteousness to believers. Goodwin contended that, corresponding to the twofold union of the human race with Adam, there exists a twofold union of believers with Christ.[150] Indeed, Goodwin appealed to the nature of union with Christ to establish the nature of union with Adam. Regarding real union with Adam, Goodwin wrote, 'he the Root, we the Branches, one man; as Christ also is'.[151] Regarding external union with Adam, he reasoned, 'As Christ was the Head of his Body, and they *one Man* in him; so were all as one Man in *Adam*, the Type of Christ therein.'[152] This latter external union, in both the cases of Adam and of Christ, results from their appointments as federal heads.[153] This parallel twofold union is crucial, Goodwin reasoned, for if Adamic guilt is imputed on the basis of an external union, then Christ's righteousness must also be imputed on the basis of an external union:

> The way by which *Adams* Sin was derived, was by imputation, he representing us all; and God ... takes the same course to Justifie us by imputing, or reckoning Christs Righteousness Ours, who represented us also in his Obedience[154]

Such logic was commonplace for federal theologians. Demonstrating that '*Union is the very ground of imputation*', Stedman likewise argued that just as the imputation of Adamic guilt is founded in a legal union, so the imputation of Christ's righteousness is also founded in a legal union.[155]

4.3.2 Union with Christ and Goodwin's tria momenta *of justification*

Given the imputation of Christ's righteousness was explained on the basis of an external union with Christ, the question raised is whether Goodwin believed justification to occur independently of real union and the Spirit's indwelling. This question prompts an examination of Goodwin's stance towards the controversial doctrine of eternal justification (i.e. justification from eternity) which advocated that the elect were justified in God's eternal decrees. Notable advocates in the

---

him and us,' Owen, *Justification*, 249. The explanation appears to be that, for Owen, union with Christ functions in some sense prior to the formation of real union with Christ. See Burger, *Being in Christ*, 38.

     150. *Works*, III, *An Unregenerate*, 20.

     151. *Works*, III, *An Unregenerate*, 20.

     152. *Works*, III, *An Unregenerate*, 20; cf. *Works*, I, *Ephesians*, part I, 62–3.

     153. As noted, the difference resides in the grounds for their appointments: whereas Adam was a covenant head by necessary implication of the law of nature, Christ was appointed by his voluntary acceptance within the *pactum salutis*. *Works*, III, *An Unregenerate*, 13–15; *Works*, I, *Ephesians*, part II, 117.

     154. *Works*, II, *Election*, 439.

     155. Stedman, *Mystical Union*, 212–13.

1640s–1650s included William Twisse (1577/8–1646), William Eyre (1612/13–1669/70) and John Crandon (d. 1654). By the time of the Westminster Assembly, the doctrine had become associated with antinomianism (although it was particularly embraced by the 'imputative' strain of antinomianism), and because of growing alarm over the spread of antinomianism, eternal justification often appeared in the debates concerning justification.[156] Jones complains of a lacuna in scholarly work on this controversy,[157] although the void has begun to be filled with the appearance of Robert McKelvey's survey.[158]

The real battle line concerned not eternal justification per se but whether actual justification occurred prior to faith; eternal justification was but the extreme position. Rutherford wrote, 'Wee hold against *Antinomians* that we are never justified till we beleeve. They say *from eternity we were justified*; or *from the time that the Messiah-dyed, all sins were finished, and wee justified*, or from our birrh.'[159] In fact, the second form (i.e. justification at satisfaction) had been advocated by the influential Pemble.[160] Antinomian figures such as John Eaton (1574/5–1630/1), Crisp and Saltmarsh, seeking to protect justification from the incursion of any human contribution and rallying around the banner of 'free grace' and 'free justification', argued along similar lines. Yet, for these 'imputative antinomians' their driving concern was not locating justification at Christ's death but locating it prior to faith. Thus, while Henry Denne (1605/6?–1666) apparently adhered to this second form, the burden of his *Seven Arguments* was, in fact, to demonstrate that justification occurs before faith.[161] These proponents, fearing that the condition of faith undermines the *sola gratia* of justification, contended that faith merely obtained assurance of justification. This was not only a reaction against legalistic tendencies among mainstream puritanism but also a reaction against Arminianism. Van Dixhoorn explains, 'Antinomians were anti-Arminian to an extreme. Arminians saw faith as the new required condition of the covenant of grace, replacing the old requirement of the covenant of works – keeping of the

---

156. For a recent examination of the Assembly's response to antinomianism, see Whitney Greer Gamble, ' "If Christ Fulfilled the Law, We Are Not Bound": The Westminster Assembly against English Antinomian Soteriology, 1643–1647' (PhD thesis, University of Edinburgh, 2014).

157. Jones, *Why Heaven Kissed Earth*, 230.

158. Robert J. McKelvey, ' "That Error and Pillar of Antinomianism": Eternal Justification', in *Drawn into Controversie: Reformed Theological Diversity and Debates within Seventeenth-Century British Puritanism*, ed. Michael A. G. Haykin and Mark Jones, *Reformed Historical Theology* (Göttingen: Vandenhoeck & Ruprecht, 2011). Also see relevant sections in Boersma, *Hot Pepper Corn*.

159. Rutherford, *Spirituall Antichrist*, part II, 19.

160. Pemble, *Vindiciæ Gratiæ*, 21.

161. See Henry Denne, *Seven Arguments to prove, that in order of working God doth justifie his Elect, before they doe actually beleeve.* (1643). See also Henry Denne, *The Doctrine and Conversation of Iohn Baptist: Delivered in a Sermon* (1642), 36–7.

moral law.'[162] However, the majority including Goodwin feared that justification before faith opened the door to licentiousness. Thus, the main battle line by the time of the Westminster Assembly was drawn at the relation of justification to faith.

It is therefore significant that, as both McKelvey and Jones highlight, Goodwin held to a 'nuanced' version of eternal justification.[163] This 'unique position' was far closer to the discredited doctrine than the majority of orthodox divines could embrace.[164] Goodwin modified and incorporated both forms of justification before faith to construct a *tria momenta* scheme of justification.[165]

The first stage occurred in eternity within the agreement between the Father and the Son in the *pactum salutis*. Christ, agreeing to become the head of the elect, covenanted to have their sins imputed to him and God covenanted the non-imputation of sin to them.[166] Thus, representing the elect, Christ received God's assurance of their pardon. This amounted to an act of justification, but justification 'in Christ' whereby Christ took possession of this assurance for the elect: 'as truly as a Feoffee in Trust may take Lands for one unborn.'[167] Goodwin declared, 'Justified then we were when first elected, though not in our own Persons, yet in our Head, as he had our Persons then given him, and we came to have a Being and Interest in him.'[168] Goodwin, therefore, insisted that this was not justification proper. Herein was the difference with proponents of eternal justification such as Eyre. Following Twisse, Eyre argued that the divine resolve not to impute sins ought to be equated with justification proper. Thus, Eyre believed that the entire act of imputation occurred in eternity: 'This act of justifying is compleat in it self, for God by his eternal and unchangeable Will, not imputing sin to his Elect, none can impute it; and he in like manner imputing Righteousness, none can hinder it.'[169] Contesting claims by Carl Trueman, both Jones and McKelvey therefore rightly conclude that Goodwin did not embrace full-blown eternal justification.[170]

---

162. Van Dixhoorn, 'Reforming the Reformation', 280.

163. See McKelvey, '"That Error and Pillar of Antinomianism"', 242–6; Jones, *Why Heaven Kissed Earth*, 230–8; Beeke and Jones, *A Puritan Theology*, 135–41.

164. McKelvey, '"That Error and Pillar of Antinomianism"', 254; Jones, *Why Heaven Kissed Earth*, 235.

165. *Works*, IV, *Object and Acts*, part I, 104; cf. part II, 130. Goodwin stated a parallel threefold scheme of effectual calling: *Works*, I, *Ephesians*, part II, 190.

166. *Works*, IV, *Object and Acts*, part I, 105.

167. *Works*, IV, *Object and Acts*, part I, 105.

168. *Works*, IV, *Object and Acts*, part I, 104; cf. *Works*, I, *Ephesians*, part I, 59, 63.

169. William Eyre, *Vindiciæ Justificationis Gratuitæ. Justification without Conditions; Or, The Free Justification of a Sinner, Explained, Confirmed, and Vindicated, from the Exceptions, Objections, and seeming Absurdities, which are cast upon it, by the Assertors of Conditional Justification* (1654), 67.

170. McKelvey, '"That Error and Pillar of Antinomianism"', 246; cf. 243; Jones, *Why Heaven Kissed Earth*, 235.

Because of the eternal transaction between God and Christ, Goodwin believed that his conception of eternal justification was stronger than the mere affirmation of the divine intent to justify the elect or of the eternal simultaneity of all events before God.[171] These weaker affirmations were as far as the anti-antinomian Rutherford, also present at the Assembly, was prepared to venture: 'Justification in Gods decree and purpose from eternity, is no more justification then Creation, sanctification, glorification, the crucifying of Christ, and all things that fall out in time; for all these were in the eternall purpose of God.'[172] Moreover, in this matter Goodwin extended beyond the pronouncement of the *Westminster Confession of Faith* (chapter 11.4):

> God did, from all eternity, decree to justifie all the elect, and Christ did, in the fulnesse of time, die for their sins, and rise again for their justification: nevertheless, they are not justified, untill the holy Spirit doth in due time, actually apply Christ unto them.[173]

As Jones observes, Goodwin's influence may be seen in the revised version found in the *Savoy Declaration*.[174] The word 'personally' was inserted so that its end reads: 'they are not justified personally untill the holy Spirit doth in due time actually apply Christ unto them.'[175] Goodwin believed that his middle position of eternal justification in Christ remained within the bounds of orthodoxy and would 'clear the great Controversy, that is now between the *Antinomians* (as they call them) and others, about being justified before Conversion'.[176]

The second stage occurred in Christ's redemptive work. Here Goodwin incorporated a modified view of justification at satisfaction. Through his death and resurrection, Christ was justified in his own person for the elect as their covenantal representative. Like the first moment, this act of justification was representative, 'in Christ', rather than comprising justification proper. Yet, whereas in the first Christ received the assurance of pardon on behalf of the elect, in the second he received 'the *actual Possession of Justification of Life*' on their behalf.[177] Goodwin therefore drew the parallel with Adam: believers were justified in Christ in the same sense that all were declared guilty in Adam.[178] Prior to birth each individual is (representatively) condemned in Adam; following birth each is condemned in their own person for Adam's sin.[179]

171. *Works*, IV, *Object and Acts*, part I, 105.
172. Rutherford, *Spirituall Antichrist*, part II, 19; cf. Leigh, *A Body of Divinity*, 515.
173. Westminster Assembly, *The Humble Advice*, 23.
174. Jones, *Why Heaven Kissed Earth*, 234.
175. Savoy Assembly, *A Declaration*, 14.
176. *Works*, I, *Ephesians*, part II, 219.
177. *Works*, IV, *Object and Acts*, part I, 105.
178. *Works*, IV, *Object and Acts*, part I, 106.
179. *Works*, I, *Ephesians*, part II, 296.

Goodwin insisted, however, that these two stages are insufficient for justification since both strictly reside in the domain of redemption accomplished, rather than redemption applied:

> But these two Acts of *Justification* are wholly out of us, immanent Acts in God; and tho they concern us, and are *towards us*, yet are not Acts of God *upon us*, they being performed towards us, not as actually existing in our selves, but only as existing in our Head, who covenanted for us, and represented us[180]

There must be a further act, he concluded, whereby believers receive justification not merely in Christ as a covenantal head but in their own persons.[181] Goodwin found support from scriptural declarations that justification follows belief and from declarations implying a '*now* of *Justification*'.[182] Upon believing, he held, there is a divine act accomplishing 'real justification' and establishing a 'real moral change' in the estate of the believer.[183] Whereas the first two stages were 'immanent Acts which lie in God's Breast', the third concerns God's judgement before creation according to his published rule that those who believe are justified.[184] Goodwin insisted, 'A Man before he believeth is unjustified, therefore he is said to be justified by Faith; and he is a Child of Wrath until he believe'.[185] This was the consensus opinion at the Assembly where Goodwin had stated, 'Justification doth follow upon beleiving, the act of faith'.[186] To hold otherwise, he contended, would be to undermine the reality of justification at conversion.[187] Thus, Goodwin believed that he had avoided the key error of denying justification *in foro divino* upon belief.[188] Pemble had maintained that justification following faith is restricted to the conscience and therefore is a matter of assurance.[189] In contrast, Goodwin stressed that the final act of justification is not simply the believer's realization of a pre-existing justified status.[190] In fact, he laboured to demonstrate that justifying faith does not entail assurance.[191]

---

180. *Works*, IV, *Object and Acts*, part I, 106.

181. *Works*, IV, *Object and Acts*, part I, 106–7; cf. *Works*, I, *Ephesians*, part II, 200–1.

182. *Works*, IV, *Object and Acts*, part I, 106.

183. *Works*, IV, *Object and Acts*, part II, 80; part I, 107.

184. *Works*, I, *Ephesians*, part II, 296–7.

185. *Works*, V, *Glory of the Gospel*, 17; cf. *Works*, IV, *Object and Acts*, part I, 106.

186. Van Dixhoorn, *Minutes*, volume 2, 173. In agreement, Seaman warned that the proposed statement on justification 'seemes to hold out that the use of faith is only to apprehend that which is already done, which doth entirely jumpe with the opinion of the Antinomians: that a man is justifyed before he repents & beleives'. Van Dixhoorn, *Minutes*, volume 2, 42.

187. *Works*, I, *Ephesians*, part II, 300.

188. *Works*, IV, *Object and Acts*, part I, 169; part II, 129–30; *Works*, I, *Ephesians*, part II, 299.

189. Pemble, *Vindiciæ Gratiæ*, 22, 49.

190. *Works*, IV, *Object and Acts*, part I, 106–7; part II, 16.

191. *Works*, I, *Ephesians*, part II, 300.

The distinctiveness of Goodwin's scheme among his contemporaries becomes apparent by comparison.[192] McKelvey claims that Crandon, contending against the neonomian Baxter, espoused a similar scheme to Goodwin's in which eternal justification is maintained, yet faith assigned a role in actual justification above mere assurance.[193] The main evidence presented by McKelvey is Crandon's summary statement:

> That the Transient Act of Justification consisteth not onely in Gods evidencing and manifesting to the beleever that he was really justified in God from eternity; but also in Gods Actual, and Judiciall pronouncing of the sentence of Absolution to the soul drawn to Gods Tribunal, and gasping for pardon thorough Christ. By means whereof the poor sinner is constituted, as well as declared actually, and personally righteous, and that before God his Justifier.[194]

However, here Crandon specified that God's declaration in justification by faith is 'to the soul', that is, *in foro conscientiae*. Crandon had explained earlier:

> the justification which is by faith consisteth not onely in a bare apprehension of our justification and pardon from God, (for this is onely mans act, and no express act of God) but first in Gods actual declaration, evidencing and certifying the conscience of man drawn to the barre of judgement (set up as it were in the conscience)[195]

Accordingly, Crandon consistently understood justification by faith to occur in the conscience of the believer.[196] Since Goodwin maintained that the final act of

---

192. Jones claims that Peter Bulkeley (1583–1659) held a similar scheme. Jones, *Why Heaven Kissed Earth*, 235. However, while Bulkeley stated a threefold scheme in passing, McKelvey rightly suggests that Bulkeley simply believed that justification was purposed in eternity and obtained in the work of Christ. McKelvey, '"That Error and Pillar of Antinomianism"', 245.

193. McKelvey, '"That Error and Pillar of Antinomianism"', 259; cf. 231. The following comment by McKelvey is perplexing and inconsistent with his own argument: 'Like Goodwin, Crandon seems content to live with the tension of embracing justification *in foro Dei* from eternity together with actual justification *in foro conscientiae* in time.' McKelvey, '"That Error and Pillar of Antinomianism"', 257–8.

194. John Crandon, *Mr. Baxters Aphorisms Exorized and Anthorized. Or An Examination of and Answer to a Book written by Mr. Ri: Baxter Teacher of the Church at Kederminster in Worcester-shire, entituled, Aphorisms of Justification. Together with A vindication of Justification by meer Grace, from all the Popish and Arminian Sophisms* (1654), part I, 246.

195. Crandon, *Aphorisms Exorized*, part I, 237.

196. Crandon's earlier words must also be interpreted similarly: 'None else but a believer, nor he, until he actually beleeveth, is thus actually justified, or hath pardon of sinnes and absolution from wrath declared and pronounced of God in his conscience.' Crandon,

justification is *in foro Dei*, Crandon's scheme is not as similar to Goodwin's as McKelvey contends.

A useful second comparator is Owen's scheme. Like Crandon, Owen opposed Baxter; yet, unlike Crandon, Owen emphatically rejected justification before faith and even the term 'eternal justification'. Nevertheless, Owen entertained sympathies with proponents of eternal justification,[197] and in his account of justification by faith struggled to avoid collapsing justification by faith to *in foro conscientiae*.[198] For reasons discussed later, Owen introduced a distinction between 'Absolution in Heaven' and 'compleat Justification', with the former occurring causally prior to faith. Although he denied that the latter is merely *in foro conscientiae*, he still felt compelled to insist that both occur simultaneously in order to distance his concept of heavenly absolution from justification before faith.[199]

Goodwin relying on the notion of justification in Christ was more successful than Crandon and Owen in avoiding actual justification before faith. Nevertheless, some orthodox writers questioned such a scheme. Admitting that notable divines including Zanchi and Johann Heinrich Alsted (1588-1638) had advocated a notion of justification in Christ before faith, Burgess recognized that those who espoused this approach did not 'strengthen the Antinomists' because faith is still required for justification proper.[200] Yet, Burgess took exception to the view: 'even the truth of this opinion may modestly be questioned … the learned men of that opinion, speak as if God then passed a formal Justification upon all (though afterwards to be applied) that are elected'.[201] Goodwin, at least, spoke in such terms, since in each of his three stages God pronounces a legal verdict.[202] Burgess objected on three grounds.[203] First, God cannot simultaneously both impute and not impute sins to the elect. Secondly, justification by faith is rendered merely a declaration in public or *in foro conscientiae* only. Thirdly, Christ cannot act as the head of the elect until they believe. Burgess, therefore, questioned whether

---

Aphorisms Exorized, part I, 233. McKelvey misconstrues Crandon's meaning by omitting the second half of this quotation. McKelvey, '"That Error and Pillar of Antinomianism"', 257.

197. John Owen, *Vindiciæ Evangelicæ Or, The Mystery of the Gospell Vindicated, and Socinianisme Examined, In the Consideration, and Confutation of A Catechisme, called A Scripture Catechisme, Written by J. Biddle M.A. And the Catechisme of Valentinus Smalcius, commonly called the Racovian Catechisme* (Oxford, 1655), appendix, 4.

198. John Owen, *Of the Death of Christ, The Price he paid, and the Purchase he made. Or, The Satisfaction, and Merit of the Death of Christ cleered, the Universality of Redemption thereby oppugned: And The Doctrine Concerning these things formerly delivered in a Treatise against Universal Redemption Vindicated from the Exceptions, and Objections of Mr Baxter* (1650), 79-80.

199. Owen, *Vindiciæ Evangelicæ*, appendix, 21, 27.

200. Burgess, *Justification (1651)*, 176.

201. Burgess, *Justification (1651)*, 176.

202. *Works*, IV, *Object and Acts*, part I, 107.

203. Burgess, *Justification (1651)*, 177-8.

the position espoused by divines such as Goodwin was coherent and avoided the alleged antinomian error. While Goodwin attempted to defend the coherency of his position by appealing to analogies of an inheritance held by a trustee, it is questionable whether a legal verdict can be possessed and transferred in the same manner as financial assets.[204]

Nevertheless, for the present purposes what must be noted is that Goodwin's distinctive *tria momenta* scheme was not arbitrarily introduced to respond to the antinomian threat but is anchored to basic structures in his soteriology. The three acts of justification correspond to the three divine persons: 'who as they have a distinct Hand in the whole Work of Redemption, so also in this main Point of our Justification.'[205] Here it is instructive to revisit the Trinitarian structure of the central treatises of Goodwin's grand project. His brief work *Man's Restauration* introduced the three succeeding treatises by arguing for a distinctive work of each person in salvation: 'the three works of *Father, Son* and *Spirit*, namely, of *Election, Redemption*, and the *Application* of both, which is the special work of the Spirit.'[206] This structure, he believed, emerges from Ephesians 1:3-14 and is particularly evident in the divine work of salvation.[207] The following three treatises – *Election, Christ the Mediator* and *The Holy Ghost* – expound each in turn.[208] Goodwin's *tria momenta* of justification, therefore, correlates with the Trinitarian structure of his grand project. The first stage he assigned to the Father's work of election, the second stage to Christ's historical act of redemption and the third stage to the work of the Spirit in application. Advancing a Trinitarian soteriological scheme subverted not only non-Trinitarian heterodox teachings but also the soteriologies of 'imputative antinomians'. As Whitney Gamble observes, there was a 'failure on the part of antinomian theology to credit adequately the Spirit with a specific role in the process of redemption.'[209] In contrast, Goodwin's Trinitarian structure demanded that justification, along with other salvific benefits, must be applied by the Spirit:

> There are three sorts of works whereby our Salvation is compleated and accomplished. 1. *Immanent* in God towards us, as his *Eternal Love* set and past upon us; out of which he chose us, and designed this and all Blessings to us. 2. *Transient*, in Christ done *for us*; in all he did or suffered representing us, and in our stead. 3. Applicatory, wrought in us, and upon us, in the endowing us with all those Blessings by the Spirit: As *Calling, Justification, Sanctification, Glorification*.[210]

---

204. E.g. *Works*, IV, *Object and Acts*, part I, 105–6.

205. *Works*, IV, *Object and Acts*, part I, 104.

206. *Works*, III, *Man's Restauration*, 11; cf. *Works*, V, *Gospel Holiness*, 89.

207. *Works*, III, *Man's Restauration*, 14–15; cf. *Works*, I, *Ephesians*, part I, 96, 217.

208. *Works*, V, *The Holy Ghost*, 40.

209. Gamble, 'The Westminster Assembly against English Antinomian Soteriology', 197.

210. *Works*, V, *The Holy Ghost*, 374.

This is significant since it implies that the very structure of both Goodwin's soteriology and his grand project demands that justification proper results from the work of the Spirit.

While the role of the Spirit is yet to be discussed, it should be further noted that for Goodwin the three acts of justification also correspond to three kinds of union existing between Christ and the elect.[211] There exists, in order: a union rooted in election, a union underpinning Christ's representative actions and a real union effected by the indwelling Spirit. Sibbes had, in fact, already proposed the same threefold scheme of union with Christ.[212] What Goodwin did was to use this scheme to ground his *tria momenta* of justification:

> All these Acts of *Justification*, as they depend upon Christ, so upon our being one with Christ; and look what kind of Union there is, answerable is the Act of Justification past forthwith. From all Eternity we were one with Christ by Stipulation, he by a secret Covenant undertaking for us, and answerably that Act of God's justifying us was but as we were considered in his Undertaking. When Christ died and rose again, we were in him by Representation, as performing it for us, and no otherwise; but as so considered we were justified. But now when we come in our Persons, by our own Consent, to be made one with him actually, then we come in our Persons through him to be personally and in our selves justified, and receive the Atonement by Faith.[213]

While Goodwin denounced views that reduce union with Christ to 'outward Relations', he did not exclude external unions as additional to real union with Christ.[214] Such external unions, however, are 'virtual and representative' in comparison to real union which is an 'actual Union'.[215] In Goodwin's mind, the significance of external union is to permit Christ's actions to be representative on behalf of the elect, whereas real union is reserved as the basis for the application of salvation. The first two unions, therefore, underpin and anticipate real union: all that Christ had obtained in promise on behalf of the elect and then received in person on behalf of the elect is subsequently delivered into the possession of the elect by real union.[216] Thus, consistent with his stress upon justification proper following the work of the Spirit and faith, Goodwin was adamant that justification

211. These three unions receive brief attention from Jones and more recently Kim. Jones, *Why Heaven Kissed Earth*, 235–7; Kim, 'Salvation by Faith', 200–1.

212. Sibbes, *An Exposition of the Third Chapter of Philippians*, 102–3.

213. *Works*, IV, *Object and Acts*, part I, 108; cf. part II, 130; *Works*, I, *Ephesians*, part I, 62–4, 71; part II, 214–15.

214. *Works*, II, *The Knowledg*, 21.

215. *Works*, I, *Ephesians*, part I, 64.

216. *Works*, I, *Ephesians*, part II, 215. Goodwin's scheme requires that the same elect persons be in view at each stage. *Works*, V, *The Holy Ghost*, 52; *Works*, I, *Ephesians*, part I, 55; part II, 135.

proper must be founded in real union with Christ.[217] This conclusion contrasted with the views of those such as Eyre who, believing that justification proper occurs in eternity, founded justification proper in a union established in divine election.[218] Typical for advocates of justification before faith, Eyre understood real union as a benefit resulting from justification. Eaton concurred,

> The third excellent benefit of the Gospel wrought upon us by *Free Iustification*, is our wonderfull *Vnion into Christ*, whereby wee are by the power of the holy Ghost though mystically and spiritually, yet, truly, really and substantially so ingraffed and united into Christ.[219]

Since, he reasoned, a lack of cleansing (i.e. justification) of the individual precludes union and indwelling.[220] Views concerning the relation of real union and justification proper, therefore, were polarized. Goodwin unequivocally contended for the majority opinion in which justification proper must result from real union with Christ.

4.3.3 Real union as the foundation of justification

Given justification proper rests upon real union by the indwelling Spirit, then, according to Goodwin, in what manner does real union cause justification and how is that compatible with an external union providing the immediate basis for imputation? What must be examined are the two parts of real union with Christ: the divine part involving the Spirit's indwelling and the human part in the act of faith. It is instructive to begin with the believer's part. Goodwin repeatedly characterized faith as the sole required condition or qualification for justification.[221] He insisted that God had set a rule in his Word that those who believe are justified.[222] In other words, there was a covenantal arrangement whereby God bound himself to justify those who fulfil the condition of faith.[223] In this sense, real union is essential for justification since it contains faith, yet the immediate basis for imputation can be identified as the external union of the covenant of grace.[224] Thus, Kim's analysis is

217. Kim comes to the same basic conclusion regarding the relationship of justification to real union, but his other comments regarding union with Christ are more problematic. Kim, 'Salvation by Faith', 201; cf. 197.

218. Eyre, *Vindiciæ Justificationis Gratuitæ*, 8.

219. Eaton, *Honey-Combe*, 429.

220. Eaton, *Honey-Combe*, 423–4, 437–8.

221. *Works*, IV, *Object and Acts*, part I, 166.

222. *Works*, I, *Ephesians*, part II, 297; cf. *Works*, IV, *Object and Acts*, part I, 107; *Christ Set Forth*, 51.

223. Here Goodwin reflected mainstream Puritan opinion. See Von Rohr, *The Covenant of Grace in Puritan Thought*, 53–8, 63–72.

224. Given this external union is conditional upon faith it cannot be simply identified with either of the two external unions in Goodwin's *tria momenta* scheme.

wrong in failing to recognize any role for an external union in Goodwin's account of justification.[225] For Goodwin, imputation is a distinct and subsequent divine act to the completion of real union by faith: upon believing 'then doth God put forth another Act, (and it is the last Act, and the Accomplishment of all) and pronounceth us righteous in our selves through him.'[226] This arrangement, widely held by mainstream puritan divines, allows imputation to occur on the basis of an external federal union with Christ, yet also upholds justification by faith in contradistinction to 'imputative antinomians'.

However, Goodwin also expressed reservations over the term 'condition' fearing it might suggest faith functions as a meritorious condition.[227] This concern was common within mainstream puritanism.[228] With English writers such as Hammond and Taylor openly rejecting the established protestant account of justification and stressing the need for moral renovation, the threat of moralism was on the rise in the 1640s and 1650s.[229] Hammond stressed the qualifications for justification as 'Faith, repentance, firme purpose of a new life, and the rest of those graces, upon which in the Gospel pardon is promised the Christian; all comprizable in the *new creature, conversion, regeneration,* &c.'[230] This emphasis upon moral reformation as the condition of justification, along with Hammond's definition of justification as merely the non-imputation of sin, evidences the Socinian influence upon Hammond's conception of justification.[231] Taylor, denying the immediate imputation of Christ's righteousness, argued that 'our Faith and sincere endevours are through Christ accepted in stead of legal righteousness: that is; we are justified through Christ, by imputation, not of Christs, nor our own righteousness: but of our faith and endevours of righteousness as if they were perfect.'[232] Even within the puritan fold, some veered in a moralistic direction in their insistence upon the condition of faith for justification. While Baxter was notorious in this regard, other divines such as John Goodwin insisted upon the condition of faith because faith itself was understood to be imputed to the believer.[233]

Seeking to avoid rising moralism on the one hand and antinomian error on the other, Goodwin retained the language of conditionality, but sought to realign

---

225. Kim, 'Salvation by Faith', 197.

226. *Works*, IV, *Object and Acts*, part I, 107.

227. *Works*, I, *Ephesians*, part II, 301; *Works*, IV, *Object and Acts*, part I, 162; part II, 61.

228. McKelvey, '"That Error and Pillar of Antinomianism"', 231; Beeke and Jones, *A Puritan Theology*, 305–10; Kim, 'Salvation by Faith', 92–6.

229. See Dewey D. Wallace, Jr, *Puritans and Predestination: Grace in English Protestant Theology, 1525–1695* (Chapel Hill: University of North Carolina Press, 1982), 126–8; Allison, *The Rise of Moralism*, 63–73, 96–106.

230. Hammond, *Practical Catechisme*, 47.

231. See especially *The Racovian Catechisme*, 152.

232. Jeremy Taylor, *An Answer to a Letter Written by the R.R. The Ld Bp of Rochester. Concerning The Chapter of Original Sin, In the Vnum Necessarium* (1656), 41.

233. Allison, *The Rise of Moralism*, 164–5.

it positively. Sharing these concerns, Owen conceded, 'There is an *obvious sense* wherein Faith may be called the *Condition of our Justification*.'[234] In particular, Goodwin stressed the instrumental nature of faith.[235] Since faith is a mere receiving, he contended, it magnifies the pure grace of justification.[236] At least in part, he believed, this explains why God ordained faith to be the requirement for justification. Here also should be noted Kim's observation that Goodwin insisted that God made 'the Covenant of Grace primarily with [Christ], and with him as for us'.[237] Thus, the primary (i.e. meritorious) conditions of the covenant were fulfilled by Christ and the conditions upon believers must be secondary and of a different (i.e. instrumental) order. Whether or not other Reformed divines advocated the same construction of covenant theology, the instrumental nature of faith was, according to Owen, the consensus view: '*Protestant Divines* until of late, have unanimously affirmed Faith to be the *instrumental cause* of our Justification.'[238] Owen's opponent, Baxter, ascribing too much to faith was the notable exception.[239] In contrast, figures such as Crisp in advocating justification before faith denied the instrumental role of faith.[240]

Moreover, Goodwin and mainstream divines emphasized that, by granting faith, God enables the covenant condition to be fulfilled.[241] For Goodwin, this point was entailed in Christ's role as the primary contracting party of the covenant. He wrote, 'in Scripture we read of Promises, not only Conditional ... but also Absolute' because God 'undertakes to fulfil the Conditions themselves, and that Covenant must needs be made with Christ first and mediately for us'.[242] Accordingly, while in one passage Goodwin insisted that union, rather than regeneration, is the grounds

234. Owen, *Justification*, 154. Thomas Warren (*c.* 1617-1694) detailed the sense in which faith is a condition. Thomas Warren, *Vnbeleevers No subjects of iustification, Nor of mystical Vnion to Christ* (1654), 128-9.

235. *Works*, IV, *Object and Acts*, part I, 104; part III, 4. Goodwin noted that strictly speaking it is the habit of faith, rather than the act which is the instrument; the act is the means. *Works*, I, *Ephesians*, part II, 300.

236. *Works*, I, *Ephesians*, part II, 200, 286, 297-8; *Works*, IV, *Object and Acts*, part II, 51; part III, 4, 11.

237. *Christ Set Forth*, 34-5; cf. *Works*, III, *Christ the Mediator*, 28. In this way, Goodwin saw an underlying unity of the covenant of grace and covenant of redemption. *Works*, III, *Election*, 355. See Kim, 'Salvation by Faith', 152-61. Kim notes that Goodwin's position here resembles the views of the more enthusiastic Petto.

238. Owen, *Justification*, 147; cf. Leigh, *A Body of Divinity*, 506, 528.

239. Boersma, *Hot Pepper Corn*, 183.

240. Crisp, *Christ Alone Exalted In the Perfection and Encouragements of the Saints*, 225.

241. E.g. *Works*, IV, *Object and Acts*, part I, 162-3. For the same point in other writers, see: Von Rohr, *The Covenant of Grace in Puritan Thought*, 80-5.

242. *Works*, III, *Christ the Mediator*, 28.

That Union with Christ is the first fundamental thing of Justification and Sanctification, and all. Christ first takes us, and then sends his Spirit. He

of justification,[243] nevertheless justification still rests on regeneration as an intermediary step, since without regeneration faith is impossible.[244] For this reason, Goodwin maintained that regeneration decisively changes the legal terms of an individual's state. Before conversion an individual exists in a state of sin and wrath but afterwards in a state of grace and life. He reasoned from the general principle: 'A state is a permanent fixed condition, whether of good or evil, continued without cessation or interruption, until the Legal Terms of that Condition be altered.'[245] Taking up the illustrations of slavery and of marriage found in Romans chapters 6 and 7, Goodwin argued that death effects a change in legal terms. Applying this to the case of conversion, he concluded, 'So then Regeneration which consists in the Mortification of Lusts, and quickning us with Christ, and Faith that marries us to him, makes the alteration, and the Resurrection of Christ follows us still.'[246] By producing faith, regeneration establishes a new legal relation to Christ, places the individual into a permanent state of justification and grants legal rights to a heavenly inheritance.[247] In this way, regeneration is necessarily inseparable from pardon and justification.[248]

In conclusion, then, the condition of faith stood behind Goodwin's insistence that justification must be applied to the believer by the Holy Spirit.[249] The Spirit applies justification by producing faith:[250] he reveals the object of faith, Christ, within the believer and infuses created grace enabling spiritual sight of Christ.[251] In fact, Goodwin contended that only real union produces the certain knowledge required for justifying faith in the understanding and can sustain justifying faith in

> apprehends us first. It is not my being regenerate that puts me into a right of all those priviledges, but it is Christ takes me, and then gives me his Spirit, Faith, Holiness, &c It is through our Union with Christ, and the perfect Holiness of his Nature, to whom we are united, that we partake of the priviledges of the Covenant of Grace.

243. *Works*, III, *Christ the Mediator*, 347. The language of this passage strains not only Goodwin's statements on the relation of justification and regeneration but also his statements elsewhere on the relation of union with Christ to the indwelling of the Spirit. See p. 56 fn. 151. While it is difficult to remove the inconsistency regarding the relation of justification and regeneration (it may represent earlier views he later abandoned), the force of his concern is clear from the context and consistent with his wider teaching: he wished to anchor justification in the certainty of union rather than progress in transformation.

244. *Works*, V, *The Holy Ghost*, 421; cf. 71.

245. *Works*, V, *The Holy Ghost*, 69.

246. *Works*, V, *The Holy Ghost*, 71.

247. *Works*, V, *The Holy Ghost*, 144; cf. 114.

248. *Works*, V, *The Holy Ghost*, 75.

249. *Works*, V, *The Holy Ghost*, 17, 54.

250. *Works*, V, *The Holy Ghost*, 16–17, 42.

251. *Works*, IV, *Object and Acts*, part II, 3–4.

the will.[252] In other words, the indwelling of the Spirit enables the faith condition of the covenant of grace to be met.[253]

The question remaining is whether the Spirit's part of real union has a distinct role as the grounds of justification. Sibbes, when defending a distinct work of the Spirit in justification, assumed not and instead merely appealed to the Spirit's work of producing justifying faith in the believer.[254] The Spirit's indwelling per se bore no significance. Consequently, this resulted in common ground with the conservative majority who rejected the indwelling of the Spirit's person. Stedman, for example, assigned justification specifically to the faith part of real union and transformation to the Spirit's part.[255] The Spirit infuses the habit of faith, but justification rests upon the act of faith.

A careful reading of Goodwin, however, reveals that he assumed a distinct significance of the Spirit's indwelling in the application of justification. It should be noted that Goodwin, in his realignment of the conditionality of faith, also stressed that faith is part of salvation.[256] Here was not only the idea that faith is a divine gift contained within regeneration but also that faith is the necessary means for experiencing the fullness of salvation. Goodwin secured this latter aspect by appealing to an analogy:

Nor indeed are those we call conditions of the Covenant on our part, as believing on Christ, turning from sin, other than necessary means of being made partakers of Christ, and Salvation: As if one should say to an hungry man, there is meat which shall be yourss, to live by it, if you will eat it and digest it, else not; In this case who will say this is barely a Condition, for it is the very partaking of the meat it self, whereby a man makes it his own.[257]

Far from understanding faith as an arbitrary condition imposed by God, Goodwin therefore contended that faith is demanded by the nature of salvation. His favourite analogy was marriage, since he was convinced that, like marriage, salvation consists in the enjoyment of interpersonal communion:

for a Father to say to one he bestows his Daughter upon in Marriage, Lo, she is your Wife, take her, and Marry her; This is not a condition of her being his Wife, as external to it, but it is that very intrinsical and essential Act, whereby she becomes his, and he her Husband[258]

252. *Works*, IV, *Object and Acts*, part II, 8, 14.

253. *Works*, II, *Election*, 37.

254. Sibbes, *The Excellencie of the Gospell*, 103–4.

255. Stedman, *Mystical Union*, 134–5.

256. *Works*, I, *Ephesians*, part II, 200; *Works*, IV, *Object and Acts*, part II, 61.

257. *Works*, II, *Election*, 65.

258. *Works*, II, *Election*, 65; cf. *Works*, IV, *Object and Acts*, part I, 200; part II, 61; part III, 6.

Because faith is the means of receiving Christ's person, Goodwin concluded that faith is the condition demanded by the nature of salvation. Here, though, Goodwin had apparently equivocated, since the issue at hand was the necessity of faith for justification rather than communion with Christ. Within his thought, however, justification is secondary to receiving Christ himself.[259] Indeed, all of Christ's benefits are received as a consequence of embracing his person. Thus, justification is a subsequent act that God performs upon the establishment of a real union between Christ and the believer. Goodwin's repeated usage of the marriage analogy points in this direction: marriage fundamentally concerns the union of two persons; legal benefits are derivative of the marriage relationship.[260]

For this reason, Goodwin particularly stressed faith as the consent of the believer. As marriage is established by mutual consent, so the believer must consent to marriage with Christ to complete union with him.[261] Because consent is the crucial factor, Goodwin was convinced that faith must be expressed in the faculty of the will:

> for the making a real Union with him (so far as on our part it is made) it lyes not primarily in believing Christ is mine, or that Christ is, but in joining my self to his Person, in shooting in of my Will into him, in taking him, and consenting to be his[262]

Justification, therefore, occurs as a result of real union forged by consent:

> e're any Man can believe his sins are forgiven, or look upon any Priviledge which is to be had by Christ as his own, he must first be united to Christ, and Christ must be made his; there must be an act of Faith closing with his Person, consenting to be his[263]

Faith, then, is the condition of justification because it is intrinsic to Goodwin's relational conception of real union with Christ.[264]

In light of the marriage analogy, the significance of the indwelling Spirit becomes clear. Goodwin equated the Spirit's indwelling with Christ taking hold of the believer: "'Tis true indeed, the Union on Christ's Part is in order of Nature first made by the Spirit: therefore ... he is said first *to comprehend us e're we can comprehend him*."[265] Thus, if believers take hold of Christ by faith, then Christ

---

259. *Works*, IV, *Object and Acts*, part I, 150; part II, 70, 77.

260. *Works*, II, *Election*, 441; *Works*, IV, *Object and Acts*, part II, 57.

261. *Works*, IV, *Object and Acts*, part I, 135.

262. *Works*, IV, *Object and Acts*, part II, 15; cf. part III, 6; *Works*, I, *Ephesians*, part I, 248.

263. *Works*, IV, *Object and Acts*, part II, 77; cf. part I, 108.

264. *Works*, IV, *Object and Acts*, part II, 130.

265. *Works*, IV, *Object and Acts*, part III, 6; cf. part II, 15.

'took hold of us by his Spirit'.[266] The external covenant permits the imputation of Christ's righteousness once Christ and the believer take hold of each other: 'When Christ by his Spirit knits us to him, and works Faith in us ... then doth God put forth another Act ... and pronounceth us righteous in our selves through him'.[267] Without the double bond of real union existing between Christ and the believer, imputation would be illegitimate since it would lack a real basis. Moreover, in Goodwin's mind, real union with Christ can only be inherently relational if the Spirit's person indwells and reveals Christ's person within the believer. Thus, justification must result from (marriage) union with Christ established by the indwelling of the Spirit's person.

Real union, therefore, is necessary but not sufficient for justification. As the marriage analogy suggests, in addition to the two parties taking hold of each other, an external covenant is required as the immediate basis of imputation. The necessity of both an external and a real union was most explicitly stated in Goodwin's early sermon on Ephesians 3:17. There he articulated a threefold scheme of unions: a relative union (i.e. external union), a real union involving the indwelling of Christ's person and a union involving Christ's indwelling by faith (i.e. through inner revelation of Christ).[268] The second and third correspond to the two parts of real union: the Spirit's indwelling and the believer's faith. Indeed, in the subsequent sermon, Goodwin combined the second and third unions, and so assumed a twofold union with Christ: 'A *Relative Union*' and 'a substantial Union, and a communicative Union'.[269] In both sermons Goodwin illustrated the necessity of both relative and real unions with Christ by appealing to the legal and real sides of marital union. Importantly, Goodwin asserted that the legal union is not completed until there is a mutual taking hold of each other: 'this Union is fully and compleatly done, when first we are turned to God, and when Christ first takes us, as ever it shall be'.[270] Since this external union is completed at regeneration, it is not to be equated with the external unions of his *tria momenta* scheme but is a distinct external union only legitimized once Christ and the believer mutually take hold of each other.

Here a difference with Owen may be detected. In his treatise on justification, Owen repeatedly stated that the immediate basis of imputation is real union with Christ:

God hath appointed that there shall be an *immediate Foundation* of the Imputation of the Satisfaction and Righteousness of Christ unto us ... this is our *actual coalescency into one mystical person* with him by Faith.[271]

266. *Works*, IV, *Object and Acts*, part I, 115.
267. *Works*, IV, *Object and Acts*, part I, 107.
268. *Works*, I, *Thirteen Sermons*, 40.
269. *Works*, I, *Thirteen Sermons*, 45–6.
270. *Works*, I, *Thirteen Sermons*, 45–6.
271. Owen, *Justification*, 307; cf. 246, 249–50, 294–5.

Christ and believers, he maintained, form a 'mystical person' not as the result of an external union but as the result of the Spirit and faith. Owen was distancing himself from Baxter who opted for an external 'political' union rather than a real union with Christ.[272] Burger observes that, while mystical union appeared elsewhere in Owen's works, the notion of a mystical person was unique and central to this treatise and was employed solely to account for the validity of imputation.[273] In contrast to Owen, Goodwin did not appeal to the notion of a mystical person as the basis for imputation.[274] In fact, denying that the guilt of believers is imputed to the indwelling Spirit, Goodwin explained that real union may only function as the immediate ground of imputation if it amounts to a hypostatic union.[275] What informed Goodwin here was the Nestorian controversy over the *communicatio idiomatum*. The Chalcedonian statement sided with Cyril of Alexandria and declared that properties of Christ's humanity may be ascribed to the divine person because of the hypostatical nature of the incarnational union. Goodwin was adamant that while real union forms Christ and the church into one mystical person, this does not amount to a hypostatic union lest the heterodox theology of the radicals be conceded. Undoubtedly, Owen would have agreed, but he did not address this matter.[276] Now the significance of Goodwin's appeals to the marriage union of two persons to ground justification is apparent. The imputation of Christ's righteousness to believers cannot be immediately grounded in real union and mystical indwelling but requires an additional external and voluntary covenant of persons akin to the marriage covenant. Here Goodwin was not alone. Concerning real union with Christ, Flavel wrote, 'The Union I here speak of, is not a *foederal Union*; or an Union by Covenant only: such a Union indeed there is betwixt Christ and believers, but that is consequential to and wholly dependent upon this.'[277] In this remark Flavel captured the relation between external and real union that Goodwin assumed. While imputation occurs on the basis of the external union of the covenant of grace, this external union grants legal rights only to those united to Christ by a real union. In this way, Goodwin maintained that justification is an implication of a real state of affairs brought about by the indwelling Spirit.

272. Boersma, *Hot Pepper Corn*, 234–5.

273. Burger, *Being in Christ*, 41, 44, 46; cf. Hunsinger, 'Justification and Mystical Union'. Burgess appealed to the same notion to validate imputation. Burgess, *Justification (1654)*, 300, 365–6.

274. For Goodwin's use of this notion, see pp. 223–4.

275. *Works*, V, *The Holy Ghost*, 35; *Works*, II, *The Knowledg*, 88.

276. Baylor argues that on occasion Owen also referred to mystical person in a legal sense prior to the indwelling of the Spirit in order to explain the basis of imputation. However, following Fesko (see p. 145), Baylor conflates the imputation of guilt to Christ and righteousness to believers. Baylor, '"One with Him in Spirit"', 444. Moreover, Baylor concedes that Owen 'finally locates the basis for the imputation of Christ's righteousness in *mystical* union with Christ'. Baylor, '"One with Him in Spirit"', 450.

277. Flavel, *The Method of Grace*, 32.

4.4 The priority of justification?

Given the apparent priority of union with Christ over justification, I will bring the argument of this chapter to culmination with an examination of the alleged priority of justification. Did Goodwin hold justification to have priority over transformation in some sense? Moreover, did Goodwin hold justification to have priority over real union with Christ? If so, did the priority of union with Christ, in fact, give way to a sequential *ordo salutis* scheme of applied soteriology?

4.4.1 The priority of justification over transformation

Like Calvin, Goodwin contended that the double grace of justification and sanctification results from real union with Christ.[278] Indeed, for Goodwin, this role of union guarantees the inseparability of justification and sanctification.[279] This argument was not exceptional among Goodwin's contemporaries; the same logic was especially emphasized by Sedgwick.[280] Yet, in Goodwin's mind justification also held a priority over transformation (although, in §4.4.2 I will show that Goodwin did not apply this principle absolutely). Such a stance was far from unique to Goodwin: Congregationalist minister Walter Marshall (1628–1679) in his treatise on sanctification contended, 'Sanctification is an Effect of Justification' alongside upholding real union with Christ.[281] However, if both justification and sanctification result from real union, then attention must be given to determine the nature of the priority of justification.

Fesko's study, intent on establishing the priority of justification over sanctification in Reformed writers, lacks sufficient care in this regard. His chief concern is to establish justification as the cause of sanctification, but he produces little evidence for this contention in his handling of Owen. He attempts to demonstrate the priority of justification by showing that Owen excluded sanctification as the cause of justification; argued for the incompleteness of sanctification in comparison to justification; believed that justification is an article of doctrine upon which the church stands or falls; and contended that acceptance before God rests solely on the imputation of Christ's righteousness.[282] However, none of these prove that justification causes sanctification.[283] Fesko fails, moreover, to comment upon a quotation he supplies in which Owen stipulated that no 'order of precedency or connection' exists between salvific benefits apart from between justification and

---

278. See also *Works*, V, *The Holy Ghost*, 204.

279. *Works*, IV, *Object and Acts*, part III, 20, 59; *Works*, V, *The Holy Ghost*, 75, 204, 212.

280. Sedgwick, *The Bowels*, 491–3.

281. Walter Marshall, *The gospel-mystery of sanctification opened in sundry practical directions suited especially to the case of those who labour under the guilt and power of indwelling sin: to which is added a sermon of justification* (1692), 323.

282. Fesko, *Beyond Calvin*, 290–3.

283. Fesko, *Beyond Calvin*, 287.

adoption.[284] Establishment of the causal priority of justification over sanctification in Owen, therefore, requires more careful analysis.

In Goodwin's case, at least, discerning the causal priority of justification can be accomplished. Goodwin assumed that justification causes transformation: 'the greatest Benefits in Grace do impress nothing upon us, make no physical Change, (tho such a Change is the Consequent of them)'.[285] He illustrated the relation of external and internal soteric benefits by appealing to the divine call to the prophetic or apostolic office. The office itself was 'but an external Privilege with Authority', yet as a consequence was accompanied with divine enablement. Goodwin pressed the application to salvation in Christ:

> many of the greatest Blessings or Benefits we receive in Christ that are an external preferring us unto a Dignity, an high Privilege in which the Benefit mainly consists, but hath for its Concomitant and its Consequence the most real Effects of any other.[286]

Taking the example of adoption he argued that, since believers will be conformed to Christ's likeness, internal grace follows this external benefit as 'its Concomitant and its Consequence'.

Thus, Goodwin believed that justification causes sanctification in the sense that imputed righteousness serves as the legal basis for imparted righteousness. In an important sermon on Ephesians, Goodwin laboured to distinguish salvation 'upon us, and towards us' from salvation 'in us'.[287] Taking the former, he offered this definition: it 'is, an investing us with a Right, a Title, a Tenure, an Interest in all Benefits of Salvation … a formal, sure, legal, authentical Interest … to all Benefits of Salvation whether in this World or in the World to come'.[288] This legal entitlement to full salvation he equated with justification (this revisits the discussion concerning the specific significance of the imputation of Christ's active obedience).[289] The second aspect is the possession of full salvation:

> in the second place, there is an actual Possession, or if you will, rather call it an Accomplishment of all the parts of Salvation and Works of God in us, which God carrieth on in us by degrees, works Holiness in us by degrees, whereof quickning is the beginning; works Glory in us by degrees, first raising us and then filling us with Glory in Heaven[290]

---

284. Fesko, *Beyond Calvin*, 290–1.
285. *Works*, IV, *Object and Acts*, part I, 25.
286. *Works*, IV, *Object and Acts*, part I, 26.
287. *Works*, I, *Ephesians*, part II, 279.
288. *Works*, I, *Ephesians*, part II, 279.
289. *Works*, I, *Ephesians*, part II, 282. See pp. 130–3.
290. *Works*, I, *Ephesians*, part II, 279–80.

Sanctification, therefore, is not only part of salvation to be possessed but is necessary for possessing final glorification.[291] Faith inducts believers into 'the present Right' and then they 'are led through Sanctification, and good works, to the Possession of Salvation.'[292] For Goodwin, then, both justification and sanctification are necessary for final salvation but for different reasons. Sedgwick stated the matter succinctly: 'Though *your Right and Title to heaven lies in Justification*, yet your *meetnesse and fitnesse for heaven lies in your Sanctification*.'[293] Since justification constitutes the legal entitlement to full salvation and sanctification is necessary for the possession of full salvation, justification therefore entitles the believer to sanctification. Justification has priority over sanctification by operating as the legal ground or meritorious cause of transformation.

This causal priority of justification coheres with Goodwin's account of original sin and the relation between original guilt and corruption. Drawing parallels between corruption/guilt and sanctification/justification,[294] he aligned the imputation of Adam's guilt with the imputation of Christ's righteousness on the one side, and the transmission of Adam's corrupt nature with sanctification on the other.[295] As sanctification is evidence of justification, so a corrupted nature is evidence of inherited guilt.[296] As guilt is the meritorious cause of corruption, so by implication justification must be the meritorious cause of sanctification. Burgess made this logic explicit: 'as *Adams* imputed sin is the cause of all our inherent corruption; so Christs imputed righteousnesse is the fountain of all our inward happinesse.'[297]

Further confirmation of the causal priority of justification can be seen in Goodwin's assumption that the extent of justification maps onto the extent of transformation. All that is promised in justification is realized through the divine work of transformation and nothing is realized which was not first promised. Corresponding to any external 'Right and Title' is 'the full accomplishment of it by Degrees'.[298] Indeed, the legal change to believers involved in salvation amounts to endowing them 'with all the Titles and Interest of whatsoever God means to bestow' upon them.[299] Again, 'this same Right to Salvation, and to the whole of Salvation, and all that ever you shall have'.[300] All transformation must have a legal grounding: 'God himself can give us nothing which he hath not given us

---

291. E.g. *Works*, I, *Ephesians*, part II, 200.

292. *Works*, I, *Ephesians*, part II, 299.

293. Sedgwick, *The Bowels*, 492.

294. *Works*, III, *An Unregenerate*, 355.

295. *Works*, III, *An Unregenerate*, 13.

296. *Works*, III, *An Unregenerate*, 27.

297. Burgess, *Justification (1654)*, 298; cf. 340; George Downame, *The covenant of grace, or, An exposition upon Luke I. 73, 74, 75* (1647), 289.

298. *Works*, I, *Ephesians*, part II, 280; cf. *Works*, III, *Christ the Mediator*, 132–3.

299. *Works*, I, *Ephesians*, part II, 281.

300. *Works*, I, *Ephesians*, part II, 281.

a Right unto.'[301] The dimensions of justification, therefore, must be matched in sanctification and final salvation. As already noted, Christ's passive obedience grounds forgiveness whereas Christ's active obedience grounds entitlement to heaven.[302] Goodwin also applied this correspondence principle to sanctification. In his argument for the imputation of both Christ's passive and active obedience, he reasoned:

> For as it is certain, that more is required to the sanctification of a Sinner, since it is described not only by a meer simple creation out of nothing, but by the Mortification of the Old Man ... to which it is necessary the New Creature be added, so the like Account is to be stated in the Justification of a Sinner (of which Sanctification is an Image) the whole of it is not accomplished in the taking away of Sins ... unless besides this an Active Conformity to the Law be added. Also to Reconciliation (which is the Effect of Justification, and bears the likeness of its cause) all that is required which is requisite to procure a new, and simple Friendship, and something more; since it is the receiving of an old Enemy into favour.[303]

Thus, both sanctification and reconciliation image justification, since like justification each contains two components. While the nature of sanctification is the premise of Goodwin's argument, by declaring it the image of justification, it is evident that Goodwin believed justification to be logically primitive. This is explicitly stated in the case of reconciliation: the twofold nature of reconciliation is a consequence of a twofold justification as its cause. In light of this evidence, it is clear that Goodwin held the conviction that justification is the meritorious cause not only of sanctification but also of the application of all real salvific benefits.

Other divines also held justification to be the legal entitlement or meritorious cause of transformation. Burgess wrote, 'the justified man is thereby put into a full possession of Gods favour ... and indeed Justification is virtually all other priviledges, for they are either Effects, or Concomitants, and Consequents of it'.[304] Here Goodwin and Burgess found themselves in agreement with 'imputative antinomian' opponents such as Eaton and Eyre.[305] However, Eyre ventured beyond mainstream opinion by delighting in pointing out that faith should be included in the effects of justification: 'Faith is not the cause or antecedent, but an effect and consequent of our Justification, procured and obtained by the death of Christ.'[306]

---

301. *Works*, I, *Ephesians*, part II, 280.
302. See p. 130.
303. *Works*, III, *Christ the Mediator*, 338–9; cf. *Works*, I, *Ephesians*, part I, 311.
304. Burgess, *Justification* (1654), 267.
305. Eaton, *Honey-Combe*, 459; Eyre, *Vindiciæ Justificationis Gratuitæ*, 179.
306. Eyre, *Vindiciæ Justificationis Gratuitæ*, 42.

4.4.2 *The priority of justification over regeneration?*

Eyre's view raises the question of whether Goodwin held justification to have priority over regeneration. In the sermon on Ephesians considered above, Goodwin stated that justification provides the legal basis for all of transformation within believers including 'quickning'.[307] Burgess too appeared to affirm the priority of justification over regeneration.[308] However, this point struck to the heart of their understanding of the relation of justification, regeneration and union with Christ. A close examination of key aspects of Goodwin's *ordo salutis* is, therefore, required.

While Kim attempts to reconstruct Goodwin's *ordo salutis*, he wrongly assumes that occasional lists of soteric benefits found within Goodwin's works (and the Savoy declaration) indicate a logical relationship between the benefits named.[309] Such an approach is far too superficial and speculative.[310] As Burgess acknowledged, discerning the *ordo salutis* taxed divines:

> It must be acknowledged a very hard task to set down the true order of the benefits bestowed upon us by God. The assigning of the priority and posteriority of them is very various according to the severall judgements of men interested in that controversie.[311]

What, therefore, must be understood are the key factors in that controversy and Goodwin's location within it.

While Goodwin did not address the *ordo salutis* at length, he made several passing references to a 'Golden Chain' of the causes of salvation, usually in relation to the *textus classicus* (Romans 8:29) and pastoral issues surrounding faith and assurance.[312] What will become apparent is that he assumed the same basic sequence as Perkins in his influential work *A Golden Chaine*, namely: effectual calling, justification, sanctification and glorification.[313] Perkins had subdivided effectual calling into election and the establishment of real union with Christ (which involves faith). While he assigned real union with Christ a foundational place in his *ordo salutis*, Perkins lacked clarity over the location of regeneration.[314]

307. *Works*, I, *Ephesians*, part II, 279–80.

308. Burgess, *Justification (1651)*, 170–1.

309. Kim, 'Salvation by Faith', 181–93.

310. Kim tries to distance himself from reconstructing Goodwin's *ordo salutis* in this manner. Kim, 'Salvation by Faith', 188. However, his argumentation is still largely based on this flawed approach, to the extent that he feels compelled to explain apparent differences between lists. Kim, 'Salvation by Faith', 191–2.

311. Burgess, *Justification (1651)*, 181.

312. See *Works*, II, *Election*, 16; *Works*, IV, *Object and Acts*, part I, 29, 100; *Works*, IV, *The Government of the Churches*, 304–5; *Works*, V, *The Holy Ghost*, 380–1.

313. Perkins, *A golden Chaine*, 114–28.

314. Since Perkins elsewhere equated the Spirit's indwelling with the infusion of created grace, by implication effectual calling ought to contain regeneration.

By the 1640s–1650s, the rise of divergent theologies put pressure on Goodwin and his mainstream colleagues to give much more careful thought to the relation of regeneration to justification, sanctification and faith. The competing factors which constrained permissible *ordo salutis* schemes came to the surface in Goodwin's discussion of the interpretation of 1 Peter 1:2.[315] Puzzling over 'how the sprinkling of the Blood of Christ should be the consequent of Sanctification', Goodwin revealed his basic *ordo salutis*. It is apparent that two main theological concerns governed the relative location of transformation and justification. On the one hand, Goodwin avoided locating sanctification before justification lest sanctification merit justification. While guarding against Catholic theology was the chief factor here, moralistic writers such as Hammond also sought to place sanctification before justification in order to promote the necessity of moral renovation. Posing the question, '*What now is the dependence between* Justification *and* Sanctification?', Hammond answered that initial sanctification precedes pardon and that sanctification must be continued in order to preserve a state of justification.[316] For Hammond, justification, both initially and continually, depends upon sanctification. In contrast, Goodwin insisted that 'the received Opinion' was that justification comprises 'the *medium* of Sanctification, and in order go afore it'.[317]

On the other hand, Goodwin embraced the twin convictions that justification follows faith and that the act of faith can only arise from the corresponding infused habit: 'as all grant justification be upon an act of Faith on Christ for justification … and that an act of Faith must proceed from a principle of Faith habitually wrought.'[318] As he wrote elsewhere, the first conviction coheres with his *tria momenta* scheme and dictated the order of faith and justification in his *ordo salutis*:

> God hath subordinated in the way, in the Chain of Salvation, one thing to another; as thus, actual Justification of our Persons upon our believing (for it is clear, we are not justified in a true sense till we believe, and then we begin to be justified in our own Persons …) Here he makes Justification to follow upon Faith, or to be concomitant to Faith[319]

While the second conviction particularly responded to Arminian theology, elsewhere Goodwin noted that some Catholics and enthusiasts understood faith to arise out of the immediate working of the Holy Spirit apart from infused grace.[320] Those who advocated this position, as Burgess noted, were able to affirm that faith

---

315. *Works*, III, *Man's Restauration*, 16.
316. Hammond, *Practical Catechisme*, 48–9.
317. *Works*, III, *Man's Restauration*, 16.
318. *Works*, III, *Man's Restauration*, 16.
319. *Works*, I, *Ephesians*, part II, 202; cf. *Works*, IV, *Object and Acts*, part I, 169.
320. *Works*, V, *The Holy Ghost*, 174–5.

precedes justification without having to concede an element of transformation before justification.[321] This approach, however, was unacceptable to both Goodwin and Burgess. The net effect of these twin convictions was to force Goodwin to concede an element of transformation prior to justification.

Constrained by these competing factors, Goodwin followed the widely accepted solution that the habit of faith must be infused prior to justification (in which the believer remains entirely passive), but the process of sanctification and ensuing acts occur after justification. Along similar lines, in order to maintain justification by faith, Rutherford refuted antinomian objections against the infusion of habits before justification.[322] While insisting upon this causal order of nature, Rutherford also contended that regeneration, the act of faith and the divine act of justification occur simultaneously.[323] Reformed orthodox writers frequently asserted such simultaneity in an attempt to minimize any possible contribution of sanctification in justification.[324] Sedgwick argued that since justification and transformation both flow from union with Christ, they must occur simultaneously.[325] While Goodwin did not stress this simultaneity point, it was widely accepted and his usage of the term 'order of nature' to denote causal rather than temporal relation of successive *ordo salutis* items is highly suggestive.[326] Burgess summarized the majority viewpoint on the *ordo salutis* that results:

> It is true, our being ingraffed into Christ, is the root and fountain of faith, and of Justification too; but yet so, that these being correlates (faith and Justification) they both flow from the root together, though with this order, that faith is to be conceived in order of nature before Justification, that being the instrument to receive it, though both be together in time. ... Neither is it any new thing in Philosophy, to say, Those causes which produce an effect, though they be in time together, yet are mutually before one another in order of nature in divers respects to their severall causalities.[327]

However, while eliminating progress in sanctification and resulting holy actions from contributing to justification, appeals to simultaneity could not remove the possibility that initial infused sanctification or the initial act of faith contributed

---

321. Burgess, *Justification (1651)*, 181.

322. Rutherford, *Spirituall Antichrist*, part II, 113.

323. Rutherford, *Spirituall Antichrist*, part II, 112.

324. E.g. Leigh, *A Body of Divinity*, 530.

325. Sedgwick, *The Bowels*, 374.

326. *Works*, III, *Man's Restauration*, 16; *Works*, IV, *Object and Acts*, part I, 168; part III, 6; *Works*, I, *Ephesians*, part I, 197. Kim claims that Goodwin envisaged a temporal interval between regeneration and justification, but he offers no substantive evidence. Kim, 'Salvation by Faith', 222.

327. Burgess, *Justification (1651)*, 182; cf. 170–1.

to justification, since, as Eyre protested, in the final analysis the order of nature is the decisive factor.[328]

Within this broad agreement, there was debate over the extent of transformation prior to justification. Goodwin was persuaded of the view that all principles of sanctification, rather than merely the habit of faith, are infused prior to the act of faith.[329] In discussing 1 Peter 1:2 he alluded to Pemble's influential work *Vindiciæ Gratiæ* which argued for the same view that regeneration as a whole precedes faith.[330] Contending against Arminians, Pemble argued that the act of faith must flow from the habit of faith and that the habit must be infused as the principal part of regeneration.[331] This position met with opposition from some quarters. George Downame (d. 1634) complained that Pemble's scheme confused vocation and sanctification and thus undermined the consensus view of the *ordo salutis*.[332] Downame instead insisted that only the habit of faith is infused prior to justification, whereas regeneration and the renewal of the *imago Dei* follow justification. These two infusions, he explained, are related as conception is to birth. Given Goodwin's willingness to embrace infused sanctification prior to justification, his sympathies clearly lay with Pemble. It is therefore unsurprising that Goodwin frequently equated regeneration and vocation.[333]

As a result of these factors, Goodwin's *ordo salutis* was: effectual calling (including regeneration), faith, justification and sanctification. The final category of sanctification referred to growth in holiness (and resulting acts) and must be distinguished from habitual sanctification which coincides with regeneration and the initial infusion of grace.[334] There is complexity in the relation of sanctification to prior links of the chain, since while justification is the meritorious cause of sanctification, sanctification and other gradual 'physical changes' are 'consequents or concomitants' of regeneration.[335] Elsewhere, Goodwin stated that sanctification and repentance are 'seminally included in Faith' and so necessarily follow regeneration.[336] Thus, sanctification has different causal relations with prior links of the chain. However, regeneration was unequivocally located prior to justification as its instrumental cause.

---

328. Eyre, *Vindiciæ Justificationis Gratuitæ*, 164.

329. See p. 99.

330. *Works*, III, *Man's Restauration*, 16.

331. Pemble, *Vindiciæ Gratiæ*, 4, 92. For a summary of Pemble's theology, see Boersma, *Hot Pepper Corn*, 71–80.

332. Downame, *Covenant of grace*, 281–3. In this context, Goodwin indicated that he had read Downame's treatise on justification. *Works*, III, *Man's Restauration*, 17.

333. *Works*, II, *Election*, 253, 279, 288, 323; *Works*, I, *Ephesians*, part I, 96; part II, 190. The category of 'calling' was important in discussions of the *ordo salutis* given its appearance in Romans 8:29.

334. *Works*, I, *Ephesians*, part I, 197.

335. *Works*, V, *The Holy Ghost*, 377.

336. *Works*, IV, *Object and Acts*, part II, 60–1.

Therefore, while Goodwin affirmed the general principle that justification functions as the legal entitlement or meritorious cause of transformation, he allowed this principle to be trumped by greater concerns. In fact, by placing regeneration and not just the infusion of faith prior to justification, Goodwin rendered the problem of maintaining justification as the meritorious cause of transformation more acute. This difficulty was pressed by Downame against Pemble's scheme.[337] It would, however, have been lost on Pemble since he held to a double justification: '*Sanctification and Inherent righteousnesse goes before our Iustification and imputed righteousnesse: but with a distinction of a double justification.*'[338] While he stipulated that imputed righteousness follows regeneration, his caveat was decisive. For Pemble, the first justification constitutes justification proper and precedes faith.[339] The second justification follows faith, but is restricted to the conscience, the view stoutly rejected by Goodwin. It is apparent that for Pemble, however, such a scheme is essential in order to maintain the priority of actual justification over transformation. Unable to follow Pemble, this problem posed by Downame, therefore, remained for Goodwin. Here Goodwin was not alone, for Eyre levelled the same charge against the mainstream majority: 'the generality of our Protestant Divines, in comparing the blessings of the Covenant, have given the precedency to Justification; some have ascribed to it, a priority of time, but all of Nature ... it a gross error, to say, That Sanctification goes before Justification' yet 'Faith is a part of Sanctification, and the same thing cannot be before it self'.[340] Defenders of free grace, such as Eyre, in effect followed Pemble and sidestepped the problem by placing justification before any real transformation. In contrast, Goodwin, along with the majority of his mainstream colleagues, insisted that regeneration and faith precede justification and allowed the causal priority of justification over transformation to be trumped. Peter Bulkeley (1583–1659) believed that the mainstream scheme had scriptural support, since it followed the order set out in Romans 8:29 of vocation preceding justification.[341]

Here it was Owen, not Goodwin, who veered closer to the free-grace proponents. Owen was more concerned to establish the legal grounding of regeneration than Goodwin. In his reply to Baxter's accusations of antinomianism, Owen directly addressed the issue of regeneration's legal basis. Arguing that the initial infusion of grace must be caused by the atoning blood of Christ, but also wanting to maintain justification by faith, Owen distinguished 'Absolution in Heaven' from 'compleat Justification':

Absolution may be considered, either as a pure Act of the Will of God in it self, or as it is *received, believed, apprehended*, in, and by the soul of the Guilty.

---

337. Downame, *Covenant of grace*, 289.
338. Pemble, *Vindiciæ Gratiæ*, 21.
339. Pemble, *Vindiciæ Gratiæ*, 21.
340. Eyre, *Vindiciæ Justificationis Gratuitæ*, 161.
341. Peter Bulkeley, *The Gospel-Covenant; Or The Covenant of Grace Opened* (1646), 322.

For Absolution in the first sense, it is evident it must proceed beleeving: as a discharge from the Effects of Anger, naturally proceeds all Collation of any fruits of Love, such as is Faith.[342]

The problem is that this absolution is tantamount to justification before faith and so, in effect, Owen was espousing Pemble's solution. In his second reply to Baxter, Owen was forced to insist upon simultaneity to compensate: 'At the *same time* wherein God *absolves us in heaven* … He *infuses a principle of life* into *our soules*.'[343] Thus, Burger inaccurately claims that Owen held regeneration, faith and imputation to occur simultaneously in order to exclude the possibility of transformation contributing to justification while maintaining justification by faith.[344] In fact, Owen stressed simultaneity to establish that justification is never chronologically separated from transformation and so answer the charge of antinomianism.[345]

Goodwin did not attempt to resolve the problem as Pemble or Owen had done. While he held to two notions of justification prior to faith, both are representative justification and, in his mind, strictly belong to the domain of redemption accomplished not applied. For Goodwin, the need to insist upon regeneration to account for justification by faith suppressed his conviction of the causal priority of justification over transformation.

4.4.3 Conclusion: The priority of union with Christ

Thus, despite affirming a general principle of the causal priority of justification, Goodwin did not believe that justification causes real union with Christ. Given faith (and by implication regeneration) belong to his conception of real union with Christ and precede justification in his *ordo salutis*, real union with Christ, therefore, necessarily precedes justification. In fact, justification could not have causal priority over the Spirit's indwelling, since Goodwin espoused a period of preparation following the Spirit's initial indwelling and before regeneration/ faith.[346] Thus, while Goodwin wanted to advance a causal priority of justification, my previously established conclusion that he understood justification to be founded in real union with Christ is not overthrown.

Here Goodwin occupied the majority position. In the English context, at least, Fesko is decidedly wrong to claim that Reformed theologians affirmed that 'justification is the *legal* ground of the believer's union with Christ'.[347] In fact, it

---

342. Owen, *Of the Death of Christ*, 79.
343. Owen, *Vindiciæ Evangelicæ*, appendix, 21.
344. Burger, *Being in Christ*, 60, 66, 75.
345. Owen, *Justification*, 174–5. See also Owen, *Pneumatologia*, 454.
346. *Works*, V, *The Holy Ghost*, 54–5.
347. Fesko, *Beyond Calvin*, 382.

was the despised antinomian champions of free grace who advocated such a view. Eaton, for instance, held real union itself to be a benefit merited by justification:

> The order also and naturall dependencie of these benefits upon one another confirme the same: for we cannot bee knit into Christ, before we have the holy Ghost dwelling in us: the holy Ghost comes not to dwell in us, before we be reconciled to God; and we are not reconciled to God, before we have all our sinnes abolished out of Gods sight.[348]

In contrast, mainstream divines, when confronted between the choice of the priority of justification or the priority of union with Christ, tended to opt for the latter.

Thus, Goodwin was adamant that real union with Christ occupies a more foundational role in his *ordo salutis* than justification. Here Goodwin was in the mainstream English Reformed tradition.[349] In Goodwin's case, the priority of union with Christ may be powerfully demonstrated by recasting his *ordo salutis* in terms of his threefold scheme of union with Christ.[350] Elective union precedes and causes representative union which in turn causes real union. Real union involves the indwelling of the Spirit causing regeneration and in turn faith. Goodwin's *ordo salutis*, therefore, may be restated: elective union (election), representative union, real union (involving: indwelling, regeneration, faith), justification, then (progressive) sanctification. In this way, the concepts of the *ordo salutis* and union with Christ can be readily integrated within Goodwin's thought. This conclusion is in contrast to Kim who, following Fesko's lead, claims that Goodwin identified union with Christ with the entire *ordo salutis* in some sense.[351] However, the evidence presented here establishes that, within Goodwin's scheme, union with Christ should be identified with the elements of the *ordo salutis* (logically) prior to justification and so union with Christ occupies a more foundational role than justification and all other soteric benefits.

4.5 Conclusion

Consistent with the wider Reformed tradition, Goodwin upheld a purely forensic understanding of justification. His doctrine of justification was an especially high doctrine, involving not only the imputation of Christ's passive and active obedience but also the imputation of Christ's holy nature. Moreover, he believed that, as the

---

348. Eaton, *Honey-Combe*, 438.

349. Muller, *Calvin and the Reformed Tradition*, 202–43.

350. Indeed, in the same way as the 'Golden Chain' was commonly used, Goodwin urged his readers to seek assurance by ascending his *tria momenta* of justification from real union to the top of the ladder. *Works*, IV, *Object and Acts*, part II, 130–1.

351. Kim, 'Salvation by Faith', 196; cf. 194.

God-man, the worth of Christ's obedience surpassed that of Adam's and merited the legal entitlement to heavenly eternal life. Goodwin's doctrine of justification, therefore, was crucial for upholding his high soteriology which not only addressed the problem of the Fall but also raised believers far above Adam's prelapsarian state. Yet, it was particularly Goodwin's modified form of eternal justification that placed him closer to antinomians than most orthodox divines were prepared to venture. Goodwin's careful distinctions, however, kept him within the bounds of accepted orthodoxy.

Importantly for this study, Goodwin was convinced that the reality of justification must be founded in union with Christ. An examination of different imputations within his thought reveals his conviction that the imputation of Christ's righteousness occurs upon the immediate basis of an external covenantal union. However, Goodwin's unique *tria momenta* scheme of justification underlines another conviction, namely, that justification proper must result from real union with Christ. Both real and external unions, therefore, are required for justification. By producing faith, real union enables the 'condition' of the covenant of grace to be fulfilled and so Christ's righteousness can be imputed on the basis of an external union. Moreover, Goodwin believed that the condition of faith is not arbitrary but natural; the believer's faith is the consent of marriage matched by Christ's taking hold of the believer by the Spirit. As in marriage, an external union permits legal benefits to be conferred on believers once a real union has been established.

Given both transformation and justification result from real union with Christ, the question of the relation of these two salvific benefits is raised. Goodwin assumed the general principle that justification functions as the legal entitlement or meritorious cause of transformation. Since transformation is necessary for final salvation and justification entitles the believer to final salvation, justification must, therefore, entitle the believer to transformation. However, Goodwin was convinced that justification follows faith (contra antinomians) and that the act of faith can only arise from the infused habit of faith (contra Arminians), therefore he was forced to place regeneration prior to justification in his *ordo salutis*. Forced to choose between the priority of justification and the priority of real union with Christ, along with the majority of his Reformed colleagues, Goodwin opted for the latter. In contrast, 'imputative antinomians' took the other option and insisted that justification must cause not only regeneration but also real union with Christ. Goodwin was convinced: real union with Christ, not justification, occupies the foundational place in his *ordo salutis*, before the application of all salvific benefits.

Chapter 5

PARTAKING OF CHRIST: THE CENTRALITY OF REAL UNION WITH CHRIST

5.1 Introduction

My study of Goodwin's doctrine of union with Christ will culminate by assessing its place within his soteriology. The basic question to be addressed may be stated: why did Goodwin set union with Christ as the means for bestowing all soteric benefits upon believers? In particular, why did he insist upon real union by the indwelling of the Spirit's person for this pivotal role? The central concern and basic shape of his applied soteriology is already evident in his sermon series on Ephesians 1:1–2:11 long before the main writing of his grand project. I will begin by revealing that in these sermons Goodwin repeatedly applied a notion of participation in Christ inherited from his mentor Sibbes in order to uphold the reality of salvation (§5.2). Widening the examination to include his grand project, in the next section I will demonstrate that this notion of participation constitutes the fundamental idea in Goodwin's soteriology and I will uncover the underlying theological rationale (§5.3). I will complete the argument by tracing how Goodwin believed his conception of real union with Christ to be essential for participation in Christ and therefore fundamental in applied soteriology (§5.4).

5.2 Ephesians *and Goodwin's rule of participation*

Goodwin's concept of participation in Christ was founded in his rule: 'whatever work God doth upon us, he doth unto Christ first.'[1] This rule asserts not only the chronological priority of Christ but also the dependence of believers upon him for receiving salvific benefits. Accordingly, Goodwin frequently designated Christ as the pattern of what God intends to work upon believers.[2] Thus, for Goodwin, participation in Christ consists in the replication upon or in the believer of aspects

---

1. *Works*, I, *Ephesians*, part I, 209.
2. E.g. *Works*, I, *Ephesians*, part I, 370.

of what is already true of Christ.[3] What his rule stresses is that all of salvation is only received by such participation in Christ.

This rule of participation Goodwin had inherited from his mentor Sibbes. While many Reformed puritans occasionally appealed to similar ideas of participation,[4] Sibbes had employed this rule extensively. For example, he wrote, 'Christ is first blessed, *we are blessed with all spirituall bleßings in Iesus Chrest*. So whatsoever is in us, we have it at the second hand.'[5] Sibbes had warned that the promises of salvation are never 'directed to us, abstracted from [Christ].'[6] For Sibbes, then, this rule provides the basic shape of soteriology. Alluding to the golden chain of salvation,[7] he wrote,

> [God] in the execution from predestination to glorification, before all worlds he loved us in Christ to everlasting: from the everlasting in election, to everlasting in glory, all is in Christ in regard of execution. We subsist in him, we are sanctified in him, we are justified in him, his righteousnesse is ours, we are glorified in him, we are loved in him: God blesseth us with all spiritual blessings in him[8]

Thus, Stephen Beck, in his study of Sibbes's soteriology, tellingly observes, 'Sibbes' soteriology is more an application of the Redeemer, than it is an explanation of redemption.'[9]

While Goodwin stated this rule only twice in his works, it applied far more extensively such that he was essentially appropriating and developing Sibbes's soteriological programme. Despite its importance, however, to date scholarship on

---

3. E.g. *Works*, I, *Ephesians*, part I, 31, 482.

4. For example, Owen wrote: 'Whatever God designeth unto us therein, he first exemplified in Jesus Christ.' Owen, *Pneumatologia*, 493; cf. Edward Leigh, *A treatise of the divine promises In five bookes* (1633), 58, 60; Hooker, *The Application of Redemption*, 94, 104; Hooker, *Christ's last Prayer*, 99, 114, 138; Flavel, *The Method of Grace*, 5–6. Similar notions also made appearances in the writings of antinomians and radicals of different varieties, although they preferred to state the stronger notion that whatever grace has been bestowed upon Christ is consequently bestowed upon believers (see §5.3.1). Where the idea was notably absent was in the writings of Socinians and moralists. They preferred to stress the duty of believers to imitate Christ's example. E.g. Jeremy Taylor, *The Great Exemplar of Sanctity and Holy Life according to the Christian Institution Described In the History of the Life and Death of the ever Blessed Jesus Christ the Saviour of the World* (1649).

5. Richard Sibbes, *Beames of Divine Light, Breaking forth from severall places of holy Scripture, as they were learnedly opened, In XXI. Sermons* (1639), 'A Description of Christ', 40.

6. Richard Sibbes, *Yea and amen: or, pretious promises, and priviledges Spiritually unfolded in their nature and vse. Driving at the assurance and establishing of weak beleevers* (1638), 28; cf. Sibbes, *Exposition: upon The first Chapter of the Second Epistle to the Corinthians*, 405.

7. See p. 167.

8. Sibbes, *Exposition: upon The first Chapter of the Second Epistle to the Corinthians*, 405.

9. Stephen Paul Beck, 'The Doctrine of *Gratia Praeparans* in the Soteriology of Richard Sibbes' (PhD thesis, Westminster Theological Seminary, 1994), 105.

this facet of Goodwin's theology is limited to a brief comment by Jones.[10] The case for the importance of this rule is best made by an examination of this notion of participation in its varied manifestations in Goodwin's sermon series on Ephesians 1:1–2:11. Preached in the early 1640s prior to the convening of the Westminster Assembly, these sermons represent Goodwin's only extended systematic exposition of a portion of Scripture. Much of the theology I have discussed in previous chapters had already been expounded in these sermons. Moreover, already in Goodwin's sights was the concern that he would carry forward into his grand project, namely, to defend Reformed soteriology and to impress upon his readers the gracious reality of salvation.[11] To this end, he repeatedly and variedly applied his rule of participation, frequently echoing Sibbes.

5.2.1 Partaking of Christ's benefits

Programmatic for Goodwin's rule was Ephesians 1:3: '*Blessed be the God and Father of our Lord Jesus Christ, who hath blessed us with all Spiritual blessings in heavenly places [or in heavenly things] in Christ.*'[12] In Goodwin's mind the final phrase 'in Christ' was pregnant with significance. It implied that believers receive salvific benefits only as a result of Christ first receiving them in his own person.[13] Believers 'partake of the same good things which he is partaker of'.[14] This idea appears in commentaries of the time. Paul Baynes (*c.* 1573–1617), in his commentary on Ephesians frequently cited by Goodwin, mentioned this idea, although it does not dominate his comments on Ephesians 1:3.[15] David Dickson (*c.* 1583–1662), in his commentary on Ephesians 1:3, also mentioned the same theological logic.[16] Here, however, Goodwin more likely was primarily influenced by his mentor Sibbes who, while not writing a commentary on the epistle, had repeatedly appealed to Ephesians 1:3 to justify the rule of participation: 'Christ is first blessed, *we are blessed with all spirituall bleßings in Iesus Chrest. So whatsoever is in us, we have it at the second hand.*'[17] For Sibbes, confirmation of this interpretation had come

---

10. Jones, *Why Heaven Kissed Earth*, 225.

11. *Works*, I, *Ephesians*, part I, 3; part II, 263.

12. *Works*, I, *Ephesians*, part I, 18.

13. *Works*, I, *Ephesians*, part I, 35.

14. *Works*, I, *Ephesians*, part I, 47.

15. Paul Baynes, *An entire commentary vpon the vvhole epistle of the Apostle Paul to the Ephesians wherein the text is learnedly and fruitfully opened, with a logicall analysis, spirituall and holy observations confutation of Arminianisme and popery, and sound edification for the dilgent reader* (1643), 31 cf. 234, 236–7.

16. David Dickson, *An Expositon of all St. Pauls Epistles together With an Explanation of those other Epistles of the Apostles St. James, Peter, John & Jude* (1659), 108.

17. Sibbes, *Beames of Divine Light*, 'A Description of Christ', 40; cf. Sibbes, *Exposition: upon The first Chapter of the Second Epistle to the Corinthians*, 405; Sibbes, *Exposition, upon The fourth Chapter of the second Epistle to the Corrinthians*, 31; Richard Sibbes, *The Christians*

from 2 Corinthians 1:20: '[Christ] must first receive all good for us, and we must have it at the second hand from him … *All the Promises of God in him are Yea, and Amen.*'[18] Where Goodwin advanced beyond Sibbes was in his twofold schema of the spiritual blessings delineated in Ephesians 1:4-9.

5.2.1.1 Benefits of Christ's person: Perfection, adoption and acceptation Goodwin identified three salvific blessings in Ephesians 1:4-6 and designated them as benefits founded upon Christ's person. That is, Christ first receives these blessings in his human nature as a result of his hypostatic union. The first blessing Goodwin interpreted to refer to the inherent 'perfect holiness' possessed by saints in glory.[19] This, he believed, was the purpose and implication of election in Christ. The hypostatic union is determinative: 'because as he being the Son of God, was to be holy, (*Luke* 1.35. *That holy thing which shall be born of thee, shall be called the Son of God,*) so are we, we being Members of him.'[20] Thus, Christ was first made holy and believers will be perfected in holiness by consequence of his holiness.[21] Ahead of Goodwin, Sibbes had likewise argued that believers are sanctified because Christ's human nature was first sanctified at his conception.[22] Again prior to Goodwin, Sibbes had similarly contended that the basis for Christ's sanctification of his human nature was its hypostatic union with the divine Son.[23]

Goodwin reckoned the second benefit, adoption, to be the highest privilege.[24] Conferring the legal status of sonship, adoption entails 'a right to the Glory of Heaven'.[25] Again, his rule of participation is evident: 'He first, and then we in a conformity to him; even as is he a Son, so are we in him.'[26] Christ operates as the pattern: '*He is my Natural Son, and I will make them my Sons through him. …* God did set up Christ as the Proto-type and principal Master-piece, and made us as little Copies and Models of him.'[27] It is as a result of the hypostatic union with

Portion, or, The Charter of a Christian (1638), 156; Richard Sibbes, *A heavenly conference between Christ and Mary after His resurrection. Wherein the intimate familiarity, and near relation between Christ and a believer is discovered* (1654), 147.

18. Sibbes, *Exposition: upon The first Chapter of the Second Epistle to the Corinthians*, 404; cf. 153–4, 405; Sibbes, *The Christians Portion*, 114; Sibbes, *Yea and amen*, 28; Richard Sibbes, *Divine meditations and holy contemplations* (1638), 194–5. Goodwin had also appealed to this verse in an earlier tract in which he had denoted Christ 'the Grand Promise'. *Christ Set Forth*, 13.

19. *Works*, I, *Ephesians*, part I, 70; cf. 67, 71, 73.

20. *Works*, I, *Ephesians*, part I, 100.

21. *Works*, I, *Ephesians*, part I, 73.

22. Sibbes, *Beames of Divine Light*, 'The Spirituall Jubile', 36–7; Sibbes, *The Saints Cordials*, 14.

23. Sibbes, *Exposition, upon The fourth Chapter of the second Epistle to the Corrinthians*, 35.

24. *Works*, I, *Ephesians*, part I, 71.

25. *Works*, I, *Ephesians*, part I, 72.

26. *Works*, I, *Ephesians*, part I, 80.

27. *Works*, I, *Ephesians*, part I, 80.

the divine Son that Christ's human nature possesses sonship.[28] All this had been a favourite theme of Sibbes. Across his works, he had repeatedly reasoned in the same manner, for example: '[Christ] was the first Son of God, we Sons in him; what he is by nature, we are by grace, and adoption.'[29] Prior to Goodwin, he had similarly drawn the same consequence: believers are heirs because Christ was first the heir.[30] And like Goodwin, Sibbes had maintained that the basis is that Christ's human nature had been hypostatically united to the divine Son.[31]

For the third benefit – the 'Acceptation of our persons in the beloved'[32] – Goodwin reasoned that as God 'hath loved Jesus Christ, and delighted in him: so in this his Beloved he loveth, pleaseth himself in, and delighteth in us'.[33] Thus, this benefit is not the acceptation entailed in justification or election[34] but a participation in God's delight and affection towards Christ that he experiences as a result of his hypostatical union.[35] Goodwin boldly concluded: 'this is the advantage of being accepted in the Beloved, God loves us with the same love wherewith he loved his Son.'[36] Here Goodwin again followed Sibbes who had written, 'God loves us with that inseparable love wherewith hee loves his owne Sonne … God loves and delights in us, because he loves, and delights in Christ Jesus.'[37] Also ahead of Goodwin, Sibbes had declared that believers experience 'the same love' that Christ experiences (differing only in degree).[38]

5.2.1.2 Benefits of Christ's merits: Redemption, justification and vocation Noting a shift in introductory formula from 'he hath' to 'in whom we have', Goodwin argued that the blessings expounded in Ephesians 1:7-9 result from Christ's merits rather than his person.[39] Christ's merits he equated with 'Christ's blood'[40] and with

---

28. *Works*, I, *Ephesians*, part I, 82.

29. Sibbes, *Exposition, upon The fourth Chapter of the second Epistle to the Corrinthians*, 31; cf. Sibbes, *Exposition: upon The first Chapter of the Second Epistle to the Corinthians*, 21; Sibbes, *Yea and amen*, 27–8; Sibbes, *The Christians Portion*, 157; Sibbes, *Light from Heaven*, 'The Chvrches Riches By Christs Poverty', 20; Sibbes, *A heavenly conference*, 151; Sibbes, *Evangelicall Sacrifices*, 'The Redemption of Bodyes', 49.

30. Sibbes, *The Christians Portion*, 158, 181.

31. Sibbes, *Exposition: upon The first Chapter of the Second Epistle to the Corinthians*, 21.

32. *Works*, I, *Ephesians*, part I, 93.

33. *Works*, I, *Ephesians*, part I, 91; cf. *Works*, II, *Election*, 307.

34. *Works*, I, *Ephesians*, part I, 92.

35. *Works*, I, *Ephesians*, part I, 93.

36. *Works*, I, *Ephesians*, part I, 94.

37. Sibbes, *Beames of Divine Light*, 'A Description of Christ', 26; cf. Sibbes, *Exposition: upon The first Chapter of the Second Epistle to the Corinthians*, 21; Sibbes, *Light from Heaven*, 'Angels Acclamations', 254–61; Sibbes, *A heavenly conference*, 148.

38. Sibbes, *Beames of Divine Light*, 'A Description of Christ', 25; Sibbes, *Yea and amen*, 88–9.

39. *Works*, I, *Ephesians*, part I, 96; cf. 100–1.

40. *Works*, I, *Ephesians*, part I, 101.

Christ's obedience to the law.[41] This identification, of course, reflected Goodwin's insistence upon the imputation of both Christ's passive and his active obedience.

Like the benefits of his person, the benefits of Christ's merits are also bestowed upon believers in Christ and so further exemplify Goodwin's rule of participation.[42] However, by Goodwin's reckoning, the first – redemption – occupied a foundational position: 'Redemption is a large word; for Christ was fain to buy all that God intended us, because we lost it.'[43] Moreover, redemption resides in Christ himself: 'He speaks not of the Redemption we receive here, but of the work of Redemption which Christ himself wrought, that is the cause of all the Redemption we receive; for he saith, it is Redemption in Christ.'[44] Here Goodwin distinguished between what Christ representatively obtained in himself and the corresponding application to believers: 'We have redemption as in a common person in Christ, we have it not only when it is applied to us, but we have it in him as we had condemnation in *Adam*, before we were born in the world, so we had redemption in Christ when he died.'[45] The application of redemption, Goodwin proposed, is contained in the remaining two benefits.

Justification constitutes the first aspect of redemption applied. While the text only named '*Remission of sins*', Goodwin interpreted it to contain the imputation of the whole of Christ's merits.[46] The distinction between adoption and justification in Goodwin's thought is now evident: whereas adoption is founded upon Christ's person, justification is founded upon his merits.[47] Since both entail an entitlement to heaven, believers have a double entitlement but on different grounds.[48] Adoption represents the fundamental entitlement; justification is added in response to the Fall. Thus, while adoption has an independent basis to justification, because of sin justification is required to secure adoption.[49]

The final benefit constitutes the second aspect of redemption applied: 'the work of *Vocation*, our first conversion to God, and of *Faith* and *Sanctification*. … It is … the blessing of Conversion, and of our Calling, and the working Faith and also our imperfect Holiness, which God works in us here.'[50] If justification represents the legal application of redemption, then vocation denotes the transformational: regeneration and progressive sanctification. The more important question for Goodwin's scheme is the relationship between vocation as a benefit of Christ's merits and perfection as a benefit of Christ's person, since both involve the transformation of the believer's nature. As outlined in Chapter 3, Goodwin

41. *Works*, I, *Ephesians*, part I, 81.
42. *Works*, I, *Ephesians*, part I, 97.
43. *Works*, I, *Ephesians*, part I, 103.
44. *Works*, I, *Ephesians*, part I, 103.
45. *Works*, I, *Ephesians*, part I, 104.
46. *Works*, I, *Ephesians*, part I, 108.
47. *Works*, I, *Ephesians*, part I, 81.
48. *Works*, I, *Ephesians*, part I, 101.
49. *Works*, I, *Ephesians*, part I, 81–2; cf. 92.
50. *Works*, I, *Ephesians*, part I, 108.

believed there exists a dual soteriological necessity for transformation: believers must be transformed both from sinful to holy and from earthly to spiritual.[51] Thus, it would be natural for Goodwin to have designated the former transformation as a benefit of Christ's merits and the latter as a benefit of Christ's person, paralleling his designation of justification and of adoption. However, Goodwin assumed a different distinction: vocation he identified with imperfect transformation prior to death, whereas perfection he identified with the final and perfect transformation at glorification.[52] Goodwin's inconsistency here, perhaps, resulted from being constrained by the text of Ephesians.

No close parallels to Goodwin's scheme for Ephesians 1:7-9 are evident in Sibbes's works. Nevertheless, as already noted, Sibbes had insisted that sanctification first occurred in Christ.[53] And, as will be examined later, Sibbes also had repeatedly insisted that justification first occurs in Christ: 'Justification from our sins, first in Christ, (he is freed from our sinnes) and then in us.'[54] Where Goodwin advanced beyond Sibbes was in his distinction between salvific benefits founded in Christ's person and those founded in Christ's merits. The significance of this distinction for Goodwin's soteriology will become evident later.[55]

5.2.2 Partaking of Christ's reunification

As Goodwin expounded Ephesians 1:10 he appealed to his rule to explain the regathering of all things in Christ. Here Goodwin advanced beyond Sibbes, who, while reflecting on the same text, had merely offered the short explanation that 'in Christ God brought all in one head againe.'[56] Elsewhere, in a longer consideration of the same doctrinal point, Sibbes had appealed to Christ's work as mediator, but desisted from arguing that the regathering of all things had first occurred in Christ's person.[57] Owen, in his chapter on this verse, also desisted from offering such an explanation and instead merely contended,

> In [Christ] they all consist, on him do they depend, unto him are they subject;
> in their Relation unto him doth their peace, union and agreement among

---

51. See §3.2.1.

52. *Works*, I, *Ephesians*, part I, 67–9, 97–101, 108.

53. See §5.2.1.1.

54. Sibbes, *Beames of Divine Light*, 'The Spirituall Jubile', 36; cf. Sibbes, *Exposition: upon The first Chapter of the Second Epistle to the Corinthians*, 405; Sibbes, *Exposition, upon The fourth Chapter of the second Epistle to the Corrinthians*, 31; Sibbes, *Evangelicall Sacrifices*, 'The Hidden Life', 32–3; Sibbes, *The Christians Portion*, 115; Sibbes, *Divine meditations and holy contemplations*, 194.

55. See §5.3.3.

56. Sibbes, *The Christians Portion*, 160–1.

57. Sibbes, *Light from Heaven*, 'Angels Acclamations', 254–61.

themselves consist. This is the *Recapitulation of all things* intended by the Apostle.[58]

In contrast to both colleagues, Goodwin provided a far more elaborate account of the regathering of all things in Christ by appealing to his rule of participation. Interpreting 'all things' to refer to all intelligent creatures in heaven and earth,[59] Goodwin argued that at the first creation 'all things' enjoyed harmony, but upon the advent of sin this original harmony was shattered.[60] He explained,

> Christ had … his gathering again in his own Person; and therefore a scattering first that befel his own Person, and what is true of us, is first true of him. And by virtue of this it was that we were All gathered; for 'tis a sure Rule, That what is done in us by him, the like was first done for us in Christ himself[61]

To Christ's incarnation, death and resurrection, Goodwin attached a united–scattered–reunited scheme which, by divine intention, is the pattern applied to 'all things'. In Christ's person the three great divisions were united: 'in the Person of the *Lord Jesus Christ* there is God, and Angels, and Men, *Jew* and *Gentile*, sum'd up in him; he partakes in his Person of all these.'[62] First, God and creature were united in him because of the hypostatic union. Secondly, humans and angels were united, since Christ assumed a human nature yet also belonged to the heavenly condition of angels.[63] Moreover, Christ's human nature, composed of both body and soul, belongs to both heaven and earth. Thirdly, having both Jewish and non-Jewish ancestry, Christ's person united Jew and Gentile.[64]

Having established this groundwork, Goodwin then moved to account for the significance of Christ's death and resurrection. In Christ's death these unions contained in his person were dissolved.[65] The hypostatic union of Christ's two natures and the union between Christ and the Father came as close as possible to disintegration. Christ was abandoned by both disciples and angels. The union of his body and soul ceased. However, in Christ's exaltation this scattering was reversed.[66] In his resurrection, Christ's body and soul were reunited, and his divine

---

58. Owen, *The Glory of Christ*, 164–5. Baynes, in his commentary on this verse, argued along similar lines. Baynes, *An entire commentary vpon the vvhole epistle of the Apostle Paul to the Ephesians*, 114–15.

59. *Works*, I, *Ephesians*, part I, 127. Goodwin conceded that other creatures are restored as a secondary effect. *Works*, I, *Ephesians*, part I, 167–8.

60. *Works*, I, *Ephesians*, part I, 134.

61. *Works*, I, *Ephesians*, part I, 165.

62. *Works*, I, *Ephesians*, part I, 131.

63. *Works*, I, *Ephesians*, part I, 130.

64. *Works*, I, *Ephesians*, part I, 131.

65. *Works*, I, *Ephesians*, part I, 165–6.

66. *Works*, I, *Ephesians*, part I, 166–7.

sonship reaffirmed. In his ascension, Christ's relation to God was re-established and he was advanced above the state of angels. The ascended Christ draws all peoples to him and so his reunification is applied to others.[67] Because this regathering was accomplished in Christ's person, Goodwin concluded that the final union of all things will enjoy a permanency and a nearness surpassing the original.[68]

In a separate sermon on Ephesians 2:14-16, published in 1651 as *Christ the Universall Peace-Maker*, Goodwin paid greater attention to the reconciliation of Jew and Gentile.[69] Insisting that the unity established in the church between Jew and Gentile was first realized in Christ himself,[70] he claimed that unity was first established in Christ's personal body (i.e. his human nature): 'This one new Man, which they are to grow up into, answereth exactly to that one Body, which was then gathered together, represented and met in him on the Cross, bearing the Image of it, and wrought by the Virtue of it.'[71] Thus, Goodwin connected the unity of the church with his rule: 'there being nothing also done for us by Christ, but the like was first done on himself.'[72]

5.2.3 Partaking of Christ's baptism

Ephesians 1:13-14 was the *textus classicus* of Goodwin's much discussed notion of personal assurance of salvation as a distinct state from conversion.[73] Equating such assurance with the sealing of the Spirit, Goodwin referred to his rule:

> The work of *Sealing* of the Holy Ghost is done by virtue of Jesus Christ, He, and his Virtue, is left out in no work that is done for us. I gave you this Rule ... That whatsoever work God doth upon us, he doth unto Christ first. Now then, are we *sealed* virtually in Christ? why then we must find the same work upon Christ himself first. ... we are sealed, because he once was sealed, and by virtue of that we come to be sealed.[74]

Prior to Goodwin, Sibbes had similarly insisted that 'Christ is the first sealed ... The same Spirit that sealed the Redeemer, seales the redeemed.'[75] For Sibbes, though,

---

67. *Works*, I, *Ephesians*, part I, 167.

68. *Works*, I, *Ephesians*, part I, 164; cf. 130, 133–4, 149.

69. Goodwin inserted a reference to this sermon in *Works*, I, *Ephesians*, part I, 160.

70. *Works*, I, *Thirteen Sermons*, 12.

71. *Works*, I, *Thirteen Sermons*, 26.

72. *Works*, I, *Thirteen Sermons*, 15.

73. E.g. Horton, 'Assurance', 289–91.

74. *Works*, I, *Ephesians*, part I, 209.

75. Sibbes, *Exposition: upon The first Chapter of the Second Epistle to the Corinthians*, 473–4; cf. Sibbes, *Yea and amen*, 107–8. Baynes, in his commentary on Ephesians, similarly remarked, 'As God did seale his Christ ... so he doth seale us who are beleevers.' Baynes, *An entire commentary vpon the vvhole epistle of the Apostle Paul to the Ephesians*, 142. Likewise,

God had sealed Christ by many events including his miracles, his resurrection and the calling of Gentiles. Elsewhere Sibbes included Christ's baptism.[76] In contrast, Goodwin identified Christ's sealing specifically with Christ's baptism, since the accompanying heavenly voice and visible descent of the Spirit confirmed Christ's sonship. If in Christ's case the outward ordinance of baptism was accompanied with divine sealing, then Goodwin reasoned that divine sealing must accompany the baptism of saints.[77] He held that this sealing, while not in the form of a heavenly voice or visible descent of the Spirit, and often separated in time from baptism, nevertheless is a consequence of Christ's own sealing.

5.2.4 Partaking of Christ's exaltation

Goodwin's rule of participation is foundational in his exposition of Ephesians 1:19-23 and 2:5-7. Throughout these verses he maintained that in Christ's exaltation Christ is presented as 'a Pattern and Prototype of what was to be done in us, and for us, until the full accomplishment of our Salvation.'[78] Here again Goodwin was following Sibbes's lead. Sibbes had often urged that the exaltation of believers was first realized in Christ: 'If we look to Resurrection, Ascension, or Glory, see it in Christ first.'[79] For both divines, participation in Christ's exaltation held special importance for in it Christ received in himself the fullness of salvific benefits. Thus, Goodwin, in keeping with his person/merits schema, maintained that Christ was exalted on the basis of both his person and his merits.[80] Consequently, he contended that the whole of salvation is comprehended in what believers receive by participation in Christ's resurrection and ascension.[81]

5.2.4.1 Christ's resurrection Citing scriptural language of Christ as the first-fruits, Goodwin saw Christ's resurrection as exemplifying his rule.[82] Both justification and transformation, he contended, were first enacted upon Christ in his resurrection.

Owen, having referred to Christ's baptism, wrote, 'Thus did God Seal the Head of the Church with the Holy Spirit; and thence undoubtedly may we best learn how the Members are sealed with the same Spirit.' John Owen, *Two discourses concerning the Holy Spirit, and His work. The one, Of the Spirit as a comforter. The other, As He is the author of spiritual gifts* (1693), 86.

76. Sibbes, *Beames of Divine Light*, 'The Fruitful Labour', 202–3.

77. *Works*, I, *Ephesians*, part I, 210.

78. *Works*, I, *Ephesians*, part II, 2.

79. Sibbes, *Exposition, upon The fourth Chapter of the second Epistle to the Corrinthians*, 238; cf. Sibbes, *Evangelicall Sacrifices*, 'The Redemption of Bodyes', 49; Sibbes, *Light from Heaven*, 'The Fountain Opened', 173; Sibbes, *A heavenly conference*, 151; Sibbes, *Divine meditations and holy contemplations*, 194–5.

80. *Works*, I, *Ephesians*, part II, 233. See §5.3.1.3.

81. *Works*, I, *Ephesians*, part II, 208.

82. *Works*, I, *Ephesians*, part II, 224–5.

To this end, Goodwin cast Christ's resurrection as Christ's justification and transformation. Conversely, he also portrayed the justification and transformation of believers as resurrection events,[83] with the pre-conversion existence of believers as a state of death in respect to both the guilt and power of sin.[84]

Justification Goodwin understood to be first bestowed upon Christ in his resurrection. To this end, he construed justification as a resurrection experience: 'Take a man condemned to die ... there is the guilt of death upon him, and you will say he is a dead man; his Pardon now would be a Resurrection from death to life.'[85] More important, however, is Goodwin's claim that Christ's resurrection was Christ's justification. By being raised from the dead, Christ was declared righteous having had guilt imputed to him in his substitutionary death (Romans 4:25).[86] Prior to Goodwin, Sibbes had repeatedly taught the same interpretation of Christ's resurrection.[87] For both divines, therefore, believers are justified by participating in Christ's resurrection.

Like justification, Goodwin understood transformation to be first bestowed upon Christ in his resurrection. This is straightforward in the case of bodily resurrection. For regeneration and progressive sanctification, Goodwin argued that both constitute resurrection experiences.[88] This is unsurprising since in his mind regeneration and bodily resurrection comprise one transformation applied in two stages.[89] To secure Christ's resurrection as the pattern of both regeneration and bodily resurrection, Goodwin argued that Christ experienced a 'double Resurrection' effected first in his soul immediately following death and then in his body on the third day.[90] Thus, Christ's double resurrection operates as the pattern for the resurrection of both the soul and body of the believer.[91] Moreover, Goodwin saw confirmation that regeneration was first enacted in Christ's resurrection from the scriptural interchange of language: 'As his Resurrection is called a begetting of him again, or a begetting him rather, so our being born again, our conversion is called a Resurrection.'[92] The parallel, however, could not be fully sustained since

---

83. *Works*, I, *Ephesians*, part II, 127; cf. 189, 207–8.

84. *Works*, I, *Ephesians*, part II, 10–11; cf. 2; part I, 367.

85. *Works*, I, *Ephesians*, part I, 383.

86. *Works*, I, *Ephesians*, part I, 141, 156, 372; part II, 189; *Christ Set Forth*, 46. Similarly, the benefit of adoption is patterned on Christ's resurrection because thence he was declared anew to be God's Son.

87. E.g. Sibbes, *Exposition: upon The first Chapter of the Second Epistle to the Corinthians*, 405; Sibbes, *Evangelicall Sacrifices*, 'The Hidden Life', 32; Sibbes, *Beames of Divine Light*, 'The Spirituall Jubile', 36; Sibbes, *Divine meditations and holy contemplations*, 194.

88. *Works*, I, *Ephesians*, part I, 382.

89. See §3.3.

90. *Works*, I, *Ephesians*, part II, 210.

91. *Works*, I, *Ephesians*, part I, 381.

92. *Works*, I, *Ephesians*, part I, 381.

Goodwin denied that Christ's human nature was corrupt. This exception was implicit in his comment: 'Christ lay under the guilt of Sin imputed to him, we lie under the *power* and *guilt* too.'[93] This difficulty was perhaps the reason that while Sibbes had freely claimed that the believer's bodily resurrection was first realized in Christ in his resurrection,[94] he had refrained from arguing that the believer's regeneration and progressive sanctification was first realized in the same.[95] For Sibbes, Christ's conception and corresponding sanctification of his human nature from original corruption appeared to have provided him with a sufficient parallel for inner transformation and which avoided the difficulty.[96]

5.2.4.2 Christ's ascension Finally, Goodwin's rule accounts for the eschatological glorification of believers. Equating Christ's ascension and heavenly session with Christ's glorification,[97] Goodwin maintained that Christ's glorification functions as the pattern of the glorification of believers such that in the final state believers will experience the same glory that Christ received first.[98] Prior to Goodwin, Sibbes had often appealed to the same logic: 'Our Ascension is in Christ, and our sitting at the right hand of God, in him first: all things that are ours, they are first his.'[99] Perhaps owing to the rise of radicals, Goodwin, however, was careful to insist that Christ alone sits at God's right hand.[100] To maintain Christ's unique glory along with believers partaking of Christ's glory, Goodwin turned to an analogy: 'Jesus Christ is the King of the other World, and you all shall be Nobles of that World, of that Kingdom, and sit together with him.'[101] As 'Nobles, and Fellows

---

93. *Works*, I, *Ephesians*, part I, 376. Goodwin was more explicit when discussing the related problem of bodily resurrection: 'Bodies that have seen Corruption; Jesus Christ's Body never saw Corruption, he was never dead in sins and trespasses, he died for sins and trespasses indeed, but we were dead in sins and trespasses.' *Works*, I, *Ephesians*, part I, 382.

94. For example, Sibbes had written, 'Our Resurrection is in Christ first, we rise, because hee is the *first begotten from the dead*.' Sibbes, *The Christians Portion*, 115; cf. Sibbes, *Exposition: upon The first Chapter of the Second Epistle to the Corinthians*, 405; Sibbes, *Exposition, upon The fourth Chapter of the second Epistle to the Corrinthians*, 31–2; Sibbes, *The Excellencie of the Gospell*, 419; Sibbes, *Beames of Divine Light*, 'The Spirituall Jubile', 36.

95. Sibbes had come close to making that identification in one passage: Sibbes, *Exposition, upon The fourth Chapter of the second Epistle to the Corrinthians*, 154.

96. See §5.2.1.1.

97. *Works*, I, *Ephesians*, part II, 226.

98. *Works*, I, *Ephesians*, part II, 221, 232–3, 247.

99. Sibbes, *The Christians Portion*, 115–16; cf. Sibbes, *Exposition: upon The first Chapter of the Second Epistle to the Corinthians*, 21, 405; Sibbes, *Exposition, upon The fourth Chapter of the second Epistle to the Corrinthians*, 32; Sibbes, *The Excellencie of the Gospell*, 419–20; Sibbes, *Beames of Divine Light*, 'The Spirituall Jubile', 36.

100. *Works*, I, *Ephesians*, part II, 233, 243.

101. *Works*, I, *Ephesians*, part II, 227.

with him', believers shall be 'Coheirs of the same Kingdom with him' and share in 'the same Glory'.[102]

5.2.5 Conclusion: Securing the reality of salvation

Inherited from Sibbes, Goodwin's rule of participation, therefore, became a crucial underlying theological principle in his exposition of Ephesians. He turned to this rule to meet his pastoral concern to impress upon his hearers the reality of salvation. First, it demonstrated the height of salvation since believers receive what Christ himself already possesses.[103] Secondly, it secured the gracious nature of salvation since salvation is entirely dependent upon Christ who has already received all salvific benefits in himself.[104] Finally, it secured the certainty of salvation since salvation has already been accomplished and received in Christ for believers.[105] Leigh concurred,

> This is a comfort to the people of God; they can never loose evangelicall blessings of grace and glory, because Christ is made the *Lord Treasurer* and *Lord Keeper* of them. We are not trusted with them our selves, for then we should loose them; but he receives them for vs, and communicates them to us.[106]

Before the bulk of his grand project was penned, Goodwin had, therefore, already embraced a powerful notion of participation which, he believed, magnified the reality of salvation. But did this rule play a fundamental role in the soteriology of his grand project?

5.3 Goodwin's soteriology of participation

What must now be demonstrated is that this notion of participation was entailed in the substructure of the soteriology of Goodwin's grand project. The foundational significance of his rule is evident from the primacy in salvation accomplished that Goodwin granted to Christ as head over other Christological categories and from the primacy in salvation applied that Goodwin granted to the exemplary cause over other causes. The net result is that Goodwin held soteriology to be the application or extension of Christology to the believer.

5.3.1 Salvation accomplished: The primacy of Christ as head

Goodwin's rule of participation was a consequence of understanding Christ as the head of the elect. Primarily here was the notion of Christ as the second

---

102. *Works*, I, *Ephesians*, part II, 233.
103. *Works*, I, *Ephesians*, part I, 64; part II, 2.
104. *Works*, I, *Ephesians*, part II, 203–4.
105. *Works*, I, *Ephesians*, part II, 217; cf. 211–12; *Christ Set Forth*, 48.
106. Leigh, *Divine Promises*, 60.

Adam. Commenting upon Paul's Adam/Christ schema, Goodwin remarked that the story of humanity reduces to two men since: 'these two betweene them, had all the rest of the sons of men hanging at their girdle'.[107] This Christological category is significant because as the head of a new humanity, whatever is true of Christ becomes true of all his members, just as was the case with Adam.[108] Goodwin's rule, therefore, was a consequence of his commitment to understanding Christ as the Adamic head of the elect.[109] The same had been the case for Sibbes's theology. Sibbes had written, 'we have all we have in *Christ*, as a Head, as the first, as our *elder brother*, as a roote, as the second *Adam*, we have all in Him, by confidence in him; we have whatsoever is good in him.'[110] What must be noted is that both Goodwin and Sibbes were, therefore, not simply advancing their rule of participation but the stronger notion that whatever is true of Christ in his human nature becomes true of believers. In this sense, soteriology is the application or extension of Christology to the believer. This stronger and more dangerous notion was loved by many radical and antinomian writers. For instance, John Everard (1584?–1640/1) wrote, 'whatever priviledge or benefit Christ hath, they shall all receive of his fulness, *grace for grace*, they shall all be made *partakers of all* the vertues of the *head*.'[111] Nevertheless, more conservative divines such as Burgess even embraced it, while qualifying the extent of application: 'Whatsoever priviledge or glory Christ hath, it is proportionably communicated to thee.'[112]

The fundamental role of participation in Goodwin's soteriology may therefore be established by demonstrating that Christ's headship was Goodwin's chief Christological category. Unfortunately, Jones in his study of Goodwin's Christology neglects its fundamental importance.[113] That it was fundamental for Goodwin is evident from several considerations. In the first instance, this Christological category had played a decisive role in unlocking his spiritual journey, for reflection upon Christ's headship had ended Goodwin's seven-year struggle for assurance. He recounted, 'I began to reflect that Jesus Christ was the Head for Salvation, as

---

107. *Christ Set Forth*, 38.

108. *Works*, I, *Ephesians*, part I, 81.

109. As will become clear in §5.4.2, Goodwin believed that Christ being the superior Adamic head entails Christ being the mystical head of the church, his mystical body. Within the head–body analogy Goodwin's rule was again implied, since a body must match its head.

110. Sibbes, *The Christians Portion*, 121.

111. John Everard, *Some Gospel-Treasures Opened: Or, The Holiest of all unvailing: Discovering yet more The Riches of Grace and Glory, to the Vessels of Mercy* (1653), 470; cf. 549; Sprigg, *Approaching Glory*, 75, 78; Tobias Crisp, *Christ Alone Exalted In fourteen Sermons preached in, and neare London* (1643), 46–7; Richard Coppin, *Divine Teachings: In three Parts* (1653), 53.

112. Burgess, *CXLV Expository Sermons*, 607.

113. The closest Jones comes to recognition of its importance is in one brief comment: Jones, *Why Heaven Kissed Earth*, 225.

Adam had been for Sin and Condemnation … this did mightily and experimentally enlighten me.'[114]

Moreover, in his sermons on Ephesians, Goodwin asserted that Christ's headship over the church is more primitive than Christ's other offices: 'above all offices belonging to himself he is above all a head to his church.'[115] Referring to the classic threefold office of prophet, priest and king, Goodwin remarked, 'this relation of *Headship* doth import all his Offices, but with that peculiarness, and with that eminency, as no other relation in Scripture doth.'[116]

However, the primacy of the headship category in salvation accomplished and its relation to Goodwin's rule is most thoroughly demonstrated by an examination of Goodwin's frequent references to Christ as a common person in his sermons on Ephesians and his tract *Christ Set Forth*. The terms 'common person' and 'head' were closely connected in Goodwin's thought and often treated as synonymous when focusing on the representative sense of headship: 'He cometh in as a Common Person, that is, as our Head.'[117] A common person he defined as an individual who not only acts on behalf of another but acts in their stead and personates them.[118] Whereas Christ is in believers by a real indwelling, believers are in Christ in this sense of legal representation. Here Goodwin's 'in Christ'/'with Christ' distinction was vital. Believers possess a privilege 'in Christ' because Christ has accomplished or received it as their representative.[119] This Goodwin distinguished from 'with Christ' whereby a benefit is possessed by believers in their own persons:

> for that is a true Rule, that those Works which were done in Christ for us, after they are begun to be wrought in us, we are said to have them wrought in us together with Christ … But when he comes to those Works which yet are to be wrought in us … of these he only saith, that they are wrought for us in Christ, but not they are wrought in us with Christ, because that we are not yet actually in our Persons Partakers of them, but only as yet in our Head[120]

The two are connected since the former grants the legal right to the latter. The representative aspect of headship, of course, was the domain of federal theology: as Adam was appointed a common or public person according to the covenant of works, so Christ was appointed a common person according to the covenant of grace. The representative actions of Adam and Christ provide the legal basis for their members to receive what each as head possesses:

114. *Life*, xvii.
115. *Works*, I, *Ephesians*, part I, 485.
116. *Works*, I, *Ephesians*, part I, 480.
117. *Works*, I, *Ephesians*, part I, 79; cf. 59, 61, 100, 481.
118. *Christ Set Forth*, 31–2, 63, 96–7.
119. *Works*, I, *Ephesians*, part II, 210.
120. *Works*, I, *Ephesians*, part II, 209; cf. 234; part I, 59.

what ever God meant to doe for us, and in us, what ever priviledge or benefit he meant to bestow upon us, he did that thing first to Christ, and (some way) bestowed the like on him as a Common person, that so it might be by a solemne formall Act ratified, and be made sure to be done to us in our persons in due time, having first been done to him representing our persons; and that by this course taken, it might (when done to us) be effected by virtue of what was first done to him. ... Now this rule holds in all blessings else bestowed[121]

Thus, Christ's designation as a common person provided the legal foundation for Goodwin's rule of participation because what Christ did as a common person believers are reckoned to have done and what befell him legally befell believers also.[122] This point was especially intrinsic to Goodwin's covenant theology because, as already observed, he contended that the covenant of grace was primarily made with Christ and only secondarily with the elect in him.[123] Consequently, all soteric benefits must be 'given in Christ, ere they are actually to us'.[124]

What should be noted is that while styling Christ as a common person was widespread among mainstream puritans,[125] Goodwin especially stressed that Christ functioned as a common person across Christ's personal history:

what Christ *was, or did,* or hath been done to him, it was all as *in,* and *to,* and *by* a common *Person* Representing us therein; which makes all, and every particular thereof (which we are capable of) as well as any part to be legally ours, and indiffeisibly must be bestowed upon in the end[126]

Since Christ served as a common person in all he did and befell him, his office as head encompasses all of his actions. Here again Goodwin was developing the thought of Sibbes who had written, 'this is a sweet meditation of *Christ!* to see our selves in him, in all the passages of his birth, and life, and death, and resurrection, and ascension, to glory in heaven: for all that he did, was as a publicke person, as the second *Adam*.'[127] For Goodwin, the implication was that believers are 'Partakers of all' that Christ was, did or befell him.[128] Accordingly, Goodwin's claim was that his rule of participation applied no less than to the entirety of what Christ did or received.

---

121. *Christ Set Forth*, 48; cf. 40.

122. *Works*, I, *Ephesians*, part II, 216.

123. See p. 157 fn. 237 for references.

124. *Works*, III, *Christ the Mediator*, 28; cf. *Christ Set Forth*, 13.

125. E.g. Flavel, *The Method of Grace*, 5–6; Burgess, *Justification (1654)*, 263; Owen, *Communion with God*, 232.

126. *Works*, II, *Election*, 322–3.

127. Sibbes, *Beames of Divine Light*, 'The Spirituall Jubile', 42; cf. 41. In contrast, Owen appealed less frequently to the notion of Christ as a common person.

128. *Works*, II, *Election*, 322; cf. *Works*, I, *Ephesians*, part I, 370.

I will now, therefore, turn to consider how, according to Goodwin, Christ operated as a common person throughout his personal history. Thus, I will demonstrate that Christ's office as head encompasses all of the stages of his existence.

5.3.1.1 Christ as common person in his pre-incarnate state Goodwin even contended that Christ acted as a common person before his incarnation.[129] Christ had to function as a representative head to Old Testament saints, he reasoned, in order for them to receive forgiveness.[130] Some divines objected to such a view, arguing that assumption of a human nature is a prerequisite for acting as a common person.[131] Goodwin, however, not only defended his view but also asserted that Christ acted as a common person in eternity past.[132] Christ, he claimed, was first appointed as a common person in election.[133] Alluding to Ephesians 1:4, he explained, 'Jesus Christ was not only a Common Person in his dying for us; but in his being chosen also ... and so we were elected in him.'[134] In Goodwin's mind the meaning of 'elected in him' is determinative: Christ was elected as an individual and also as the representative head of the church; believers were elected as individuals and also elected in Christ, that is, with Christ as their head.[135] Both Christ and the church were elected in eternity, but Christ was elected first in the order of nature.[136] Goodwin's rule of participation is, therefore, rooted in the divine decrees of election: 'we were *Chosen in Christ* as the *Pattern* unto whom we should be conformed.'[137] Moreover, as the elected head Christ represented believers in the making of the *pactum salutis*: 'so a Covenant was as truly struck between God and Us, through Christ's representing us, as the Covenant of Works was between God and Us, as considered in *Adam*.'[138] Christ as a common person thereby took possession of the promises on behalf of the elect.

5.3.1.2 Christ as common person in his earthly state However, Goodwin held that Christ most clearly functions as a common person in his earthly life because in that state Christ fulfilled the obligations God had laid upon humans. In *Christ Set Forth*, he explained,

129. *Works*, I, *Ephesians*, part I, 481; cf. 61.
130. *Works*, I, *Ephesians*, part I, 61.
131. *Works*, I, *Ephesians*, part I, 60.
132. *Works*, V, *Glory of the Gospel*, 76.
133. *Works*, I, *Ephesians*, part I, 72; cf. *Works*, IV, *Object and Acts*, part I, 105; *Works*, V, *The Knowledg*, 76.
134. *Works*, I, *Ephesians*, part I, 59; cf. *Works*, II, *The Knowledg*, 171.
135. Dickson briefly stated a similar scheme when commenting on Ephesians 1:4. Dickson, *An Expositon of all St. Pauls Epistles*, 108.
136. *Works*, I, *Ephesians*, part I, 62; cf. *Works*, II, *The Knowledg*, 111. Here Goodwin followed the exposition of Baynes in his commentary on Ephesians. Baynes, *An entire commentary vpon the vvhole epistle of the Apostle Paul to the Ephesians*, 32–3.
137. *Works*, I, *Ephesians*, part I, 64.
138. *Works*, I, *Ephesians*, part I, 63; cf. *Works*, III, *Christ the Mediator*, 28.

if you aske, wherein Christ was a *Common person*, representing us, and standing in our stead; I answer, If in any thing, then in all those conditions and states wherein he was, in what *he did*, or *befell him*, whilst *here on earth especially*: For he had no other end to come downe into this world, but to sustaine our persons, and to act our parts, and to have what was to have been done to us, acted upon him.[139]

In the same tract, Goodwin argued that Christ only operated as a common person with respect to what humans were obliged to do under the covenant of works, and so concluded that Christ did not function as a common person in the incarnation event itself.[140] Here Goodwin's thought was inconsistent, since such a condition would prohibit Christ from operating as a common person in election. Yet, in the same work, Goodwin argued that Christ functioned as a common person in the sanctification of his nature occurring at his incarnation.[141] Furthermore, in later works Goodwin argued that the benefits founded in Christ's person were received in Christ himself as the immediate result of the incarnation and subsequently bestowed upon the church.[142] Perhaps the mature Goodwin had abandoned the narrower understanding of Christ as a common person. Nevertheless, what was unequivocal was Goodwin's repeated insistence upon the incarnation as 'the Foundation of all, that Christ, as a public Person, did for us'.[143] In this sense, at least, the incarnation was essential to Christ's office as a common person.

For Goodwin, Christ acted as a common person in all of his actions on earth.[144] In particular, he acted as a common person in his life of obedience under the law and in his atoning death.[145] Owen contended for the same: 'Christ in his obedience, death and sacrifice was a publick person.'[146] Goodwin's dual contention here was,

---

139. *Christ Set Forth*, 38.

140. *Christ Set Forth*, 97.

141. *Christ Set Forth*, 48.

142. E.g. *Works*, V, *The Holy Ghost*, 387–8.

143. *Works*, II, *The Creatures*, 87; cf. 81; *Works*, V, *Glory of the Gospel*, 76. Here he followed Sibbes who had insisted that the incarnation was the essential foundation for Christ acting as a public person. E.g. Sibbes, *Beames of Divine Light*, 'The Spirituall Jubile', 37; Richard Sibbes, *Christs exaltation purchast by humiliation Wherein you may see mercy and misery meete together. Very vsefull I. For instructing the ignorant. II. For comforting the weake. III. For confirming the strong* (1639), 8–9; Sibbes, *Exposition: upon The first Chapter of the Second Epistle to the Corinthians*, 406, 437; Sibbes, *Yea and amen*, 30.

144. *Works*, V, *Glory of the Gospel*, 76.

145. *Works*, III, *Christ the Mediator*, 293.

146. John Owen, *Salus electorum, sanguis Jesu, or, The death of death in the death of Christ a treatise of the redemption and reconciliation that is in the blood of Christ with the merit thereof, and the satisfaction wrought thereby: wherin the proper end of the death of Christ is asserted ... and the whole controversie about universall redemption fully discussed* (1648), 240. Elsewhere, specifically insisting upon Christ's obedience under the law, Owen

of course, shared by many like-minded divines because it was required to secure justification as the imputation of both Christ's active and passive obedience.[147] On behalf of the elect, Christ fulfilled the law's demands for both obedience and punishment. Importantly, as Goodwin stressed, Christ in his death acted not only as a surety but also as a common person.[148] As a surety, Christ was a substitute, so the believer no longer faces the penalty of death; as a common person, Christ was a representative, so the believer participates in Christ's death (i.e. the believer is counted as having died in his death).[149] The former requires the imputation of guilt to Christ; the latter entails the imputation of Christ's righteousness to the believer.

Further, Goodwin held that Christ acted as a common person in his death with regard not only to justification but also to sanctification. Since Christ died as a common person, so the mortification of believers occurs as a result.[150] However, since Goodwin held to the sinless humanity of Christ, Christ's death and mortification of sin in believers fell short of an exact correspondence. Here it should also be noted that Goodwin refrained from embracing Saltmarsh's claim that Christ's sanctification on behalf of the elect included him repenting and believing on their behalf.[151] This notion was stoutly rejected by mainstream puritans. Burgess, for example, believed Saltmarsh's position implied that Christ saved himself.[152]

Finally, since Christ represented the whole of the elect, Goodwin understood Christ to operate as a common person in regard to the unity of believers.[153] Christ's body (i.e. his human nature) represented his mystical body. Goodwin attempted to explain this in terms of a penal substitutionary understanding of the atonement: as well as bearing the penalty for the enmity between God and the elect in his death to achieve vertical reconciliation, Christ bore the penalty for enmity between fellow members of the elect to accomplish horizontal reconciliation.[154] This work in Christ's own person was representative in nature and so to be distinguished from

---

wrote, 'Christ obeyed as a publick Person.' Owen, *Justification*, 375 cf. 377. Sibbes, however, had put more stress on Christ acting as a common person in his death than in his life of obedience under the law. For example, Sibbes had written, 'when Christ died, then we were in him as a publike person.' Sibbes, *An Exposition of the Third Chapter of Philippians*, 102; cf. Richard Sibbes, *Two sermons: preached by that faithfull and reverend divine, Richard Sibbes, D.D. and sometimes preacher to the honorable society of Grayes Inne; and master of Katherine Hall in Cambridge* (1639), 63; Sibbes, *Christs exaltation*, 131.

147. *Works*, I, *Ephesians*, part II, 218; *Christ Set Forth*, 40.
148. *Works*, III, *Christ the Mediator*, 293; *Christ Set Forth*, 31–3.
149. In contrast, Adam acted as a common person but not as a surety.
150. *Works*, II, *Election*, 322–3; *Christ Set Forth*, 42.
151. Saltmarsh, *Free-Grace*, 84.
152. Burgess, *Justification (1654)*, 123–4, 366.
153. *Works*, I, *Thirteen Sermons*, 24; cf. 13, 25–6.
154. *Works*, I, *Thirteen Sermons*, 15.

the subsequent work of application.[155] There was 'a virtual, influential making us one in his own Person, before we are made one in our selves'.[156]

5.3.1.3 Christ as common person in his exalted state In his exaltation, Goodwin held, Christ acted as a common person by taking possession of salvation on behalf of the elect. Christ therefore became the repository of all salvific benefits upon which believers may draw: 'God ordained him as the Store-House, and Treasury of all that Grace and Glory which he means to bestow on his Children.'[157] This idea was widely held among Reformed puritans and frequently associated with Christ as an Adamic head and common person.[158] Goodwin insisted that Christ took possession on the basis of both his person and his merits.[159] The latter was not universally accepted: as Burgess noted, there was some debate over whether Christ merited his exaltation.[160] Goodwin here again followed Sibbes.[161] In Goodwin's case this point was essential, since in his system Christ in his exaltation received the full benefits of his merits as well as of his person.

For Goodwin, Christ acted as a common person in his resurrection,[162] in respect to both justification and transformation.[163] Goodwin gave particular consideration to the former. Since Christ bore the guilt of the elect, his resurrection constituted justification from their guilt.[164] Thus, by Christ's resurrection the elect were justified in Christ.[165] While Goodwin was not alone in holding Christ's

---

155. *Works*, I, *Thirteen Sermons*, 5, 11.

156. *Works*, I, *Thirteen Sermons*, 12.

157. *Works*, V, *The Holy Ghost*, 203.

158. Hooker, *The Application of Redemption*, 121; Samuel Rutherford, *The Covenant of Life Opened: Or, A Treatise of the Covenant of Grace* (Edinburgh, 1655), 296; Owen, *Pneumatologia*, 362; Dickson, *An Expositon of all St. Pauls Epistles*, 108; Sibbes, *The Christians Portion*, 121.

159. *Works*, I, *Ephesians*, part I, 399, 402; part II, 223, 233; *Works*, III, *Christ the Mediator*, 407.

160. Burgess, *CXLV Expository Sermons*, 25. For background on this debate, see: T. Robert Baylor, '"With Him in Heavenly Places": Peter Lombard and John Calvin on the Merits and Exaltation of Christ', *International Journal of Systematic Theology* 17, no. 2 (2015): 152–75.

161. Sibbes, *Christs exaltation*, 28.

162. *Works*, I, *Ephesians*, part II, 211; cf. *Works*, V, *Gospel Holiness*, 34. Sibbes had stated the same, e.g. Sibbes, *Christs exaltation*, 16–17, 72, 132–3.

163. *Works*, I, *Ephesians*, part I, 400; part II, 11; *Christ Set Forth*, 40. Sibbes had also contended that Christ was a common person in his resurrection in respect of transformation. Sibbes, *Christs exaltation*, 16–17.

164. *Works*, I, *Ephesians*, part II, 189.

165. *Works*, I, *Ephesians*, part I, 373, 378; *Christ Set Forth*, 48. Admittedly, Goodwin did not connect Christ's resurrection with Christ's active obedience. However, Christ's

resurrection to be the justification of the elect,[166] he was particularly influential in promoting this notion.[167] Evans's claim that after Ames there was an 'almost total absence of this idea' therefore must be questioned.[168] Yet, some like Burgess, fearing the antinomian threat, expressed reservations about this interpretation of Christ's resurrection.[169] Goodwin, however, believed that his 'in Christ'/'with Christ' distinction was vital and resolved the disagreement between mainstream divines and '*Antinomians*' over justification before faith.[170] At Christ's resurrection individuals were justified 'in Christ', but only upon believing are justified 'with Christ'.[171] Justification at Christ's resurrection was representative and therefore equated to the second act of justification in Goodwin's *tria momenta* scheme.[172]

As on earth, Christ continues to operate as a representative head in heaven.[173] Christ, therefore, ascended as a common person: 'He *entred into Heaven in our very names*, and so is to be considered in that act as a *Common person* ... and so representing us, and also taking *possession* in our right, and *we in him*; as a guardian takes possession for Heirs under age'.[174] Whereas in his resurrection Christ obtained possession of freedom from condemnation, in his ascension he obtained possession of eternal life.[175] In this sense, believers are presently seated in heaven. Goodwin compared this understanding to alternative interpretations of the present heavenly session of believers.[176] Some understood the expression to denote that Christ's heavenly session serves as a guarantee of the future sitting of believers, others that Christ functions as the pattern of future sitting and finally others that Christ's heavenly session grants the right to future glory. The final interpretation was Goodwin's opinion. The same view was articulated by Burgess,[177] and also had been assumed by Sibbes when he wrote that Christ 'hath taken Heaven in our place as our Husband, and we sit in heavenly places with

---

resurrection could be readily understood as divine approval of his active obedience alongside acquittal from imputed guilt.

166. Robert Towne, *A Re-assertion of Grace. Or, Vindiciæ Evangelii. A Vindication of the Gospell-truths, from the unjust censure and undue aspersions of Antinomians* (1654), 22; Dickson, *An Expositon of all St. Pauls Epistles*, 11; Sibbes, *Beames of Divine Light*, 'A Description of Christ', 40.

167. Saltmarsh, *Free-Grace*, 212, 215–16; Eyre, *Vindiciæ Justificationis Gratuitæ*, 71, 147.

168. Evans, *Imputation and Impartation*, 56–7.

169. Burgess, *Justification (1654)*, 124.

170. *Works*, I, *Ephesians*, part II, 219.

171. *Works*, I, *Ephesians*, part II, 218.

172. See §4.3.2.

173. *Works*, I, *Ephesians*, part I, 286; *Christ Set Forth*, 96–7; *Works*, V, *Glory of the Gospel*, 76.

174. *Christ Set Forth*, 68; cf. *Works*, I, *Ephesians*, part II, 213, 242.

175. *Christ Set Forth*, 69. This, Goodwin claimed, corresponds to the passive and active obedience parts of justification.

176. *Works*, I, *Ephesians*, part II, 211–12.

177. Burgess, *Justification (1651)*, 178.

him'.[178] Goodwin stressed that this interpretation may only be properly grounded if Christ is understood to sit as a common person and so believers already sit in Christ as their representative head.[179] Nonetheless, the other two interpretations, he contended, are also implications of Christ sitting as a common person.[180] Thus, in Goodwin's mind, Christ's ascension as a common person was the basic idea.

However, Goodwin denied that Christ operates as a common person in his heavenly intercession: 'he intercedes not as a *Common person*, (which relation in all other forementioned acts he still bore …) for we must not, cannot be said to intercede in him, for this last work lay not upon us to doe.'[181] Nevertheless, Christ's heavenly ministry pertains to his role as common person because it consists in the application of all that Christ accomplished and received as a representative head.[182] Indeed, it was because Christ's intercession concerns the application of salvation that Goodwin concluded that it must be unique to Christ as the mediator.[183]

5.3.1.4 Christ as head in Goodwin's grand project

While the term 'common person' is less dominant in the treatises belonging to Goodwin's grand project, crucially the notion of Christ as a superior Adamic head of the elect nevertheless provides the substructure of its soteriology.[184] To set a foundation for the whole project, Goodwin dedicated the bulk of the opening treatise, *The Creatures*, to a comparison of Adam and Christ.[185] Christ is presented as the second Adam, superior to the first. The following treatise, *An Unregenerate*, expounds how Adam as head brought the human race into misery. Against this backdrop, Goodwin further presented Christ as the second Adam. The three central treatises continue to present Christ as head. *Election* sets forward two divine decrees corresponding to two offices of Christ – head and redeemer – and states that headship is

---

178. Sibbes, *Exposition, upon The fourth Chapter of the second Epistle to the Corrinthians*, 237. In his commentary, Dickson likewise assumed the same view: 'In Christs ascension into heaven, the Redeemed judicially ascend with him; In Christs sitting, or glorious possession of eternal life, the Redeemed in a judicial way do sit, and are placed with him.' Dickson, *An Expositon of all St. Pauls Epistles*, 113.

179. *Works*, I, *Ephesians*, part II, 212.

180. See also: *Works*, I, *Ephesians*, part II, 218, 231–3.

181. *Christ Set Forth*, 96–7. Here Goodwin assumed his narrower definition of Christ's office as a common person.

182. *Works*, I, *Ephesians*, part II, 217–18.

183. *Christ Set Forth*, 97.

184. While Kim's purview is limited to the themes of faith and covenant, he correctly surmises that the natural/supernatural distinction founded upon Adam/Christ plays a fundamental role in Goodwin's soteriology: 'Goodwin's sharp distinction between Adam's natural faith and our supernatural faith leads to another clear distinction between Adam's representation of the natural order in *the covenant of works* and Christ's representation of the supernatural order in *the covenant of grace*. This contrast between Adam and Christ is a key parallel, penetrating throughout Goodwin's soteriology.' Kim, 'Salvation by Faith', 127.

185. *Works*, II, *The Creatures*, 31.

fundamental: 'the Office of *Redeemer* and *Saviour* superadded in his Election, unto that of *Headship*'.[186] Accordingly, this treatise is opened by grounding the necessity of election not in hamartiology which would require a redeemer but in the mutable condition of Adam by creation which necessitated a superior Adamic head.[187] This theme continues into *Christ the Mediator*, which although focused upon Christ's office as redeemer assumes that Christ's headship is more basic: 'Christ being originally and primitively constituted an *head* to them, this drew him to be a *Saviour*.'[188] In *The Holy Ghost*, Christ is presented as the head anointed with the Spirit which leads to the anointing of the church.[189] Many of these points will be elaborated below. While Christ's role as an Adamic head falls from view in the final treatise, *Blessed State*, this is because, by Goodwin's admission, he had already pre-empted discussing the final state in his opening work and so restricted himself to the narrow question of the intermediate state.[190] What, then, is clear is that Goodwin's grand project assumed that Christ's office as head of the elect is fundamental for articulating salvation accomplished. The implication is that Goodwin's rule of participation constitutes the basic principle in the soteriology of his grand project.

5.3.2 Salvation applied: The primacy of the exemplary cause

The primacy of Christ as head in salvation accomplished is matched by the primacy of the exemplary cause in salvation applied. This is evident from an examination of Goodwin's fragmentary comments concerning the various causal connections between Christ's work and the application of salvation. His tract *Christ Set Forth* is structured by the sequence of Christ's work – his death, resurrection, ascension and intercession – and he described this sequence as a '*golden chaine* of the *Causes of our salvation*'.[191] While each part of Christ's work in the chain holds a general causal relation to salvation applied, Goodwin contended that each part especially causes a corresponding aspect of salvation applied:

> though all the works of Christ for us have an Influence into his work in us, and upon us; yet so, as some are more especially attributed to some work of Christ than to another and some things in every work in us, more peculiarly to some of his Works for us, than to others.[192]

Each part of Christ's work, therefore, possesses both a general and a specific causal relationship with salvation applied. Here Goodwin's example was regeneration: 'this

---

186. *Works*, II, *Election*, 93; cf. 91, 305, 308–9; *Works*, I, *Ephesians*, part I, 98; part II, 233.
187. *Works*, II, *Election*, 1–3.
188. *Works*, III, *Christ the Mediator*, 302.
189. *Works*, V, *The Holy Ghost*, 8–10.
190. *Works*, V, *Blessed State*, 8.
191. *Christ Set Forth*, 82; cf. 85–6.
192. *Works*, V, *The Holy Ghost*, 419–20.

New Birth is thus peculiarly attributed to his Resurrection.'[193] This was not to deny other causes: 'to speak properly, His death is the *Meritorious* Cause, his Intercession, the *Applicatory* Cause: But his Resurrection is the *Virtual* Cause; as by virtue of which, it is wrought.'[194] The category '*Virtual* Cause' was employed to denote both that the resurrection contains the transforming power and that it is 'the exemplary Cause of our Regeneration'.[195] The former involves Christ's reception of the Spirit's power. The latter implies that the Spirit regenerates believers according to the pattern of Christ's resurrection.[196] Thus, in Goodwin's mind a twofold causal relation exists between Christ's resurrection and regeneration. Since Christ rose as a common person, the two ideas are readily integrated: Christ received resurrection power in his own resurrection in order for the same to be caused in the elect. Thus, 'When he rose all rose, and his Resurrection had all the power of all Resurrections contracted in it.'[197] Yet, it was the exemplary cause that is responsible for Christ's resurrection functioning as the special cause of regeneration.

The special role of the exemplary cause becomes clearer through an examination of the case of mortification. Goodwin particularly assigned mortification to the influence of Christ's death[198] and, importantly, interpreted the power of Christ's death in mortification in two ways. Often he interpreted it as a meritorious power: 'this a certain Rule, that whatever you can reckon and account to have been his Sufferings, they acquired and merited (in every tittle of them) a redeeming power, a purchasing power of something of like nature for us.'[199] He repeatedly stressed that Christ's death merited the power and grace to overcome corruption.[200] This was commonplace among Reformed orthodox divines.[201] Goodwin moved beyond the conservative majority by claiming that 'Christ purchased not only all the Graces of the Spirit for us, but the Spirit himself ... to dwell in us.'[202] Thus, whereas the power of Christ's resurrection equated to the actual power of the Spirit,[203] the power of Christ's death was to purchase the Spirit. As with vivification, Goodwin identified the actual mortifying power in terms of the Spirit: 'As Christ, after he was Condemned, was brought to the Cross, and there Executed, Crucified; so also the Spirit of God in true Christians, comes with the power of Christ, naileth his Lusts to the Cross of Christ.'[204] By implication, as in the case of vivification the

193. *Works*, V, *The Holy Ghost*, 420.
194. *Works*, V, *The Holy Ghost*, 420.
195. See also *Works*, I, *Ephesians*, part I, 81.
196. *Works*, V, *The Holy Ghost*, 420–1.
197. *Works*, I, *Ephesians*, part I, 378.
198. *Works*, V, *The Holy Ghost*, 420.
199. *Works*, II, *Election*, 313.
200. *Works*, I, *Ephesians*, part I, 486; *Works*, II, *The Knowledg*, 175.
201. E.g. Burgess, *Justification (1654)*, 417–18.
202. *Works*, V, *The Holy Ghost*, 45; cf. 47; *Works*, III, *An Unregenerate*, 48.
203. *Works*, V, *The Holy Ghost*, 420.
204. *Works*, V, *The Holy Ghost*, 211.

actual transforming power of mortification also resides in Christ's resurrection. This is consistent with Goodwin's claim that mortification occurs by vivification, that is, the infusion of new life displaces corruption.[205] For both mortification and vivification, then, Christ's death is the meritorious power, whereas his resurrection contains the actual transformative power.[206] However, elsewhere Goodwin equated 'the Power of Christs Death' with the exemplary cause:

> though the whole Sanctifying Vertue, and Energy flow together from his Death and Resurrection, yet Mortification is rather ascribed to the Vertue, and the Power of Christs Death, as quickening, or vivification to his Resurrection. Because Mortification hath a greater similitude with his Death, as the Effect useth to have with its cause.[207]

Christ's death, therefore, possesses a twofold causation in mortification: meritorious and exemplary. As with vivification, it was the exemplary cause in mortification that occupied a special place in Goodwin's thought.[208]

A similar pattern emerges from Goodwin's comments concerning bodily resurrection: the efficient cause is Christ's bestowal of his Spirit upon believers; the meritorious cause is the virtue of his death; the exemplary cause is his resurrection. The resurrection therefore operates as the pattern to which believers will be conformed.[209] The same also applies to glorification: Christ having entered heaven as a human is the efficient cause, his death the meritorious cause and his glorification the exemplary cause.[210] Again, Goodwin indicated that the exemplary cause is the special causal relation:

> I proceed ... to the exemplary Cause; and the greatness of this Glory appears from this. This exemplary Cause is the Glory of Jesus Christ himself ... He is not only made the efficient and meritorious Cause, but also the exemplary Cause of this Glory[211]

Here Goodwin again followed Sibbes. Sibbes had stressed that Christ's resurrection was 'both the cause and the patterne; the efficient and the exemplary cause' of the

205. See pp. 97–8.

206. *Works*, V, *The Holy Ghost*, 210–11.

207. *Works*, III, *Christ the Mediator*, 345.

208. Here Goodwin can be contrasted with enthusiastic preachers such as Saltmarsh who tended to avoid causation categories altogether and conceived mortification in mystical terms: 'they who are *mystically* and *spiritually planted* into *Christ*, are partakers of the power of his death, which is that *highest, purest,* and most *mystical mortification* that any have; and with this there goes a *spiritual power*, transforming and changing the whole man from former lusts.' Saltmarsh, *Free-Grace*, 66.

209. *Works*, I, *Ephesians*, part II, 223–4.

210. *Works*, I, *Ephesians*, part II, 232–3; *Works*, V, *Blessed State*, 108–10.

211. *Works*, V, *Blessed State*, 109.

resurrection of believers.[212] Regarding glorification, Sibbes wrote that Christ 'is not onely the efficient of all *glory* within and without, but he is the exemplary cause'.[213]

Regarding justification Goodwin also assumed that each part of Christ's work has a causal influence.[214] As the *materiale* of justification, Christ's obedience and death is its meritorious cause.[215] As before, Goodwin reserved the applicatory cause for Christ's intercession.[216] Regarding Christ's resurrection, the widespread opinion was that it causes justification by working faith in the believer.[217] Goodwin argued that Christ's resurrection has an additional 'reall causall influence into Justification'.[218] As already discussed, Christ's resurrection causes the justification of believers because it was his justification from the guilt of the elect.[219] While Goodwin refrained from employing the language of exemplary cause in this matter, he stated that the justification of believers is 'in a conformity' to Christ's justification.[220] Moreover, Burgess, while he could not accept Christ's resurrection as Christ's justification, nevertheless characterized this view as treating Christ's resurrection as the 'exemplar cause' of justification.[221]

Thus, while mainstream puritans commonly embraced the notion of the exemplary cause in the application of salvation, the case of justification suggests that Goodwin assumed it applied more widely. For Goodwin, every part of Christ's work has a special causal relation with a corresponding part of salvation applied in the believer: 'we may apply all in Christ, piece by piece, to the like to be done in our selves.'[222] While each part of Christ's work causes the whole of salvation, each part also causes a specific part 'in a more eminent manner … for what is in Christ is but the Idea, the meer Pattern and Exemplar of a Christian'.[223] The exemplary cause, therefore, constitutes the dominant causation in Goodwin's applied soteriology. It is of little surprise that the same can be said of Sibbes's soteriology. Sibbes wrote, 'Christ is an exemplary cause, we have all in him and through him, and by him, as an exemplary paterne.'[224] For both divines, salvation primarily

---

212. Sibbes, *Evangelicall Sacrifices*, 'The Redemption of Bodyes', 48; cf. Sibbes, *An Exposition of the Third Chapter of Philippians*, 243, 246.

213. Sibbes, *Light from Heaven*, 'The Fountain Opened', 173; cf. Sibbes, *Exposition: upon The first Chapter of the Second Epistle to the Corinthians*, 100.

214. *Christ Set Forth*, 8.

215. *Christ Set Forth*, 29; *Works*, IV, *Object and Acts*, part I, 103.

216. *Christ Set Forth*, 82.

217. *Works*, IV, *Object and Acts*, part I, 106; *Christ Set Forth*, 30; cf. *Works*, V, *The Holy Ghost*, 421.

218. *Christ Set Forth*, 29.

219. *Works*, IV, *Object and Acts*, part I, 106.

220. *Christ Set Forth*, 53.

221. Burgess, *Justification (1654)*, 263–4.

222. *Works*, I, *Ephesians*, part II, 218; cf. part I, 81.

223. *Works*, I, *Ephesians*, part II, 218.

224. Sibbes, *The Christians Portion*, 122.

involves the replication of each part of Christ's *historia salutis* upon and in the believer. Goodwin wrote that Christ's work as a common person was performed in stages: 'Christ he came, and by Degrees he did purchase it, fulfilled the Law, died, rose again, ascended, sitteth in Heaven.'[225] Salvation applied is the replication of these stages in the believer by the Spirit: 'when it comes to be wrought in our Persons, there indeed he goes by Degrees, as it is applied unto us.'[226] In this way, Goodwin contended for a tight connection between Christ's work for, and Christ's work in, believers, such that salvation consists in the replication of Christ's personal history in their persons. In this passage Goodwin identified three stages, namely, Christ's double resurrection and his ascension, subsequently realized in three stages in a believer, namely, regeneration, bodily resurrection and glorification.[227] Elsewhere, however, Goodwin extended this principle of replication to include other aspects of Christ's work:

> 'tis a sure Rule That whatsoever Christ did for a Christian, he doth in Him also, there being a Likeness and Proportion and an Assimulation in his Works of Grace in us and for us. He is Conceived, Formed, Born again in us ... the Conversion of a Sinner is but the acting over again of Christ's part.[228]

Believers receive salvation, then, by experiencing Christ's *historia salutis* replicated in their persons. In other words, salvation is a participation in the life of Christ: 'It is all but the Life of Jesus Christ, which doth spring and by degrees rise up in us, and he as our Life doth sit in Heaven for us.'[229] Thus, while Goodwin gave careful consideration to an *ordo salutis* especially relating to conversion,[230] what captivated his imagination more was the idea of the replication in believers of the *historia salutis* sequence first enacted in Christ. Ahead of Goodwin, Sibbes had likewise contended for the same: 'when we heare in the Gospel, in the Articles of the Creed, of Christ crucified, of Christ dying, of Christ rising, ascending, and sitting at the right hand of God: let us see our selves in him, see our selves dying in him, and rising in him, and sitting at the right hand of God.'[231] This vision of soteriology is what emerges from privileging the exemplary cause.

Here Goodwin (and Sibbes) resembled the teachings of 'perfectionist antinomians'. Cradock, one of the more respectable proponents, also taught that believers participate in all of Christ's actions: 'We have a share in all his *actions*; we are one with him in his *graces*, in his *life*, and *death*, and *resurrection*, and *ascension*: There is nothing in *Christ*; there is nothing that *Christ is*, or *hath*, but we

---

225. *Works*, I, *Ephesians*, part II, 217.

226. *Works*, I, *Ephesians*, part II, 217.

227. *Works*, I, *Ephesians*, part II, 217; cf. 213, 221.

228. *Works*, V, *The Holy Ghost*, 210.

229. *Works*, I, *Ephesians*, part II, 217.

230. See §4.4.

231. Sibbes, *Exposition: upon The first Chapter of the Second Epistle to the Corinthians*, 21–2.

are *one with him* in it.'[232] More mystical teachers tended to stress that the entire life of Christ must be replayed mystically within the believer. Como identifies Everard as the foundational figure of this strain of antinomianism.[233] Central to Everard's soteriology is the idea that Christ's historical actions were a type of spiritual actions performed within the believer:

> Christ Jesus himself, he is the *resemblance* and type of himself; his *outward, temporal* and *visible* actions in the flesh, were a type of his *inward* and *internal* actions in the souls of all Believers, he being their *life* and *resurrection*[234]

Types included Christ's nativity, circumcision, holiness, teaching, miracles, death and resurrection. Everard wrote, 'When you read the Story of the *Conception, Birth, Life, Death, Resurrection of Christ*; of his *Whipping, Crowning* with *Thorns, Buffeting, Spitting upon*, you shall be able *experimentally* to say, and cry out, Alas! *this day is this Scripture fulfilled in me.*'[235] Como remarks, 'Such a view was anathema to the mainstream puritan tradition … one is hard-pressed to find any puritan arguing that to be saved, the entire life of Christ needed to be lived over again in the believer's experience.'[236] Yet, contra Como, Goodwin's soteriology resembled Everard's scheme.

Critically, however, Goodwin departed from Everard's scheme in certain key respects. Everard insisted that Christ's historical actions were in the domain of the flesh, whereas Christ's actions within the believer belong to a higher spiritual order. Embracing a similar theology, Sprigg wrote, 'The same things are done in the Saints in the Spirit, that were done in, and upon Christ in the flesh.'[237] Regarding the difference in order, he contended,

> here is the difference of that work of God within us, from that work of God in *Christ*. The latter is the truth of the former; *sanctifie them through thy Truth*, that is, do thou act those things really in them, which are done in a figure for them upon me[238]

In contrast, Goodwin avoided such a distinction. This is readily demonstrated in the case of Christ's bodily resurrection. Como notes that perfectionist writers neglected the bodily resurrection of believers in favour of a mystical

---

232. Cradock, *Divine Drops*, 230.

233. Although the idea was already present in the writings of Familist founder Niclaes. Marsh, *The Family of Love*, 24. See p. 22 fn. 103.

234. Everard, *Gospel-Treasures*, 545.

235. Everard, *Gospel-Treasures*, 77.

236. Como, *Blown by the Spirit*, 238.

237. Sprigg, *Approaching Glory*, 41; cf. 99.

238. Sprigg, *Approaching Glory*, 103.

resurrection.[239] Goodwin held that Christ's resurrection caused not only regeneration (i.e. inner resurrection) but also future bodily resurrection. For Goodwin, this parity of cause and effect reflected his concern to consistently maintain Christ as the exemplary cause of salvation.

Also in contrast to Goodwin, the mystical emphasis of these radicals tended to demote Christ's historical representative actions. Rutherford accused '*Familists*' of so stressing the inner spiritual work that Christ's historical work was rendered immaterial.[240] Goodwin, however, was emphatic regarding the primacy of Christ's historical actions. Erbery, one of the radicals, critiqued Goodwin for writing 'much according to the flesh; for he meddles not with the Mystery of Christ in us, of his dying in us ... but all of Christ without us, which though a truth, yet not the whole truth, nor that spirit and truth which Christ spake of'.[241] While Erbery's analysis was limited to Goodwin's early and popular tract *Christ Set Forth*, even Goodwin's later comments regarding the work of Christ within the believer were consistently presented as secondary to and dependent upon the historical work of Christ for believers.[242] For Goodwin, Christ could only operate as the exemplary cause because his actions were representative as a common person.

Thus, while Goodwin's soteriology resembled the scheme of many perfectionist antinomians, he remained within the bounds of orthodoxy by stressing the primacy of Christ's representative actions, by refusing to limit the replication of Christ's historical actions to the inner mystical life of the believer and by employing causal categories rather than simply appealing to mystical participation.

All this considered, the exemplary cause enjoyed a primacy above other causes in Goodwin's soteriology. His framing of Christ's acts as exemplary causes expressed his rule of participation in causal language. So the primacy of the exemplary cause further demonstrates the fundamental place of participation in Goodwin's soteriology. On one occasion, Goodwin explained why the exemplary cause was the dominant causal relation:

> although an exemplary Cause, hath of all ordinary Causes the least influence; yet this hath more than such ordinary Causes use to have ... by virtue of a Decree, or Ordinance given out by God. That we should as well *bear the Image of the Heavenly, as of the Earthly Adam.* ... The Rule being, That that in Christ should have an Influence more special to work in us that which was most like thereto.[243]

Ultimately, then, the exemplary cause owed its superior influence to God's decree to establish Christ as an Adamic head. Elsewhere, Goodwin claimed that God had

239. Como, *Blown by the Spirit*, 38–9.
240. Rutherford, *Spirituall Antichrist*, part I, 167, 198.
241. Erbery, *The Testimony*, 68.
242. See also Fienberg, 'Puritan Pastor and Independent Divine', 73.
243. *Works*, V, *The Holy Ghost*, 420–1.

appointed Christ in predestination as the exemplary cause, such that believers are predestined to be conformed to Christ.[244]

5.3.3 The glory of Christ and Goodwin's soteriology of participation

To conclude this analysis of the substructure of Goodwin's soteriology the significance of God's decrees, therefore, must be examined. Here Goodwin's concern for Christ's glory was determinative. As Jones and Beeke remark, Goodwin 'more than any of his British contemporaries, had an intense focus on the glory of the God-man, Jesus Christ'.[245] Accordingly, Goodwin advocated what they describe as a 'christological supralapsarian position' on the order of divine decrees:[246] supralapsarian because the decree to election is more primitive than the decree ordaining the Fall;[247] Christological because the decree to election was chiefly concerned with Christ's glory, with believers elected in him as head.[248] Here Goodwin should be compared with two influential colleagues. Sibbes, according to Mark Dever, was 'decidedly agnostic' on the order of the decrees.[249] According to Trueman, Owen's infralapsarian view can be compared with Goodwin's 'more vigorously supralapsarian theology'.[250] To be more exact, Goodwin actually held to 'two several parts of God's Decree':

> The One is, the Decree of the *End* that God hath ordained to bring us unto, *Decretum finis*. The other is *Decretum viæ*, or *medii*, the Decree of the *Way* through which God leads us in bringing us to that End.[251]

It was the decree concerning the end of election, wherein the divine intention was to establish Christ's glory, that Goodwin held to be supralapsarian.[252] In contrast, the decree concerning the means was infralapsarian and motivated by the human predicament. Importantly, Goodwin correlated these two decrees to Christ's two relations to the church as head and redeemer.[253] The decree concerning the end ordained Christ to be head over the church. This relation is founded upon Christ's

---

244. *Works*, I, *Ephesians*, part I, 80.

245. Beeke and Jones, *A Puritan Theology*, 159.

246. Beeke and Jones, *A Puritan Theology*, 150.

247. *Works*, I, *Ephesians*, part II, 132–3; *Works*, II, *Election*, 79–88.

248. *Works*, II, *Election*, 80, 89–94.

249. Mark Dever, *Richard Sibbes: Puritanism and Calvinism in Late Elizabethan and Early Stuart England* (Macon, GA: Mercer University Press, 2000), 102–3.

250. Carl R. Trueman, *The Claims of Truth: John Owen's Trinitarian Theology* (Carlisle, UK: Paternoster Press, 1998), 138.

251. *Works*, I, *Ephesians*, part I, 97; cf. 91.

252. Horton mistakenly writes, 'With respect to the end, the decree to elect was infralapsarian.' Horton, 'Assurance', 64.

253. *Works*, I, *Ephesians*, part I, 100; cf. 440; *Works*, II, *Election*, 305–6.

person, since he must be hypostatically united to a human nature to function as an Adamic head. The relation of head allows Christ to receive the utmost glory by having a multitude conformed to him and so he is constituted the prime end of God's decree.[254] Consequently, the church is formed and elected ultimately for Christ's glory: 'if he be their Head, that then they were created for him; they were ordained for him, and not he for them.'[255] The decree concerning the means ordained Christ as redeemer (an office founded upon Christ's merits) in response to the Fall. While Christ gains glory from his work of redemption,[256] Goodwin believed that this glory is eclipsed by the glory from Christ's headship over the church.[257]

The crucial point to be noted is Goodwin's belief that the decree concerning the end represents the fundamental divine purpose:

> He had a primary Plot, which was first in his intention; and he had an after plot subordinate to the other. His first Plot was to choose us to that state which we shall be in in Heaven, His after plot that he had towards us whilst we are in our way, was to Redeem us, and reconcile us unto himself by his Son Jesus Christ.[258]

This claim was in apparent tension with comments in *Election* where Goodwin stated that 'neither had a Priority or *Posteriority*.'[259] However, his intention there was to establish that the decree concerning the means was not dependent upon the decree concerning the end, rather than to exclude primacy in God's motives. There he also stated that 'the first Design in God's Intention' concerns establishing Christ's role as head which, unlike his role as redeemer, endures into the eschaton.[260] Elsewhere Goodwin declared that Christ's ordination to be head is 'the fundamental Decree of all'.[261]

The priority of Christ's office as head over his office as redeemer is manifested in Goodwin's claim that the benefits founded in Christ's person are more fundamental than those founded in his merits.[262] The former are more primitive since they

---

254. *Works*, I, *Ephesians*, part I, 82.

255. *Works*, I, *Ephesians*, part I, 83; cf. 82; *Works*, II, *The Knowledg*, 139.

256. *Works*, I, *Ephesians*, part I, 101; cf. *Works*, II, *Election*, 91–2, 325–7. Indeed, Goodwin held that God ordained a multitude of causal connections between Christ's work for and in believers in order to multiply Christ's glory: 'That Christ may be magnified, and have a praise in it, as he is God-Man, Mediator, as well as God, he saith, that all this is done in Christ and with Christ, as the instrumental Cause, and representative Head, and meritorious Cause of all this.' *Works*, I, *Ephesians*, part II, 128.

257. *Works*, II, *The Knowledg*, 135; *Works*, I, *Ephesians*, part I, 86.

258. *Works*, I, *Ephesians*, part I, 100.

259. *Works*, II, *Election*, 82.

260. *Works*, II, *Election*, 94.

261. *Works*, V, *Gospel Holiness*, 95.

262. *Works*, I, *Ephesians*, part I, 95. Goodwin repeatedly made this distinction. *Christ Set Forth*, 18; Works, II, *The Knowledg*, 121, 168, 171–2.

represent the original divine intention for eschatological glory.[263] In his opening work to his grand project, referring to 1 Corinthians 15:47-48, Goodwin wrote,

> the Apostle doth put our carrying to Heaven ... not so much upon the merit of Christ's Death, as upon his being *the Lord from Heaven*;] because Heaven was his Natural Due, and he descended from his Right, when he came down upon Earth: And so, because he was thus from Heaven, therefore he is now gone thither himself, as unto his Natural Place, and advanceth us up thither also[264]

The benefits of Christ's merits, in contrast, address the condition of fallen man: 'These latter blessings are but the removings of those Obstacles which by reason of Sin stood in our way to that intended Glory.'[265] Moreover, Christ's law-obedience and atoning death only have such merit because of the high worth of his person.[266] In other words, even the benefits of Christ's merits require Christ's person as a foundation.

Consequently, Goodwin contended that the primary reason for the incarnation was not the human predicament but Christ's glory.[267] Alarmingly, this is a point that Jones's thesis entirely overlooks despite primarily addressing the question of '*Cur Deus Homo?*' On this question Goodwin differed from Owen. Changlok Oh states, 'Owen would be willing to say with Calvin that "the sole purpose of Christ's incarnation was our redemption." '[268] Goodwin rejected this position, arguing that if so, believers would displace Christ's glory as the end of the divine purposes.

In the final analysis, then, Goodwin's rule of participation was central to his soteriology because Christ's glory represents the chief end of God's decree. Christ was appointed as an Adamic head principally to be glorified as the head of a new humanity conformed to him. Prior to Goodwin, Sibbes had similarly justified salvation by participation in Christ by appealing to Christ's pre-eminence:

> Christ is the prime creature of all, he is Gods Masterpiece, that is the reason why nothing can be ours, but it must be Christs first. Hee is the first begotten of every creature, both as God and man: he is the first begotten, because he is more excellent in order and dignity, than any other whatsoever.[269]

---

263. *Works*, I, *Ephesians*, part I, 93.

264. *Works*, II, *The Creatures*, 46.

265. *Works*, I, *Ephesians*, part I, 100.

266. *Works*, II, *The Knowledg*, 136.

267. *Works*, I, *Ephesians*, part I, 84.

268. Changlok Oh, 'Beholding the Glory of God in Christ: Communion with God in the Theology of John Owen (1616–83)' (PhD thesis, Westminster Theological Seminary, 2006), 111; cf. Baylor, ' "One with Him in Spirit" ', 439.

269. Sibbes, *The Christians Portion*, 114.

However, Goodwin's Christological supralapsarian scheme, accompanied by his application of the distinction between Christ's person and merits, grounded this soteriology in a far more robust and developed framework.

It is evident, then, that Christ's office as head over the church (and so his rule of participation) provides the substructure of Goodwin's soteriology in his grand project. For this reason, Christ's work as redeemer was understood within his office as head: 'he is *first* said to be the *Head*, and then the *Saviour:* And *Saviour* as an additional *unto* that Relation of *Head.*'[270] Redemption, Goodwin declared, is 'the super-added Project'.[271] Even in his treatise devoted to Christ as redeemer, *Christ the Mediator*, Goodwin wrote, 'Christ being originally and primitively constituted an *head* to them, this drew him to be a *Saviour.*'[272] Crucially, Goodwin insisted that the benefits of Christ's work of redemption are not applied directly to the believer without reference to Christ's person, but instead the benefits must first be bestowed upon Christ himself 'as our Head'.[273] He concluded,

> all Blessings which God in time bestows, are said to be given in Christ, ere they are actually to us. ... The Promise of Life is said to be in Jesus Christ: Now the Phrase notes out a transaction, an endowment of all these on us, not first immediately in ourselves, but in Christ for us, and on us in him.[274]

Since in this way the incarnation is more fundamental than the atonement, Blackham is correct in his claim that 'Goodwin ... places the Work of Christ in the Person of Christ as the God-Man.'[275] While Goodwin held to a strong doctrine of sin and that salvation requires redemption from the plight of sin, he was convinced that salvation fundamentally concerns advancing individuals to a state surpassing that of the prelapsarian Adam.[276] This fundamental movement rests upon Christ's person and his relation as head over the church.

Missing from this account of the substructure of Goodwin's soteriology is his conviction that more fundamental than Christ's office as head is Christ's person as the God-man. Christ possesses a glory owing to his person surpassing not only his glory as redeemer but even his glory as head.[277] This conviction was but the extension of Goodwin's concern for Christ's person to take precedence over any other factor. Ultimately, this was the reason that Goodwin refused to found the incarnation chiefly upon the Fall. To do so, he argued, would render Christ's

270. *Works*, II, *Election*, 305.

271. *Works*, II, *The Knowledg*, 117; cf. 99.

272. *Works*, III, *Christ the Mediator*, 302.

273. *Works*, III, *Christ the Mediator*, 9.

274. *Works*, III, *Christ the Mediator*, 28.

275. Blackham, 'Pneumatology', 194.

276. *Works*, II, *Election*, 306–7.

277. *Works*, II, *The Knowledg*, 96–9, 138–53

person inferior to his salvific benefits.[278] The implication for the believer is that salvation first concerns receiving Christ himself: 'his Person thus given us, is more worth than all those his Benefits.'[279] Indeed, by locating all salvific benefits in Christ's person, Goodwin ensured that believers must receive Christ's person before any benefits. More fundamental than Christ's office as head, therefore, is Christ's person as the God-man. Nevertheless, the two are closely related since, as Goodwin stated, Christ's person as the God-man is what qualifies him to assume the office of headship.[280] Thus, in my analysis of the substructure of Goodwin's soteriology I must ultimately turn to examine participation in Christ in terms of participation in his person as the God-man.

5.4 *The centrality of real union with Christ*

It was Goodwin's notion of participation in Christ that demanded that union with Christ occupy a pivotal role in his soteriology. Partaking of Christ, he wrote, rests upon union with him: 'Our Union or Oneness with Christ, it is the Foundation of our Communion and Fellowship with him, and being made partakers with him of all he did for us.'[281] To explicate this further, Goodwin appealed to his threefold scheme of union with Christ underpinning his *tria momenta* of justification.[282] The first two unions are extrinsic and allow believers to participate in Christ merely in the sense of him performing representative actions on their behalf. Entailed is a weak sense of participation: 'we are not yet actually in our Persons Partakers of them, but only as yet in our Head.'[283] The third union, corresponding to real union with Christ, allows personal participation, such that the Holy Spirit applies to the individual all that Christ as a common person has accomplished and possesses for the church.[284] Sibbes, in stating the same threefold scheme of union with Christ, also viewed the Spirit as the means of participation.[285] Elsewhere he wrote, 'The Holy Ghost fetcheth all from Christ … for whatsoever is in Christ, the Holy Ghost … workes in us, as it is in Christ.'[286] Goodwin and Sibbes were not alone. Sedgwick wrote,

---

278. *Works*, I, *Ephesians*, part I, 84.

279. *Works*, II, *The Knowledg*, 121; cf. *Works*, V, *The Holy Ghost*, 51; *Works*, I, *Ephesians*, part I, 103, 105; part II, 132; *Works*, IV, *Object and Acts*, part I, 150; *Works*, V, *Christ's Reward*, 130–1.

280. See §5.4.2. While Christ's person also qualified Christ for the office of redeemer, in Goodwin's mind there was a tighter connection between Christ's person and Christ's office of headship, since this latter office is only founded upon his person and not upon his merits.

281. *Works*, I, *Ephesians*, part II, 214–15.

282. *Works*, I, *Ephesians*, part II, 215. See §4.3.2.

283. *Works*, I, *Ephesians*, part II, 209.

284. *Works*, I, *Ephesians*, part II, 215.

285. Sibbes, *An Exposition of the Third Chapter of Philippians*, 102–3.

286. Sibbes, *Beames of Divine Light*, 'A Description of Christ', 42.

For *applying of Christ unto them*, and for the applying of them unto Christ; that there is a conjunction or union between Christ the Head, and his Mystical body the Church, is an unquestionable truth. And how Christ who locally in heaven, should be joyned or united to his Church here on earth; this cannot be done but by the Spirit who doth knit or joyn Christ to us, and us to Christ[287]

Owen stated the same: 'The Lord Christ is the Head Fountain and Treasure of all actual supplyes: And the *Spirit* is the *Efficient Cause* communicating them unto us from him.'[288]

Why, then, was real union forged by the indwelling of the Spirit necessary for participation? And why must the Spirit be responsible for bestowing all soteric benefits?[289] In part, this arose from Goodwin's desire to ascribe to each person of the Trinity a distinct role, yet more specifically it arose from the determinative role of Christology in his soteriology. Since soteriology is fundamentally participation in Christ, the nature of Christ's person as God-man determines the nature of union required for participation in him.

5.4.1 Partaking of Christ's humanity by the same Spirit

Goodwin believed that the Holy Spirit played a determinative role in Christ's incarnate life.[290] In his treatise *The Holy Ghost*, he traced the Spirit's 'Operation upon Christ our Head'.[291] The Spirit formed Christ's human nature in the womb, united the human nature to the divine nature,[292] anointed Christ at his baptism, empowered Christ in his ministry, enabled Christ to perform miracles, raised Christ from the dead, filled Christ with glory in his ascension, anointed Christ as king in heaven and proclaims him as the Christ to the world.[293] In short, Goodwin declared, 'the Spirit made him Christ.'[294]

In this matter, Goodwin was again following Sibbes's lead. Despite several studies devoting attention to this aspect of Owen's Christology,[295] Nuttall rightly

---

287. Sedgwick, *The Bowels*, 587–8.

288. Owen, *Pneumatologia*, 344; cf. Owen, *Communion with God*, 232. As will become clear, this point had wide acceptance even including notable 'imputative antinomians'. See, e.g. Crisp, *Christ Alone Exalted In the Perfection and Encouragements of the Saints*, 354.

289. *Works*, I, *Ephesians*, part I, 42.

290. Both Blackham and Jones have provided expositions of Goodwin's Spirit-christology. Blackham, 'Pneumatology', 37–65; Jones, *Why Heaven Kissed Earth*, 165–8. See also Woo's comments. Woo, *The Promise of the Trinity*, 197–205, 227–30.

291. *Works*, V, *The Holy Ghost*, 8.

292. Although Goodwin was ambivalent on this point. See p. 57.

293. *Works*, V, *The Holy Ghost*, 8–10.

294. *Works*, V, *The Holy Ghost*, 43–4.

295. Stephen R. Holmes, 'Reformed Varieties of the Communicatio Idiomatum', in *The Person of Christ*, ed. Murray Rae and Stephen R. Holmes (London: T&T Clark, 2005);

identifies the seminal role Sibbes played.[296] Citing various factors, Nuttall argues that pneumatology had suffered neglect in the pre-Reformation period and despite Calvin's attention to the doctrine, it had again receded into the background.[297] Sibbes broke new ground by devoting considerable attention to the role of the Spirit upon Christ.[298] Indeed, the Spirit was so determinative for Sibbes's Christology that he declared, 'whatsoever Christ did as man he did by the Spirit.'[299]

If Goodwin made a contribution, then it was to elucidate the Spirit's work upon the ascended Christ. At his heavenly enthronement, Christ's human nature was massively enlarged, so that all divine action towards the church could be mediated through Christ's human nature.[300] Accordingly, Christ's glorified human nature received the Spirit in the greatest measure possible and so came to possess colossal knowledge, power and affections.[301] Here Goodwin presented Christ as the head who governs and has intimate knowledge of all that befalls his body, the church.

Since both Sibbes and Goodwin understood soteriology to be the application or the extension of Christology, this Spirit-Christology was vital for their soteriologies. Christ first received the Spirit, they contended, in order for the Spirit to be bestowed upon the church.[302] For Goodwin, the bestowal of the Spirit upon the church was especially a consequence of Christ's heavenly enthronement, rather than his baptism, because in heaven he received 'the whole of the Spirit' with the very purpose of bestowing the Spirit upon the church (Acts 2:33).[303] Employing a favourite analogy, Goodwin explained that this exemplifies his rule of participation:

> it is a certaine rule, that *whatsoever* we receive from Christ, *that* he himselfe first receives in himselfe for us. And so one reason why this oile ran then so plentifully downe on the skirts of this our High-priest, that is, on his members the Apostles and Saints, (and so continues to do unto this day) is because our High-priest and Head himselfe was then afresh anointed with it. ... according to that rule, that whatever God doth unto us by Christ, he first doth it unto Christ; all promises are made and fulfilled unto him first, and so unto us in him; all that he bestows on us, he receives in himselfe.[304]

Alan Spence, *Incarnation and Inspiration: John Owen and the Coherence of Christology* (London: T&T Clark, 2007), 54–9; Carl R. Trueman, *John Owen: Reformed Catholic, Renaissance Man*, Great Theologians Series (Aldershot, UK: Ashgate, 2007), 92–8. See especially Owen, *Pneumatologia*, 128–53.

296. Nuttall, *The Holy Spirit in Puritan Faith*, 14, 145–6.

297. Nuttall, *The Holy Spirit in Puritan Faith*, 2–9.

298. E.g. Sibbes, *Beames of Divine Light*, 'A Description of Christ', 32–62.

299. Sibbes, *Beames of Divine Light*, 'A Description of Christ', 39.

300. *The Heart of Christ*, 178–9.

301. *The Heart of Christ*, 210–11, 217.

302. *Works*, V, *The Holy Ghost*, 45; cf. 7.

303. *Works*, II, *Election*, 314; cf. *The Heart of Christ*, 177.

304. *The Heart of Christ*, 178.

This anointing analogy was frequently employed by Sibbes as well as enthusiastic preachers and conservative divines,[305] although, as discussed below, the latter interpreted the analogy in terms of the Spirit's graces alone.

Since all that Christ accomplished or received occurred by the Spirit, Goodwin reasoned, therefore, by receiving the same Spirit believers receive the same salvific benefits. Indeed, by receiving the Spirit at his heavenly enthronement, Christ received all benefits in himself for the church: 'when he first ascended into Heaven, he as an Head, received every whit, and the whole of all that should be given us by the Spirit from God.'[306] For this reason, the same Spirit who determined Christ's human existence determines the existence of the church, both corporately and individually.[307] Mediated through Christ, the Spirit replicates in believers all his operations in and upon Christ's human nature. In this way, Goodwin wrote, 'the Grace and Vertue of all that Christ did, suffered, descends to them that receive the anointing of him.'[308]

Ahead of Goodwin, Sibbes had stated the matter in reverse: 'whatsoever the Holy Ghost doth in us, he doth the same in Christ first, and hee doth it in us because in Christ.'[309] Thus, 'we must partake of the same Spirit that Christ hath, or else wee are none of his members … if we have the Spirit of Christ, it will worke the same in us as it did in Christ'.[310] The Spirit, then, makes effective Christ as the exemplary cause.[311] Beck comments, 'It is crucial to see that in Sibbes' pneumatology, the Holy Spirit's central work is to Christ, and only by extension and application, to Christ's people.'[312] As both Beck and Bert Affleck Jr. observe, central to Sibbes's vision of soteriology, therefore, was the application of his Spirit-Christology.[313] It was this 'same Spirit' theology that not only Goodwin but also other divines such as Sedgwick and Owen espoused.[314]

For Goodwin, believers partake of Christ's humanity in the first instance by having the same Spirit operate upon them as upon Christ. Here the *textus classicus* was Romans 8:11, from which Goodwin contended that the same Spirit who raised

---

305. E.g. Sibbes, *Beames of Divine Light*, 'A Description of Christ', 46; Sprigg, *Approaching Glory*, 148–9; Cradock, *Divine Drops*, 229–30; Bulkeley, *The Gospel-Covenant*, 376.

306. *Works*, II, *Election*, 319.

307. *Works*, V, *The Holy Ghost*, 10–32. The church mystical is formed and united by the same Spirit indwelling believers as indwells Christ. *Works*, I, *Thirteen Sermons*, 5–6, 11; *Works*, IV, *The Government of the Churches*, 251.

308. *Works*, V, *The Holy Ghost*, 204.

309. Sibbes, *Beames of Divine Light*, 'A Description of Christ', 41.

310. Sibbes, *Beames of Divine Light*, 'A Description of Christ', 50.

311. Sibbes, *The Christians Portion*, 122–3; Sibbes, *Beames of Divine Light*, 'A Description of Christ', 42.

312. Beck, 'Gratia Praeparans', 107.

313. Bert Affleck, Jr, 'The Theology of Richard Sibbes, 1577–1635' (PhD thesis, Drew University, 1969), 58–60; Beck, 'Gratia Praeparans', 95.

314. Sedgwick, *The Bowels*, 526, 589; Owen, *Pneumatologia*, 493.

Christ from the dead will also raise believers in the future bodily resurrection.[315] Goodwin extended this principle to argue that the same Spirit also inwardly raises believers in regeneration.[316] In stressing that the same Spirit who raised and glorified Christ will perform the same in believers, Goodwin followed the lead of Sibbes and was of one accord with Sedgwick and Owen.[317]

However, perhaps inconsistently Goodwin refrained from arguing that the Spirit's operation in Christ's death is repeated in believers. The Spirit, Goodwin assumed, strengthened Christ to endure the trial of his passion: 'all that while the Holy Ghost supported and upheld him, and he was filled with the Spirit beyond measure for Strength to stand under the Weight of the Father's Wrath, for no created Strength could have done it.'[318] Furthermore, by connecting the Spirit with the fire that consumed Old Testament sacrifices, Goodwin apparently held that the Spirit mediated the divine wrath in Christ's sufferings. It would have, therefore, been natural for Goodwin to have argued that the same Spirit who performed this dual operation in the crucified Christ both enables believers to endure trials and, as a purifying fire, refines believers also.[319] Such theology, however, was the domain of the radicals.[320] Higgenson argued that the same Spirit who crucified sin in Christ will mortify sin in believers.[321] Dell argued that Christ endured and overcame the trials of his passion 'through the power of the Spirit' and that believers can endure and overcome evils through 'the same power'.[322] Sprigg explored similar theology but, reasoning from the sinlessness of Christ's human nature, differentiated the sanctification of Christ and of believers.[323]

Instead, foremost in Goodwin's theology is the idea that the same Spirit who formed Christ's human nature at the incarnation forms the new nature in believers.[324] Goodwin repeatedly stressed that the Spirit formed Christ's human

---

315. *Works*, I, *Ephesians*, part I, 221; *Works*, V, *The Holy Ghost*, 35, 418–21.

316. *Works*, I, *Ephesians*, part II, 188.

317. Sibbes, *Exposition: upon The first Chapter of the Second Epistle to the Corinthians*, 100; Sedgwick, *The Bowels*, 586; Owen, *Pneumatologia*, 149.

318. *Works*, IV, *Object and Acts*, part I, 113; cf. *Works*, III, *Christ the Mediator*, 279–83.

319. *Works*, V, *The Holy Ghost*, 24, 30, 41; cf. *Works*, III, *An Unregenerate*, 560–5.

320. Although Owen gave some consideration of similar theology. See Trueman, *John Owen*, 97–8.

321. Higgenson, *Glory sometimes afar off*, 7–10; cf. William Dell, *Baptismōn Didaché: Or, The Doctrine of Baptisme's, Reduced from its Ancient and Moderne Corruptions: And Restored to its Primitive Soundnesse and Integrity, According to {The Word of Truth, The Substance of Faith, and The Nature of Christ's Kingdome* (1648), 22.

322. William Dell, *Power from on high, or, The power of the Holy Ghost dispersed through the whole body of Christ, and communicated to each member according to its place and use in that body* (1645), 13.

323. Sprigg, *Approaching Glory*, 64, 99.

324. *Works*, V, *The Holy Ghost*, 43.

nature and bestowed all graces upon it.[325] Since believers have the same Spirit, the analogous work of regeneration and sanctification will be performed in believers.[326] Reflecting upon John 17:19, Goodwin contended that the very purpose of the sanctification of Christ's humanity was for the same to be wrought in them.[327] Thus, 'Christ and his Graces are the perfect Original and Exemplar' to which the Spirit conforms believers, such that 'there is not a letter or tittle, added in the Copy, which is not found in him'.[328] All moral virtues grow from union with Christ, since they were first formed in Christ.[329] Goodwin pressed this logic extensively in his popular 1642 tract *The Heart of Christ*. Aiming to prove that the ascended Christ remains affectionately disposed towards believers, he reasoned that the Spirit who formed Christ's human nature and fitted it with a compassionate heart continues to indwell Christ in heaven and, therefore, Christ's affections must remain unchanged.[330] In fact, he contended that since the glorified Christ received the Spirit in an even greater measure, Christ's affections must have been enlarged to care for the worldwide church.[331] Significantly, Goodwin reinforced this argument by appealing to the affections wrought in believers by the same Spirit: 'the same Spirit dwelling in Christs heart in Heaven, that doth in yours here, and alwayes working in his heart first for you, and then in yours by commission from him'.[332] Taking the apostle Paul's example, Goodwin concluded that Paul's affectionate dispositions must have originated from the ascended Christ.[333]

Along with Goodwin, other like-minded divines also held that the same Spirit who first formed graces in Christ forms the same graces in believers.[334] This differed from certain 'perfectionist antinomians'. Some accepted inherent graces in Christ but denied the replication of inherent graces in believers, arguing that Christ worked immediately by the Spirit. This was an 'error' identified by heresiographers. Rutherford warned of those who taught: '*That there is no inherent grace in the Saints, but Christ immediately worketh all in them, and grace is onely in Christ*'.[335] The radical Traske, for example, argued for this position: 'the sanctified person is no further foorth sanctified, then he is in union with the Lord *Iesus* Christ; and

325. *Works*, II, *Election*, 339; *Works*, V, *The Holy Ghost*, 23; *Works*, III, *Christ the Mediator*, 58–9.

326. *Works*, V, *The Holy Ghost*, 146.

327. *Works*, V, *The Holy Ghost*, 77, 205.

328. *Works*, V, *The Holy Ghost*, 14.

329. *Works*, V, *The Holy Ghost*, 206.

330. *The Heart of Christ*, 170, 173–4.

331. *The Heart of Christ*, 210–11, 217.

332. *The Heart of Christ*, 179.

333. *The Heart of Christ*, 172–3, 186.

334. E.g. Sedgwick, *The Bowels*, 635; Owen, *Pneumatologia*, 95.

335. Rutherford, *Spirituall Antichrist*, part I, 125; cf. Thomas Edwards, *The First and Second Part of Gangræna: Or, A Catalogue and Discovery of many of the Errors, Heresies, Blasphemies and pernicious Practices of the Sectaries of this time* (1646), 20.

it is not he that hath any habit of grace in his flesh; but the Lord *Iesus* dwelling in him.'[336] To Goodwin and others following Sibbes, Traske's scheme denied the key principle: the same Spirit produces the same salvific benefits.

For Goodwin and like-minded divines, then, it was crucial that if believers are to participate in Christ's human nature, the same Spirit who indwelt Christ should also indwell them. Owen wrote,

> And this belongs unto the Establishment of our Faith, that he who *Prepared*, *Sanctified*, and *Glorified* the Humane Nature, the Natural Body of Jesus Christ, the Head of the Church, hath undertaken to *Prepare*, *Sanctifie*, and *Glorifie* his Mystical Body, or all the Elect given unto him of the Father.[337]

The Spirit indwelt Christ and consequently granted his human nature all salvific privileges; the same Spirit must indwell believers for them to partake of the same benefits already possessed by Christ. Thus, believers partake of Christ's human nature by receiving the same Spirit. It is not a direct participation in the substance of Christ's humanity but participation mediated by the Spirit where Christ's humanity operates as the exemplary cause.

The necessity of real union by the Spirit is, therefore, a consequence of Goodwin's Spirit-Christology. Indeed, from this same Spirit theology, Goodwin argued that the Spirit must have the same mode of indwelling in believers as in Christ: 'the manner of the Indwelling of the Holy-Ghost's Person; it is no Error to affirm that it is the same in us and the Man Christ Jesus.'[338] Here Goodwin believed that he had won the argument, for 'I suppose none will say that the Person of the Spirit, nor of the Son, dwells in the Man Jesus only by means of his Graces.'[339] From Romans 8:11, Sedgwick similarly argued that since the person of the Spirit raised Jesus from the dead, his person must also indwell believers.[340]

By itself, however, this same Spirit theology is inadequate to account for Goodwin's conception of real union with Christ. Here it is instructive to locate Goodwin's position between enthusiasts and radicals on one side and the conservative majority on the other. Each side raises a crucial question for Goodwin's scheme. On the one side were enthusiasts and radicals who revelled in the idea of the same Spirit indwelling believers as in Christ.[341] Cradock wrote, 'For

---

336. Traske, *The True Gospel Vindicated*, 22–3; cf. Sprigg, *Approaching Glory*, 163–4.

337. Owen, *Pneumatologia*, 155.

338. *Works*, V, *The Holy Ghost*, 58.

339. *Works*, V, *The Holy Ghost*, 58.

340. Sedgwick, *The Bowels*, 585–6.

341. 'Imputative antinomians' also advocated this 'same Spirit' theology. Parnham argues that Crisp avoided this theology because of his stress upon the corruption of believers. David Parnham, 'The Covenantal Quietism of Tobias Crisp', *Church History* 75, no. 3 (2006): 532; David Parnham, 'Motions of Law and Grace: The Puritan in the Antinomian', *Westminster Theological Journal* 70, no. 1 (2008): 91. However, Parnham overstates his case.

if thou be a *Saint,* thou hast the *Spirit of God really dwelling* in thee in its measure, as truly as in the *Lord Jesus Christ*.'[342] More extreme preachers concluded that the only difference between Christ and believers is chronological priority. Erbery employed the anointing analogy in a less restrained manner: 'The Saints are the anointed of God with Christ ... The same Spirit ... oil poured forth on the Son, is poured forth on the Saints, and that in the same fulnesse.'[343] The saints 'have all the fulnesse of the Godhead as the Son'.[344] Christ simply has 'preeminence in manifestation'.[345] By arguing that the same Spirit indwells believers, Dell appeared to come to the same conclusion:

> For *Christ* is the *self same* both in *Himself* the *Head,* and in *Believers* his *Members.*
> ... *These* partake of the same *Divine Nature,* and have the *same Word* and *Spirit*
> dwelling in them ... there is no *difference* between *Christ* and *them,* but what is
> between the *Head* and the *Members,* the *firstborn* and his *Brethren.*[346]

Fox, even while defending himself against accusations of similar teaching, maintained that 'he that hath the same Spirit that raised up Jesus Christ, is equal with God'.[347] Fry employed the head–body analogy to defend his view that Christ partakes of divinity in the same sense as believers.[348] The incipient danger, therefore, of the same Spirit theology was to deny Christ's unique hypostatic union and collapse the difference between Christ and believers to mere chronological priority. Even Goodwin in handling scriptural references to the 'Spirit' in Christ was capable of equivocating between interpreting 'Spirit' as the Holy Spirit and Christ's divine nature, so leaving himself vulnerable to the radical position.[349] Indeed, Nuttall alleges that Goodwin and Sibbes advocated an adoptionist Christology.[350] This raises a critical question of Goodwin's scheme: how does Christ's divine nature and hypostatic union play a vital and unique role?

While far more restrained, Crisp and Towne both advocated this idea. Crisp, *Christ Alone Exalted In fourteene Sermons,* 127–8; Towne, *A Re-assertion of Grace,* 122.

342. Cradock, *Divine Drops,* 215; cf. 229; Sprigg, *Approaching Glory,* 85.

343. Erbery, *Nor Truth, nor Errour,* 24; cf. 10.

344. Erbery, *Nor Truth, nor Errour,* 23.

345. Erbery, *Nor Truth, nor Errour,* 15.

346. Dell, *The Stumbling-Stone,* 34–5; cf. William Dell, *The building and glory of the truely Christian and spiritual church. Represented in an exposition on Isai. 54, from vers. 11. to the 17* (1646), 11.

347. George Fox, *Saul's errand to Damascus: with his packet of letters from the high-priests, against the disciples of the Lord* (1653), 8; cf. 5–7; George Fox, *Newes coming up out of the north, sounding towards the south. Or, A blast out of the north up into the south, and so to flie abroad into the world* (1653), 16.

348. Fry, *The Accuser sham'd,* 15.

349. *Works,* I, *Ephesians,* part I, 334; cf. 486; part II, 186–8; *Christ Set Forth,* 46.

350. Nuttall, *The Holy Spirit in Puritan Faith,* 145–6.

On the other side was the conservative majority who were alarmed by the teaching of the radicals. In his catalogue of dangerous tenets, Edwards listed the teaching: 'That God is in our flesh as much as in Christs flesh; he is as much in the flesh of the members, as in the Head.'[351] Accordingly, in a sermon preached in 1638, the staunch anti-antinomian Stephen Denison (d. 1649) contended that the Spirit indwelt Christ in a superior mode to the believer: 'it is not meant wee must be filled with the essence of the spirit of god as though the spiritt of god did dwell in us … It is sufficient that the Spirit of god doth Dwell in Christ in that Sence.'[352] Dell condemned this strategy as subtracting from Christ:

> I say, some hold, that the *Eternal Word* or *Divine Nature* came indeed into that *flesh* which was born of the *Virgin*, but they will by no meanes allow it to come into *ours*; onely, they say, some *created habits* or *gifts of grace* come in our *flesh*, but not *Christ himself*, or the *divine nature*, or *Son of the living God*: and so these men set up these *Created Gifts*, and *graces* in the *members*, instead of *Christ* Himself the Head.[353]

Here it must be recalled that many conservatives excluded the special indwelling of the Spirit's person in believers on the basis of his omnipresence.[354] Consistency, however, demanded that they likewise deny the indwelling of the Spirit's person in the case of Christ's human nature.[355] The logical conclusion was to also restrict the Spirit's indwelling of Christ's human nature to graces alone. Scriptural language of Christ receiving the Spirit in order to be bestowed upon believers was interpreted accordingly.[356] This raises a second critical question for Goodwin's scheme: why must the person of the Spirit indwell believers? Is not his indwelling by graces sufficient?

5.4.2 Partaking of Christ's divinity by the indwelling Spirit

Both questions may be addressed by examining the significance of Christ's divinity and his hypostatic union. In Goodwin's mind, the hypostatic union granted Christ's human nature rights belonging to the second person of the Trinity. Christ's hypostatic union, therefore, was the grounds for Christ receiving the benefits of his person. The benefits of Christ's merits also required the hypostatic union, since Christ's divinity multiplied the worth of his merits.[357] Thus, all salvific benefits could only be received in Christ as head because of his status as the God-man. This point allowed Goodwin to distance himself from

---

351. Edwards, *The third Part of Gangræna*, 10; cf. Rutherford, *Spirituall Antichrist*, part I, 65.

352. Quoted in Como, *Blown by the Spirit*, 167.

353. Dell, *The Tryal of Spirits*, 16.

354. See p. 60.

355. Perkins, *An Exposition of the Symbole*, 388–9.

356. Perkins, *A golden Chaine*, 115; Hooker, *Christ's last Prayer*, 84; Bulkeley, *The Gospel-Covenant*, 175–6.

357. See p. 206 cf. p. 133.

enthusiasts who placed saints on the same level as Christ.[358] Whereas Christ receives soteric benefits in his own right on the basis of the hypostatic union, Goodwin insisted that believers receive these benefits derivatively from Christ and thus in an inferior measure.

Yet, Goodwin believed that Christ's divinity plays a more fundamental role in Christ's headship and this consideration reveals the core of Goodwin's conception of real union with Christ. In the opening treatise of his grand project, *The Creatures*, Goodwin stated his intention to introduce the project with a comparison of Adam and Christ:

> these I thought best in this place to give the brief entire view of, not only for the pleasantness of the prospect, when in brief set together, but because it will serve as the clearest Introduction or general Preface unto all the Treatises that are to follow, which have for their particular and set Subjects these several Estates and Conditions: This discourse being to handle the State of *Adam* in his purest naturals, with a Comparison between him and Christ, and his State, and our State of Grace under the Gospel.[359]

For Goodwin, the superiority of the state of grace over the state of nature is founded upon the superiority of Christ's person over Adam's. Taking his lead from 1 Corinthians 15:45, he expounded the significance of Christ's designation as a 'quickning Spirit' in contrast to Adam as a 'living soul'. Goodwin was emphatic that 'Spirit' refers not to the Holy Spirit but to Christ's divine nature.[360] Thus, as Adam became a 'living soul' by the union of soul and body in one person, so Christ became a 'quickning Spirit' by virtue of the hypostatic union of his two natures. The adjective 'quickning' he took to describe the 'transcendent Power of giving Life and Glory' inherent in divine nature. Christ's divine nature can therefore grant spiritual life to his human nature: 'Christ's Godhead supplies Life, Motion, Quickning, Vigour, Power, and all unto his Human Nature immediately from it self.'[361] This is not merely the spiritual life of created grace examined in Chapter 3 but the spiritual life of uncreated grace.[362] As noted there, the former results from and is continually dependent upon the latter.

Significantly, while Goodwin adopted a Sibbesian soteriology, in this matter Goodwin departed from his mentor. Sibbes had also discussed Christ as the quickening Spirit but interpreted 'Spirit' as the Holy Spirit.[363] This reflects his conviction that the Holy Spirit operates as the buffer between Christ's two natures:

---

358. *Works*, I, *Ephesians*, part I, 31; *Works*, II, *The Knowledg*, 148.
359. *Works*, II, *The Creatures*, 31.
360. *Works*, II, *The Creatures*, 74; cf. *Works*, II, *The Knowledg*, 86.
361. *Works*, II, *The Creatures*, 74.
362. See especially §3.2.3.
363. Sibbes, *The Excellencie of the Gospell*, 33–4.

Christ is both God and Man, Christ as God gives the Spirit to his humane nature, so hee communicates his Spirit, the Spirit is his Spirit as well as the Fathers, the Spirit proceeds from them both. … so Christ both gives and receives the Spirit in diverse respects[364]

This conviction was in turn an implication of Sibbes's insistence that the Spirit is always the immediate operator of the Trinity upon creation.[365] Owen followed Sibbes in both matters, likewise insisting that the Holy Spirit is

the immediate Operator of all Divine Acts of the Son himself, even on his own Humane Nature. Whatever the Son of God, wrought in, by, or upon the *Humane* Nature, he did it by the Holy Ghost, who is his Spirit[366]

Thus, Sibbes and Owen both held that the Holy Spirit functions as the principle of spiritual life in Christ.[367]

Goodwin appeared to embrace similar theological logic in one passage where he refuted the Socinian denial of Christ's agency in his resurrection. Applying the maxim that the *ad extra* works of the Trinity are indivisible, he reasoned that all three divine persons resurrected Christ.[368] In other words, he understood the second person to grant resurrection life to his human nature by the Holy Spirit. This readily explains Goodwin's designation elsewhere of the Holy Spirit as the 'immediate cause' of Christ's resurrection.[369] However, this was not Goodwin's main mode of thought. What dominated was that whereas the Holy Spirit constitutes spiritual life in believers, Christ's divine nature fulfils this role in Christ.[370]

Goodwin was determined to establish the unique role of Christ's divine nature in his soteriological scheme. Arguably, Goodwin could have accomplished this and embraced the view of Sibbes and Owen by contending that Christ's divine nature grants his human nature the right to the Holy Spirit as the life principle in him and in believers.[371] After all, the unique privilege of Christ's humanity was not the indwelling of divine nature but the hypostatic union which Goodwin frequently treated as significant in bestowing the rights of the divine Son upon the human nature. However, for Goodwin, such legal considerations were insufficient. Instead, he contended that Christ's divine nature must directly constitute Christ's

---

364. Sibbes, *Beames of Divine Light*, 'A Description of Christ', 38.

365. Sibbes, *The Excellencie of the Gospell*, 577–8.

366. Owen, *Pneumatologia*, 130.

367. Sibbes, *Exposition: upon The first Chapter of the Second Epistle to the Corinthians*, 464; Sibbes, *Beames of Divine Light*, 'The Spirituall Jubile', 34–6; Sibbes, *The Excellencie of the Gospell*, 14–44; Owen, *Saints Perseverance*, 194–7.

368. *Works*, I, *Ephesians*, part I, 401–2; cf. 405, 439.

369. *Works*, V, *The Holy Ghost*, 10.

370. *Works*, II, *The Creatures*, 118.

371. See pp. 216–17.

spiritual life in order to grant Christ 'Life in himself independently'.[372] In other words, whereas natural life is reliant on external (created) resources, Christ's spiritualized human nature depends only upon his own divinity. Since the Holy Spirit is distinct from Christ's person, being neither of his two natures, Goodwin assumed that Christ would not possess independent life if the Holy Spirit operated as his life principle.

At one level Goodwin's departure from Sibbes can be explained on the basis of heterodox Christologies that rose to prominence after Sibbes's death.[373] It should be recalled that Lawrence argues that *The Creatures* Book II was particularly written to refute Socinian teaching.[374] More relevant, though, is the radical view mentioned in Book II which alleged that believers, like Christ, enjoy hypostatic union.[375] In contrast to radical teaching, Goodwin insisted upon Christ's divine nature as his independent spiritual life in order to secure the unique necessity of Christ's hypostatic union. However, it should also be recalled that in Goodwin's early sermon on Ephesians 3:17 he had already departed from Sibbes on a related matter.[376] Whereas Sibbes had held that Christ indwells believers by the proxy of the Spirit, the early Goodwin stressed the immediate and primary indwelling of Christ's divine nature. While Goodwin's theology underwent pneumatological revision, this revision was restricted to the case of believers, rather than to Christ himself. Goodwin's departure from Sibbes regarding the spiritual life of Christ's human nature, therefore, is better explained from his desire to uphold a higher soteriology in which nothing short of Christ's divine nature functions as the immediate spiritual life of believers. To state the same matter differently, Goodwin laboured to maintain a soteriology in which believers commune with Christ's divine person and not just his human nature.

Thus, Goodwin sought to uphold two competing concerns. On the one hand, he wanted to uphold a Sibbesian conception of the work of the Holy Spirit upon Christ's human nature. On the other, he wanted to advance further and construct a higher soteriology founded in Christ's divine nature. (These conflicting concerns may explain why both Blackham and Jones give attention to Goodwin's Spirit-Christology, yet fail to notice Goodwin's distinctive views concerning the significance of Christ's divinity for his humanity.) In effect, Goodwin integrated these two concerns by distinguishing Christ's principle of spiritual life from the enablement of his actions and transformation. The former was accredited to Christ's divine nature, whereas the latter to the Holy Spirit.

---

372. *Works*, II, *The Creatures*, 74.

373. Perhaps, Goodwin also feared the incipient Nestorian danger of isolating the two natures of Christ from direct contact by treating the Holy Spirit as a buffer between the two. This would explain his ambivalence in designating the Holy Spirit as the bond of union between Christ's two natures, see pp. 56–7.

374. Lawrence, 'Transmission', 43.

375. *Works*, II, *The Creatures*, 105.

376. See §2.3.

Moreover, Goodwin held that the Spirit played an active role in establishing the union of two natures in Christ, such that the Spirit 'made the Man Christ Partaker of the Divine Nature'.[377]

For Goodwin, then, Christ's divine nature is decisive for constituting Christ as the superior Adamic head. As Adam's created soul was 'the Supream immediate Principle of Life' to his body, so Christ's divine nature occupies the analogous relation to his human nature.[378] Indeed, Goodwin contended that Adam was a type of Christ in this respect.[379] As this scheme suggests, Adam's natural life is far surpassed by the spiritual life in Christ's divine nature.[380] As a superior Adamic head, Christ can advance believers to a heavenly state, but they must partake of his divinity if they are to share in his spiritual life. Here Goodwin assigned further uniqueness to Christ's divine nature. Not only is Christ's divinity crucial in supplying spiritual life to his human nature, but it is also crucial for him giving the same life to believers. Christ's hypostatic union grants Christ the right to bestow the Spirit upon others.[381] More importantly, since the hypostatic union supplies Christ with spiritual life in himself without external reliance, Christ is able to be the permanent source of spiritual life to others. Thus, Goodwin argued that the title 'quickning Spirit' not only imported that Christ has life in himself but also that he can bestow spiritual life upon others.[382]

Since Christ's human nature enjoys spiritual life by the indwelling of a divine person, Goodwin insisted the same must be the case for believers. He frequently compared the incarnational union and the union of believers with Christ, since both involve the indwelling of a divine person constituting spiritual life. Yet, Goodwin was adamant that believers are not hypostatically united to a divine person and therefore, unlike Christ, cannot possess independent spiritual life. Instead, believers enjoy the same life by continual dependence upon Christ. Here, however, it is instructive to return to the development in Goodwin's theology of union with Christ.[383] In his early sermon on Ephesians 3:17, he explained that whatever operates as the principle of life must indwell: 'it is certain, all Principles of Life ... must be the most intimate Indwellers in them which are said to live thereby'.[384] Specifically, a divine person must indwell, since only divinity can supply spiritual life. The indwelling of created grace would be insufficient, Goodwin explained, because the life-giving power of divinity would be too removed from the believer:

---

377. *Works*, V, *The Holy Ghost*, 43.

378. *Works*, II, *The Creatures*, 74.

379. *Works*, II, *The Creatures*, 87, 89–90.

380. *Works*, II, *The Creatures*, 74.

381. *Works*, II, *The Creatures*, 90–1.

382. *Works*, II, *The Creatures*, 75.

383. See §§2.3– 2.4.

384. *Works*, I, *Thirteen Sermons*, 31–2.

whereas you will say, the Graces wrought are an inward Principle of Spiritual Life … yet he is *intimior intimo nostro*; more within us, than we our selves are within our selves or our own Graces.[385]

Goodwin pressed this logic to justify the immediate and primary indwelling of Christ's divine nature in believers. He concluded,

Christ our Life, notes this, That that spiritual Life we begin to live here, is not so much a Life different from his Life, *as it is the very Life that Christ lives himself, the very same in Number; that same very Life, and no other extends to us*, so far as we are capable[386]

Despite his theology undergoing pneumatological revision, Goodwin continued to maintain that enjoyment of spiritual life required the indwelling of a divine person as a principle of life. In *The Creatures*, he claimed that Christ conveys 'the same Life which Christ himself hath'.[387] The difference is that Christ conveys spiritual life to believers by the indwelling of the Holy Spirit:

He saith of Jesus Christ, that he is a *quickning Spirit*, the Godhead being personally united to him, quickned his Human Nature; but so it shall not be with us: That's his prerogative alone; but he hath put his Spirit, the third Person of the Trinity, into us, who doth dwell in us … what *Adam's* Soul was to his Body, that shall the Holy Ghost be to our Bodies in a transcendent manner; though not by a Personal Union, yet by such an Union as is between the Human Nature of Christ and the Holy Ghost[388]

The Spirit, therefore, indwells believers as a soul of the soul and so functions as a new spiritual principle of life.[389] Sibbes and Owen, likewise, contended for the Holy Spirit indwelling as the principle of spiritual life.[390] Unlike Goodwin, however, both were able to maintain that the same divine person operated as the spiritual life in Christ and believers. Where Goodwin saw consistency was that the Spirit played an active role in establishing spiritual life in both.[391]

Nevertheless, a key question remains for Goodwin's scheme. If Christ's divine nature is responsible for his spiritual life, yet the Holy Spirit is responsible for the spiritual life of believers, then how could Goodwin maintain that believers experience the very same spiritual life as Christ? While he did not directly address

---

385. *Works*, I, *Thirteen Sermons*, 32.

386. *Works*, I, *Thirteen Sermons*, 32.

387. *Works*, II, *The Creatures*, 90; cf. *Works*, V, *Glory of the Gospel*, 73.

388. *Works*, II, *The Creatures*, 118; cf. 111; *Works*, V, *The Holy Ghost*, 43.

389. *Works*, V, *The Holy Ghost*, 54, 62–3.

390. Sibbes, *Beames of Divine Light*, 'The Dead-Man', 142; Owen, *Saints Perseverance*, 194.

391. *Works*, V, *The Holy Ghost*, 43. See p. 57.

this question, Goodwin likely assumed that the procession of the Spirit from the Son is the fundamental reason.[392] Two additional factors must also be noted. First, Goodwin argued that the Spirit unites believers directly to Christ's divine nature. Indeed, in his early sermons it was salvation as the reception of spiritual life that led Goodwin to reject the view that believers are first united to Christ's human nature. That believers are first united to Christ's divine nature was entailed in the immediate and primary indwelling of Christ's divine nature.[393] Following his pneumatological revision, Goodwin continued to argue that in order to partake of Christ's divine life believers must first be united to Christ's divine nature.[394] If the Spirit united believers first to Christ's human nature, then the divine life of Christ would be buffered from the believer. Significantly, Goodwin differed from both Sibbes and Owen on this point;[395] for both colleagues the prime focus of union with Christ is participation in Christ's human nature.

Secondly, in one passage, Goodwin assumed that reception of Christ's spiritual life via the Spirit is dependent upon the Spirit's work of inwardly revealing Christ. Reflecting upon John 6, Goodwin argued that reception of spiritual life depends upon the Spirit's work of causing Christ to indwell by faith.[396] As believers 'by Faith chew upon the Word that describeth' Christ, so the Spirit reveals Christ to the believer and supplies life from Christ. Thus, as believers are transformed by Christ, they become empty of themselves, and increasingly the life of Christ dominates.[397] In Goodwin's thought, then, spiritual life apparently equates to communion with Christ and, by extension, to communion with God.[398]

What results, then, from Goodwin's account of how believers partake of Christ's divinity is his conception of real union with Christ involving the indwelling of the Spirit's person. Moreover, since the Holy Spirit sent from Christ operates as the principle of life in believers, the church becomes an extension of Christ's person. The higher principle of life that believers experience is not the life of their own persons but Christ's own spiritual life (Galatians 2:20). Hence, believers possess both a lower and higher principle of life: the lower from their own person; the higher supplied from Christ by the Holy Spirit.[399] When

392. See pp. 57–8.

393. *Works*, I, *Thirteen Sermons*, 38–40.

394. *Works*, V, *Glory of the Gospel*, 76.

395. Sibbes, *The Saints Cordials*, 105. Oh states that Owen held the same view as Goodwin but fails to provide clear evidence. Oh, 'Beholding the Glory of God in Christ', 109–13. Moreover, union of believers with Christ's divine nature would run counter to the logic of Owen's stress upon union with Christ as consisting in the same Spirit indwelling the human natures of Christ and the believer. See Owen, *Saints Perseverance*, 194; Owen, *Pneumatologia*, 419.

396. *Works*, V, *Glory of the Gospel*, 75.

397. *Works*, V, *Glory of the Gospel*, 73–4.

398. *Works*, I, *Ephesians*, part II, 188.

399. Because of the hypostatic union, for Christ both principles of life belonged to the same person.

viewed from the perspective of spiritual life, Christ and believers comprise one (mystical) person.

It was natural then for Goodwin's chief analogy of union with Christ to be the head–body relation.[400] Here Christ's headship entailed more than a representative office. While Christ was the representative head of the church from eternity past, Goodwin asserted that Christ operates as an influential head from the time of his ascension.[401] Christ exerts influence by communicating life, motion and strength to the church.[402] Thus, as Christ's divine nature acts as the principle of life to his human nature, by the Spirit he acts in the same way in believers: 'He is first the Fountain of all Spiritual life, the uniter of us to himself, the principle of all union is from the head; he is Secondly the fountain of all motion; and thirdly of all strength.'[403] To help his readers to grasp Christ as head of the church, Goodwin asked them to imagine a giant:

> Suppose ... there were a Man that were as high as that his head were in Heaven, and his feet were here upon Earth, and his hands stretched all over the World: No sooner did the head that was in Heaven think of moving the toe, but it would move in an instant.[404]

Regarding the place of the Holy Spirit, he wrote,

> He beareth the part of the Spirits that run up and down in the Nerves and Sinnews and Blood, (which is called the life of a Man,) that carry all the commissions for actions to be done,& that part indeed the Holy Ghost hath between the head and us.[405]

Elsewhere, Goodwin cast the Spirit as the soul of the head and body.[406] Like-minded divines Sedgwick and Owen employed similar analogies and insisted that the Spirit binds the head to the body and causes it to move.[407]

---

400. The marriage analogy mainly appeared when accounting for participation in Christ's legal benefits and sometimes for illustrating interpersonal communion. Nevertheless, the category of Christ as head allowed Goodwin to switch between the two metaphors as convenient.

401. *Works*, I, *Ephesians*, part I, 481

402. *Works*, I, *Ephesians*, part I, 482–3.

403. *Works*, I, *Ephesians*, part I, 483.

404. *Works*, I, *Ephesians*, part I, 483; cf. 486.

405. *Works*, I, *Ephesians*, part I, 483; cf. 486; part II, 215–16.

406. *Works*, V, *The Holy Ghost*, 11; cf. 13.

407. Sedgwick, *The Bowels*, 588; Owen, *Saints Perseverance*, 196; Owen, *Pneumatologia*, 486. Sibbes had used the analogy of a giant tree, see: Sibbes, *An Exposition of the Third Chapter of Philippians*, 102.

Furthermore, as the higher principle of life, Goodwin contended that the spiritual life of a believer is stronger than their natural life. Regarding the resurrection body, he wrote, 'What will be the Life of our Bodies at the last Day? The Holy-Ghost; not only our own Souls, but the Holy-Ghost shall possess us more than our own Souls; he that shall be the Life of our Bodies then, he is the Root of our spiritual Life.'[408] It is, therefore, unsurprising that Goodwin claimed that the union between Christ and believers is far stronger than the union of a natural head and body: 'There is more reality and nearness betwixt the Church and him, than between the Natural Head and the Body; that other is but a shadow of this.'[409] Seeking to impress upon his hearers the reality of their salvation, Goodwin urged, 'Let me say to godly men, Agree, you are the body of Christ, remember that, let your mistical relation to Christ, that mistically you are his body, prevail over all considerations whatsoever. It is the strongest tie in the World.'[410]

Here Goodwin was again close to many enthusiasts. Higgenson wrote, 'is not the union between the head and members of a body natural more real and substantial then the union of Christ and Saints? or is not Christ the head of all things less to his Church then the head of an earthly Creature to its body?'[411] While conservatives who restricted indwelling to created grace employed the language of Christ's mystical person, this was inevitably a much weaker notion. Higgenson, outraged by such theology, complained that if infused grace alone acts as the principle of spiritual life, then the union of Christ's mystical person is stripped of its glory and rendered inferior to the union of a natural head and body.[412]

5.4.3 Conclusion: Goodwin's soteriology of Reformed Christocentric deification

For Goodwin, then, real union with Christ equates to participation in Christ's divinity by the indwelling Spirit. Other salvific benefits result from this notion of union with Christ. Referring to all that Christ possesses by and accomplished as a representative, Goodwin contended that 'the Power and Virtue of all these communicated to you by [Christ] being in you'.[413] In terms of the head–body analogy, Goodwin wrote that Christ, as the head of his mystical body, uses his influence to conform the church to himself: 'what Christ did to his Natural body, that he doth to his Mystical body, to conform them to him.'[414] Thus, believers partake of the benefits of Christ's humanity by first partaking of his divinity. For Goodwin, then, participation in Christ by replication of his benefits remains secondary to

408. *Works*, I, *Ephesians*, part II, 187.
409. *Works*, I, *Ephesians*, part I, 478.
410. *Works*, I, *Ephesians*, part I, 490.
411. Higgenson, *Glory sometimes afar off*, 31.
412. Higgenson, *Glory sometimes afar off*, 14.
413. *Works*, V, *Glory of the Gospel*, 76.
414. *Works*, I, *Ephesians*, part I, 489; cf. 129, 132, 482, 493.

partaking of his divine nature. The latter represents a more fundamental notion of participation.

This stance is significant. Goodwin was convinced that real union must involve partaking of Christ's divinity because such participation is the primary content of salvation above mere restoration. He insisted upon an 'eminently transcendent difference' between the mode in which Adam conveys natural life to his descendants and the mode in which Christ conveys spiritual life to the elect: 'The one, that of *Adam*, is by Natural Generation, to make us Men, like himself: But Christ's conveyance is by immediate quickning and causation of his new Life.'[415] Whereas Adam not only conveyed life to his offspring but also conveyed the ability to give life to others, Christ cannot give the latter for it requires his unique hypostatic union. The corollary is a continual dependence of believers upon Christ. Employing an analogy, Goodwin explained that Adam's conveyance of life is like 'the Communication of Light from a Candle to another' whereas Christ's is like 'the Sun doth to the Moon and Stars: He makes them light and bright, with that Light which is in himself; but he makes them not to be Suns, as himself is.'[416] Herein was a marked contrast with those who restricted indwelling to created grace alone. Such writers conceived the relation of Christ to the elect in much the same terms as Adam to the race. Indeed, Perkins employed the candle analogy to vindicate his model of real union with Christ by the indwelling of created grace.[417] However, for Goodwin, Christ's hypostatic union to his divinity and the corresponding indwelling Spirit in believers established a much higher state of affairs than the original created order. While Goodwin departed from Sibbes on the relationship of Christ's divine nature to union with Christ, both divines shared the same concern that the state of salvation must rise far above mere restoration.[418]

Moreover, while Goodwin conceded that the Spirit indwelt Adam, the mode of indwelling was drastically inferior to believers. In several early sermons, he stated that the prelapsarian Adam was indwelt by graces alone (thus not precluding

415. *Works*, II, *The Creatures*, 90–1.
416. *Works*, II, *The Creatures*, 91.
417. Perkins, *An Exposition of the Symbole*, 389.
418. Sibbes wrote,

> And therefore as there be many differences which advance the state of grace above the state of nature; so this is one, that our state in grace is more stable and firm, as being stablished upon a better ground, even upon Jesus Christ the second *Adam*. God never mends, but he mends for the better: and he never restores, but he restores for the better: the new heaven and the new earth shall be better then the first, so the new creature, the new *Adam* is more glorious then the first: and as that which we recover in Christ is more and better then that we lost in *Adam*, so the certainty and security of our estate in grace, is far beyond the other, this being stablished in Christ.

Sibbes, *Exposition: upon The first Chapter of the Second Epistle to the Corinthians*, 444.

the Fall).[419] In *The Holy Ghost* Goodwin conceded that the Spirit indwelt Adam, otherwise Adam could not possess created grace, yet stipulated that the Spirit indwelt only in the same manner as common to all of creation and conditional on obedience within the covenant of works.[420] In contrast, the Spirit indwells believers permanently as the Spirit of Christ.[421] What is crucial is that the Spirit did not operate as Adam's principle of life, as a soul to his soul, as is the case with believers.[422] Thus, Goodwin maintained that believers enjoy the spiritual life of Christ far surpassing Adamic natural life.

Goodwin's scheme of soteriology, therefore, amounted to what could be described as a Reformed Christocentric doctrine of deification. Gösta Hallonsten has brought much needed clarification to what constitutes deification. Warning of equating deification with vague notions of union or participation with God, he argues that it properly involves a comprehensive scheme of salvation, from creation through the incarnation to the eschaton.[423] Conforming to Hallonsten's definition, Goodwin saw the incarnation as more fundamental than the atonement in soteriology, advocated an anthropology anticipating the incarnation and contended for the necessity of the exaltation of believers from an earthly to a spiritual state involving participation in the divine nature. Where Goodwin differed from Hallonsten's definition was in his rejection of a platonic conception of participation[424] and instead defined participation in the divine nature in terms of interpersonal communion with God,[425] reception of qualities equivalent to the divine nature[426] and the indwelling of the divine Spirit uniting believers to Christ's divine nature.[427] Since the latter notion is the cause of the other two, reception of the indwelling Spirit as a spiritual life principle (along with the hypostatic union of Christ) is the key foundation of Goodwin's soteriology of Christocentric deification. Goodwin summarized his soteriology thus:

> And that Person, as now become God-Man, when united to us, we thereby becomes Partakers of his Divine Nature; and so to have the Divine Nature to

---

419. *Works*, I, *Thirteen Sermons*, 34; *Works*, I, *Ephesians*, part I, 134; cf. 221.

420. *Works*, V, *The Holy Ghost*, 47–8.

421. *Works*, V, *The Holy Ghost*, 47–8.

422. *Works*, V, *The Holy Ghost*, 62–3; *Works*, I, *Ephesians*, part II, 186.

423. Gösta Hallonsten, 'Theosis in Recent Research: A Renewal of Interest and a Need for Clarity', in *Partakers of the Divine Nature: The History and Development of Deification in the Christian Traditions*, ed. Michael J. Christensen and Jeffery A. Wittung (Cranbury, NJ: Fairleigh Dickinson University Press, 2007).

424. Thus, neither did Goodwin appeal to the essence/energies distinction in order to protect the God/creation ontological distinction.

425. See pp. 74–5.

426. See p. 92.

427. *Works*, V, *The Holy Ghost*, 43.

dwell in us first: As he by his Union, hath the Divine Nature of the God-head to dwell in him.[428]

Both the incarnational union and believers' union with Christ, therefore, are essential for reception of spiritual life. This revisits Goodwin's chain of three unions:[429] the Son enjoys divine life through the Trinitarian union; the human nature of Christ enjoys divine life through the hypostatic union with the Son; and, finally, believers enjoy divine life through their union with Christ.

This deification scheme rooted in the incarnational and mystical unions applied to other salvific benefits. Both legal and real salvific benefits are first received in Christ because of his hypostatic union and are conveyed to believers as a result of the indwelling Spirit. And, since these benefits are founded upon participation in Christ's divinity, the character of these benefits also surpasses the Adamic state. As demonstrated in previous chapters, justification and adoption founded in the worth of Christ's person entitle the believer to heavenly life;[430] transformation into the divine qualities of Christ's person enables the enjoyment of that life.[431]

Goodwin's grand vision of salvation differed from the soteriology of the conservative majority and instead resembled radical teaching. Rutherford found the idea of the Spirit indwelling as a principle of spiritual life incomprehensible and warned that Familism resulted:

> If there be an union of the person of the Holy Ghost with the soule, and not an in-dwelling by graces, the beleever as a beleever, must live by the uncreated and eternall life of the Holy Ghost ... neither any man, nor the man Christ can in any capacity be elevated so above it selfe, as to partake of the infinite life of God[432]

In contrast, Goodwin upheld a far higher soteriology than conservatives such as Rutherford could accept. Those who denied the Spirit's person indwelling tended to view salvation as mere restoration. While they freely advocated that the state of salvation is greater because it rests upon the covenant of grace rather than the covenant of works, Higgenson complained this was mere external change establishing little more than permanency. Higgenson called his readers to consider the height of salvation in Christ:

> it is worthy of consideration, whether the state of the new Creature in Christ be no more nor higher then the state of the first man in his pure Paradisical

---

428. *Works*, II, *The Knowledg*, 146. Elsewhere, referring to the Spirit's role in establishing unions, Goodwin wrote, 'The same Person that made the Man Christ Partaker of the Divine Nature, maketh us also.' *Works*, V, *The Holy Ghost*, 43.

429. See §2.2.

430. See p. 133.

431. See §3.2 and §3.5.3.

432. Rutherford, *Christ Dying*, 467.

nature, before the transgression; if no more, then the administration of light and glory from God upon *Adam*, and *Adams* union with that light, was as high and spiritual as is the light and union which by the Gospel is administred to a man in Christ; and the first man who was made but a living soul, had as much glory in him as the second man who is made a quickning spirit.[433]

Like Higgenson, Goodwin was convinced that the edifice of soteriology is at stake. Only the indwelling of uncreated grace allows salvation to surpass mere restoration of Adamic natural life. Where Goodwin differed from Higgenson and other radical voices was in holding the hypostatic union to be essential for Christ to function as the spiritual Adamic head. By insisting upon the unique hypostatic union of Christ, Goodwin therefore maintained a higher soteriology than the conservative majority but remained firmly within the bounds of orthodoxy.

Moreover, Goodwin's grand vision of soteriology even surpassed like-minded puritan colleagues. As already discussed, in comparison to both Sibbes and Owen, Goodwin's scheme was more ambitious and advanced a more immediate participation of believers in Christ's divine nature. While Sibbes and Owen affirmed the indwelling of uncreated grace in believers, both denied that Christ's divine nature was the immediate source of spiritual life to his human nature and both denied that believers are immediately united to Christ's divine nature. As a consequence, their notion of believers partaking of the divine nature was much more restrained and struggled to rise above transformation into the likeness of Christ's human nature.

Goodwin's high soteriology constructed on his conviction that union with Christ is participation in Christ's divine nature, therefore, constitutes a significant attempt at a Reformed doctrine of deification. To date, however, scholarship has largely ignored the notion of deification in puritan writers and the wider early Reformed tradition.[434] Discussion has been limited to whether Calvin's doctrine of union with Christ entailed a notion of deification.[435] Bruce McCormack has forcefully answered that question in the negative, arguing that such cannot be the case since Calvin insisted that believers are merely united to Christ's human nature.[436] Goodwin's grand soteriological vision, with its central stress upon believers being united to, and so participating in, Christ's divine nature, may well

---

433. Higgenson, *Glory sometimes afar off*, 32–3.

434. The notable exception is Paul Dominiak's recent doctoral thesis 'The Architecture of Participation in the Thought of Richard Hooker' (Durham, 2017).

435. The quest to explore Calvin's theology in this regard was prompted by the so-called 'The New Finnish Interpretation of Luther', which contends that Luther's soteriology was close to an Eastern Orthodox notion of deification.

436. Bruce L. McCormack, 'Union with Christ in Calvin's Theology: Grounds for Divinization Theory?', in *Tributes to John Calvin: A Celebration of His Quincentenary*, ed. David W. Hall (Phillipsburg, NJ: Presbyterian & Reformed, 2010).

represent the clearest and most developed Reformed account of deification, an account that is inherently Christocentric.

5.5 Conclusion

Why, then, did union with Christ occupy a fundamental place in Goodwin's soteriology? In his sermons on Ephesians, Goodwin repeatedly turned to a rule of participation according to which all salvific benefits are first bestowed upon Christ and, consequently, replicated upon and in believers. This notion of participation, inherited from Sibbes, constituted a fundamental principle in Goodwin's soteriology which he carried forward into his grand project. In salvation accomplished, Goodwin principally understood Christ as the Adamic head of a new humanity who in all his actions represented the church. Thus, Christ is the head to whom all the elect must be conformed. In salvation applied, Goodwin stressed that Christ's work as the exemplary cause is the dominant cause. Accordingly, salvation applied chiefly involves the replication of Christ and his *historia salutis* in/upon believers. In Goodwin's mind, this account of salvation accomplished and applied is demanded by the fundamental divine decree ordaining Christ's glory as the head of a new humanity conformed to him. Thus, Christ's work as redeemer must be understood within Christ as the Adamic head of an eschatological humanity.

Union with Christ, therefore, is central for Goodwin's soteriology because it allows the elect to participate in Christ. Since Goodwin's soteriology is the extension of Christology, his conception of real union with Christ is an implication of the nature of Christ's person. Again inherited from Sibbes, Goodwin advocated a rich Spirit-Christology, such that all that Christ accomplished and received as the head of a new humanity occurred by the Spirit. Only by the elect's reception of the same Spirit can Christ's human nature be replicated in them. However, Goodwin advanced beyond Sibbes by insisting that union with Christ is primarily union with Christ's divine nature. For Goodwin, Christ's divinity is fundamental for Christ to act as the head of a glorified humanity superior to Adam. Christ's human nature enjoys (uncreated) spiritual life by consequence of the hypostatic union with his divine nature. Believers may share in the same spiritual life through constant dependence upon Christ's divine nature by the Spirit. In other words, the Spirit, by indwelling as a new principle of life in believers, extends the very life of Christ to them. Believers, therefore, become part of Christ's mystical person. Herein lay Goodwin's fundamental conception of union with Christ. The union between Christ and the church is stronger and more real than even the union of a natural head and body. In the final analysis, Goodwin believed that union with Christ as participation in Christ's divine nature is essential for maintaining a soteriology beyond mere restoration to the Adamic state: a soteriology amounting to a Reformed Christocentric doctrine of deification.

Chapter 6

CONCLUSION AND ASSESSMENT

6.1 Goodwin's doctrine of union with Christ

My main argument in this study has been to demonstrate that Goodwin founded the application of every aspect of salvation upon a particular conception of real union with Christ (i.e. mystical union with Christ forged by his indwelling within the believer) rather than upon mere relative union (i.e. legal union external to the believer).[1] Goodwin's conception of real union with Christ has been unfolded in the four main chapters of this book.

In Chapter 2 I showed that Goodwin contended for a strong notion of real union with Christ. In his mind, the strongest unions involve indwelling; the union of believers with Christ must therefore involve indwelling if a high doctrine of salvation is to be maintained. Goodwin was careful to insist that such union is not essential, unlike the Trinitarian union, or hypostatic, unlike the incarnational union. Nonetheless, he refused to reduce union with Christ to the indwelling of created grace alone. Instead, he insisted that real union with Christ must involve the indwelling of a divine person. In his mature thought, he held that the person of the Holy Spirit indwells and enables Christ's mystical indwelling by revealing Christ within the believer (Goodwin tied this revelation to the external means of the New Testament Scriptures and the sacraments). On this conception, union with Christ must be completed by faith expressed in the will. Real union with Christ, therefore, is twofold in nature: the divine part involving the Spirit's indwelling and the human part in the response of faith. Yet, even faith results from the Spirit's revelation of Christ and infusion of created grace (hence real union includes an element of transformation). The Spirit is qualified to act as the bond of union with Christ's divine nature because from there he proceeds. The application of every aspect of salvation, Goodwin claimed, is founded in his conception of real union with Christ. This is primarily evident in the ultimate goal of salvation: communion with God. For Goodwin, real union must intrinsically involve a person-to-person union in order to found interpersonal communion with the Trinitarian persons.

In Chapter 3 I revealed Goodwin's conviction that the transformation of believers must be founded in his conception of real union with Christ. In his

---

1. See §1.5.1.

account of regeneration and bodily resurrection, Goodwin insisted that a radical transformation is necessary for final salvation, not just for addressing corruption but also for fitting the believer for a heavenly existence. To avoid capitulating to the view that the believer's essence becomes divine, Goodwin pressed the widely accepted distinction of qualities and substance, arguing that transformation consists in a change of qualities only. Nevertheless, the new quality, he maintained, is the quality equivalent of the divine substance not only in terms of divine holiness but also in terms of divine substance as a spirit. This quality functions as (created) spiritual life: initially infused into the soul at regeneration, increased in sanctification and completed at death, then infused into the body at the resurrection. Goodwin contended that this created grace is secondary to and continually dependent upon the indwelling Spirit; created grace must be primarily understood as enabling the reception of the Spirit's immediate work within believers. The renewal of the *imago Dei* represents the totality of transformation and occurs as the believer beholds the inner revelation of Christ by the indwelling Spirit. In this way, Goodwin grounded transformation in his conception of real union with Christ.

Chapter 4 showed that Goodwin likewise insisted that even legal benefits, most notably justification, are also founded in real union with Christ. Despite the claims of previous studies, Goodwin advocated a purely forensic understanding of justification. He contended for a high conception of justification in which Christ's passive and active righteousness along with his holy nature are imputed to believers. Moreover, because Christ's person as the God-man ascribes a corresponding worth to his merits, Christ's righteousness exceeds Adamic righteousness, meriting even participation in God. This reality of justification, Goodwin insisted, must be founded in union with Christ. Advancing a *tria momenta* view of justification, Goodwin founded each moment of justification in a distinct notion of union. On the basis of external unions with Christ, believers were justified representatively in Christ both in God's decree of election and in Christ's representative work. Justification proper follows faith and so requires the formation of real union with Christ. However, while real union is necessary, Goodwin believed it to be insufficient for the imputation of Christ's righteousness. Like marriage, an external covenantal union is also required to legitimize the exchange of legal benefits but only given the existence of a real union. What complicated matters was Goodwin's adherence to the general principle that justification functions as the legal grounds or meritorious cause of transformation and salvation. While he applied this principle to sanctification, he allowed it to be trumped in the case of regeneration and real union. Goodwin, therefore, maintained the causal priority of regeneration and of real union with Christ over justification. Thus, real union with Christ occupies a central place in his *ordo salutis*, with all salvific benefits causally dependent upon it.

In Chapter 5 I demonstrated that real union with Christ occupies a foundational role in Goodwin's soteriology because of his conviction that salvation chiefly involves participation in Christ. Fundamental is a notion of participation inherited from Sibbes whereby all salvific benefits bestowed upon believers were first bestowed upon Christ himself. In salvation accomplished, this was an implication of Goodwin's chief Christological category of Christ as an Adamic head (since what is true of Christ as a common person is replicated in his members). In salvation applied, it was an implication of the exemplary cause being the dominant causal relation. This vision of soteriology was motivated by Goodwin's desire to uphold Christ's glory as the head of a new humanity. Consequently, the fundamental movement in his soteriology is not redemption from the Fall but the advancement of believers from an earthly to a heavenly state in Christ. Thus, union with Christ has a foundational role because salvation fundamentally involves participation in Christ. In other words, Goodwin's soteriology is the extension of Christology. The nature of the union required for participation, therefore, is dictated by the nature of Christ's person. Real union is required because all that Christ accomplished and received in his human nature was by the Spirit and so believers can only participate in Christ's human nature by the operation of the same Spirit. Furthermore, real union must involve the indwelling of the Spirit's person, since believers must partake of Christ's divinity. Christ's divine nature functions as the spiritual principle of life to his human nature, thus raising it to a spiritual state surpassing Adam's earthly state. Believers share in Christ's (uncreated) spiritual life by the Spirit sent from Christ operating in them as a higher principle of life. Ultimately, then, Goodwin's conception of real union with Christ equates to participation in Christ's divine life and is the basis for upholding a Reformed deification soteriology.

6.2 Union with Christ in Goodwin's grand project

This assessment now turns to the place of union with Christ within Goodwin's thought and, in particular, within his grand project: the defence of Reformed soteriology. The importance of union with Christ to Goodwin is evident from his earliest sermons, dated to the 1620s.[2] There Goodwin stressed the immediacy of indwelling as the basis of union and, while certain key aspects of his views later underwent revision, there was considerable consistency in his doctrine of union with Christ throughout the rest of his writings. In the early 1640s, Goodwin preached an extended series on Ephesians 1:1–2:10 in which union with Christ and related soteriological categories featured extensively. The numerous interpretative and theological decisions made in those sermons reinforced the basic shape of his applied soteriology which remained unchanged into the 1650s when he wrote the bulk of his grand project. Also important was Goodwin's polemical work *The Knowledg*, penned in the 1650s, in which he defended union with Christ against heretical teachings that had sprung up since the early 1640s.[3] His views

2. See §2.3.
3. See §2.2.

were already sufficiently robust not to require significant modification; instead he pressed key distinctions to define the true bounds of union with Christ.

Examining union with Christ has uncovered the architectonic substructures of Goodwin's soteriology. A deliberate Trinitarian structure was especially evident in the central treatises of his grand project.[4] Alongside seeking to retain an orthodox conception of the Trinity, Goodwin particularly stressed the distinctiveness of the three divine persons and their respective operations. Each divine person has distinct honour, he reasoned, arising from a distinct work. In salvation, election belongs to the Father, redemption to the Son and application to the Holy Spirit. The central treatises were organized in a corresponding Trinitarian structure. *Man's Restauration* introduced three treatises each devoted to a divine person: *Election*, *Christ the Mediator* and *The Holy Ghost*. For Goodwin, salvation began with the Father's eternal decree for Christ to be the head of a new humanity; it was enacted in the historical representative work of Christ whereby he accomplished salvation from the problem of sin in his own human nature; and it is brought to completion by the Spirit indwelling believers and applying to them what had first become true of Christ himself. Goodwin's doctrine of union with Christ, therefore, must be understood in light of this Trinitarian substructure. To each divine person and associated work Goodwin attached, in accordance with his *tria momenta* scheme, a notion of union with Christ. Crucially, the application of salvation rests upon real union forged by the Spirit and thus found fullest exposition in his work *The Holy Ghost*. The necessity of real union with Christ, therefore, is entailed in his Trinitarian scheme. Moreover, Goodwin's Trinitarian concerns dictated that the Spirit must indwell in person rather than by graces. First, the particular way the Spirit is seen to be worthy of divine honour is by his person indwelling sinful believers. Secondly, the goal of salvation is participation in the interpersonal communion of the Trinity (possible because the divine persons are distinct). Thus, union with Christ must be forged by the indwelling of the person of the Spirit; indwelling by graces alone would render the three persons too removed. Finally, conceiving the Trinity as distinct persons was necessary to maintain Goodwin's covenant soteriology. As distinct persons, the divine persons agree to the terms of the *pactum salutis*. Indeed, federal theology assumes a notion of persons as agents consenting to the contractual terms of a covenant. The covenant of grace, likewise, involves persons in all transactions and therefore the Spirit's person must be given to believers.[5]

Although the central treatises were Trinitarian in structure, more fundamental in Goodwin's grand project as a whole was the Adam/Christ schema basic to federal theology.[6] This schema, focused on Christ as an Adamic head, was introduced at length in Goodwin's opening treatise, *The Creatures*, and developed further in *An Unregenerate*. While this was not present in the final treatise, *Blessed*

---

4. See pp. 8, 153.
5. *Works*, V, *The Holy Ghost*, 52.
6. See §5.3.1.

State, Goodwin admitted that he had already pre-empted an exposition of the eschatological state in *The Creatures* and instead restricted himself to defending the intermediate state. The Adam/Christ schema, therefore, should be understood as framing his exposition of soteriology. This underlying structural role is also evident in the three central treatises. *Election* sets forward two divine decrees corresponding to two offices of Christ – head and redeemer – and states that headship is fundamental. Although *Christ the Mediator* is focused upon Christ as redeemer, his work of redemption is incorporated within his headship, for Christ first receives all salvific benefits in himself. *The Holy Ghost* presents Christ as the head anointed with the Spirit. Crucially, this Adam/Christ schema had important implications for Goodwin's conception of union with Christ, since as Adam is united to the human race, so Christ is united to the elect. Moreover, just as all that was true of Adam is conveyed to the human race, so all that is true of Christ as the second Adam is conveyed to the elect. In particular, as Adam brought the dual problem of guilt and corruption upon his members, so Christ brings a commensurate solution of justification and transformation. The Adam/Christ schema therefore allowed Goodwin to defend a strong Reformed doctrine of sin and redemption.

Yet, for Goodwin the difference between Adam and Christ was even more significant than the commonalities.[7] Christ's superiority over Adam dictated the superiority of salvation above mere restoration. Whereas Adam and all in him live under a covenant of works, Christ fulfilled the covenant of works and therefore all in him live under a covenant of grace. This difference grants a stability and permanency to salvation. This much was commonplace among federal theologians. For Goodwin, however, there was a far more significant difference entailed in Christ's hypostatic union with his divine nature. Christ's divinity, Goodwin contended, grants his humanity spiritual life superior to Adam's earthly life. By the indwelling of the divine Holy Spirit, believers partake of Christ's divine nature and so enjoy the same spiritual life. Goodwin's conception of real union with Christ, therefore, equated to participating in Christ's divine nature and was vital for maintaining a soteriology of Christocentric deification. He advocated three notions of partaking of the divine nature: interpersonal communion with the divine persons, infusion of qualities equivalent to the divine nature and the indwelling of the divine Holy Spirit as spiritual life. Rigidly protecting the God/creature distinction, platonic construals of participation are absent. Goodwin's Christocentric account of deification rests upon Christ's hypostatic union, and real union with Christ by the indwelling of the divine Spirit. These two represented the fundamental pillars of Goodwin's soteriology. Even justification constitutes the legal entitlement to participation in God only because it is the imputation of the righteousness of the God-man.[8] None of this diminishes Goodwin's strong Reformed doctrine of redemption from sin but rather reveals that it was

7. See §5.4.2.
8. See p. 133.

incorporated, as the means to the end, within a more fundamental scheme of deification. Goodwin, therefore, demonstrates how a strong Reformed soteriology may be combined with a deification soteriology.

6.3 Locating Goodwin in his immediate historical context

Widening the assessment, Goodwin's doctrine of union with Christ may now be located within the landscape of mid-seventeenth-century English theology. Lawrence's historical reassessment uncovered not only that the majority of Goodwin's extended treatises were intended to form a grand project defending Reformed soteriology but also that these treatises were largely composed when Goodwin was at the height of his powers in the 1650s, rather than in the post-Restoration period as had previously been assumed. While Catholic and Arminian theology remained a concern for puritans such as Goodwin, Lawrence particularly highlights the growing alarm during the 1640s–1650s over Socinianism and moralistic teaching on the one hand, and numerous radical and antinomian teachers on the other. Consequently, this study has examined Goodwin's soteriology in light of the debates and concerns of the Reformed orthodox in that historical context and paid close attention to key theological distinctions employed by Goodwin to defend Reformed soteriology.

Confirming Lawrence, Goodwin's grand project can be readily understood in the context of the 1650s or earlier. The topics discussed along with the concerns and issues raised in his treatment of union with Christ may all be accounted for by a composition date prior to 1660.[9] However, in this study I have questioned Lawrence's suggestion, taken up and absolutized by Jones, that Goodwin's chief opponent and motive for writing was the Socinian threat. While Goodwin undoubtedly abhorred Socinianism, a more prominent concern was to refute and demarcate his position from the radicals, especially regarding the themes explored here. He warned of enthusiastic and pantheistic ideas far more frequently than Socinian teachings. Moreover, as Lawrence observes, the original impetus for Goodwin's grand project was not to respond to heterodox teachings but to expound the grace of salvation. In the final analysis, Goodwin's chief concern was pastoral: to impress upon his readers the height and reality of salvation. Union with Christ was central to this endeavour.

However, Goodwin had to demonstrate how his high soteriology did not collapse into radical and antinomian teachings. Particularly in view was an array of heterodox teachers who advocated a union with God so close that it jeopardized, or even explicitly undermined, orthodox Christology and the God/creation distinction: figures such as Erbery, Higgenson, Dell, Fry, Bauthumley and Clarkson. While these radicals were far from a homogeneous grouping, the basic impetus common to their theology can be traced to the influence of Familism and

---

9. The one exception is a single chapter inserted later into *The Holy Ghost*. See Appendix B.

the perfectionist strand of antinomianism brewing prior to the Civil War. Such proponents prized the immediacy of the divine indwelling them. In this respect, Goodwin, following the lead of Sibbes, held views resembling these radicals and enthusiasts. In contrast, the conservative majority followed Perkins who restricted the indwelling of the Spirit to created grace alone. By the 1640s–1650s, this division fell roughly along ecclesiological lines: Congregationalists typically shared Goodwin's opinion, whereas the majority of Presbyterians feared that strong notions of indwelling led to the tenets of the radicals.

Yet, Goodwin remained firmly within the bounds of orthodoxy by careful application of key theological distinctions. Important distinctions include: first, Goodwin affirmed a strong notion of real union with Christ but demarcated this from a union of essence and hypostatic union; secondly, he advocated the mystical indwelling of Christ by the Spirit's illumination but tied this inner revelation to the external means of Scripture and sacraments; thirdly, he maintained immediate communion with God but avoided collapse of the God/creature distinction by stressing communion of distinct persons; fourthly, he insisted upon the indwelling of uncreated grace but avoided perfectionism by also affirming the indwelling of created grace; fifthly, he contended for transformation into divine nature but limited it to transformation of qualities rather than substance; sixthly, he allowed for a notion of justification before faith but limited it to representative justification in Christ and argued that actual justification results from real union;[10] finally, he understood salvation as the replication of Christ's humanity but insisted that Christ possesses salvific benefits by virtue of his hypostatic union, whereas believers possess them derivatively.

Moreover, Goodwin's work should be recognized to occupy a significant place within English puritanism. His basic conception of soteriology was inherited from Sibbes and it was a broadly Sibbesian soteriology that Goodwin defended into the 1640s–1650s. Goodwin, however, provided a much more systematic and detailed account, such that the scale of his exposition not only surpassed Sibbes but was unmatched among English puritans. Furthermore, Goodwin advanced upon Sibbes's soteriology by equating union with Christ with participation in Christ's divine nature (rather than Christ's human nature). While much of Goodwin's theology was shared in common with other Reformed orthodox writers also opposed to Catholic and Arminian theology, Goodwin represented the end of the Reformed orthodox spectrum which particularly strove to maintain a high soteriology. Even Owen, who embraced a similar high soteriology, did not follow Goodwin's lead in advocating such a strong account of salvation surpassing mere restoration and involving participation in Christ's divine nature. It is both the scale and height of Goodwin's soteriology that ought to establish firmly the unrivalled significance of his grand project within mid-seventeenth-century Reformed puritanism and even within the early Reformed tradition.

---

10. Here Goodwin demarcated his view from 'imputative antinomians'.

6.4 *Significance for contemporary debate over union with Christ*

The contribution of this study to the contemporary debate over the place of union with Christ and related *loci* within Reformed theology may now be assessed. The debate, so far, has suffered from a lack of detailed analysis of individual theologians from the post-Reformation period. While a number of puritan studies have mentioned union with Christ, extended rigorous doctrinal analysis of the notion within an individual theologian's works has been lacking. Goodwin's significant place within seventeenth-century British Reformed orthodoxy and the unmatched scale of his exposition of soteriology render Goodwin an important case study. While many of his contemporaries assumed union with Christ occupies a central role, the doctrine remained largely undeveloped in their works. In contrast, Goodwin's grand project allows for an examination of the nature and function of union with Christ in his wider soteriology. This study, therefore, allows important new light to be shed on the conflicting claims of Evans and Fesko.[11]

What has emerged is that, in common with mainstream puritan opinion, Goodwin's applied soteriology was governed by the priority of a real union with Christ involving both the Spirit's indwelling and the response of faith. Goodwin, like his colleagues, founded the application of both real and forensic salvific benefits in real union. For Goodwin, applied soteriology must be structured in this way because salvation primarily consists in participation in Christ, first in his person, then in his benefits. Goodwin, therefore, vindicates Evans's overarching contention that Reformed soteriology was characterized by the priority of real union with Christ, rather than the priority of justification as Fesko contends. However, this summary oversimplifies the debate and when more fully considered both Evans's and Fesko's accounts require significant revision.

Fesko contends that Reformed orthodox divines embraced the notion of the *ordo salutis* and granted priority to the forensic alongside affirming union with Christ. This finds some support in Goodwin's writings. First, Goodwin assumed an *ordo salutis* scheme compatible with his notions of union with Christ.[12] However, Fesko's stronger claim that union with Christ was identified with the *ordo salutis* as a whole finds no support in Goodwin.[13] Indeed, Goodwin's *tria momenta* scheme of threefold union with Christ maps on to specific elements within his *ordo salutis*. Moreover, Goodwin believed it crucial that real union with Christ in particular appears before both justification and sanctification in the *ordo salutis*.

Secondly, Goodwin held justification to have priority over sanctification alongside holding transformation and justification to flow from real union with Christ.[14] Thus, both real union and justification cause sanctification but with

---

11. See §1.6.

12. See §4.4.3.

13. Kim follows Fesko and makes this claim for Goodwin in particular. Kim, 'Salvation by Faith', 196.

14. See §4.4.1.

differing causal relations. While Fesko often equivocates on the precise nature of the priority of justification, for Goodwin it was limited to legal grounding, that is, meritorious causation. As guilt is the legal ground or meritorious cause of corruption, so the same relation exists between justification and sanctification. However, while this priority is evident, Fesko overlooks a key factor which trumped the causal priority of justification. Since Goodwin was adamant that justification occurs as a result of faith, and faith as a result of regeneration, he insisted that justification occurs subsequently to regeneration.[15] Despite this being typical for mainstream puritans, Fesko not only fails to recognize this concern in his account of Owen but even attempts to demonstrate that justification precedes real union. Having cited Owen's declaration that justification finds its immediate ground in mystical union, Fesko makes an arguably incoherent claim that Owen also taught that 'imputation occurs prior to its application to the believer through union with Christ'.[16] Fesko's desire to find in Owen justification prior to real union and all transformation is wrong-headed, since the majority of puritan divines opposed 'imputative antinomians' for promoting precisely such teaching. At best, Fesko could appeal to features of Owen's and Goodwin's soteriologies which resemble justification before faith. For example, Owen's concept of absolution in heaven is causally prior to mystical union and Goodwin's representative justification in Christ is prior to real union.[17] However, both Owen and Goodwin denied that justification proper occurs before real union. This was more convincing in Goodwin's case, since his notion of representative justification belonged to redemption accomplished, not applied. Thus, Goodwin was adamant that, while prior legal considerations exist, justification proper cannot cause real union. It is striking that in this matter 'imputative antinomians' aligned themselves with Luther's soteriology, accusing mainstream divines of deviating from Luther's vision.[18] Although Fesko rejects accusations of his having a 'Lutherizing' tendency in championing the priority of justification over sanctification,[19] the accusation may have validity in his prioritizing of justification over regeneration and real union.

In his handling of Owen's soteriology, Fesko's desire to discover the priority of justification over real union results in him underplaying the significance of real union with Christ. Tudor Jones remarks that it was particularly the substantive reality of union with Christ which captivated the imaginations of puritan preachers.[20] Mainstream puritan divines prized the idea that salvation could be

---

15. See §4.4.2.

16. Fesko, *Beyond Calvin*, 296.

17. See §4.3.2. For Owen's scheme, see pp. 152 and 171–2.

18. See J. Wayne Baker, '*Sola Fide, Sola Gratia*: The Battle for Luther in Seventeenth-Century England', *Sixteenth Century Journal* 16, no. 1 (1985): 115–33; Tim Cooper, *Fear and Polemic in Seventeenth-Century England: Richard Baxter and Antinomianism* (Aldershot, UK: Ashgate, 2001), 35.

19. Fesko, 'Methodology, Myth, and Misperception', 399–402.

20. See R. Tudor Jones, 'Union with Christ: The Existential Nerve of Puritan Piety', *Tyndale Bulletin* 41, no. 2 (1990): 186–208.

applied only on the basis of a real union involving the Spirit's indwelling and the response of faith. Fesko's account, however, treats this role of real union as a problem to be circumvented. He gives little attention to the nature of union with Christ and how its nature permits the application of salvific benefits. Moreover, he fails to grasp the Christocentric shape of Owen's soteriology. For puritans such as Owen, Sibbes and Goodwin, soteriology is the application or extension of their Spirit-Christology to the believer.[21] Christ was conceived as the storehouse of salvific benefits and so salvation consists in partaking of him through real union by the Spirit. For Goodwin, at least, the glory of Christ is at stake: union with Christ must have this central role lest Christ be robbed of glory as the Adamic head of the elect.[22]

Turning to Evans, Goodwin's soteriology constitutes evidence for Evans's overarching contention that applied soteriology in the Reformed tradition was structured by the priority of union with Christ. It is ironic, however, that Evans argues that by the seventeenth century the priority of union with Christ had been displaced or severely revised in Reformed orthodox theology. The narrative of development Evans advances for this period, therefore, requires significant revision. Considering the main factors examined by Evans in light of Goodwin's theology, a more accurate picture may be established regarding the nature of development. In particular, Evans overlooks puritan divines who defended the indwelling of uncreated grace.[23]

Evans claims that Reformed orthodox theologians departed from Calvin's scheme by appropriating the scholastic category of infused *habitus* to account for the transformation of believers.[24] While Evans helpfully traces the reintroduction of *habitus* into Reformed theology, he pays insufficient attention to the significance of this notion among Reformed puritans. Mainstream opinion judged that Arminian theology severely underestimated the degree of transformation in regeneration and so the necessity of infused grace became a hallmark of orthodoxy. For this reason, Goodwin insisted upon infused grace in more profound terms than Catholic divines allowed.[25] More importantly, Evans's analysis could be significantly improved by identifying the crucial differences within mainstream puritanism over the mode of the Spirit's indwelling. The conservative majority denied the indwelling of uncreated grace. They not only appropriated created grace to account for sanctification, but actually equated it to the Spirit's part of real union with Christ.[26] Yet, Goodwin was an important representative of a minority who defiantly refused this view. In his mind, indwelling by mere graces markedly

21. See §5.4.1.

22. See §5.3.3.

23. See §2.4.

24. Evans, *Imputation and Impartation*, 47–51.

25. See §3.2.3.

26. In a footnote, Evans recognizes a tendency for union with Christ to be identified with the indwelling of created grace. Evans, *Imputation and Impartation*, 52.

weakened the reality of union with Christ. In effect, such indwelling merely amounts to a moral union whereby Christ and saints are one in affections and dispositions. In this way, the conservative majority had considerably weakened the doctrine of union with Christ and departed from Calvin's scheme. In contrast, Goodwin cast created grace as continually dependent upon the indwelling of the Spirit's person. By holding to the primacy of the Spirit's person, he incorporated the notion of *habitus* while preserving a scheme truer to Calvin's conception of union with Christ. In Goodwin's mind, the issue was not the appropriation of created grace but whether that displaced the primacy of the Spirit's person. On the other side of Goodwin were radical antinomians who denied created grace and advocated the indwelling of the person of the Spirit alone. For Goodwin, such theology was inadequate because it failed to respond to Arminianism and could also lead to radical ideas of the Spirit overriding human agency or indeed of the transubstantiation of believers into the divine substance.

Evans highlights the related development of the bifurcation of union with Christ into legal and real unions underpinning justification and sanctification respectively.[27] Here he points to the influence of the development of the doctrine of original sin and federal theology. This alleged departure from Calvin is partially discernible in the case of Goodwin.[28] Explicitly referring to a twofold union between Adam and the human race, with real and external unions accounting for inherited corruption and guilt respectively, Goodwin asserted that the equivalent twofold scheme of union exists between Christ and the elect. In Goodwin's mind, the immediate basis for imputation is an external legal union. Yet, he also insisted that justification is founded in a real union.[29] Here the marriage analogy was crucial: like marriage, where a legal covenant legitimizes the conveying of legal benefits between individuals who mutually consent, so the covenant of grace conveys legal benefits to persons united to Christ in a real union.[30] Thus, despite bifurcation of union, the application of justification and sanctification was not as neatly separated into different unions as Evans suggests. However, among those who rejected the indwelling of the Spirit's person, some explicitly assigned sanctification to the Spirit's part of real union and justification to the believer's part (which was aligned with legal union). In this case, Evans's further claim that one consequence of the bifurcation of union was that real union was no more than sanctification proves true.[31] However, for Goodwin real union could not collapse to sanctification because real union is forged by the indwelling of the Spirit's person (i.e. it is distinct from transformation).

More problematic is Evans's claim that the rise of the *ordo salutis* displaced union with Christ as the central organizing idea of applied soteriology.[32] Evans

27. Evans, *Imputation and Impartation*, 55.
28. See §4.3.1.3.
29. See §4.3.2.
30. See §4.3.3.
31. Evans, *Imputation and Impartation*, 55.
32. Evans, *Imputation and Impartation*, 52–7.

contends that whereas for Calvin salvation was applied simultaneously, for the later Reformed orthodox salvation was applied sequentially. Polarizing two conceptions of the application of salvation, he writes,

> Either all the benefits of salvation reside in Christ and are communicated to the believer through spiritual union with him, or they are communicated through a series of successive and discrete acts, the coherence and unity of which can only be grounded in divine intention and sovereignty[33]

Goodwin, however, held that all salvific benefits reside in Christ first and cannot be communicated apart from real union, alongside employing the idea of an *ordo salutis*, adopting a high view of the divine decrees and holding a sequential application of salvation. Several factors meant that Goodwin transcended Evans's division. First, the divine decrees principally concern Christ and the elect in relation to him.[34] Secondly, Christ received salvation sequentially and so believers must receive it likewise, since salvation is the repeating of Christ's *historia salutis* upon the believer.[35] Finally, Goodwin's notion of union with Christ was integrated within his *ordo salutis*.[36] Conceding this point, Evans writes that the Reformed orthodox tended to maintain 'the formal umbrella function of union with Christ while, at the same time, revising it along lines compatible with the *ordo salutis* structure.'[37] For Goodwin, real union consists in a causal sequence: the indwelling of the person of the Spirit is primary; this causes both regeneration and the inner revelation of Christ, which in turn evoke the response of faith. Evans's criticism has more force regarding those who denied the indwelling of the Spirit's person, since in that case union with Christ collapses to regeneration and faith without remainder. For Goodwin, union principally consists in indwelling, which is distinct from transformation and justification, and thus not normally included in *ordo salutis* descriptions. Moreover, while he accepted the necessity of an *ordo salutis*, largely pressed upon him to navigate a middle course between Arminianism and 'imputative antinomianism', Goodwin fitted it around his chief conviction that soteriology consists in the application of Christ.

Evans's final claim to be considered is that later puritans tended to allow communion with Christ to displace union with Christ. Having cited Goodwin as proof, he alleges,

> A result of this trend was that 'communion with Christ' (a devotional matter) tended to displace 'union with Christ' (a theological concept) for many of the later Puritans. Calvin had focused on union with Christ's incarnate humanity

---

33. Evans, *Imputation and Impartation*, 54.
34. See §5.3.3.
35. See §5.3.2.
36. See §4.4.3.
37. Evans, *Imputation and Impartation*, 55.

as the means whereby redemption is applied to the Christian, but the later Puritans viewed the humanity of Christ more as an object of contemplation and devotion.[38]

Undeniably, works such as *The Heart of Christ* revealed Goodwin's interests in communion with Christ and especially with his human nature, but this did not displace union with Christ in his thought. In fact, Goodwin was convinced that communion, as the pinnacle of salvation, must be founded upon union.[39] Here again the decisive importance of the nature of real union is manifest: since union involves the indwelling of the Spirit's person who mediates Christ's person, union is inseparable from interpersonal communion. For the conservative majority, however, language of interpersonal communion was more restrained. Evans's further claim, therefore, was applicable to the majority:

> For federal theology, however, the sanctifying work of the Holy Spirit *represents* rather than *mediates* Christ. In other words, the Holy Spirit functions as a surrogate for an absent Christ instead of mediating a personal presence, a perspective often reflected in federal views of the eucharist.[40]

This construal of the Holy Spirit's role was, in fact, an implication of the conservative majority denying the indwelling of the Spirit's person and thus treating created grace as a buffer between the believer and the divine persons. In contrast, Goodwin from his earliest sermons strove to maintain that the person of Christ indwells the believer. Even with his pneumatological recasting of the doctrine, Goodwin insisted that the Spirit does not merely replace an absent Christ but mediates his presence through his work of revealing Christ within the believer. For Goodwin, immediacy of believers with the divine persons is the pinnacle of the Christian faith.

Nevertheless, the question of whether believers are united to Christ through his human nature requires evaluation. On the one hand, Goodwin was committed to the idea that Christ in his human nature receives all salvific benefits first and consequently these benefits are applied to the believer.[41] Goodwin's insistence that the Spirit is first poured out upon Christ as head and subsequently on to the church as his body suggests that union occurs through Christ's humanity.[42] On the

---

38. Evans, *Imputation and Impartation*, 78. Won makes the same judgement regarding Goodwin in particular. Won, 'Communion with Christ', 257; cf. abstract.

39. See §2.6.

40. Evans, *Imputation and Impartation*, 83.

41. See §5.2.

42. The strongest statement appeared in a sermon on Ephesians: 'He sendeth down the Holy Ghost, and he works all, the Manhood doth it instrumentally, the Godhead doth it Virtually, the fulness of the Godhead dwelleth in him and runneth, overfloweth through the Humane Nature as the instrument of it and filleth all in all.' *Works*, I, *Ephesians*, part I, 486.

other hand, Goodwin explicitly rejected the idea that believers are united to Christ through his human nature. At one level, he argued that this must be the case because Old Testament saints were united to Christ before his incarnation.[43] This appears to confirm Evans's claim that the Reformed orthodox increasingly denied union via Christ's human nature to affirm continuity between the old and new dispensations. However, the argument from Old Testament saints assumes the necessity of union with Christ's divinity for salvation, so in Goodwin's mind it was this factor that decided the issue. Reasoning that believers must share Christ's spiritual life, Goodwin was convinced that believers must be united directly to Christ's divinity.[44] In this scheme, Christ's humanity merely provides the legal precondition; that is, Christ's human nature constitutes the moral but not the physical cause. Goodwin's case, therefore, supports Evans's contention that union with Christ was no longer understood to be mediated through Christ's human nature, but instead his humanity merely provides the precondition for union. However, Goodwin may well have been in the minority. Goodwin's stance came from his conviction that salvation involves partaking of Christ's divine life and therefore believers must be both indwelt by the divine Spirit and united to Christ's divine nature. Sibbes and Owen, more restrained in their deification language, agreed with the former but denied the latter. Perkins, who restricted union to the indwelling of created grace, also contended that believers are united to Christ's human nature. This suggests that the conservative majority who restricted indwelling to created grace were especially likely to advocate union with Christ's human nature, since to receive the same created grace as Christ corresponds to receiving his human nature (as well as avoiding conceding immediacy of believers with the divine nature). As Evans recognizes, however, for Calvin union with Christ's humanity meant that the Spirit conveys to the believer the life of Christ's ascended human nature.[45] In this light, Goodwin's theology of the indwelling Spirit conveying the spiritual life of Christ was closer to Calvin's concerns than the theology of the conservative majority.

In conclusion, the narrative of development must be realigned around the issue of the nature of union with Christ. It was commonplace for mainstream Reformed puritans to insist that applied soteriology rests upon real union with Christ by the Holy Spirit's indwelling; the question was the mode of indwelling. The conservative majority who restricted indwelling to created grace indulged in the most significant departure from Calvin's scheme. Many of the developments claimed by Evans were a consequence of this key denial and so bear more weight regarding these divines. In contrast, Goodwin and like-minded divines promoted the indwelling of the Spirit's person and so were much closer to Calvin's vision of the priority of a strong notion of real union with Christ in applied soteriology. In effect, faced with new challenges, Goodwin retained the same basic scheme of applied soteriology but incorporated new distinctions and theological structures.

---

43. *Works*, I, *Thirteen Sermons*, 39.
44. See §5.4.2.
45. Evans, *Imputation and Impartation*, 27.

Where Goodwin departed from Calvin was in his insistence that believers are first united to Christ's divine nature in order to advance a soteriology of deification.

However, as Fesko and Muller have highlighted, Calvin, while important, was not considered definitive of the Reformed tradition. Indeed, while Goodwin was influenced by a range of Reformed writers, what I have highlighted in this study is the significant role played by Sibbes in shaping Goodwin's vision of soteriology. Moreover, the ambitious scale of Goodwin's exposition of soteriology demands that his doctrine of union with Christ must not be merely assessed by the degree of alignment with previous Reformers but instead deserves to be recognized as a definitive contribution itself. Arguably, the most important writers on this doctrine were not those who wrote a dedicated tract on union with Christ but those who expounded the doctrine within a comprehensive scheme of soteriology. As it is of Calvin's *Institutes*, so this is the significance of Goodwin's grand project. Therein Goodwin advanced a plan of salvation that not only addresses the devastating effects of the Fall but did so within what amounts to a Reformed Christocentric doctrine of deification. This high soteriology, surpassing both Calvin's and Sibbes's, requires nothing less, Goodwin contended, than believers partaking of Christ's divine nature through real union with Christ's divine nature by the indwelling of the divine Spirit.

Appendix A

EDITIONS OF GOODWIN'S *WORKS*

Two editions of Goodwin's *Works* have been published: the original five-folio edition (1681–1704)[1] and the nineteenth-century James Nichol twelve-volume edition (1861–6).[2] While most studies have used the Nichol edition, Lawrence departed from this practice and referenced the original printed edition instead. Following his lead, Jones mounts an argument for the superiority of the original edition.[3] Vickery, however, takes issue with Jones's main argument and returns to the practice of citing the Nichol edition.[4] It is, therefore, necessary to address this matter and to provide the rationale for the choice of edition I have used in the present study.

Jones's main argument for the superiority of the original edition is that a comparison of a specific passage cited from both editions reveals that they significantly disagree in content. This is an alarming claim, yet Vickery presents devastating evidence against Jones's case:

> What Jones has failed to recognize is that Goodwin wrote two treatises of very similar titles, and of largely similar content. One was an expansion upon the other. The earlier title, *The Glory of the Gospel*, is a shorter version of the larger discourse, *A Discourse of the Glory of the Gospel*.[5]

Furthermore, Vickery cannot find any substantive differences between the two editions. He concludes: 'There is no need to distrust the Nichol edition, and it remains, as the editors claimed, an edition that has brought greater clarity to the original.'[6]

---

1. Note: Jones incorrectly reports the date of the original edition as 1691–1704. Jones, *Why Heaven Kissed Earth*, 19.

2. Thomas Goodwin, *The Works of Thomas Goodwin, D.D.*, 12 vols, ed. W. Lindsay Alexander, Thomas J. Crawford, William Cunningham, D. T. K. Drummond, William H. Goold and Andrew Thomson, Nichol's Series of Standard Divines: Puritan Period (Edinburgh: James Nichol, 1861–6).

3. Jones, *Why Heaven Kissed Earth*, 19–21.

4. Vickery, 'A Most Lawful Pleasure', 18–22. In 'Salvation by Faith', Kim also reverts to the practice of referencing the Nichol edition.

5. Vickery, 'A Most Lawful Pleasure', 20.

6. Vickery, 'A Most Lawful Pleasure', 22.

However, irrespective of the strengths of the Nichol edition, the original edition remains the standard by which it may be assessed. Unless Vickery has verified the accuracy of the entire Goodwin corpus in the newer edition, he is undertaking a risky venture by relying on it. If the critical edition merely corrects typographical errors, erratic punctuation, verse reference inaccuracies and so on, then surely scholarly research should work with the original edition and only employ the later edition as an aid for clarification. Rather than providing a positive argument for the newer edition, Vickery has merely dismissed Jones's main grounds for the superiority of the old one.

Besides, positive reasons remain for using the original edition. As Jones notes, for various reasons the 'later twelve-volume edition is missing a lot of the marginalia';[7] Vickery ignores this comment, yet the marginalia of the original edition provided Lawrence with important evidence for uncovering Goodwin's intentions and scheme underlying the *Works*. For instance, Lawrence observes a marginal note in the original edition of *An Unregenerate* Book VI explaining that the neighbouring content was originally preached in 1629.[8] Yet, Book VI is omitted from the Nichol edition, the editor noting that, apart from a few minor verbal variations, the Book is identical to Goodwin's separately published tract *The Vanity of Thoughts*. The marginal note was consequently omitted in the Nichol edition.

Moreover, on occasion the Nichol edition wrongly corrects the original edition. For example, one line in the original edition reads: 'Man had ras'd and defaced that image.'[9] Here it is evident that Goodwin was referring to the destruction of the *imago Dei* and thus 'ras'd' should be taken as 'razed'.[10] Yet, in the Nichol edition the same line reads: 'man had raised and defaced that image.'[11] A second example reveals the failure of the Nichol edition to consult the errata of the original edition. One line in the Nichol edition reads: 'So as well might the apostle, comparing this gift of Christ's righteousness and obedience imparted, with that one disobedience of Adam imputed.'[12] While the word 'imparted' reproduces the main text of the original edition,[13] it was corrected as 'imputed' in the appended errata.[14] In both examples, the incorrect word signifies the opposite meaning to that intended.

In conclusion, while the Nichol edition is largely accurate, it is inadequate for serious scholarship and so in this study I have provided references to the original printed edition.

---

7. Jones, *Why Heaven Kissed Earth*, 19.

8. *Works*, III, *An Unregenerate*, 240. See Lawrence, 'Transmission', 31–2.

9. *Works*, V, *The Holy Ghost*, 361.

10. The *Oxford English Dictionary* lists 'rased' as a variant spelling for 'razed' in the seventeenth century. Elsewhere, Goodwin declares the image to be 'razed'. E.g. *Works*, II, *The Creatures*, 43.

11. Nichol Edition, *Works*, VI, *The Holy Ghost*, 392.

12. Nichol Edition, *Works*, IX, *Election*, 309.

13. *Works*, II, *Election*, 272.

14. *Works*, II, errata, n.p.

Appendix B

DATING OF SELECT TREATISES FROM GOODWIN'S *WORKS*

In this appendix I consider the evidence for dating the composition of select treatises and sermons published in the *Works* referenced in this study.[1] In the main, Lawrence's arguments are repeated here but supplemented where necessary. A full analysis of the provenance of each of Goodwin's works, however, must await future research. The difficulty in this task is that many of Goodwin's works do not contain clear internal evidence for the date of composition and matters are further complicated by an editing process. This process involved the stitching together of various discourses into treatises composed at different times and also the insertion of cross-references to other works. Thus, the dating of one part of a treatise is not necessarily evidence for other parts and cross-references to other treatises seldom constitute firm evidence for establishing a date of composition.

B.1 Treatises in Goodwin's grand project

The first seven treatises comprise Goodwin's grand project and the evidence supplied here must be combined with Lawrence's arguments for the existence of a grand project substantially underway by the end of the 1650s.[2]

B.1.1 The Creatures (Works *II*)

This treatise was largely, if not entirely, composed in the 1650s.[3] Book I includes a description of Goodwin's opponents which readily matches the tenets of the 'ranters' and matches Goodwin's description in *The Knowledg*.[4] Lawrence argues that this identification suggests a probable date for Book I to the aftermath of the

---

1. Treatises in the *Works* not relevant to this study will be ignored. Goodwin also separately published a number of tracts during his lifetime; details of those cited in this study can be found in the bibliography.
2. See §1.3.
3. See Lawrence, 'Transmission', 23–9, 41–4.
4. *Works*, II, *The Creatures*, 1–2.

'ranter' sensation of 1649–50. This Book appears to have been delivered as sermons and therefore not composed retrospectively.[5] Book II, Lawrence contends, is more difficult to date since these opponents fall from view, but was most likely targeted against Socinian teachings and thus also composed in the 1650s. Lawrence identifies the Socinians on the basis of one passing reference by Goodwin and by the set of topics addressed. This is plausible, but additionally it should be noted that Goodwin also made reference to radical teaching prevalent in the 1650s.[6] Also suggestive of composition in the 1650s is Goodwin's comment in *Blessed State* that he chose to focus on the intermediate state because he had already sufficiently addressed the final state in *The Creatures* Book II.[7]

B.1.2 An Unregenerate (Works III)

Lawrence comments that dating this treatise is difficult, yet it appears that a considerable proportion was penned before Goodwin's resignation from Holy Trinity in 1633 and then updated and expanded much later in his career. Lawrence provides detailed consideration of the evidence for this conclusion.[8] The first few chapters of Book I contain various references to other works, likely dating them to the 1650s.[9] These do not appear to be later editorial insertions, since they are embedded in the flow of the discourse. However, the remainder of Book I, expounding Romans 5:19-20, appears to date from the 1620s and reflects Goodwin's own overwhelming awareness of his inherited guilt and corruption during 1620-7.[10] Furthermore, a marginal note in Book I identifies one chapter with a sermon preached in 1626.[11] Lawrence suggests that Book II should be dated to the same period as it continues themes closely integrated with the second half of Book I. Of importance for dating the rest of the treatise, a marginal note relating to Book VI reads: 'These Sermons were preached in the year 1629 in the course of my Lectures at *Cambridge*.'[12] Book VI was originally printed as *The Vanity of Thoughts* (1637). Moreover, the sermons of Book VI were but one set in a series, of which the other titles agree with the various Book headings of *An Unregenerate* (Books III, IV, V, VII and VIII). It is therefore likely that Books III–VIII were originally delivered in 1629. Book IX is more difficult to date. Books X and XI can be tentatively dated to 1627 because their contents correspond with a description provided by Hartlib in a 1634 diary entry and also cohere with the end of Goodwin's seven-year struggle for assurance (by expounding the problem of human depravity).[13] Book XII must

5. *Works*, II, *The Creatures*, 14.
6. *Works*, II, *The Creatures*, 105.
7. *Works*, V, *Blessed State*, 8.
8. Lawrence, 'Transmission', 29–38.
9. E.g. *Works*, III, *An Unregenerate*, 15–16.
10. *Life*, xv.
11. *Works*, III, *An Unregenerate*, 28.
12. *Works*, III, *An Unregenerate*, 240.
13. Lawrence, 'Transmission', 34–5.

be dated to the 1620s–1630s, since it was published as *Aggravation of Sinne* in 1637. Book XIII is again difficult to date, but an early date is plausible and would also fit with Goodwin's seven-year struggle. In addition to Lawrence's evidence, the Nichol edition of Goodwin's works reprinted anonymous sermon notes which date various sermons of this treatise to the autumn of 1629.[14] In conclusion, this treatise was largely composed in the late 1620s but later expanded, quite possibly in the 1650s.

B.1.3 Man's Restauration (Works III)

It does not appear possible to date this short treatise.

B.1.4 Election (Works II)

This treatise contains a central and extended section on the union of creatures with God. Goodwin's concerns here overlap considerably with *The Knowledg*.[15] Moreover, his discussion is carried out in particular relation to John 17 with Goodwin approvingly citing Hooker's treatise on this chapter of John.[16] Since Goodwin had brought Hooker's work to publication in 1654, it is plausible, then, that this part of *Election* should be dated to the mid-1650s. Two factors suggest a date in the late 1650s for at least some sections. References to Hammond's annotations on the New Testament, published in 1653, suggest a later date.[17] Moreover, in a probable reference to the 1640s–1650s, Goodwin refers to 'the Complexion of Twenty years last past' as an age of both gospel witness and heresy.[18] This part of the treatise should therefore be dated near the end of the 1650s.

B.1.5 Christ the Mediator (Works III)

This treatise is much more difficult to date, yet it is likely to have been written in the 1650s. In this treatise, Socinian teachings are mentioned twice, whereas radical teachings are absent; however, the subject matter probably dictated this emphasis.[19] A composition date of the 1650s is tentatively suggested by internal references. The treatise makes reference to *The Knowledg* which was penned in the early 1650s.[20] Goodwin also makes reference to 'the Levellers'.[21] However, it is unlikely to have been composed later than the 1650s because Goodwin's treatise *The Holy Ghost*,

---

14. Nichol Edition, *Works*, XII, appendix, 130–48.
15. *Works*, II, *Election*, 79–144.
16. *Works*, II, *Election*, 105.
17. *Works*, II, *Election*, 257, 265.
18. *Works*, II, *Election*, 177.
19. *Works*, III, *Christ the Mediator*, 46, 121, 196, 415.
20. *Works*, III, *Christ the Mediator*, 21, 42, 186.
21. *Works*, III, *Christ the Mediator*, 325.

largely written during the 1650s, made reference to central chapters in *Christ the Mediator*, suggesting that it too was penned in the 1650s.[22]

B.1.6 The Holy Ghost (Works V)

It is strange that Lawrence does not consider important internal evidence that this treatise began life as sermons delivered in Oxford during Goodwin's tenure in the 1650s.[23] The treatise contains several descriptions and refutations of radical teachings of the 1650s (but no references to Socinians). It also includes a reference to the Quakers indicating a composition date in the second half of the 1650s for that sermon at least.[24] Moreover, Goodwin wrote in Book III:

> We have seen the greatest outward Alterations that ever were in any Age, Kingdoms turned and Converted into Commonwealths … In this University of *Oxford* we have had puttings out and puttings in … Where do we hear … of Students running home weeping to their Studies, crying out *What shall I do to be saved?*[25]

Chang also notes this evidence but wrongly judges that the later Books of the treatise were written after 1673 because of a reference in Book VIII to the 'late Mr. *Caryl*' who died in that year.[26] However, this is problematic given the same audience still appears to be in view in Books IX–X (the last two Books) of the treatise:

> What is then, the Glory of the Church, and so should be of Universities? Even this, that multitudes of Converts are Born again therein, and they fill'd with such. … And whilst former times have boasted they have sent forth out of such a Colledge so many *Bishops*, *Deans*, &c. or Famous Writers, Men of such and such Learning, and Renown, the Memory of whom you continue in your Windows, let the Glory which you affect be, that such and such a Man was *Born again* here; and blessed are the Colledges that have their Quiver full of them as the *Psalmist* there goes on.[27]

> You that are young Students, and God hath turn'd your Hearts unto him; you have, in Doctrine, a Foundation laid of the greatest encouragement to the work of the Ministry.[28]

---

22. *Works*, V, *The Holy Ghost*, 109–10.

23. This is despite Fienberg's observation that the treatise began life as sermons. Fienberg, 'Puritan Pastor and Independent Divine', 278–81.

24. *Works*, V, *The Holy Ghost*, 309.

25. *Works*, V, *The Holy Ghost*, 145.

26. *Works*, V, *The Holy Ghost*, 351; Chang, 'Christian Life', 357.

27. *Works*, V, *The Holy Ghost*, 383.

28. *Works*, V, *The Holy Ghost*, 473.

Moreover, the reference to the 'late Mr. *Caryl*' is more readily explained in light of the manuscript catalogue and arrangement of the treatise provided by Goodwin's son in the preface to the *Works* V.[29] There it is evident that *The Holy Ghost* is a composition of twenty discourses with a degree of rearrangement from the original catalogue order provided in *Works* III.[30] Crucially, the reference in question appears in a short discourse which comprises a single chapter in the published treatise inserted in the middle of a longer discourse. Thus, there is strong evidence that this reference represents part of a later insertion made as Goodwin enlarged the treatise ready for publication. What is not clear is whether the original catalogue order reflected (1) the order of composition; (2) the intended order for publication; or (3) the order in which the manuscripts happened to be stored. There is an approximate correlation between the original catalogue order and the order found in the published treatise, suggesting (2), but that correlation is far from decisive. It is, however, unlikely that the original catalogue order reflected the exact order of composition because the discourse containing the 'late Mr. *Caryl*' (composed after 1673) appears immediately before the discourse including sections addressed to students.[31] What may be concluded concerning this treatise is that it largely began life as a series of sermons delivered in Oxford during the 1650s, but following the Restoration Goodwin inserted at least one extra section.

B.1.7 Blessed State (*Works V*)

The bulk of this treatise may be dated with confidence to the mid-1650s.[32] Lawrence notes that chapters XI and XII correspond verbatim to a sermon preached on 2 Corinthians 5:5 before the Lord Mayor at St Paul's, London, on 30 August 1657 and published shortly afterwards. In the dedication, Goodwin wrote that the sermon was but the final instalment in a sermon series preached 'just afore elsewhere upon those foregoing Verses' and he hoped that the whole series would eventually be published. This series readily corresponds to chapters IV–XII and by implication must have been preached earlier in 1657 or not long before. Lawrence wrongly claims that no marginal notes aid the dating of this treatise. In fact, a reference to Hammond's annotations on the New Testament dates chapter V to at least 1653.[33] Moreover, a passing reference to '*The University*' suggests Oxford as the probable original location for the sermon series given Goodwin's office there.[34] While the remaining chapters cannot be dated with the same precision, a reference in chapter III to *The Creatures* Book II also dates that chapter to the 1650s.[35] Chapter II refers

29. *Works*, V, contents, iv.

30. *Works*, III, *A Catalogue of the Authors Writings in M.S.*, n.p.

31. *Works*, V, *The Holy Ghost*, 473.

32. See Lawrence, 'Transmission', 38–40.

33. *Works*, V, *Blessed State*, 35.

34. *Works*, V, *Blessed State*, 72.

35. *Works*, V, *Blessed State*, 8.

to a recent denial of the intermediate state which Lawrence contends is a probable reference to Socinian teachings and therefore dates that chapter to the 1650s.[36] (Although, as already noted, radicals of the time also denied the intermediate state.[37]) The exception is the final chapter, XV, which Lawrence notes is almost identical to a sermon printed in 1638 entitled *The Happinesse of Saints in Glory, or, A Treatise of Heaven on Rom 8:18.*

B.2 Other sermons and treatises

I will consider more briefly the dating of other treatises important to the themes of this study.

B.2.1 Thirteen Sermons (Works I)

Of these sermons, five are important for this study. Goodwin's two sermons on Ephesians 3:17[38] are included in a set of sermons 'preached in his younger Time at Cambridge in his Lecture at Trinity Church'.[39] They, therefore, date to the late 1620s or early 1630s. Also in this group are two sermons entitled *Glory of the Gospel*, discussed separately below. In addition to these early sermons, Goodwin's sermon on Ephesians 2:14 is also important.[40] This was originally preached and published as *Christ the Universall Peace-Maker* in 1651 and called for greater unity between Presbyterians and Congregationalists.[41]

B.2.2 Glory of the Gospel (Works I and V)

This work was a significant expansion upon two sermons bearing the same title preached in 1625 delivered at Trinity Church.[42] As Lawrence convincingly argues, the original sermons were responding to the provocative publications of the Laudian Richard Montagu (1575?–1641).[43] He further suggests that, since Goodwin was still a preacher at St Andrew's in 1625, the location of the original sermons must have been wrongly reported by Goodwin's son.[44]

Of greater importance, however, is the dating of the later extended treatise. A marginal note indicates that it was '*Preach'd in his Younger Time, when he was*

---

36. *Works*, V, *Blessed State*, 6.
37. See p. 88 fn. 54.
38. *Works*, I, *Thirteen Sermons*, 29–50.
39. *Works*, I, *Thirteen Sermons*, 'To the Reader', n.p.
40. *Works*, I, *Thirteen Sermons*, 1–28.
41. Lawrence, 'Transmission', 147.
42. *Works*, I, *Thirteen Sermons*, 'To the Reader', n.p.; 61–89.
43. Lawrence, 'Transmission', 83.
44. Lawrence, 'Transmission', 81–2.

Fellow of Katherine *Hall in* Cambridge'.[45] This is confirmed by his son's comment that, Goodwin called these sermons 'his *Primitiæ Evangelicæ*, or his evangelical First-Fruits' because they were the fruit of his newfound conviction in 1627 to preach Christ.[46] Moreover, the longer work can be specifically dated to the years following 1627 given a remark by Goodwin that 'lately one of the *Septuagint* written 1300 Years ago was sent over'.[47] This was in the context of a veiled attack upon the Laudian desire to obtain ancient manuscripts. The manuscript in question must be the *Codex Alexandrinus* presented to Charles I in 1627.[48] This evidence suggests that the discourse should be dated in the period between 1627 and Goodwin's resignation from Trinity Church in 1634. This time frame is confirmed by: (1) a reference to the location of the preaching in a city which has been 'the greatest Mart of Truth, for this last Age, of any Part of the World';[49] (2) lists of heterodox teaching including Socinianism, Catholic teaching, Arminianism and antinomianism, but excluding 'ranters' and other radical teachings which came to prominence in the late 1640s;[50] and (3) a reference to 'the king'.[51] Admittedly, the last chapter contains a reference to 'the *Quakers*'.[52] However, since Goodwin's son listed a separate discourse on Galatians 1:15-16 in his proposed programme for publication, this chapter appears to be a separate sermon appended to the main discourse.[53]

B.2.3 Ephesians (Works I)

This series of sixty sermons on the opening chapters of Ephesians was delivered in London during the early 1640s before the convening of the Westminster Assembly.[54] A sermon towards the end of the series contains a reference to events that had unfolded in 1641.[55]

45. *Works*, V, *Glory of the Gospel*, 39.

46. *Life*, xvii.

47. *Works*, V, *Glory of the Gospel*, 27–8.

48. See Matthew Spinka, 'Acquisition of the Codex Alexandrinus by England', *Journal of Religion* 16, no. 1 (1936), 10–29.

49. *Works*, V, *Glory of the Gospel*, 50. A very similar description appeared in the original sermons and was more clearly a reference to Cambridge. *Works*, I, *Thirteen Sermons*, 79.

50. *Works*, V, *Glory of the Gospel*, 16–18, 41–2. The inclusion of Socinianism in Goodwin's list likely reflected his concerns over its presence on the continent, rather than an immediate local threat.

51. *Works*, V, *Glory of the Gospel*, 57.

52. *Works*, V, *Glory of the Gospel*, 78.

53. *Works*, III, 'A Catalogue', n.p.

54. *Works*, I, *Ephesians*, part I, preface. See Lawrence, 'Transmission', 19, 29, 196.

55. *Works*, I, *Ephesians*, part II, 230.

B.2.4 The Knowledg (Works II)

Lawrence judges this treatise to be written in the early 1650s, since Goodwin stated in the opening chapters that it was written in response to 'ranter' theology.[56] Because the 'ranter' sensation occurred in 1649–50, this likely locates the treatise in the early 1650s. Confirmation comes from scattered references to Socinian errors.[57] Lawrence highlights that both the *Principles* (1652) and the *New Confession* (1654) shared the same set of concerns. Finally, the same concerns are even more starkly articulated in Goodwin's preface to Hooker's treatise on John 17 published in 1656.[58]

B.2.5 Object and Acts (Works IV)

Beeke incorrectly reports the date of this work as 1642.[59] In fact, Goodwin stated therein that his 1642 treatises *Christ Set Forth* and *The Heart of Christ* were 'long since published to the World'.[60] Presumably, then, *Object and Acts* was composed at the earliest in the late 1640s. Goodwin included quotations from Bulkeley's discourse on covenants published in 1646 as well as from Hammond's annotations on the Psalms published in 1659.[61] While the latter quotation suggests a composition date into the 1660s, this may represent a later editorial insertion. Furthermore, the quotation appears in part I and there is some indication that part II was composed earlier: there is a reference in part I to part II which indicates this.[62] The preface also identifies one chapter from part II as having been composed in Goodwin's time in Cambridge,[63] and Lawrence notes that part II contains a second sermon that Goodwin preached in 1622 on Hebrews 3:10.[64] Nevertheless, these parts are exceptionally early; part II not only contains the aforementioned reference to *Christ Set Forth* and *The Heart of Christ* but also contains refutations of radical teachings of the 1650s, and so must have been largely composed in the 1650s.[65]

---

56. *Works*, II, *The Knowledg*, 3–4, 13. Lawrence, 'Transmission', 159, 200.

57. *Works*, II, *The Knowledg*, 52, 156, 157, 159, 180.

58. Hooker, *Christ's last Prayer*, 'To the Reader', n.p.

59. Joel R. Beeke, *Assurance of Faith: Calvin, English Puritanism, and the Dutch Second Reformation*, American University Studies 7, Theology and Religion (New York: Peter Lang, 1991), 334.

60. *Works*, IV, *Object and Acts*, part II, 16; cf. part I, 163.

61. *Works*, IV, *Object and Acts*, part I, 163, 15–16; cf. 73.

62. *Works*, IV, *Object and Acts*, part I, 164.

63. *Works*, IV, preface, ii. Chang wrongly claims that *The Acts of Justifying Faith* (i.e. part II of this work) was composed in 1630 on this basis. Chang, 'Christian Life', 355.

64. *Works*, IV, *Object and Acts*, part II, 62–70; *Life*, vii; Lawrence, 'Transmission', 80–1.

65. *Works*, IV, *Object and Acts*, part II, 104–6.

B.2.6 Gospel Holiness *(Works V)*

There is little evidence to date this work. Goodwin appeared to have 'imputative antinomians' in view, which likely locates composition in the 1640s–1650s.[66] Internal references to *Christ the Mediator* suggest that this was written in the late 1650s.[67]

B.2.7 Three Several Ages *(Works V)*

The strongest evidence from this treatise is a veiled reference to and critique of Hammond's controversial work *A Practicall Catechisme* which dates this work to at least 1645.[68]

B.2.8 The Government of the Churches *(Works IV)*

Internal evidence strongly suggests that this was written during the time of the Westminster Assembly. Carter lists six pieces of evidence:[69] (1) references to the king as alive; (2) descriptions of Presbyterianism in terms common to the 1640s; (3) a marginal reference to 1646 as the year of composition; (4) veiled references to the pamphlet war of the 1640s; (5) a parallel with the introduction to Hooker's *A Survey of the Summe of Church-Discipline*, which was published in 1648;[70] (6) the Assembly is mentioned in the present tense as though it was still sitting.[71] Carter further suggests that since Goodwin requested permission in 1645 to be absent from the Assembly in order to develop his model of church government, this treatise is likely to be the product of his six-month break.[72]

---

66. *Works*, V, *Gospel Holiness*, 20, 104.

67. E.g. *Works*, V, *Gospel Holiness*, 104, 113, 116.

68. *Works*, V, *Several Ages*, 184.

69. Carter, 'The Presbyterian-Independent Controversy', 14–15.

70. Thomas Hooker, *A Survey of the Summe of Church-Discipline. Wherein, The Way of the Churches of New-England is warranted out of the Word, and all Exceptions of weight, which are made against it, answered* (1648).

71. *Works*, IV, *The Government of the Churches*, 221.

72. Carter, 'The Presbyterian-Independent Controversy', 10–12.

BIBLIOGRAPHY

Primary sources were published in London unless otherwise indicated. Long titles have been shortened.

Goodwin's works

Goodwin, Thomas. *Aggravation of sinne and sinning against knowledge.* 1637.

Goodwin, Thomas. *A childe of light vvalking in darknesse: or A treatise shewing the causes, by which God leaves his children to distresse of conscience.* 1636.

Goodwin, Thomas. *Christ Set Forth In his {Death, Resurrection, Ascension, Sitting at Gods right hand, Intercession,} As the {Cause of Justification [&] Object of Justifying Faith. Upon Rom. 8. ver. 34. Together with A Treatise Discovering The Affectionate tendernesse of Christs Heart now in Heaven, unto Sinners on Earth.* 1642. Reprint 1651.

Goodwin, Thomas. *Christ the Universall Peace-Maker: Or, The Reconciliation of All the People of God, Notwithstanding all their {Differences, Enmities.* 1651.

Goodwin, Thomas. *Encouragements to Faith: Drawn from severall Engagements Both of {Gods Christs} Heart To {Receive Pardon} Sinners.* 1642. Reprint 1645.

Goodwin, Thomas. *The Happinesse of the Saints in Glory, Or, A Treatise of Heaven, On Rom. 8. 18.* 1638.

Goodwin, Thomas. *The Returne of Prayers. A Treatise wherein this Case [How to discerne Gods answers to our prayers] is briefly resolved.* 1636. Reprint 1638.

Goodwin, Thomas. *The tryall of a Christians growth in mortification, or purging out corruption, vivification, or bringing forth more fruit: a treatise affording some helps rightly to judge of growth in grace by resolving some tentations, clearing some mistakes, answering some questions about growth.* 1641.

Goodwin, Thomas. *The Vanity of Thoughts Discovered: with Their Danger and Cure.* 1637. Reprint 1638.

Goodwin, Thomas. *The Works of Thomas Goodwin, D.D.: Sometime President of Magdalene Colledge in Oxford.* 1681–1704.

Goodwin, Thomas. *The Works of Thomas Goodwin, D.D.* Nichol's Series of Standard Divines: Puritan Period, 12 vols, edited by W. Lindsay Alexander, Thomas J. Crawford, William Cunningham, D. T. K. Drummond, William H. Goold and Andrew Thomson. Edinburgh: James Nichol, 1861–6.

Goodwin, Thomas, Philip Nye, and Sidrach Simpson. *The Principles of Faith, presented by Mr. Tho. Goodwin, Mr. Nye, Mr. Sydrach Simson, and other Ministers, to the Committee of Parliament for Religion, by way of explanation to the Proposals for propagating of the Gospel.* 1654.

Primary works

The Racovian Catechism, with Notes and Illustrations, Translated from the Latin: To Which Is Prefixed a Sketch of the History of Unitarianism in Poland and the Adjacent Countries. Translated by Thomas Rees. 1818.

The Racovian Catechisme; vvherein You have the substance of the Confession of those Churches, which in the Kingdom of Poland, and Great Dukedome of Lithuania, and other Provinces appertaining to that Kingdom, do affirm, That no other save the Father of our Lord Jesus Christ, is that one God of Israel, and that the man Jesus of Nazareth, who was born of the Virgin, and no other besides, or before him, is the onely begotten Sonne of God. Amsterledam, 1652.

Ashwood, Bartholomew. *The best treasure, or, The way to be truly rich being a discourse on Ephes. 3.8, wherein is opened and commended to saints and sinners the personal and purchased riches of Christ.* 1681.

Bauthumley, Jacob. *The Light and Dark sides of God: Or a plain and brief Discourse of The light side {God, Heaven and Angels.} The dark side} Devill, sin, and Hell. As also of the Resurrection and Scripture.* 1650.

Baxter, Richard. *Of the imputation of Christ's righteousness to believers in what sence sound Protestants hold it and of the false divised sence by which Libertines subvert the Gospel.* 1675.

Baxter, Richard. *The saints everlasting rest, or, A treatise of the blessed state of the saints in their enjoyment of God in glory.* 1650.

Baynes, Paul. *An entire commentary vpon the vvhole epistle of the Apostle Paul to the Ephesians wherein the text is learnedly and fruitfully opened, with a logicall analysis, spirituall and holy observations confutation of Arminianisme and popery, and sound edification for the dilgent reader.* 1643.

Best, Paul. *Mysteries Discovered. Or, A Mercuriall Picture pointing out the way from Babylon to the holy City, for the good of all such as during that night of generall Errour and Apostasie.* 1647.

Biddle, John. *The Apostolical And True Opinion concerning the Holy Trinity, revived and asserted; partly by Twelve Arguments Levyed against the Traditional and False Opinion about the Godhead of the Holy Spirit: partly by A Confession of Faith Touching the three Persons.* 1653.

Biddle, John. *A Brief Scripture-Catechism for Children: Wherein, notwithstanding the brevity thereof, all things necessary unto Life and Godliness are contained.* 1654.

Biddle, John. *A confession of faith touching the Holy Trinity, according to the Scripture.* 1648.

Biddle, John. *A Twofold Catechism: The One simply called A Scripture-Catechism; The Other, A brief Scripture-Catechism for Children. Wherein the chiefest points of the Christian Religion, being Question-wise proposed, resolve themselves by pertinent Answers taken word for word out of the Scripture, without either Consequences or Comments.* 1654.

Bulkeley, Peter. *The Gospel-Covenant; Or The Covenant of Grace Opened.* 1646.

Burgess, Anthony. *CXLV Expository Sermons upon The whole 17th Chapter of the Gospel According to St. John: Or, Christs Prayer Before his Passion Explicated.* 1656.

Burgess, Anthony. *The Doctrine of Original Sin Asserted & Vindicated against The old and new Adversaries thereof, both Socinians, Papists, Arminians and Anabaptists.* 1659.

Burgess, Anthony. *Spiritual Refining: Or A Treatise of Grace and Assurance.* 1652.

Burgess, Anthony. *The True Doctrine of Justification Asserted & Vindicated From the Errours of many, and more especially Papists and Socinians: Or A Treatise of the Natural Righteousness of God, and Imputed* Righteousness of Christ. 1654.

Burgess, Anthony. *The True Doctrine of Justification Asserted and Vindicated, From The Errours of Papists, Arminians, Socinians, and more especially Antinomians. In XXX. Lectures.* 1651.

Burgess, Anthony. *Vindiciæ Legis: Or, A Vindication of the Morall Law and the Covenants, From the Errours of Papists, Arminians, Socinians, and more especially, Antinomians.* 1646.

Burton, Henry. *The Christians bulvvarke, against Satans battery. Or, The doctrine of iustification so plainely and pithily layd out in the severall maine branches of it as the fruits thereof may be to the faithfull, as so many preservatives against the poysonous heresies and prevailing iniquities of these last times.* 1632.

Calvin, J. *Institutes of the Christian Religion.* Translated by F. L. Battles. Library of Christian Classics 20. 2 vols. Philadelphia, PA: Westminster Press, 1960. Reprint, Louisville, KY: Westminster John Knox Press, 2006.

Case, Thomas. *Movnt Pisgah, or, A prospect of heaven being an exposition on the fourth chapter of the first epistle of St. Paul to the Thessalonians.* 1670.

Cheynell, Francis. *An Account Given to the Parliament by the Ministers sent by them to Oxford. In which you have the most remarkable passages which have fallen out in the six Moneths service there, divers Questions concerning the Covenant of Grace, Justification, &c. are briefly stated.* 1647.

Cheynell, Francis. *The Divine Trinunity of the Father, Son, and Holy Spirit: Or, The blessed Doctrine of the three Coessentiall Subsistents in the eternall Godhead without any confusion or division of the distinct Subsistences, or multiplication of the most single and entire Godhead.* 1650.

Church of England. *The Proceedings of the Assembly of Divines upon the Thirty nine Articles of the Church of England.* 1647.

Claxton [pseud.], Laurence. *A Single Eye: All Light, no Darkness; or Light and Darkness One.* 1650.

Coppin, Richard. *Divine Teachings: In three Parts.* 1653.

Cotton, John. *The Covenant of Grace: Discovering The Great Work of a Sinners Reconciliation to God.* 1655.

Cradock, Walter. *Divine Drops Distilled from the Fountain of Holy Scriptures: Delivered in several Exercises before Sermons, upon Twenty and three Texts of Scripture.* 1650.

Cradock, Walter. *Glad Tydings from Heaven; To The Worst of Sinners on Earth.* 1648.

Cradock, Walter. *Gospel-Holinesse: Or, The saving Sight of God. Laid open from Isa. 6.5. Together with The glorious Priviledge of the Saints. From Rom. 8.4,5.* 1651.

Cradock, Walter. *The Saints Fulnesse of Joy in their fellowship with God:* Presented In a Sermon preached July 21. 1646. Before the Honorable House of Commons. 1646.

Crandon, John. *Mr. Baxters Aphorisms Exorized and Anthorized. Or An Examination of and Answer to a Book written by Mr. Ri: Baxter Teacher of the Church at Kederminster in Worcester-shire, entituled, Aphorisms of Justification. Together with A vindication of Justification by meer Grace, from all the Popish and Arminian Sophisms.* 1654.

Crisp, Tobias. *Christ Alone Exalted In fourteene Sermons preached in, and neare London.* 1643.

Crisp, Tobias. *Christ Alone Exalted In the Perfection and Encouragements of the Saints, notwithstanding Sins and Trialls.* 1646.

Crisp, Tobias. *Christ Alone Exalted; In seventeene Sermons: Preached In or neare London.* 1643.

Dell, William. *Baptismōn Didaché: Or, The Doctrine of Baptisme's, Reduced from its Ancient and Moderne Corruptions: And Restored to its Primitive Soundnesse and Integrity, According to {The Word of Truth, The Substance of Faith, and The Nature of Christ's Kingdome.* 1648.

Dell, William. *The building and glory of the truely Christian and spiritual church. Represented in an exposition on Isai. 54, from vers. 11. to the 17.* 1646.

Dell, William. *A Plain and Necessary Confutation Of divers gross and Antichristian Errors Delivered ... by Mr. Sydrach Simpson.* 1654.

Dell, William. *Power from on high, or, The power of the Holy Ghost dispersed through the whole body of Christ, and communicated to each member according to its place and use in that body.* 1645.

Dell, William. *Right Reformation: Or, The Reformation of the Church of the New Testament, Represented in Gospel-Light.* 1646.

Dell, William. *The Stumbling-Stone, Or, A Discourse touching that offence which the World and Worldly Church do take against {1. Christ Himself. 2. His true Word. 3. His true Worship. 4. His true Church. 5. His true Government. 6. His true ministry.}.* 1653.

Dell, William. *The Tryal of Spirits Both in Teachers & Hearers. Wherein is held forth The clear Discovery, and certain Downfal of the Carnal and Antichristian Clergie of These Nations.* 1653.

Dell, William. *The Way of True Peace and Unity among The Faithful and Churches of Christ, In all humility and bowels of love presented to them.* 1649.

Denne, Henry. *The Doctrine and Conversation of Iohn Baptist: Delivered in a Sermon.* 1642.

Denne, Henry. *Seven Arguments to prove, that in order of working God doth justifie his Elect, before they doe actually beleeve.* 1643.

Dickson, David. *An Expositon of all St. Pauls Epistles together With an Explanation of those other Epistles of the Apostles St. James, Peter, John & Jude.* 1659.

Downame, George. *The covenant of grace, or, An exposition upon Luke I. 73, 74, 75.* 1647.

Eaton, John. *The Honey-Combe of Free Justification by Christ alone. Collected out of the meere Authorities of Scripture, and common and unanimous consent of the faithfull interpreters and Dispensers of Gods mysteries.* 1642.

Edwards, Thomas. *The First and Second Part of Gangræna: Or, A Catalogue and Discovery of many of the Errors, Heresies, Blasphemies and pernicious Practices of the Sectaries of this time.* 1646.

Edwards, Thomas. *The third Part of Gangræna. Or, A new and higher Discovery of the Errors, Heresies, Blasphemies, and insolent Proceedings of the Sectaries of these times.* 1646.

Erbery, William. *Nor Truth, nor Errour, Nor day, nor Night; But in the Evening There shall be Light. Zach. 14. 6, 7. Being the Relation of a Publike Discourse in Maries Church at Oxford, Between Master Cheynel and Master Erbury, January 11. 1646.* 1647.

Erbery, William. *The North Star: Or, Some Night-Light Shining in North-Wales. With some Dark Discoveries Of the day of God approaching, that is, the second coming or appearing of Christ in us the hope of Glory.* 1653.

Erbery, William. *The Testimony of William Erbery, Left Upon Record for The Saints of succeeding Ages being A Collection of the Writings of the aforesaid Authour, for the benefit of Posterity.* 1658.

Everard, John. *Some Gospel-Treasures Opened: Or, The Holiest of all unvailing: Discovering yet more The Riches of Grace and Glory, to the Vessels of Mercy.* 1653.

Eyre, William. *Vindiciæ Justificationis Gratuitæ. Justification without Conditions; Or, The Free Justification of a Sinner, Explained, Confirmed, and Vindicated, from the Exceptions, Objections, and seeming Absurdities, which are cast upon it, by the Assertors of Conditional Justification.* 1654.

Flavel, John. *The Method of Grace, In bringing home the Eternal Redemption, Contrived by the Father, and accomplished by the Son through the effectual application of the Spirit unto God's Elect; being the Second Part of Gospel Redemption.* 1681.

Fox, George. *A Message from the Lord, to the Parliament of England.* 1654.

Fox, George. *Newes coming up out of the north, sounding towards the south. Or, A blast out of the north up into the south, and so to flie abroad into the world.* 1653.

Fox, George. *Saul's errand to Damascus: with his packet of letters from the high-priests, against the disciples of the Lord.* 1653.

Freeman, Francis. *Light vanquishing darknesse. Or a vindication of some truths formerly declared, from those aspersions which have been (by reason of some misapprehensions) cast upon them; now published for the satisfaction and benefit of others.* 1650.

Fry, John. *The Accuser sham'd: Or, A pair of Bellows To Blow off that Dust cast upon John Fry, A Member of Parliament, by Col: John Downs, likewise a Member of Parliament, Who by the Confederacy and Instigation of some, charged the said John Fry of Blasphemy & Error To the Honorable House of Commons.* 1648.

Gataker, Thomas. *An Antidote Against Errour Concerning Justification, Or, The True Notion of Justification, and of Justifying Faith.* 1670.

Hammond, Henry. *A Practical Catechisme.* 1645.

Higgenson, Thomas. *Glory sometimes afar off, Now stepping in; Or, The great Gospel-Mysterie of The Spirit, or Divine Nature in Saints.* 1653.

Hollingworth, Richard. *The Holy Ghost on the Bench, other Spirits at the Bar: Or the Judgment of the Holy Spirit of God upon the Spirits of the Times.* 1656.

Hooker, Thomas. *The Application of Redemption, By the effectual Work of the Word, and Spirit of Christ, for the bringing home of lost Sinners to God.* 1656.

Hooker, Thomas. *A Comment upon Christ's last Prayer In the Seventeenth of John. Wherein is opened, The Union Beleevers have with God and Christ, and the glorious Priviledges thereof.* 1656.

Hooker, Thomas. *An Exposition of the Principles of Religion.* 1645.

Hooker, Thomas. *The Paterne of Perfection: Exhibited in Gods Image on Adam: And Gods Covenant made with him.* 1640.

Hooker, Thomas. *The Soules Exaltation. A Treatise containing The Soules Union with Christ, on I Cor. 6. 17. The Soules Benefit from Union with Christ, on I Cor. 1. 30. The Soules Justification, on 2 Cor. 5. 21.* 1638.

Hooker, Thomas. *A Survey of the Summe of Church-Discipline. Wherein, The Way of the Churches of New-England is warranted out of the Word, and all Exceptions of weight, which are made against it, answered.* 1648.

Leigh, Edward. *A Systeme or Body of Divinity: Consisting of Ten Books.* 1654.

Leigh, Edward. *A treatise of the divine promises In five bookes.* 1633.

Love, Christopher. *The Combate between the Flesh and Spirit. As also The wofull withdrawing of the Spirit of God, with the Causes thereof: And walking in, and after the Spirit, together with the blessednesse thereof.* 1654.

Manton, Thomas. *A second volume of sermons preached by the late reverend and learned Thomas Manton.* 1684.

Marshall, Walter. *The gospel-mystery of sanctification opened in sundry practical directions suited especially to the case of those who labour under the guilt and power of indwelling sin: to which is added a sermon of justification*. 1692.

More, William. *A short and plaine tractate of the Lords Supper grounded upon I Cor. II, 23, &c.* 1645.

Nicholls, Henry. *The Shield Single against The Sword Doubled. To defend the Righteous against the Wicked*. 1653.

Overton, Richard. *Mans Mortalitie: Or, A treatise Wherein 'tis proved, both Theologically and Philosophically, that whole Man (as a rationall Creature) is a Compound wholly mortall, contrary to that common distinction of Soule and Body: And that the present going of the Soule into Heaven or Hell is a meer Fiction: And that at the Resurrection is the beginning of our immortality, and then Actual Xondemnation, and Salvation, and not before*. Amsterdam, 1644.

Owen, John. *Christologia, Or, A Declaration of the Glorious Mystery of the Person of Christ, God and Man*. 1679.

Owen, John. *The Doctrine of Justification by Faith Through the Imputation of the Righteousness of Christ, Explained, Confirmed, & Vindicated*. 1677.

Owen, John. *The Doctrine of the Saints Perseverance, Explained and Confirmed. Or, The certain Permanency of their {1. Acceptation with God, & 2. Sanctification from God. Manifested & Proved from the {1. Eternal Principles 2. Effectuall Causes 3. Externall Meanes} Thereof*. 1654.

Owen, John. *Exercitations on the Epistle to the Hebrews, Concerning the Priesthood of Christ. Wherein, The Original, Causes, Nature, Prefigurations, and Discharge of that Holy Office, are Explained and Vindicated*. 1674.

Owen, John. *Meditations and Discourses on the Glory of Christ, in His Person, Office, and Grace with The differences between Faith and Sight*. 1684.

Owen, John. *Of Communion with God The Father, Sonne, and Holy Ghost, Each Person Distinctly; in Love, Grace, and Consolation: Or, The Saints Fellowship With the Father, Sonne, and Holy Ghost, Unfolded*. Oxford, 1657.

Owen, John. *Of the Death of Christ, The Price he paid, and the Purchase he made. Or, The Satisfaction, and Merit of the Death of Christ cleered, the Universality of Redemption thereby oppugned: And The Doctrine Concerning these things formerly delivered in a Treatise against Universal Redemption Vindicated from the Exceptions, and Objections of Mr Baxter*. 1650.

Owen, John. *Pneumatologia: Or, A Discourse Concerning the Holy Spirit. Wherein An Account is given of his Name, Nature, Personality, Dispensation, Operations, and Effects*. 1674.

Owen, John. *Salus electorum, sanguis Jesu, or, The death of death in the death of Christ a treatise of the redemption and reconciliation that is in the blood of Christ with the merit thereof, and the satisfaction wrought thereby: wherin the proper end of the death of Christ is asserted ... and the whole controversie about universall redemption fully discussed*. 1648.

Owen, John. *Theomachia A'vtexousiatike: Or, A Display of Arminianisme*. 1643.

Owen, John. *Two discourses concerning the Holy Spirit, and His work. The one, Of the Spirit as a comforter. The other, As He is the author of spiritual gifts*. 1693.

Owen, John. *Vindiciæ Evangelicæ Or, The Mystery of the Gospell Vindicated, and Socinianisme Examined, In the Consideration, and Confutation of A Catechisme, called A Scripture Catechisme, Written by J. Biddle M.A. And the Catechisme of Valentinus Smalcius, commonly called the Racovian Catechisme*. Oxford, 1655.

Pemble, William. *Vindiciæ Gratiæ. A Plea For Grace. More especially the Grace of Faith. Or, Certain Lectures as touching the Nature and Properties of Grace and Faith.* 1627.

Perkins, William. *A Commentarie or Exposition, vpon the fiue first Chapters of the Epistle to the Galatians.* Cambridge, 1604.

Perkins, William. *An Exposition of the Symbole or Creede of the Apostles, according to the Tenour of the Scriptures, and the consent of Orthodoxe Fathers of the Church: reuewed and corrected.* Cambridge, 1596.

Perkins, William. *A golden Chaine: Or, The Description of Theologie, containing the order of the causes of Saluation and Damnation, according to Gods word.* Cambridge, 1600.

Petto, Samuel. *The Voice of the Spirit. Or An Essay towards a Discoverie of the witnessings of the Spirit.* 1654.

Preston, John. *An elegant and lively description of spirituall life and death.* 1632.

Preston, John. *The saints qualification: or A treatise I. Of humiliation, in tenne sermons. II. Of sanctification, in nine sermons whereunto is added a treatise of communion with Christ in the sacrament.* 1633.

Reeve, John, and Lodowick Muggleton. *A Divine Looking-Glass: Or, The third and last Testament of our Lord Jesus Christ, Whose personal Residence is seated on his Throne of Eternal Glory in another world.* 1661.

Reeve, John, and Lodowick Muggleton. *A Transcendent Spiritual Treatise Upon several heavenly Doctrines, from the holy spirit of the man Jesus, the only true God.* 1652.

Reynolds, Edward. *Three Treatises of the Vanity of the Creature. The Sinfulness of sinne. The Life of Christ.* 1631.

Rollock, Robert. *A Treatise of Gods Effectual Calling.* Translated by Henry Holland. 1603.

Rutherford, Samuel. *Christ Dying and Drawing Sinners to Himself. Or, A survey of our Saviour in his soule-suffering, his lovelynesse in his death, and the efficacie thereof.* 1647.

Rutherford, Samuel. *The Covenant of Life Opened: Or, A Treatise of the Covenant of Grace.* Edinburgh, 1655.

Rutherford, Samuel. *Influences of the Life of Grace. Or, A Practical Treatise concerning The way, manner, and means of having and improving of Spiritual Dispositions, and quickning Influences from Christ the Resurrection and the Life.* 1659.

Rutherford, Samuel. *A Survey of the Spirituall Antichrist. Opening the secrets of Familisme and Antinomianisme in the Antichristian Doctrine of John Saltmarsh, and Will. Del, the present Preachers of the Army now in England, and of Robert Town, Tob. Crisp, H. Denne, Eaton, and others.* 1648.

Saltmarsh, John. *The Fountaine of Free Grace Opened by Questions and Answers: Proving the Foundation of Faith to consist only in Gods Free Love in giving Christ to dye for the sins of all, and Objections to the contrary Answered.* 1645.

Saltmarsh, John. *Free-Grace: Or, The Flowings of Christs Blood freely to Sinners. Being an Experiment of Iesus Christ upon one who hath been in the bondage of a troubled Conscience at times for the space of about twelve years, till now upon a clearer discovery of Iesus Christ and the Gospel.* 1648.

Savoy Assembly. *A Declaration of the Faith and Order Owned and practised in the Congregational Churches in England: Agreed upon and consented unto By their Elders and Messengers in Their Meeting at the Savoy, Octob. 12. 1658.* 1659.

Scudder, Henry. *The Christians daily walke in holy securitie and peace.* 1631.

Sedgwick, Obadiah. *The Bowels of Tender Mercy Sealed in the Everlasting Covenant wherein is set forth the Nature, Conditions and Excellencies of it, and how a Sinner should do to enter into it, and the danger of refusing this Covenant-Relation.* 1661.

Shower, John. *Sacramental discourses, on several texts, before, and after the Lord's Supper.* 1693.

Sibbes, Richard. *Beames of Divine Light, Breaking forth from severall places of holy Scripture, as they were learnedly opened, In XXI. Sermons.* 1639.

Sibbes, Richard. *The Christians Portion, or, The Charter of a Christian.* 1638.

Sibbes, Richard. *Christs exaltation purchast by humiliation Wherein you may see mercy and misery meete together. Very vsefull I. For instructing the ignorant. II. For comforting the weake. III. For confirming the strong.* 1639.

Sibbes, Richard. *Divine meditations and holy contemplations.* 1638.

Sibbes, Richard. *Evangelicall Sacrifices. In XIX. Sermons.* 1640.

Sibbes, Richard. *The Excellencie of The Gospell above the Law.* 1639.

Sibbes, Richard. *Exposition of the Third Chapter of the Epistle of St. Paul to the Philippians.* 1639.

Sibbes, Richard. *A Fountain Sealed: Or, The duty of the sealed to the Spirit, and the worke of the Spirit in Sealing.* 1637.

Sibbes, Richard. *A heavenly conference between Christ and Mary after His resurrection. Wherein the intimate familiarity, and near relation between Christ and a believer is discovered.* 1654.

Sibbes, Richard. *A Learned Commentary or Exposition upon The first Chapter of the Second Epistle of S. Paul to the Corinthians.* 1655.

Sibbes, Richard. *A Learned Commentary or, Exposition, upon The fourth Chapter of the second Epistle of Saint Paul to the Corrinthians.* 1656.

Sibbes, Richard. *Light from Heaven, Discovering The {Fountaine Opened. Angels Acclamations. Churches Riches. Rich Povertie.* 1638.

Sibbes, Richard. *The Saints Cordials.* 1629.

Sibbes, Richard. *Two sermons: preached by that faithfull and reverend divine, Richard Sibbes, D.D. and sometimes preacher to the honorable society of Grayes Inne; and master of Katherine Hall in Cambridge.* 1639.

Sibbes, Richard. *Yea and amen: or, pretious promises, and priviledges Spiritually unfolded in their nature and vse. Driving at the assurance and establishing of weak beleevers.* 1638.

Sprigg, Joshua. *Christus Redivivus, The Lord is risen being Some Account of Christ, what, and where he is; of the glory and mystery of his Person and Office, so miserably mangled now adaies.* 1649.

Sprigg, Joshua. *A Testimony to An Approaching Glory Being An Account of certaine Discourses lately delivered.* 1649.

Stedman, Rowland. *The Mystical Union of Believers with Christ. Or, A Treatise wherein, That great Mystery and Priviledge, of The Saints Union with the Son of God is opened.* 1668.

Synod of Dort. *The Iudgement of the Synode Holden at Dort, Concerning the fiue Articles: As also their sentence touching Conradus Vorstius.* 1619.

Taylor, Jeremy. *An Answer to a Letter Written by the R.R. The Ld Bp of Rochester. Concerning The Chapter of Original Sin, In the Vnum Necessarium.* 1656.

Taylor, Jeremy. *Deus justificatus. Two Discourses of Original Sin.* 1656.

Taylor, Jeremy. *The Great Exemplar of Sanctity and Holy Life according to the Christian Institution Described In the History of the Life and Death of the ever Blessed Jesus Christ the Saviour of the World.* 1649.

Taylor, Jeremy. *Vnum Necessarium. Or, The Doctrine and Practice of Repentance.* 1655.

Towne, Robert. *A Re-assertion of Grace. Or, Vindiciæ Evangelii. A Vindication of the Gospell-truths, from the unjust censure and undue aspersions of Antinomians.* 1654.

Traske, John. *The True Gospel Vindicated, From the Reproach of A new Gospel. In which many things are opened that tend to the comfort of sad Soules, and for their understanding of the Scriptures and their assurance of Faith*. 1636.

Warren, Thomas. *Vnbeleevers No subjects of iustification, Nor of mystical Vnion to Christ*. 1654.

Webster, John. *The Saints Guide, Or, Christ the Rule, and Ruler of Saints*. 1653.

Westminster Assembly. *The Confession of Faith, And the Larger and Shorter Catechisme, First agreed upon by the Assembly of Divines at Westminster*. Edinburgh, 1649.

Westminster Assembly. *The Humble Advice of the Assembly of Divines, Now by Authority of Parliament sitting at Westminster, Concerning A Confession of Faith: With the Quotations and Texts of Scripture annexed*. 1647.

Whitefoote, John. *A discourse upon I Peter IV. VIII. wherein the power and efficacy of charity as it is a means to procure the pardon of sin is explained and vindicated*. Cambridge, 1695.

Wilkinson, Henry. *The hope of Glory, Or, Christs Indwelling in true Believers Is an Evident Demonstration of their hope of Glory*. Oxford, 1657.

Williams, Roger. *The Hirelings Ministry None of Christs, Or, A Discourse touching the Propagating the Gospel of Christ Jesus*. 1652.

Zanchi, Girolamo. *An excellent and learned treatise, of the spirituall mariage betvveene Christ and the church, and every faithfull man*. Translated by [anon.]. [Cambridge?], 1592.

Secondary works

Affleck, Bert, Jr. 'The Theology of Richard Sibbes, 1577–1635'. PhD thesis, Drew University, 1969.

Allison, C. FitzSimons. *The Rise of Moralism: The Proclamation of the Gospel from Hooker to Baxter*. Wilton, CT: Morehouse Barlow, 1966.

Baker, J. Wayne. '*Sola Fide, Sola Gratia*: The Battle for Luther in Seventeenth-Century England'. *Sixteenth Century Journal* 16, no. 1 (1985): 115.

Barbour, Hugh. *The Quakers in Puritan England*. Yale Publications in Religion 7. New Haven, CT: Yale University Press, 1964.

Baylor, T. Robert. ' "One with Him in Spirit": Mystical Union and the Humanity of Christ in the Theology of John Owen'. In *'In Christ' in Paul: Explorations in Paul's Theology of Union and Participation*, edited by Michael J. Thate, Kevin J. Vanhoozer and Constantine R. Campbell. Wissenschaftliche Untersuchungen Zum Neuen Testament. 2. Reihe 384, 427–52. Tübingen, Germany: Mohr Siebeck, 2014.

Baylor, T. Robert. ' "With Him in Heavenly Places": Peter Lombard and John Calvin on the Merits and Exaltation of Christ'. *International Journal of Systematic Theology* 17, no. 2 (2015): 152–75.

Beck, Stephen Paul. 'The Doctrine of *Gratia Praeparans* in the Soteriology of Richard Sibbes'. PhD thesis, Westminster Theological Seminary, 1994.

Beeke, Joel R. *Assurance of Faith: Calvin, English Puritanism, and the Dutch Second Reformation*. American University Studies 7, Theology and Religion 89. New York: Peter Lang, 1991.

Beeke, Joel R., and Mark Jones. *A Puritan Theology: Doctrine for Life*. Grand Rapids, MI: Reformation Heritage Books, 2012.

Blackham, Paul. 'The Pneumatology of Thomas Goodwin'. PhD thesis, University of London, 1995.

Boersma, Hans. *A Hot Pepper Corn: Richard Baxter's Doctrine of Justification in Its Seventeenth Century Context of Controversy*. Netherlands: Boekencentrum, 1993. Reprint, Vancouver: Regent College Publishing, 2004.

Brown, Paul Edward. 'The Principle of the Covenant in the Theology of Thomas Goodwin'. PhD thesis, Drew University, 1950.

Budiman, Kalvin S. 'A Protestant Doctrine of Nature and Grace as Illustrated by Jerome Zanchi's Appropriation of Thomas Aquinas'. PhD thesis, Baylor University, 2011.

Burger, Hans. *Being in Christ: A Biblical and Systematic Investigation in a Reformed Perspective*. Eugene, OR: Wipf & Stock, 2009.

Carter, Rembert Byrd. 'The Presbyterian-Independent Controversy with Special Reference to Dr. Thomas Goodwin and the Years 1640–1660'. PhD thesis, University of Edinburgh, 1961.

Chang, Paul Ling-Ji. 'Thomas Goodwin (1600–1680) on the Christian Life'. PhD thesis, Westminster Theological Seminary, 2001.

Cleveland, Christopher Harold. 'Thomism in John Owen'. PhD thesis, Aberdeen University, 2011.

Como, David R. *Blown by the Spirit: Puritanism and the Emergence of an Antinomian Underground in Pre-Civil-War England*. Stanford, CA: Stanford University Press, 2004.

Cooper, Tim. *Fear and Polemic in Seventeenth-Century England: Richard Baxter and Antinomianism*. Aldershot, UK: Ashgate, 2001.

Dallison, Anthony R. 'The Latter-Day Glory in the Thought of Thomas Goodwin'. *Evangelical Quarterly* 58, no. 1 (1986): 53–68.

Davis, J. C. *Fear, Myth and History: The Ranters and the Historians*. Cambridge: Cambridge University Press, 1986.

Dever, Mark. *Richard Sibbes: Puritanism and Calvinism in Late Elizabethan and Early Stuart England*. Macon, GA: Mercer University Press, 2000.

Dixon, Philip. *'Nice and Hot Disputes': The Doctrine of the Trinity in the Seventeenth Century*. London: T&T Clark, 2003.

Dominiak, Paul Anthony. 'The Architecture of Participation in the Thought of Richard Hooker'. Durham, 2017.

Ebel, Julia G. 'The Family of Love: Sources of Its History in England'. *Huntington Library Quarterly* 30, no. 4 (1967): 331–43.

Edwards, William R. 'John Flavel on the Priority of Union with Christ: Further Historical Perspective on the Structure of Reformed Soteriology'. *Westminster Theological Journal* 74, no. 1 (2012): 33–58.

Ellis, Mark A. *Simon Episcopius' Doctrine of Original Sin*. American University Studies 7, Theology and Religion 240. New York: Peter Lang, 2006.

Engel, Mary Potter. *John Calvin's Perspectival Anthropology*. American Academy of Religion Academy Series 52. Atlanta, GA: Scholars Press, 1988.

Evans, William B. 'Déjà Vu All over Again? The Contemporary Reformed Soteriological Controversy in Historical Perspective'. *Westminster Theological Journal* 72, no. 1 (2010): 135–51.

Evans, William B. *Imputation and Impartation: Union with Christ in American Reformed Theology*. Studies in Christian Thought and History. Milton Keynes, UK: Paternoster, 2008.

Evans, William B. 'Of Trajectories, Repristinations, and the Meaningful Engagement of Texts: A Reply to J. V. Fesko'. *Westminster Theological Journal* 72, no. 2 (2010): 403–14.

Fesko, J. V. *Beyond Calvin: Union with Christ and Justification in Early Modern Reformed Theology (1517–1700)*. Reformed Historical Theology 20. Göttingen: Vandenhoeck & Ruprecht, 2012.

Fesko, J. V. *The Covenant of Redemption: Origins, Development, and Reception*. Reformed Historical Theology 35. Göttingen: Vandenhoeck & Ruprecht, 2016.

Fesko, J. V. 'Methodology, Myth, and Misperception: A Response to William B. Evans'. *Westminster Theological Journal* 72, no. 2 (2010): 391–402.

Fienberg, Stanley. 'Thomas Goodwin, Puritan Pastor and Independent Divine'. PhD thesis, University of Chicago, 1974.

Fisher, George P. 'The Augustinian and the Federal Theories of Original Sin Compared'. *New Englander and Yale Review* 27, no. 3 (1868): 468–516.

Frost, Ronald Norman. 'Richard Sibbes' Theology of Grace and the Division of English Reformed Theology'. PhD thesis, University of London, 1996.

Gamble, Whitney Greer. '"If Christ Fulfilled the Law, We Are Not Bound": The Westminster Assembly against English Antinomian Soteriology, 1643–1647'. PhD thesis, University of Edinburgh, 2014.

Hall, David D. *The Antinomian Controversy, 1636–1638: A Documentary History*, 2nd edn. Durham, NC: Duke University Press, 1990.

Halley, Robert. 'Memoir of Thomas Goodwin, D.D.'. In *The Works of Thomas Goodwin, D.D.*, vol. 2, edited by W. Lindsay Alexander, Thomas J. Crawford, William Cunningham, D. T. K. Drummond, William H. Goold and Andrew Thomson. Nichol's Series of Standard Divines: Puritan Period. Edinburgh: James Nichol, 1861.

Hallonsten, Gösta. 'Theosis in Recent Research: A Renewal of Interest and a Need for Clarity'. In *Partakers of the Divine Nature: The History and Development of Deification in the Christian Traditions*, edited by Michael J. Christensen and Jeffery A. Wittung, 281–93. Cranbury, NJ: Fairleigh Dickinson University Press, 2007.

Harrison, Peter. *The Fall of Man and the Foundations of Science*. Cambridge: Cambridge University Press, 2007.

Herzer, Mark A. 'Adam's Reward: Heaven or Earth?'. In *Drawn into Controversie: Reformed Theological Diversity and Debates within Seventeenth-Century British Puritanism*, edited by Michael A. G. Haykin and Mark Jones. Reformed Historical Theology 17, 162–82. Göttingen: Vandenhoeck & Ruprecht, 2011.

Hillerbrand, Hans J. *The Oxford Encyclopedia of the Reformation*, 4 vols. Oxford: Oxford University Press, 1996.

Holmes, Stephen R. 'Reformed Varieties of the Communicatio Idiomatum'. In *The Person of Christ*, edited by Murray Rae and Stephen R. Holmes, 70–86. London: T&T Clark, 2005.

Horton, Michael S. 'Calvin's Theology of Union with Christ and the Double Grace: Modern Reception and Contemporary Possibilities'. In *Calvin's Theology and Its Reception: Disputes, Developments, and New Possibilities*, edited by J. Todd Billings and I. John Hesselink, 72–94. Louisville, KY: Westminster John Knox Press, 2012.

Horton, Michael S. 'Thomas Goodwin and the Puritan Doctrine of Assurance: Continuity and Discontinuity in the Reformed Tradition, 1600–1680'. PhD thesis, University of Coventry, 1995.

Hughes, Ann. *Gangraena and the Struggle for the English Revolution*. Oxford: Oxford University Press, 2004.

Hunsinger, George. 'Justification and Mystical Union with Christ: Where Does Owen Stand?'. In *The Ashgate Research Companion to John Owen's Theology*, edited by Kelly M. Kapic and Mark Jones, 199–211. Farnham, UK: Ashgate, 2012.

Jones, Mark. *Why Heaven Kissed Earth: The Christology of the Puritan Reformed Orthodox Theologian, Thomas Goodwin (1600–1680)*. Reformed Historical Theology 13. Göttingen: Vandenhoeck & Ruprecht, 2010.

Jones, R. Tudur. 'Union with Christ: The Existential Nerve of Puritan Piety'. *Tyndale Bulletin* 41, no. 2 (1990): 186–208.

Jue, Jeffrey K. 'The Active Obedience of Christ and the Theology of the Westminster Standards: A Historical Investigation'. In *Justified in Christ: God's Plan for Us in Justification*, edited by K. Scott Oliphint, 99–130. Ross-shire: Christian Focus, 2007.

Kapic, Kelly M. 'Communion with God: Relations between the Divine and the Human in the Theology of John Owen'. PhD thesis, University of London, 2001.

Kim, Hyo Nam. 'Salvation by Faith: Faith, Covenant, and the Order of Salvation in Thomas Goodwin (1600–1680)'. PhD thesis, Calvin Theological Seminary, 2016.

Lawrence, Thomas Michael. 'Transmission and Transformation: Thomas Goodwin and the Puritan Project 1600–1704'. PhD thesis, University of Cambridge, 2002.

Lim, Paul Chang-Ha. *Mystery Unveiled: The Crisis of the Trinity in Early Modern England*. Oxford Studies in Historical Theology. Oxford: Oxford University Press, 2012.

Macleod, Donald. 'Original Sin in Reformed Theology'. In *Adam, the Fall, and Original Sin: Theological, Biblical and Scientific Perspectives*, edited by Hans Madueme and Michael Reeves, 129–46. Grand Rapids, MI: Baker Academic, 2014.

Marsh, Christopher W. *The Family of Love in English Society, 1550–1630*. Cambridge Studies in Early Modern British History. Cambridge: Cambridge University Press, 1994.

McCormack, Bruce L. 'Union with Christ in Calvin's Theology: Grounds for Divinization Theory?'. In *Tributes to John Calvin: A Celebration of His Quincentenary*, edited by David W. Hall, 504–29. Phillipsburg, NJ: Presbyterian & Reformed, 2010.

McDonald, Suzanne. 'The Pneumatology of the 'Lost' Image in John Owen'. *Westminster Theological Journal* 71, no. 2 (2009): 323–35.

McGraw, Ryan M. *A Heavenly Directory: Trinitarian Piety, Public Worship and a Reassessment of John Owen's Theology*. Reformed Historical Theology 29. Göttingen: Vandenhoeck & Ruprecht, 2014.

McGregor, J. F., and Barry Reay. *Radical Religion in the English Revolution*. Oxford: Oxford University Press, 1984.

McKelvey, Robert J. '"That Error and Pillar of Antinomianism": Eternal Justification'. In *Drawn into Controversie: Reformed Theological Diversity and Debates within Seventeenth-Century British Puritanism*, edited by Michael A. G. Haykin and Mark Jones. Reformed Historical Theology 17, 223–62. Göttingen: Vandenhoeck & Ruprecht, 2011.

Mortimer, Sarah. *Reason and Religion in the English Revolution: The Challenge of Socinianism*. Cambridge Studies in Early Modern British History. Cambridge: Cambridge University Press, 2010.

Muller, Richard A. *Calvin and the Reformed Tradition: On the Work of Christ and the Order of Salvation*. Grand Rapids, MI: Baker Academic, 2012.

Muller, Richard A. *Post-Reformation Reformed Dogmatics: The Rise and Development of Reformed Orthodoxy, ca. 1520 to ca. 1725*, 2nd edn. 4 vols. Grand Rapids, MI: Baker Academic, 2003.

Nuttall, Geoffrey F. *The Holy Spirit in Puritan Faith and Experience*. Oxford: Basil Blackwell, 1946. Reprint, Chicago, IL: University of Chicago Press, 1992.

Oh, Changlok. 'Beholding the Glory of God in Christ: Communion with God in the Theology of John Owen (1616–83)'. PhD thesis, Westminster Theological Seminary, 2006.

Parnham, David. 'The Covenantal Quietism of Tobias Crisp'. *Church History* 75, no. 3 (2006): 511–41.

Parnham, David. 'Motions of Law and Grace: The Puritan in the Antinomian'. *Westminster Theological Journal* 70, no. 1 (2008): 73–104.

Pederson, Randall J. *Unity in Diversity: English Puritans and the Puritan Reformation, 1603–1689*. Brill's Series in Church History 68. Leiden: Brill, 2014.

Powell, Hunter. *The Crisis of British Protestantism: Church Power in the Puritan Revolution, 1638–44*. Politics, Culture and Society in Early Modern Britain. Manchester, UK: Manchester University Press, 2015.

Reay, Barry. *The Quakers and the English Revolution*. London: Temple Smith, 1985.

Schultz, Robert C. 'Original Sin: Accident or Substance: The Paradoxical Significance of FC I, 53-62 in Historical Context'. In *Discord, Dialogue, and Concord: Studies in the Lutheran Reformation's Formula of Concord*, edited by Lewis W. Spitz and Wenzel Lohff, 38–57. Philadelphia, PA: Fortress Press, 1977.

Shields, James L. 'The Doctrine of Regeneration in English Puritan Theology, 1604–1689'. PhD thesis, Southwestern Baptist Theological Seminary, 1965.

Spence, Alan. *Incarnation and Inspiration: John Owen and the Coherence of Christology*. London: T&T Clark, 2007.

Spinka, Matthew. 'Acquisition of the Codex Alexandrinus by England'. *Journal of Religion* 16, no. 1 (1936): 10–29.

Stoever, William K. B. *'A Faire and Easie Way to Heaven': Covenant Theology and Antinomianism in Early Massachusetts*. Middletown, CT: Wesleyan University Press, 1978.

Strange, Alan D. 'The Imputation of the Active Obedience of Christ at the Westminster Assembly'. In *Drawn into Controversie: Reformed Theological Diversity and Debates within Seventeenth-Century British Puritanism*, edited by Michael A. G. Haykin and Mark Jones. Reformed Historical Theology 17, 31–51. Göttingen: Vandenhoeck & Ruprecht, 2011.

Torrance, Thomas F. *Calvin's Doctrine of Man*. London: Lutterworth Press, 1949.

Trueman, Carl R. *The Claims of Truth: John Owen's Trinitarian Theology*. Carlisle, UK: Paternoster Press, 1998.

Trueman, Carl R. *John Owen: Reformed Catholic, Renaissance Man*. Great Theologians Series. Aldershot, UK: Ashgate, 2007.

Van Dixhoorn, Chad B. *The Minutes and Papers of the Westminster Assembly, 1643–1652*, 5 vols. Oxford: Oxford University Press, 2012.

Van Dixhoorn, Chad B. 'Reforming the Reformation: Theological Debate at the Westminster Assembly, 1643–1652'. PhD thesis, University of Cambridge, 2005.

Van Vliet, Jason. *Children of God: The Imago Dei in John Calvin and His Context*. Reformed Historical Theology 11. Göttingen: Vandenhoeck & Ruprecht, 2009.

Vickery, Jon M. 'A Most Lawful Pleasure: The Marriage of Faith and Reason in the Thought of Thomas Goodwin'. PhD thesis, University of Toronto, 2011.

Von Rohr, John. *The Covenant of Grace in Puritan Thought*. American Academy of Religion Studies in Religion 45. Atlanta, GA: Scholars Press, 1986.

Wallace, Dewey D., Jr. *Puritans and Predestination: Grace in English Protestant Theology, 1525–1695*. Chapel Hill: University of North Carolina Press, 1982.

Won, Jonathan Jong-Chun. 'Communion with Christ: An Exposition and Comparison of the Doctrine of Union and Communion with Christ in Calvin and the English Puritans'. PhD thesis, Westminster Theological Seminary, 1989.

Woo, B. Hoon. *The Promise of the Trinity: The Covenant of Redemption in the Theologies of Witsius, Owen, Dickson, Goodwin, and Cocceius*. Reformed Historical Theology 48. Göttingen: Vandenhoeck & Ruprecht, 2018.

INDEX

Printed in the USA
CPSIA information can be obtained
at www.ICGtesting.com
LVHW020432191023
760260LV00024B/198